THE ART AND THOUGHT
OF HERACLITUS

The art and thought of Heraclitus

An edition of the fragments with translation and commentary

CHARLES H. KAHN
Professor of Philosophy, University of Pennsylvania

CAMBRIDGE UNIVERSITY PRESS

CAMBRIDGE
LONDON   NEW YORK   NEW ROCHELLE
MELBOURNE   SYDNEY

Published by the Press Syndicate of the University of Cambridge
The Pitt Building, Trumpington Street, Cambridge CB2 1RP
32 East 57th Street, New York, NY 10022, USA
296 Beaconsfield Parade, Middle Park, Melbourne 3206, Australia

First published 1979
First paperback edition 1981
Reprinted 1983

Printed in Great Britain at the
University Press, Cambridge

Library of Congress catalogue card number: 77-82499

British Library Cataloguing in Publication Data
Heraclitus
The art and thought of Heraclitus.
1. Philosophy, Ancient
I. Title II. Kahn, Charles H.
182'.4   B220.E5
ISBN 0 521 21883 7 hard covers
ISBN 0 521 28645 X paperback

for Charalampos S. Floratos

a true friend and scholar, master of the
classical tradition and hierophant of
the beauty of Cephalonia

Contents

Preface

Heraclitus was a great prose artist, one of the most powerful stylists not only of Greek antiquity but of world literature. He was also a major thinker, perhaps the only pre-Socratic philosopher whose thought is of more than historical interest today. His reflections upon the order of nature and man's place within it, upon the problems of language, meaning and communication still seem profound; and many of his insights will remain illuminating for the modern reader, not merely for the specialist in ancient thought.

The aim of the present work is to demonstrate the truth of these claims by making Heraclitus accessible to contemporary readers as a philosopher of the first rank. With this in mind I have tried to re-arrange the fragments in a meaningful order, to give a translation that reflects as far as possible the linguistic richness of the original, and to provide a commentary designed to make explicit the wealth of meaning that cannot be directly conveyed in a translation but is latent in Heraclitus' own words, in his tantalizing and suggestive form of enigmatic utterance.

The Greek text is given here together with the translation, since any interpretation is obliged to make continual reference to the original wording. And I think it should be possible to read the fragments in a meaningful order, even if one reads them in Greek. No attempt has been made to produce a new critical edition, and I have generally followed the text of Marcovich where he diverges from Diels. But in some nine cases my text differs from both Diels and Marcovich in such a way that the interpretation of the fragment is altered, sometimes radically (see p. 26). The notes to the translation are designed to provide the minimum of information required to understand Heraclitus' words without a knowledge of Greek. The commentary is there for those readers who would go further. But in the commentary too all Greek words have been given in transliteration, and the element of scholarly controversy has been kept to a minimum (although I have tried to acknowledge my debt to my predecessors, and to take

some account of their views even where I disagree). The aim throughout has been not to add another book to the secondary literature on
Heraclitus but to make the thought of Heraclitus accessible to the
general reader in the way that a good translation and commentary on
the *Divine Comedy* tries to make the poetry of Dante accessible to
one who knows little or no Italian.

The comparison to Dante is chosen deliberately. Despite the vast
difference in scale between the two works, and despite the fact that
our text is only partially preserved, even from these shattered remains
we can see that the literary art of Heraclitus' composition was comparable in technical cunning and density of content to that of Dante's
masterpiece. As a thinker, Heraclitus was even more original. And in
both cases the reader who approaches his author without any scholarly assistance is likely to get quickly lost. May this serve as my
excuse for such a lengthy commentary to such a brief text.

The first draft was written in Athens in 1974–75, when I held a
senior fellowship from the National Endowment for the Humanities
and was in residence as visiting professor at the American School of
Classical Studies. I am happy to express my appreciation to the
Endowment for its support, and to thank the American School, its
then director James McCredie, and the staff of the Blegen Library
for their friendly help and hospitality. I am greatly obliged to the
Research Center for Greek Philosophy and the Academy of Athens
for cordial assistance, and in particular to Dr E.N. Roussos of that
Center who permitted me to use his typescript of Wiese's dissertation,
Heraklit bei Klemens von Alexandrien. Among the colleagues who
improved this work by their criticism I must mention G.E.L. Owen
and Edward Hussey. The translation has benefited from suggestions
by Diskin Clay, Jenny Strauss Clay, Martin Ostwald and John van
Sickle. Barbara Hernnstein Smith kindly served as my Greekless
reader, and made many valuable suggestions for a more idiomatic
translation as well as for the presentation of notes and commentary.
Finally, both the reader and I are indebted to R.J. Mynott of the
Cambridge University Press for showing me how to condense the
commentary; it is not his fault if it is still a bit long.

June 1977   Charles H. Kahn

A free man thinks of death least of all things, and his wisdom is not a meditation upon death but upon life.

Spinoza, *Ethics* IV.67

The longing not to die, the hunger for personal immortality, the effort by which we strive to persevere in our own being, this is the emotional basis for all knowledge and the intimate point of departure for all human philosophy.

Unamuno, *The Tragic Sense of Life*

Bibliography and abbreviations

Adkins, A.W.H. *Merit and Responsibility: A Study in Greek Values* (Oxford, 1960)

AJP: *American Journal of Philology*

Anaximander: C.H. Kahn, *Anaximander and the Origins of Greek Cosmology* (New York, 1960)

'A new look at Heraclitus': C.H. Kahn in *American Philosophical Quarterly* 1 (1964), 189–203

Bollack, J. and H. Wismann. *Héraclite ou la séparation* (Paris, 1972)

Bronowski, J. *The Ascent of Man* (London, 1973)

Burnet, J. *Early Greek Philosophy* (4th ed. London, 1930)

Bywater, I. *Heracliti Ephesii reliquiae* (Oxford, 1877)

Deichgräber, K. 'Bemerkungen zu Diogenes' Bericht über Heraklit', *Philologus* 93 (1938), 12–30

Diels, H. *Doxographi graeci* (Berlin, 1879; reprint, 1929)

Diels, H. *Herakleitos von Ephesos* (1st ed. Berlin, 1901; 2nd ed. 1909)

DK: H. Diels, *Die Fragmente der Vorsokratiker*, 6th ed. by W. Kranz (Berlin, 1951)

D.L.: Diogenes Laertius, *Lives of the Philosophers* (ed. H.S. Long, Oxford, 1964)

Dodds, E.R. *The Greeks and the Irrational* (Berkeley, 1951)

Fränkel, H. *Dichtung und Philosophie des frühen Griechentums* (1st ed. New York, 1951; 2nd ed. Munich, 1962)

Fränkel, H. *Wege und Formen frühgriechischen Denken* (3rd ed. Munich, 1968)

Furley, D. and R.E. Allen (eds.). *Studies in Presocratic Philosophy*, Vol. I (London, 1970)

Gigon, O. *Untersuchungen zu Heraklit* (Basel dissertation, Leipzig, 1935)

Gigon, O. *Der Ursprung der griechischen Philosophie* (Basel, 1945)

Gomperz, H. 'Ueber die ursprüngliche Reihenfolge einiger Bruchstücke Heraklits', *Hermes* 58 (1923), 20ff.

Guthrie, W.K.C. *A History of Greek Philosophy*, Vol. I (Cambridge, 1962)

Hölscher, U. *Anfängliches Fragen: Studien zur frühen griechischen Philosophie* (Göttingen, 1968)

Hussey, E. *The Presocratics* (London, 1972)

JHS: *Journal of Hellenic Studies*

Kerschensteiner, J. *Kosmos. Quellenkritische Untersuchungen zu den Vorsokratikern* (Munich, 1962)

Kirk, G.S. *Heraclitus, The Cosmic Fragments* (Cambridge, 1954)

Kirk and Raven: G.S. Kirk and J.E. Raven, *The Presocratic Philosophers* (Cambridge, 1957)

Lebeck, A. *The Oresteia: A Study in Language and Structure* (Washington, 1971)

LSJ: Liddell-Scott-Jones, *A Greek-English Lexicon* (Oxford, 1925–40)

Mansfeld, J. *Die Offenbarung des Parmenides und die menschliche Welt* (Assen, 1964)

Marcovich, M. *Heraclitus, editio maior* (Merida, Venezuela, 1967)

Marcovich, PW: article 'Herakleitos' in PW Supplement-Band X (1965), 246–320

Mondolfo, R. and L. Tarán. *Eraclito. Testimonianze e Imitazioni* (Florence, 1972)

North, H. *Sophrosyne: Self-Knowledge and Self-Restraint in Greek Literature* (Cornell, 1966)

'On early Greek astronomy': C.H. Kahn in *JHS* 90 (1970), 99–116

Powell, J.E. *A Lexicon to Herodotus* (Cambridge, 1938; reprint, Hildesheim, 1960)

PW: *Real Encyclopädie der classischen Altertumswissenschaft*, ed. Pauly-Wissowa-Kroll (Stuttgart, 1894–)

Reinhardt, K. *Parmenides und die Geschichte der griechischen Philosophie* (Bonn, 1916; reprint, 1959)

Reinhardt, K. *Vermächtnis der Antike. Gesammelte Essays zur Philosophie und Geschichtsschreibung*, ed. C. Becker (Göttingen, 1966)

Schleiermacher, F. *Herakleitos der dunkle, von Ephesos*, in *Sämtliche Werke* Abt. III, Bd. 2 (Berlin, 1839), pp. 1–146

Snell, B. *Die Entdeckung des Geistes* (3rd ed. Hamburg, 1955)

Snell, B. 'Die Sprache Heraklits', *Hermes* 61 (1926), 353–81; in *Gesammelte Schriften* (Göttingen, 1966)

Stokes, M.C. *One and Many in Presocratic Philosophy* (Cambridge, Mass., 1971)

The Verb 'Be' in Ancient Greek: C.H. Kahn, *The Verb 'Be' and its*

Synonyms, Part 6, ed. J.W.M. Verhaar (Foundations of Language Suppl. Series, Vol. 16, Reidel, Dordrecht, 1973)

Verdenius, W.J. 'A psychological statement of Heraclitus', *Mnemosyne* Series 3.11 (1943), 115–21

Vlastos, G. 'On Heraclitus', *AJP* 76 (1955), 337–68, reprinted in part in Furley and Allen

von Arnim, H. *Stoicorum Veterum Fragmenta*, 3 vols. (Leipzig, 1903–5)

Walzer, R. *Eraclito, Raccolta dei frammenti* (Florence, 1939; reprint, 1964)

West, M.L. *Early Greek Philosophy and the Orient* (Oxford, 1971)

Wiese, H. *Heraklit bei Klemens von Alexandrien* (Kiel dissertation, 1963, typescript)

Zeller-Nestle: E. Zeller, *Die Philosophie der Griechen in ihrer geschichtlichen Entwicklung*, I, 6th ed. by W. Nestle (Leipzig, 1919–20)

Zuntz, G. *Persephone. Three Essays on Religion and Thought in Magna Graecia* (Oxford, 1971)

General introduction

1 The Man, the Time, and the Place

The details of Heraclitus' life are almost completely unknown. Reliable information is limited to the fact that he was a native of Ephesus, on the coast of Asia Minor north of Miletus, and that his father's name was Bloson. His approximate date is fixed by a synchronism with the reign of Darius, 521 to 487 B.C.; his traditional 'acme' in the 69th Olympiad, 504–501 B.C., is probably nothing more than a simplified version of the same synchronism.[1] The rough accuracy of this date, on the threshold of the fifth century, is guaranteed by fragment XVIII (D. 40), where Pythagoras, Xenophanes, and Hecataeus are cited as older contemporaries or figures of the recent past. All three men seem to have died between 510 and 480 B.C.[2] The book dates itself, then, in or near this period. The same approximate date could be inferred from the presence or absence of various philosophical influences: there are clear debts to the sixth-century Milesians, to Pythagoras and Xenophanes, but none to Parmenides or to any thinker of the fifth century.

The 'life' of Heraclitus by Diogenes Laertius is a tissue of Hellenistic anecdotes, most of them obviously fabricated on the basis of statements in the preserved fragments. (The unusually disgusting reports of his final illness and death reveal a malicious pleasure in mocking a figure whom the Stoics venerated as the source of their own philosophy.) Suggestive, if not entirely credible, are the stories which describe Heraclitus as refusing to engage in politics or to legislate for Ephesus, in sharp contrast with the public activities of most early philosophers. Such stories may reflect no more than the expressions of contempt for his fellow-citizens found, for example, in LXIV (D. 121). A related anecdote, probably more worthy of belief, tells us that he relinquished the hereditary and largely honorific title of 'king' to his younger brother.[3] If true, this would imply that Heraclitus was the eldest son of one of the most aristocratic

families in Ionia, the Androclids, who traced their descent back to
Androclus, son of King Codrus of Athens, reputed leader of the
Ionian migration to Asia Minor and founder of Ephesus.

Heraclitus is said to have deposited his book as a dedication in the
great temple of Artemis, where the general public would not have
access to it.[4] The dimensions of this archaic Artemesium, built not
long before Heraclitus' birth, are still recognizable in the picturesque
remains of a later rebuilding: the sheer scale of the enterprise is evidence for the wealth, the power, and the civic pride of Ephesus in
the middle of the sixth century.[5] The temple was constructed about
560 B.C. 'in emulation of the temple of Hera which had just been
built on Samos, but larger — indeed one of the largest ever to be
attempted by a Greek architect'.[6] This architectural rivalry between
the new Ephesian temple and its slightly older neighbor, the Heraion
of Samos, prefigures a generation in advance the philosophic emulation that will oppose Heraclitus to his famous Samian predecessor,
Pythagoras. (Compare XVIII, D. 40 and XXV–XXVI, D. 129 and 81.)

Like other Ionian cities of Asia Minor, the destiny of Ephesus in
the sixth century was linked to the rise of Lydia as dominant power
under Croesus, and to the latter's overthrow by Cyrus the Persian in
547 or 546 B.C. Ephesus seems to have remained on good terms with
the ruling powers in the east. Croesus of Lydia contributed to the
construction of the Artemesium. And when her great neighbor
Miletus was destroyed by the Persians after the disastrous Ionian
revolt of 494, Ephesus was spared. In the earlier period Miletus had
surpassed all other Ionian cities in maritime enterprise and colonial
expansion, while serving at the same time as the birthplace for western science and philosophy: it was in sixth-century Miletus that
Thales, Anaximander, and Anaximenes created the tradition of
natural philosophy. The destruction of Miletus at the beginning of
the fifth century left Ephesus as the major Greek city of Asia Minor,
a position she retained until the end of antiquity, as we can see today
from the resurrected splendor of her Roman ruins.

It was in this opulent city, in the days of rivalry between Ephesus,
Samos, and Miletus, under Persian control but before the unsuccess-
ful Ionian revolt, that Heraclitus grew up as the eldest son of the
noblest family in the city. (The presence of the Persians in and around
Ephesus may be reflected in a scornful reference to *magoi* in D. 14.
See below on CXV.) We have no information on the struggles between
the poor and the rich, the pro-Persian and the anti-Persian parties
that must have dominated the civic life of Ephesus at this time.

Heraclitus' attack upon his fellow-citizens for the expulsion of Hermodorus (in LXIX, D. 12) certainly presupposes local autonomy and probably also some form of popular government. Heraclitus will himself have had small sympathy for democracy understood in the Greek sense as rule by the greater number, or by the lower classes, as we see from his contemptuous reference to the *dēmos* or 'mob' in LIX (D. 104). On the other hand, there is no reason to think of him as an unconditional partisan of the rich.[7] The fragments and the later anecdotes agree in portraying him as an observer *audessus de la mêlée*, withdrawn from competing factions. I imagine his civic attitude by analogy with the quasi-neutral stance of Solon, but without any of the active political involvement of the latter. Solon saw himself as a mediating force, opposing the excesses of the rival parties, 'standing like a boundary mark between the warring factions' (fr. 25) in order to preserve the common interests of the city as a whole. So Heraclitus, who discovered in what is shared or common to all (*to xynon*) the essential principle of order in the universe, recognized within the city the unifying role of the *nomos*, the structure of civic law and moral custom which protects the demos as the city wall protects all the inhabitants of the city (LXV, D. 44). The only political attitude which we can safely extrapolate from the fragments is a lucid, almost Hobbesian appreciation of the fact that civilized life and communal survival depend upon loyalty to the *nomos*, the law in which all citizens have a share (XXX, D. 114), but which may be realized in the leadership of a single outstanding man.[8]

2 The Book

Heraclitus is, as Diels put it, 'the most subjective and, in a sense, the most modern prose author of antiquity'.[9] A loner among a gregarious race, he seems to have had no personal disciples or associates. (One anecdote has him fleeing human society in disgust and going to live like a hermit in the mountains.) In a literary age which we think of as still primarily 'oral', Heraclitus' influence made itself felt exclusively through the power of his written word. Within a generation or two 'his book acquired such fame that it produced partisans of his doctrine who were called Heracliteans'.[10] The best known of fifth-century Heracliteans is Cratylus of Athens, a rather taciturn participant in the Platonic dialogue that bears his name, whose eccentric ideas are reported more fully by Aristotle (*Metaphysics* 1010a11). Aristotle strangely names Cratylus as one of Plato's teachers (ibid.

987a32), perhaps because he regarded him as a source of the Heraclitean influence which he rightly recognized in Plato's own thought. The stylistic impact of Heraclitus' book is well documented in fifth-century literature, notably in the fragments of Democritus, several of which seem to be composed as a direct response to statements by Heraclitus.[11] The Hippocratic treatise *On Regimen*, probably from the same period, shows a more systematic attempt to imitate the enigmatic, antithetical style of Heraclitus' prose.[12] There is enough evidence for widespread interest in Heraclitus among the intellectuals who represent what is called the Enlightenment of the late fifth century B.C. to establish the plausibility, if not the literal truth, of the story that it was the tragedian Euripides himself who gave the book to Socrates and asked for his opinion of it.[13]

It is in the fourth-century works of Plato and Aristotle that we find the first detailed discussion of Heraclitean doctrine, but few literal quotations from his book. The doctrine itself is seen from a perspective far removed from the intellectual atmosphere of the early fifth century. For Plato Heraclitus is the theorist of universal flux (*panta rhei* 'all things flow') in contrast to Parmenides, the partisan of a fixed and stable reality. For Aristotle Heraclitus was a material monist who derived the entire physical world from fire as its underlying element. Both characterizations cast a long shadow over later readings of Heraclitus' text. Before turning to the book itself, I will briefly survey its influence over the next few centuries and indicate the principal sources from which our knowledge of it is derived. Like all Greek prose authors before Herodotus and all philosophical writings before Plato, the original text of Heraclitus is lost. We are entirely dependent upon quotations, paraphrases, and reports in later literature that happens to have survived the collapse of ancient civilization and the destruction of its papyrus libraries.

A full account of Heraclitus' doctrine as he understood it, along the lines traced by Aristotle, was given by the latter's pupil Theophrastus in his great doxographical survey, *The Opinions of the Natural Philosophers* (*Physikōn Doxai*). Theophrastus' own work is lost, but a good excerpt from the relevant sections, including close paraphrases of several extant fragments, is preserved in Diogenes Laertius' *Life* of Heraclitus, IX.7–11 (translated below in Appendix IIA). The high point of Heraclitus' philosophical influence was reached a generation later in the work of Zeno, the founder of the Stoic school in the early third century B.C., and in that of Zeno's successor Cleanthes. Cleanthes wrote a commentary on Heraclitus in four books, of which no certain trace has been preserved; but the surviving sections of his famous *Hymn to Zeus* contain elaborate echoes of Heraclitean phrasing and imagery.[14] The Stoics saw Heraclitus through the deforming lens of their own system, but that system was itself based upon a deep study of his written words. I believe the Stoic interpretation is, in its broad outlines, more faithful to Heraclitus' own thought than is generally recognized. In their dogmatic way, and without his subtlety of thought and expression, the Stoics are the true Heracliteans of antiquity.

Interest in Heraclitus remained intense throughout the Hellenistic period, partly but not exclusively as a result of Stoic influence. Diogenes (IX.15) lists seven other authors who wrote commentaries on the book.[15] By the fourth century B.C. Heraclitus had acquired the status of a literary classic, a status which he kept as long as ancient civilization endured.

The various full-length commentaries are lost, and the earliest extant author to quote extensively from Heraclitus is Plutarch, the Platonic philosopher and biographer of the late first century A.D. The work was still familiar in the next century, as we can see from many quotations and from the witty parody by Lucian in his *Sale of Philosophic Lives*, which reflects — and presupposes on the reader's part — an accurate knowledge of the text.[16] The most abundant and most faithful quotations are found in the works of two Christian bishops writing about A.D. 200: Clement of Alexandria and Hippolytus of Rome. Several good verbatim citations are preserved by another early Church father, Origen of Alexandria. Plotinus in the third century A.D. and other later Neoplatonists also quote from Heraclitus, but they are not much concerned with literal citation. Our last important source of original fragments is the anthology of wise sayings on moral topics put together by John Stobaeus in the fifth century A.D., almost a millenium after the original composition of the book.

Stobaeus is probably drawing upon earlier anthologies; and other late authors may have got their quotations at second hand. (Origen tells us he is citing Heraclitus from the pagan philosopher Celsus; and Porphyry once quotes the text from a neo-Pythagorean named Numenius.) But I see no reason to doubt that down to the time of Plutarch and Clement, if not later, the little book of Heraclitus was available in its original form to any reader who chose to seek it out. Some authors obviously made selections of quotations for particular purposes, like the excerpts in Hippolytus (who wants to show that

Heraclitus is the source of a Christian heresy) and in Sextus Empiricus who presents Heraclitus as a Stoic rationalist in epistemology. The selection of quotations in Diogenes' *Life* of Heraclitus (IX.1–2) is motivated by the special interest in illustrating the philosopher's personality. The existence of such excerpts has led some modern scholars to suppose that the work circulated in Stoic or Hellenistic 'editions'. But it is one thing to cite a few passages for some special purpose, and another thing to edit or rearrange the text as a whole. For the latter there is really no evidence. The book itself must have been so short that the project of an abridged edition would have had no point.[17] Plutarch and Clement both know Heraclitus by heart, and frequently quote him from memory. It seems obvious that these two extraordinarily learned and literary authors each possessed his own copy of the book. The same may be true for others who quote from memory, as Marcus Aurelius does in the second century A.D. and Plotinus a century later.

Is it possible to form some general idea of a work that was so continuously read, quoted, imitated, and interpreted for more than seven centuries, and from which we have nearly a hundred literal citations? Early editors, such as Bywater, tried to group the fragments by subject matter.[18] After 1901, however, the standard arrangement became that of Diels, who lists the fragments in alphabetical order according to the name of the author citing them. This apparently irrational procedure can be justified on sound philological grounds. Recognizing that any arrangement by subject matter was to some extent arbitrary, Diels wished above all to avoid imposing any personal interpretation upon his edition of the texts. In fact, by the atomistic character of his arrangement he has largely succeeded in imposing his own view of Heraclitus' work as lacking in literary structure. For Diels was motivated not only by the impossibility of reconstructing the original sequence of the fragments. He also called attention to their aphoristic style, their resemblance to the sayings of the Seven Sages, and (with Nietzsche's *Zarathustra* in mind) he suggested that these sentences had originally been set down in a kind of notebook or philosophical journal, with no literary form or unity linking them to one another. He thus implied, after all, that the chaotic pattern of his arrangement gave a true picture of Heraclitus' own composition. In the case of Heraclitus, arrangement and interpretation are inseparable from one another, as Diels saw in the work of his predecessors. His mistake was to imagine that his own order could be an exception.

The arrangement of the fragments presented here is based upon a

different assumption: that Heraclitus' discourse as a whole was as
carefully and artistically composed as are the preserved parts, and
that the formal ordering of the whole was as much an element in its
total meaning as in the case of any lyric poem from the same period.
The true parallel for an understanding of Heraclitus' style is, I suggest,
not Nietzsche but his own contemporaries, Pindar and Aeschylus.
The extant fragments reveal a command of word order, imagery, and
studied ambiguity as effective as that to be found in any work of
these two poets. I think we can best imagine the structure of
Heraclitus' work on the analogy of the great choral odes, with their
fluid but carefully articulated movement from image to aphorism,
from myth to riddle to contemporary allusion. Yet the intellectual
unity of Heraclitus' composition was in a sense greater than that of
any archaic poem, since its final intent was more explicitly didactic,
and its central theme a direct affirmation of unity: *hen panta einai*,
'all things are one'. The content of this perfectly general formula
seems to have been filled in by a chain of statements linked together
not by logical argument but by interlocking ideas, imagery, and
verbal echoes. Theophrastus found the result 'incomplete and inconsistent', but he was looking for a prosaic exposition of physical
theories.[19] Heraclitus is not merely a philosopher but a poet, and one
who chose to speak in tones of prophecy. The literary effect he
aimed at may be compared to that of Aeschylus' *Oresteia*: the solemn
and dramatic unfolding of a great truth, step by step, where the sense
of what has gone before is continually enriched by its echo in what
follows.[20]

That Heraclitus' discourse possessed an artistic design of this type
can scarcely be demonstrated, but is strongly suggested by clear evidence of artistry in every fragment where the original wording has
been preserved. The impression that the original work was a kind of
commonplace book, in which sentences or paragraphs were jotted
down as they occurred to the author, is largely due to the fact that
Heraclitus makes use of the proverbial style of the Sages, just as he
invokes the enigmatic tones of the Delphic oracle. But Heraclitus has
many literary strings to his bow; he does not always speak in riddles
or aphorisms. Among the quotations are four or five long passages of
several connected sentences. Fragment I is a carefully wrought proem,
which suggests the beginning of a well planned book.[21] XXX (D.
114) exhibits a complex literary structure elaborated by word play,
phonetic resonance, and syntactical ambiguity. And other long
quotations show that Heraclitus' prose could be supple and ironic as

well as massive and stately. XXII (D. 56) reports a traditional story
in a narrative style that suggests the naive manner of a folk tale.
CXVII (D. 5) is unique in its unrestrained sarcasm on the subject of
blood purification and praying to man-made gods. The nearest parallel to such plainness of speech is in LXIV (D. 121), where the outburst on the men of Ephesus who deserve hanging utilizes, but does
not exemplify, the proverbial style of wisdom literature.

This diversity of artistic technique does not prove that the work as
a whole was carefully composed. It does indicate that Heraclitus was
master of his medium and could impose an artistic shape upon it if
he chose. And there is a general consideration that tells strongly in
favor of his having done so. If we survey the plastic and literary arts
of archaic Greece, we are struck in almost every case by the remarkable sense of form that characterizes the individual work. Since the
pre-classical notion of poetic structure does not coincide with the
logical or psychological pattern of beginning, middle and end that is
typical of later Greek literature, scholars have not always recognized
this older style of literary form, just as they once failed to appreciate
the peculiar dynamism of archaic sculpture. But today this notion of
archaic form has become familiar to us again, in part from its redis-
covery by artists working in our own century. Whether we are considering an ode of Pindar, a narrative in Herodotus, or a sculptured
frieze, it would be difficult to find an art work from archaic Greece
that is finely wrought in detail but unshapely as a whole.

The preceding argument tends to show that the fragments were
originally arranged in a significant order. It does not claim to show
that the original order has been recovered here. The present arrangement is largely my own contrivance, the result of much trial and
error, and it has no special title to historical authenticity. I have
worked on the assumption that, if Heraclitus' own order was a meaningful one, it is the interpreter's task to present these incomplete and
shattered fragments in the most meaningful order he can find. How
close I have come to duplicating Heraclitus' own order may depend
in part upon how successful I have been in grasping his meaning.[22]

There are, however, a few formal points of reference on which I
have relied. The existence of an introduction is guaranteed by fragment I, which suggests that Heraclitus' initial emphasis was upon
men's failure to grasp the universal *logos* which he proclaims. Accordingly, I have grouped the fragments of a critical and polemical nature
at the beginning. Following a hint of Reinhardt, I take XXXVI (D.
50) as the transition from this introduction to the exposition

proper.[23] For the structure of the exposition itself, there is one much-maligned piece of external evidence: 'the book is divided into three discourses (*logoi*), on the universe, on politics [and ethics], and on theology'.[24] I have followed this clue by presenting the more explicitly cosmological statements immediately after the introductory polemic, and reserving for the end those fragments which refer to cult and deity. Since in my view Heraclitus' psychology is inseparable from his theology, I have put most of the fragments dealing with the psyche immediately before the last section on the gods.

3 The Doctrine: Heraclitus and his Predecessors

From the time of Cratylus and Plato with their special interest in the doctrine of flux, down to the Christian Church fathers who were fascinated by a *logos* that they could so easily assimilate to the word that was 'in the beginning with God', every generation and every school construed the doctrine of Heraclitus from its own particular vantage point. We will return to the deeper problems of hermeneutical perspective in the introduction to the commentary, 'On reading Heraclitus'. Here I want only to provide a modest historical corrective: a survey of the early Greek tradition that can help us to see the thought of Heraclitus against the intellectual background of his own time and place.

As a first approximation, I distinguish two traditions in the intellectual heritage of Heraclitus, that is, in the body of thought he is responding to and which he is, by this very response, in the act of transforming. On the one hand there is the popular tradition of wisdom represented by the poets and by the sages of the early sixth century, including Solon and Bias. Note that Solon was both a poet and a sage, and that the term *sophos*, which means 'wise (man)', originally referred to skill in any art, and particularly in the art of poetry. On the other hand, there is the new technical or scientific culture which took shape in Miletus in this same century. Under circumstances which we can only dimly perceive, natural philosophy began as the work of a handful of men, the circle around Thales and Anaximander. (The origin of the new tradition as an offshoot from the older one, as well as the failure of the ancients to distinguish between the two, is symbolized by the figure of Thales, who is regularly counted among the Seven Sages but also named as the first natural philosopher.) By the time of Heraclitus at the end of the sixth century, the scientific tradition had begun to spread from Miletus to other neighboring cities (Samos, Colophon, Clazomenae, Ephesus) and had also been carried to the distant west by Ionian refugees. Thus sometime in the last half of that century Pythagoras migrated from Samos to Croton and Metapontum on the southern shores of Italy; perhaps a bit later, Xenophanes travelled from Colophon to Sicily and to Elea on the west coast of Italy, below Paestum and Naples. In the fifth century this philosophical culture will be brought to Athens by such men as Anaxagoras (from the Ionian city of Clazo-menae) and the Sophists (including Gorgias, from Sicily). The con-sequent generalization and popularization of these new ideas, above all in Athens in the so-called Enlightenment of the late fifth century, is reflected for us in the extant works of Euripides, Aristophanes, and Thucydides, and in the earliest Hippocratic treatises. It is carried on by the orators, philosophers and scientists of the fourth century. Through the work and influence of Isocrates, Plato, and Aristotle, and mathematician-astronomers like Eudoxus of Cnidos, this new scientific and philosophic culture became the intellectual heritage of the whole civilized west.

It is necessary to bear in mind the fact that this scientific culture, which every educated person today can take for granted no matter how little he knows of its technical detail, was something quite new in Heraclitus' day and still restricted to a small circle of initiates. For the most part, the overwhelmingly dominant culture was what I shall call the popular tradition: the culture of Homer, the poets, and the early sages.

Neither the popular nor the scientific tradition is internally simple or uniform, and the radical difference between the two is much clearer to us than it was to Heraclitus himself.[25] But the originality of Heraclitus can be fully appreciated only in the light of this dis-tinction. For both his historical position and his role as a sage for the centuries are most clearly seen as a bridge between these two tra-ditions.

The underlying assumption common to both traditions (and to all Greek thought) is a basic antithesis between gods and men, between the divine and the human, and an interpretation of the human con-dition in the light of this contrast. Human nature for the Greeks is thus essentially characterized by mortality and fallibility: by the brevity of human life and by the weakness of our intellectual vision. (Heraclitus is expressing this basic assumption when he says 'human nature has no insights, but the divine has them', LV, D. 78.) Where the two traditions diverge most sharply is in their conception of what is divine. For the poets of the popular tradition the gods have human form, even though they are vastly superior in strength, clairvoyance, ability of all sorts, and in their total freedom from the shadow of death. The clearest symptom (though not the original source) of the new world view is a radical break with this anthropomorphism. When Xenophanes complained that 'Homer and Hesiod ascribed to the gods everything that is a shame and reproach among men' (fr. 11), he is not departing in principle from the popular view. For it was part of this tradition that 'bards tell many a lie', and that every poet has the right to correct his predecessors by rejecting or reshaping a familiar story.[26] The new tendency to require that tales about the gods conform with human moral standards can be seen as completing rather than denying the traditional conception of the gods as superior, but generally similar, to human beings. And the origins of this moralizing tendency in Greek theology can be traced back at least as far as the *Odyssey*, which opens with a scene in which Zeus complains that mortals always blame the gods for disaster when they are themselves at fault. The whole structure of the *Odyssey* implies the thesis upon which Hesiod insists with such vehemence: that the actions of Zeus will respect and enforce recognizable principles of justice.[27]

But it is something else again when Xenophanes attacks the views of mortals who 'imagine that the gods are born, and that they have the same clothes and voice and body as men do' (fr. 14; cf. frs. 15–16), and when he announces instead that there is 'one god, greatest among gods and men, similar to mortals neither in body nor in thought' (fr. 23), who remains forever stationary in one place but 'agitates all things with the effortless thought of his mind' (frs. 25–6). What we encounter here, for the first time in surviving literature, is a total rejection of the basis upon which the traditional theology rests. For within this tradition divine genealogies and family connections, as well as direct personal intervention in the affairs of mankind, were fundamental features of the popular and poetic conception of the gods.

This new conception of divinity as birthless and not merely deathless, as radically different from men in every respect, is essentially the conception of a *cosmic god*: a deity conceived not as the supreme patriarch of a quasi-human family but as the ruling principle of an orderly universe. And such a view presupposes the work of the scientists or natural philosophers whom Aristotle called the *physikoi*, students of the nature of things (*physis*). More specifically, the theology of Xenophanes presupposes the cosmology of the first *physikoi*, the Milesians of the sixth century.[28]

(a) The popular tradition

Before turning to the new tradition I want to summarize the moral conceptions of the popular view, as presented in the early poets. The discussion will be limited to the notion of *aretē* or human excellence, generally translated 'virtue', and to some discrepancies between different notions of excellence attested in the early literature.

The Homeric conception of *aretē* is strikingly expressed in a few familiar verses. *Aien aristeuein kai hypeirochon emmenai allōn* is the advice which a heroic father gives to his son (*Iliad* VI.208), as Peleus to Achilles (XI.784): 'Always be first and best, and ahead of everyone else.' This unabashed striving for individual pre-eminence, in the spirit of an athletic competition or a contemporary race for the American presidency, is specified for the Homeric hero by two ranges of activity in which he may achieve distinction: 'to be a speaker of words and a doer of deeds' (*Iliad* IX.443). The deeds are those of military and athletic prowess; the words are those of wise counsel and planning. This ancient duality of speech and action remains as a permanent paradigm for the classification of achievements: it is echoed in Heraclitus' opening reference to the 'words and works (*erga*) which I set forth' (in fragment I), as in the later Sophistic antithesis between 'in word' (*logos*) and 'in deed' (*ergon*). It is natural to take the heroes of the two Homeric epics as supreme examples of success in these two fields: Achilles as the greatest warrior at Troy, and Odysseus as the wiliest and most sagacious of mortal men. For a good 'speaker of words' is of course a man of discretion and foresight: language stands here for intelligence. We may speak of a contrast between the active and the calculating or the military and the intellectual virtues, as long as we realize that the intelligence which is prized is the practical use of words and wits to guide successful action.

Thus we find in the early heroic code, whose grip on classical and even on modern Greece is extraordinarily persistent, no recognition of intellectual or moral excellence that might be distinct in principle from the successful pursuit of whatever goals one has in view. With some oversimplification, we can say that according to the heroic code an action is judged wrong, shameful or foolish only if and because it will lead to failure or disaster for the agent himself.

This statement is oversimplified in two respects. In the first place, the success or failure of the agent is generally inseparable from the fortunes of his family, his friends, and other close associates. To this extent heroic individualism falls considerably short of egoism strictly understood.[29] Secondly, and more significantly, the heroic code also recognizes independent standards of unseemly behavior and unjust dealing, behavior for which one may rightly be punished or at least despised. Thus the beating of Thersites in the *Iliad*, the killing of the suitors in the *Odyssey* are both presented as justified punishment for the violation of a code whose rules cannot be defined exclusively in terms of success and failure in the heroic competition for *aretē*. Recent discussions of the early Greek moral tradition have recognized this distinction between the 'competitive' excellences and other more 'quiet' or 'cooperative' virtues, to use Adkins' terminology, and have stressed the extent to which the heroic conception of *aretē* favors the former over the latter.[30] The contrast is real, but shifting and complex; and it cannot be fully captured by any single pair of antithetical terms. In some cases it seems more accurate to speak of a tension between individualistic and social virtues; in other cases the opposition is rather between the virtues of *achievement* and those of *restraint*.

It is the last pair of terms that best characterizes the disparity between the heroic conception of excellence and a quite different moral ideal enshrined in the sayings of the Seven Sages and associated in classical literature with the term *sōphrosynē*.[31] In epic poetry *sōphrosynē* (in its old form *saophrosynē*) has the literal meaning of 'good sense' or 'soundness of mind', the opposite of folly; it implies little more than the ability to take rational action in pursuit of one's own interest. In later usage, however, the same term comes to denote a certain restrained mode of speech and action that is socially esteemed, modest behavior that is likely to meet with approval from one's fellow men and also from the gods.[32] It is this general preference for moderation and restraint which must account for the curious fact that a word meaning 'good sense' comes to designate something like 'temperance'. Chastity in sexual matters, moderation in eating and drinking, are then seen as concrete manifestations of *sōphrosynē*: a decent sense of one's place within the social setting and one's limitations as a human being. So *sōphrosynē* comes to be the watchword for the very un-Homeric conception of excellence summed up in the aphorisms of the Seven Sages: 'Know thyself', 'Nothing in excess', 'Measure is best'.[33]

Since the heroic ideal of 'always be first and best' is clearly predominant in the Homeric epics (composed around 700 B.C.), while the ideology of self-restraint tends to prevail in later literature beginning with Hesiod and gets canonized in the wisdom of the sixth-century sages, there has been much speculation about the nature and the causes of this moral 'development'.[34] My own view is that this chronological shift from one ideal to the other is more literary than sociological. The Homeric poems do not portray a real society, neither that of the poets nor that of any other definite historical period. They present us with a highly stylized picture in which cultural traits from many periods are combined in an essentially fictive world, created over the centuries by the tradition of epic poetry and organized according to principles that are proper to the heroic poem as such, an art form designed to create and preserve a tradition of individual glory. Hence the code of individual achievement and uninhibited self-assertion is much stronger in the epic world than it can ever have been in any real society.[35]

For our purposes, however, it does not matter how far the contrast between the ideal of self-assertion and the morality of self-restraint is the result of an ideological shift between two stages in the development of Greek society. The important fact is that both views, the selfish and the social conception of *aretē*, and the deep tension between the two, were there in the moral bloodstream of the Greeks long before philosophy appeared on the scene. This discrepancy between two views of excellence must be taken into account not only in reading Greek tragedy and Greek moral philosophy but also in attempting to understand the political careers of men like Themistocles and Alcibiades. Most pertinently, it is in the light of this ideological tension that we must interpret those utterances of Heraclitus that refer to excellence and self-knowledge, to the best men and the vile, and to *sōphronein* or 'thinking well'.

Here as elsewhere we find that the characteristic achievement of Heraclitus lies in articulating a view within which the opposites can be seen together as a unity. For Heraclitus there will be no conflict between the selfish and the social conception of *aretē*, since the deepest structure of the self will be recognized as co-extensive with the universe in general and the political community in particular. Men may live as if they had a private world of thinking and planning, but the *logos* of the world order, like the law of the city, is common to all (III, D. 2 with XXX, D. 114). So true self-knowledge will coincide with knowledge of the cosmic order, and true self-assertion will mean holding fast to what is shared by all. The best of men, including those who die in battle in defense of their city, choose everlasting glory as did the Homeric hero. But what they choose is not their own interest in any private sense but what is common and shared (*to xynon*), that 'one thing in exchange for all' which represents the divine unity of the cosmos (XCVII, D. 29 with C, D. 24).

A later generation enlightened by the Sophists will oppose *physis* to *nomos*, nature to convention. And the freethinkers of the late fifth century will challenge all moral claims and restrictions that rest upon *nomos* alone. A precursor of the Enlightenment in other respects, Heraclitus is in this regard a conservative. For him there is no split in principle between *nomos* and nature. As an institution, law is neither man-made nor conventional: it is the expression in social terms of the cosmic order for which another name is Justice (*Dikē*). Heraclitus' political doctrine can be seen as a development of Hesiod's old insight, that the order allotted by Zeus to mankind is to follow justice and shun violence: 'for to fish and beasts and winged birds he gave the rule (*nomos*) that they eat one another, since there is no justice among them; but to human beings he gave justice (*dikē*)' (*Works and Days* 275ff.).

I note that Heraclitus' restatement of this traditional view marks the birth of political philosophy proper and the beginnings of the theory of natural law, which will receive its classic statement by the Stoics working under his inspiration. Heraclitus' own formulation is novel in three respects. He generalizes the notion of Justice to apply to every manifestation of cosmic order, including the rule of the jungle by which birds and beasts eat one another (LXXXII, D. 80). Secondly, human law is conceived as the unifying principle of the political community, and thus as grounded in the rational order of nature which unifies the cosmos. Finally, the unique status of human *nomos* and the political order is interpreted as a consequence of the common human possession of speech (*logos*) and understanding (*noos*), that is, as a consequence of the rational capacity to communicate one's thoughts and come to an agreement (*homologein* in XXXVI, D. 50, echoing *xyn legontas* in XXX, D. 114). Thus it is the very thought and word play of Heraclitus that Plato will echo when, in defending the natural basis of the moral order against the relativists and nihilists of his own time, he defines law (*nomos*) as the arrangement disposed by reason (*nous*).[36] Heraclitus, like Plato, had seen his city conquered in war and torn by civil strife. He was all the more sensitive to the fundamental requirement, for a minimally decent life, of a human community upon whose legal and moral structure all the citizens can rely.

(b) The tradition of natural philosophy

This synthesis between the selfish and social ideals of the Greek tradition was made possible by a deeper sense of unity articulated in Heraclitus' interpretation of the Milesian cosmology. Despite a wide range of mythic and poetic antecedents, the Ionian conception of the world as a *kosmos* was something new, and its novelty is identical with the emergence of western science and philosophy as such. What we find in sixth-century Miletus is a scientific revolution in Kuhn's sense, the creation of a new paradigm of theoretical explanation, with the peculiar distinction that this world view is the first one to be recognizably scientific, so that the innovation in this case is not so much a revolution *within* science as a revolution *into* science for the first time. The Milesian cosmologies are scientific, in the sense in which for example the world picture of Hesiod is not, because the new view of the *kosmos* is connected both with a geometric model and with empirical observation in such a way that the model can be progressively refined and corrected to provide a better explanation for a wider range of empirical data.

Astronomical observation, like numerical calculation, had long been practiced with great skill in the East; and for several centuries after Thales and Anaximander the Greeks remained the pupils of the Babylonians in this respect. But Anaximander provided what it seems that no Babylonian and no Greek had ever conceived before him: a simple geometrical model by which to comprehend the observed movements of the heavenly bodies. In its general outlines, with the earth situated in the middle of a system of concentric circles, the Milesian scheme remained the standard one in scientific astronomy down to Copernicus. But in all its details it was subject to systematic and in some cases very rapid improvement. The conception of the fixed stars as revolving in a stellar sphere, if it does not go back to Anaximander or Anaximenes, must have been articulated soon afterwards. The shape of the earth, a flat disk for Anaximander, was soon recognized as spherical. The explanation of solar and lunar eclipse, which Anaximander seems to have provided for by an *ad hoc* hypothesis of fire-holes opening and closing, begins to take on a more accurate optical and geometric form by the time of Parmenides. The true explanation, according to essentially correct principles of celestial

geometry, was given by Anaxagoras within a century after Anaximander's initial formulation of the model. The Greeks learned how
to compute eclipses from the Babylonians; but they were the first to
explain them. And the very possibility of such an explanation was
created by the idea of a clear geometric model for the heavens.

It is this celestial geometry that constitutes the radically new and
revolutionary aspect of the Milesian cosmology, considered as a contribution to science in the strict sense. And it is revealing for
Heraclitus' relationship to the new science that it is precisely this
aspect of Milesian cosmology that interested him least. What little we
know about his pronouncements on astronomical matters suggests an
almost deliberate preference for more primitive conceptions: for the
view that the sun is the size of a human foot, that it is extinguished
every night and relit every morning.[37] What fascinated him in the
new world view was not its geometrical clarity and the possibilities
this offered for the development of exact science, but something else,
something more directly continuous with older, pre-scientific concerns.

The early natural philosophers were not mere theoreticians; they
were practical astronomers, interested in forecasting seasonal changes
of weather, measuring the agricultural seasons, and establishing a
reliable calendar.[38] The Babylonians had used the *gnōmōn* or sundial
for this purpose, and the Greek tradition has it that the Ionians (more
specifically Anaximander according to some reports) had taken over
the instrument from them and began to make accurate measurements
of the astronomical seasons, as marked by solstice and equinox.[39]
The result was a progressively more accurate scientific calendar, based
upon a convergence of lunar and solar cycles estimated first at 8 and
then at 19 years. The cycles themselves were probably discovered in
Mesopotamia. But their use in Greece (where the highly accurate
'Metonic' cycle of 19 years was known about 450 B.C.) testifies to an
increasingly sophisticated tradition of observational astronomy.

The astronomical study of daily, monthly, and annual cycles is
connected not only with agricultural applications but also with the
seafaring enterprises in which Miletus excelled: thus Thales was
credited with one of the earliest handbooks (in verse) of *Nautical
Astronomy*.[40] Both agricultural and navigational concerns require
continuous attention to the atmospheric phenomena of evaporation
and precipitation involved in drought and rain, clouds and wind. It is
characteristic of Ionian cosmology to connect these with other, less
immediately obvious phenomena of earth, sea, and sky — such as the

silting process that has gradually transformed the ancient harbors of
Ephesus and Miletus into marshy plains 3 and 5 miles from the sea,
or the up-and-down changes in the level of the coastline that are
found throughout the Aegean area, as well as in southern Italy — and
to interpret them all in terms of a conflict between opposing powers:
the wet and the dry, the hot and the cold, the bright and the dark.
The natural philosophers construed this conflict as a cycle of elemental
interchange, within which each of the opposing powers dominates in
turn, as the hot and dry does in summer, the cold and wet in winter.
It was such a cycle that Anaximander described in the one surviving
quotation from his book:

> Out of those things [namely, the opposing powers] from which
> their generation comes, into these again does the destruction of
> things take place, in accordance with what is right and necessary;
> for they make amends and pay the penalty to one another for
> their aggression (*adikia*, injustice) according to the ordinance of
> Time. (DK 12.B1)

Here the pattern of physical change and transformation, the birth of
what is new and the death of what is old, is seen as a conflict regu-
lated by an 'ordinance of time', where the contestants appear in turn
as victor and vanquished. And this ordering is itself described in the
language of justice, where the wrongdoer must pay the penalty for his
aggression or excess. This Milesian notion of cosmic order as one of
opposition, reciprocity, and inevitable justice, is faithfully taken over
by Heraclitus, with all its poetic resonance and association with older,
mythical ideas: 'War is shared [for the killer will be killed in his turn],
and [hence] Conflict is Justice.' (See LXXXII, D. 80, with commentary.)

I have so far characterized the new Ionian cosmology by three
fundamental features: (1) a geometric model for the heavens, (2)
observation and numerical measurement of astral cycles, and (3) the
interpretation of physical change as a conflict of elemental powers
within a periodic order of reciprocity and symmetry recognized as
just. To these must be added a fourth, less original feature: the tendency to explain the present state of affairs by deriving it from some
initial situation or first beginning. In place of Hesiod's theogony, the
natural philosophers give us cosmogony. The reports on Anaximander
and the quotations from Anaxagoras show that Ionian cosmology
began, like Hesiod and the book of Genesis, 'in the beginning'. It
described the emergence of the world order as a gradual process of
generation or development from an *archē*, a starting point or 'what

came first of all' (*Theogony* 115). And there is some evidence to suggest that Anaximander, like Empedocles and the atomists later, applied the principle of symmetry to foresee a reversal of the cosmic process, so that the earth which had emerged from the sea would sink into it again, and perhaps the whole world process might begin anew.[41]

These four principles characterize the original Greek conception of the natural world as a *kosmos*, an orderly arrangement whose structure can be rationally understood. For the early cosmologists, as later for Plato, Aristotle and the Stoics, this conception entailed a fifth principle to which I have alluded: the idea of the cosmos brought with it the idea of the cosmic god.[42] Although this new theological view, with its radical departure from the traditional notion of the gods, is first clearly attested in the surviving fragments of Xenophanes, it seems likely that here too Anaximander was the precursor. For we are told that he described his primary cosmic principle, the *apeiron* or Boundless, as eternal and unaging, which is to say divine. And he said of this divine principle that it 'circumscribes all things and steers them all' (DK 12.A 15).

Now if Heraclitus shows little interest in the geometric model for the heavens or the scientific explanation of nature in detail, his thought is nevertheless penetrated by the new conception of the cosmos. Although not himself a *physikos* or natural philosopher proper, his own system can only be understood as a response to the world view of the Milesian physicists. This will appear most clearly if we compare his doctrine of Fire with the latest Milesian cosmology, that of Anaximenes.

In place of the indeterminate Boundless of Anaximander, Anaximenes proposed the more definite physical form of *aēr* as starting point for the cosmic process. Before the word come to denote atmospheric air, *aēr* had meant 'mist' or 'vapor'; and Anaximenes must have chosen this principle because of its close association with the atmospheric cycle of evaporation and condensation. He appears to have taken that cycle as the paradigm for understanding physical change in general and explaining the origin of the world order: all things are derived from *aēr* by being condensed through cooling or by being rarefied through heating.[43] This doctrine of Anaximenes, restated in later conceptual terms by Diogenes of Apollonia in the next century, was taken by Aristotle as the pattern for the material monism which he ascribes to most of the early *physikoi*. Thus Thales is said to have derived all things from water, as Anaximenes and Diogenes derived everything from air. And Heraclitus is named

together with a certain Hippasus of Metapontum as having chosen
fire as the starting point (*Met.* A 3, 983b—984a). This interpretation
of Heraclitus' doctrine by analogy with that of Anaximenes is more
fully stated in the Theophrastean doxography in Simplicius:

> They [sc. Hippasus and Heraclitus] produce all things from fire by
> thickening and rarefaction and they dissolve them back into fire,
> maintaining that this is the underlying nature or substrate of things.
> For Heraclitus says all things are an exchange (*amoibē*) for fire.
> (DK 22.A 5)

The last sentence of this report is a paraphrase of XL (D. 90): 'All
things are requital (*antamoibē*) for fire, and fire for all things, as
goods for gold and gold for goods.' Thus Theophrastus, following the
example of Aristotle, understood Heraclitus' doctrine of fire as the
statement of a physical theory along the lines of Anaximenes and
Diogenes of Apollonia, but differing from them by the substitution
of fire for air. And in doing so, Theophrastus was both right and
wrong. For the assertion that all things are exchanged for fire must
have been intended as an *allusion* to Anaximenes' doctrine; just as
statements like 'for water it is death to become earth, but out of
earth water arises' (CII, D. 36), or the listing of sea, earth and lightning storm as 'reversals' of fire (XXXVIII, D. 31A) and the statement
that 'sea pours out, and it measures up to the same amount it was
before becoming earth' (XXXIX, D. 31B) can only be understood by
reference to Ionian theories of elemental transformation.[44] Such
texts provided a *prima facie* case for grouping Heraclitus together
with the natural philosophers. Theophrastus' mistake (continued in
the tradition, both ancient and modern, that treats Heraclitus' doctrine of fire as a physical theory of the same sort as Anaximenes')
lies in ignoring the poetic and paradoxical nature of these statements
concerning elemental change, and thus treating the mode of
expression as irrelevant to the meaning. To make such a mistake is to
disregard the hint that Heraclitus himself had given in speaking of the
oracle which 'neither declares nor conceals but gives a sign' (XXXIII,
D. 93). The sign, in Heraclitus' case, is the very form of his discourse,
the nature of the *logos* which he has composed as an expression of
his own view of wisdom, in contrast to that piling up of erudition
which he despises as *polymathiē*, 'the learning of many things', in the
work of his predecessors. It is precisely in the use of such words as
antamoibē 'requital' and *tropai* 'turnings', 'reversals', as in the description of elemental change as a cycle of 'birth' and 'death' with the
soul (*psychē*) placed both at the beginning and at the end of the cycle

(CII, D. 36), that Heraclitus gives the sign of his own deeper meaning. These signs, and the riddling nature of his whole discourse, were systematically ignored by Theophrastus and the doxographers who followed him. Theophrastus could only regard the paradoxical style of the work as the symptom of some mental derangement, some *melancholia*, which caused Heraclitus to express himself 'sometimes incompletely and sometimes in inconsistent fashion'.[45]

We come closer to a correct reading of the signs with a Hellenistic critic named Diodotus, who declared that the book was not about the nature of things (*peri physeōs*) after all but about man's life in society (*peri politeias*), and that the physical doctrines serve only as illustration.[46] This is an overstatement, but it points in the right direction. Diels came still closer to the mark when he observed that Heraclitus was interested only in the most general conceptions of Ionian physics, and that his real starting point was 'I went in search of myself.' Once he had encountered the law of the microcosm within himself, 'he discovered it for a second time in the external world'.[47]

I believe that Diels was right in locating the central insight of Heraclitus in this identity of structure between the inner, personal world of the psyche and the larger natural order of the universe. The doctrines of fire, cosmic order, and elemental transformations serve as more than illustrations; but they are significant only insofar as they reveal a general truth about the unity of opposites, a truth whose primary application for human beings lies in a deeper understanding of their own experience of life and death, sleeping and waking, youth and old age. If I have chosen as epigraph for this book two quotations from Spinoza and Unamuno, that is not because they assert doctrines with which Heraclitus would have agreed but because they locate more precisely the focal point of his own philosophical reflection: a meditation on human life and human destiny in the context of biological death. In Heraclitus' view such an understanding of the human condition is inseparable from an insight into the unifying structure of the universe, the total unity within which all opposing principles — including mortality and immortality — are reconciled. It is this insight and this understanding which Heraclitus prizes as wisdom (*sophia*) and which his whole discourse struggles to express. The war of opposites, the cosmic fire, the divine one which is also wisdom itself or 'the wise one' — all these provide the framework within which human life and death are to be understood, and to be understood means to be seen in their unity, like day and night (XIX, D. 57). The ignorance of men lies in their failure to comprehend the

logos in which this insight is articulated, the *logos* which is at once
the discourse of Heraclitus, the nature of language itself, the structure of the psyche and the universal principle in accordance with
which all things come to pass. Heraclitus' grasp of this insight would
have been impossible without the new, philosophic conception of
cosmic order; and this sets him apart from the older Wise Men. But
he belongs with them in the concern for wisdom as an insight into
the pattern of human life and the limits of the human condition.
What they did not see — and could not see before the birth of natural
philosophy — is that the pattern of human life and the pattern of cosmic order is one and the same.

A fuller defense of this interpretation will be the task of the commentary. I conclude these introductory remarks by a glance at the
most striking of the 'physical' fragments, in which Heraclitus is
clearly responding to and transforming the doctrines of the natural
philosophers.

> The ordering (*kosmos*), the same for all, no god or man has made,
> but it ever was and is and will be: fire everliving, kindled in
> measures and in measures going out. (XXXVII, D. 30)

Modern interpreters who look for a physical theory in Heraclitus have
seen here a denial that the world order was generated as a result of
any cosmogonic process such as the other natural philosophers had
assumed. But the emphasis of the wording and imagery suggests something quite different.

The Milesians were concerned to show how the order of the world
had come into being, how it was maintained, and (very probably) how
it would eventually perish, only to be produced anew out of its
eternal and inexhaustible source. Anaximander had conceived this
order as governed from without, by the primordial Boundless; Xenophanes had replaced the Boundless with an intelligent deity who
moves all things by thought. Heraclitus accepts the Milesian view of a
world order in which the opposition and transformation of elementary powers is governed by measure and proportion. But he denies
that this order is imposed upon the world by any power from without. Instead, he deifies one of its internal constituents. For to say
that fire is 'everliving', that it 'ever was and is and will be' is to say,
simply, that it is eternal and divine. Yet Heraclitus insists upon the
fact that this god participates in the changing life of nature, 'kindled
in measures and in measures going out'. There is a genuine parallel
here to Anaximenes' conception of the primordial Air. But Anaximenes would scarcely have emphasized the extinction of his principle

at the very moment that he asserts its eternity; nor would he have identified his elemental principle with the cosmos as such. What is striking about Heraclitus' statement is that it confronts us with the double paradox of a world order identified with one of its constituent parts, and an eternal principle embodied in the most transitory of visual phenomena.

The resolution of these antinomies, concerning what is 'whole and not whole' (CXXIV, D. 10), what is both mortal and everliving, must await the fuller commentary. The point of importance here is that the choice of fire as a substitute for air can scarcely have been motivated by the desire for a more adequate physical theory: nothing is literally derived from fire in the way that winds, clouds, and water may be derived from air. Heraclitus' aim is not to improve the Milesian cosmology by altering a particular doctrine but to reinterpret its total meaning by a radical shift in perspective. The advantage of fire for the new point of view is that it signifies both a power of destruction and death − as in a burning city or a funeral pyre − and also a principle of superhuman vitality; a temporary phenomenon that dies out or is quenched and an eternal principle that is everywhere one and the same, whether in the altar flame, the domestic hearth, the forest fire lit by lightning, or the blazing torches of war. By meditating on the fire one who knows how to read oracular signs can perceive the hidden harmony that unifies opposing principles not only within the cosmic order but also in the destiny of the human psyche.

From Pythagoras of Samos, his neighbor and near contemporary, Heraclitus had learned a new conception of the destiny of the psyche, and perhaps also a new sense for the power of number, proportion, and measure in the rational organization of the world. But Pythagoras, like Xenophanes, provokes his particular scorn, for these two have tried to expand the philosophy of nature into a general vision of god and man and have, in his view, conspicuously failed.

It is precisely this task which Heraclitus undertakes. His real subject is not the physical world but the human condition, the condition of mortality. But by its participation in the eternal life cycle of nature and also by its capacity to master this pattern in cognition, the structure of the psyche is unlimited (XXXV, D. 45). Mortals are immortal, immortals mortal (XCII, D. 62). The opposites are one; and this deathless structure of life-and-death is deity itself.

Introductory note to text and translation

I give here as a 'fragment' every ancient citation or report that seems to provide information about the content of Heraclitus' book not otherwise available. Out of these 125 fragments, only 89 qualify as fully verbatim citations, and even this figure may be a bit too generous. The other 36 texts, marked here by square brackets, form a mixed bag. They include partial quotations blended with the citer's own text, free paraphrases that may or may not preserve some of the original wording, and some reports of doctrine that do not even claim to represent Heraclitus' words. Thus this second group of texts ranges from borderline quotations, that might be counted among the literal fragments, to doctrinal statements that could be listed with the doxography (in Appendix II). At either end the division is arbitrary. More significant, and less controversial, is the difference in principle between those passages where we have Heraclitus' own words and those where we do not. It is this distinction that I have tried to mark by the use of square brackets.

The translation aims at giving a readable version of Heraclitus' text, with as much literal accuracy as is compatible with the primary goal of not making Heraclitus more obscure in English than he is in Greek. In some cases, for example in LXXIII, D. 58, this means that the translation will deviate slightly from what I print as the most plausible text. In five cases (XLII, LXXII, LXXXI, XCV, and CXIII) I have combined two paraphrases in the translation or rendered the more reliable version. The glosses to the translation are designed to provide the minimum of lexical and other information required for a fair reading of the fragments. All substantive questions of scholarship and interpretation are postponed to the commentary.

In presenting the Greek text I follow Marcovich's edition wherever possible, but without his spacing and occasionally without his punctuation. The critical notes are designed to indicate significant discrepancy between Marcovich ('M.') and Diels-Kranz ('D.'), and my own divergences from Marcovich. The most important differences are the following. In the case of XXXVII (D. 30), LXIII (D. 49), LXXXII (D. 80), LXXXVI (D. 86), CVIII (D. 77), CIX (D. 118), and CXXIII (D. 67), I reject an interpolation or emendation made by Bywater or Diels and accepted by most subsequent editors (except Bollack-Wismann, with whom I agree in these cases). In XXXII (D. 112) I accept the punctuation given by Bollack-Wismann, which crucially alters the sense. In the desperate case of LXXIII (D. 58) I follow the text of Kirk, against both Diels and Marcovich.

The fragments

I

I (D. 1, M. 1) Sextus Empiricus, *Adversus Mathematicos* VII.132

τοῦ δὲ λόγου τοῦδ᾿ ἐόντος αἰεὶ ἀξύνετοι γίνονται ἄνθρωποι καὶ
πρόσθεν ἢ ἀκοῦσαι καὶ ἀκούσαντες τὸ πρῶτον· γινομένων γὰρ
πάντων κατὰ τὸν λόγον τόνδε ἀπείροισιν ἐοίκασι πειρώμενοι καὶ
ἐπέων καὶ ἔργων τοιουτέων ὁκοίων ἐγὼ διηγεῦμαι κατὰ φύσιν
διαιρέων ἕκαστον καὶ φράζων ὅκως ἔχει· τοὺς δὲ ἄλλους
ἀνθρώπους λανθάνει ὁκόσα ἐγερθέντες ποιοῦσιν ὅκωσπερ ὁκόσα
εὕδοντες ἐπιλανθάνονται.

II

II (D. 34, M. 2) Clement, *Stromateis* V.115.3

ἀξύνετοι ἀκούσαντες κωφοῖσιν ἐοίκασι· φάτις αὐτοῖσι μαρτυρεῖ
παρεόντας ἀπεῖναι.

III

III (D. 2, M. 23b) Sextus Empiricus, *Adversus Mathematicos* VIII.133

[διὸ δεῖ ἔπεσθαι τῷ κοινῷ · ξυνὸς γὰρ ὁ κοινός.] τοῦ λόγου δ᾿
ἐόντος ξυνοῦ ζώουσιν οἱ πολλοὶ ὡς ἰδίαν ἔχοντες φρόνησιν.

IV

IV (D. 17, M. 3) Clement, *Stromateis* II.8.1.

οὐ γὰρ φρονέουσι τοιαῦτα πολλοὶ ὁκοίοις ἐγκυρέουσιν, οὐδὲ μαθόντες
γινώσκουσιν, ἑωυτοῖσι δὲ δοκέουσι.

III With Bywater and Bollack-Wismann, I take the words in brackets as a comment by
Sextus. In the belief that they contain a genuine quotation Bekker inserted <ξυνῷ, τουτέστι
τῷ> after τῷ and before κοινῷ; followed by D., M., and others.
IV For ὁκοίοις ἐγκυρέουσιν D. reads ὁκόσοι ἐγκυρεῦσιν; others otherwise. The MSS have
ὁκόσοι ἐγκυρσεύουσιν.

I

Although this account holds forever, men ever fail to comprehend, both before hearing it and once they have heard. Although all things come to pass in accordance with this account, men are like the untried when they try such words and works as I set forth, distinguishing each according to its nature and telling how it is. But other men are oblivious of what they do awake, just as they are forgetful of what they do asleep.

II

Not comprehending, they hear like the deaf. The saying is their witness: absent while present.

III

Although the account is shared, most men live as though their thinking were a private possession.

IV

Most men do not think things in the way they encounter them, nor do they recognize what they experience, but believe their own opinions.

I   **account:** *logos*, saying, speech, discourse, statement, report; account, explanation, reason, principle; esteem, reputation; collection, enumeration, ratio, proportion; *logos* is translated 'account' here (twice) and also in III, XXVII, LX and LXII; it is rendered 'report' in XXXV, XXXVI and CI; 'amount' in XXXIX.

    holds forever: text is ambiguous between 'this account is forever, is eternal' and 'this account is true (but men ever fail to comprehend)'.

III   **shared:** *xynos*, common, in common, together: cf. same term in VI, XXX, LXXXII, XCIX.

    thinking: *phronēsis*, intelligence, understanding.

IV   **think:** *phroneousi*, understand, think straight; act with intelligence.

    recognize: *ginōskousi*, know, be acquainted with; a recurrent theme: cf. XIX, XX, XXII, XXVII, etc.

    believe their own opinions: *heōutoisi dokeousi*, lit. 'seem to themselves (to recognize and understand)', or 'imagine for themselves': cf. LXXXIV–LXXXV.

V

V (D. 71–3, M. 69b[1], 4, 3c, 1h[1]) Marcus Aurelius IV.46

[[ἀεὶ τοῦ Ἡρακλειτείου μεμνῆσθαι . . .
(there follows a version of XLI, D. 76)
μεμνῆσθαι δὲ καὶ τοῦ ἐπιλανθανομένου ᾗ ἡ ὁδὸς ἄγει· καὶ ὅτι ᾧ
μάλιστα διηνεκῶς ὁμιλοῦσι (λόγῳ τῷ τὰ ὅλα διοικοῦντι) τούτῳ
διαφέρονται, καὶ οἷς καθ᾽ ἡμέραν ἐγκυροῦσι, ταῦτα αὐτοῖς ξένα
φαίνεται. καὶ ὅτι οὐ δεῖ ὥσπερ καθεύδοντας ποιεῖν καὶ λέγειν.]]

VI

VI (D. 89, M. 24) Plutarch, *De Superstitione* 166C

[[ὁ Ἡράκλειτός φησι τοῖς ἐγρηγορόσιν ἕνα καὶ κοινὸν κόσμον εἶναι,
τῶν δὲ κοιμωμένων ἕκαστον εἰς ἴδιον ἀποστρέφεσθαι.]]

VII

VII (D. 18, M. 11) Clement, *Stromateis* II.17.4

ἐὰν μὴ ἔλπηται ἀνέλπιστον οὐκ ἐξευρήσει, ἀνεξερεύνητον ἐὸν καὶ
ἄπορον.

VIII

VIII (D. 22, M. 10) Clement, *Stromateis* IV.4.2

χρυσὸν οἱ διζήμενοι γῆν πολλὴν ὀρύσσουσι καὶ εὑρίσκουσιν ὀλίγον.

V

[[Men forget where the way leads . . . And they are at odds with that with which they most constantly associate. And what they meet with every day seems strange to them . . . We should not act and speak like men asleep.]]

VI ⁄

[[The world of the waking is one and shared, but the sleeping turn aside each into his private world.]]

VII

He who does not expect will not find out the unexpected, for it is trackless and unexplored.

VIII

Seekers of gold dig up much earth and find little.

V   From Marcus Aurelius: 'Always bear in mind what Heraclitus said . . . about the man who forgets . . . '
   at odds with: *diapherontai*, differ from; quarrel with: cf. LXXVIII and CXXIV; most of this text seems to be a reminiscence of other fragments (CVI, D. 117; IV, D. 17; and I or VI, D. 89).

VI   From Plutarch: 'Heraclitus says that . . . '

32

IX

IX (D. 35, M. 7) Clement, *Stromateis* V.140.5

χρὴ εὖ μάλα πολλῶν ἵστορας φιλοσόφους ἄνδρας εἶναι καθ᾽ Ἡράκλειτον.

X

X (D. 123, M. 8) Philo, Themistius, etc.

φύσις κρύπτεσθαι φιλεῖ.

XI

XI (D. 47, M. 113) Diogenes Laertius IX.73

μὴ εἰκῇ περὶ τῶν μεγίστων συμβαλλώμεθα.

XII

XII (D. A23, M. 6a[1]) Polybius IV.40.2

[[οὐκ ἄν ἔτι πρέπον εἴη ποιηταῖς καὶ μυθογράφοις χρῆσθαι μάρτυσι περὶ τῶν ἀγνοουμένων, ὅπερ οἱ πρὸ ἡμῶν πεποιήκασι περὶ τῶν πλείστων, ἀπίστους ἀμφισβητουμένων παρεχόμενοι βεβαιωτὰς κατὰ τὸν Ἡράκλειτον.]]

IX

Men who love wisdom must be good inquirers into many things indeed.

X

Nature loves to hide.)

XI

Let us not concur casually about the most important matters.

XII

[[In taking the poets as testimony for things unknown, they are citing authorities that cannot be trusted.]]

IX   Men who love wisdom: *philosophoi andres*, philosophers: cf. *sophon*, wise, in XXVII, etc.

inquirers: *histores*, researchers, investigators; judges; eye-witnesses; Ionian science was called *peri physeōs historiē*, inquiry into the nature of things.

X   Nature: *physis*, character or nature of a thing.

loves: *philei*, tends; alternate rendering: 'The true character of a thing likes to be in hiding.'

XI   casually: *eikē*, at random, perhaps with a play here on *eikēi*, (concur) with likelihood.

XII   From Polybius: 'It would no longer be fitting to take poets and story-tellers as witnesses for things unknown, as our ancestors did in most cases, citing untrustworthy authorities on disputed points as Heraclitus says.'

34

XIII

XIII (D. 74, M. 89) Marcus Aurelius IV.46 (following citation V above)

[[καὶ ὅτι οὐ δεῖ <ὡς> παῖδας τοκεώνων (sc. ποιεῖν καὶ λέγειν), τουτέστι κατὰ ψιλόν· καθότι παρειλήφαμεν.]]

XIV

XIV (D. 55, M. 5) Hippolytus, *Refutatio* IX.9.5

ὅσων ὄψις ἀκοὴ μάθησις, ταῦτα ἐγὼ προτιμέω.

XV

XV (D. 101a, M. 6) Polybius XII.27.1

[[κατὰ τὸν Ἡράκλειτον· ὀφθαλμοὶ γὰρ τῶν ὤτων ἀκριβέστεροι μάρτυρες.]]

XVI

XVI (D. 107, M. 13) Sextus Empiricus, *Adversus Mathematicos* VII.126

κακοὶ μάρτυρες ἀνθρώποισιν ὀφθαλμοὶ καὶ ὦτα βαρβάρους ψυχὰς ἐχόντων.

XVII

XVII (D. 19, M. 1g) Clement, *Stromateis* II.24.5

ἀκοῦσαι οὐκ ἐπιστάμενοι οὐδ᾽ εἰπεῖν.

XIII

[[We should not listen like children to their parents.]]

XIV

Whatever comes from sight, hearing, learning from experience: this I prefer.

XV

[[Eyes are surer witnesses than ears.]]

XVI

Eyes and ears are poor witnesses for men if their souls do not understand the language.

XVII

Not knowing how to listen, neither can they speak.

XIII   From Marcus Aurelius (continuing V above); alternate rendering: 'we should not <act and speak> like children of our parents, in other words, in the way that has been handed down to us.'

XIV   **learning from experience:** *mathēsis*, cognate with *mathontes*, they experience, in IV.

XV   From Polybius: 'According to Heraclitus . . . '
   Eyes i.e. direct experience.
   ears i.e. hearsay.

XVI   Literally, 'if they have barbarian souls (*psychai*)', souls that do not speak Greek. For *psychē*, see on XXXV.

36

XVIII

XVIII (D. 40, M. 16) Diogenes Laertius IX.1

πολυμαθίη νόον οὐ διδάσκει · Ἡσίοδον γὰρ ἂν ἐδίδαξε καὶ
Πυθαγόρην, αὖτίς τε Ξενοφάνεά τε καὶ Ἑκαταῖον.

XIX

XIX (D. 57, M. 43) Hippolytus, *Refutatio* IX.10.2

διδάσκαλος δὲ πλείστων Ἡσίοδος · τοῦτον ἐπίστανται πλεῖστα
εἰδέναι, ὅστις ἡμέρην καὶ εὐφρόνην οὐκ ἐγίνωσκεν · ἔστι γὰρ ἕν.

XX

XX (D. 106, M. 59) Plutarch, *Camillus* 19.1

[[Ἡράκλειτος ἐπέπληξεν Ἡσιόδῳ τὰς μὲν (sc. ἡμέρας) ἀγαθὰς
ποιουμένῳ, τὰς δὲ φαύλας, ὡς ἀγνοοῦντι φύσιν ἡμέρας μίαν οὖσαν.]]

XXI

XXI (D. 42, M. 30) Diogenes Laertius IX.1

τόν τε Ὅμηρον ἔφασκεν ἄξιον ἐκ τῶν ἀγώνων ἐκβάλλεσθαι καὶ
ῥαπίζεσθαι, καὶ Ἀρχίλοχον ὁμοίως.

XVIII

Much learning does not teach understanding. For it would have taught
Hesiod and Pythagoras, and also Xenophanes and Hecataeus.

XIX

The teacher of most is Hesiod. It is him they know as knowing most,
who did not recognize day and night: they are one.

XX

[[Hesiod counted some days as good, others as bad, because he did
not recognize that the nature of every day is one and the same.]]

XXI

Homer deserves to be expelled from the competition and beaten with
a staff — and Archilochus too!

XVIII Much learning: *polymathiē*, learning many things, cognate with *mathontes, mathēsis*
in IV and XIV; term apparently coined by Heraclitus.
    understanding: *noos*, mind, good sense, as in XXX and LIX.
    Hesiod, epic poet of early seventh century B.C., author of *Theogony* and *Works and
Days*.
    Pythagoras of Samos, philosopher and social leader of late sixth century.
    Xenophanes of Colophon, poet and philosopher-theologian of same period.
    Hecataeus of Miletus, contemporary world-traveller and rationalizing student of myth,
author of lost works on geography and legendary genealogies.

XIX   day and night: referring to *Theogony* 748—57, where Day and Night meet one
another as mythical figures moving in opposite directions.

**XX   ** From Plutarch: 'Heraclitus attacked Hesiod for counting some days as good . . . ',
referring to *Works and Days* 765ff., where lucky and unlucky days are distinguished.

XXI   beaten with a staff, with a *rhabdos*, standard instrument of bards and rhapsodes who
competed in poetic performances.
    Archilochus, lyric poet and author of comic invectives, seventh century B.C.

38

XXII

XXII (D. 56, M. 21) Hippolytus, *Refutatio* IX.9.5

ἐξηπάτηνται οἱ ἄνθρωποι πρὸς τὴν γνῶσιν τῶν φανερῶν
παραπλησίως Ὁμήρῳ, ὃς ἐγένετο τῶν Ἑλλήνων σοφώτερος
πάντων· ἐκεῖνόν τε γὰρ παῖδες φθεῖρας κατακτείνοντες ἐξηπάτησαν
εἰπόντες· ὅσα εἴδομεν καὶ κατελάβομεν, ταῦτα ἀπολείπομεν, ὅσα δὲ
οὔτε εἴδομεν οὔτ᾽ ἐλάβομεν, ταῦτα φέρομεν.

XXIII

XXIII (D. 105, M. 63a) Scholia A T in *Iliad* XVIII.251

[[Ἡράκλειτος... ἀστρολόγον φησὶ τὸν "Ὅμηρον.]]

XXIV

XXIV (D. 38, M. 63b) Diogenes Laertius I.23

[[δοκεῖ δὲ (sc. Θαλῆς) κατά τινας πρῶτος ἀστρολογῆσαι καὶ ἡλιακὰ
ἐκλείψεις καὶ τροπὰς προειπεῖν, ὥς φησιν Εὔδημος ἐν τῇ περὶ τῶν
ἀστρολογουμένων ἱστορίᾳ· ὅθεν αὐτὸν καὶ Ξενοφάνης καὶ Ἡρόδοτος
θαυμάζει· μαρτυρεῖ δ᾽ αὐτῷ καὶ Ἡράκλειτος καὶ Δημόκριτος.]]

XXV

XXV (D. 129, M. 17) Diogenes Laertius VIII.6

Πυθαγόρης Μνησάρχου ἱστορίην ἤσκησεν ἀνθρώπων μάλιστα πάντω
καὶ ἐκλεξάμενος ταύτας τὰς συγγραφὰς ἐποιήσατο ἑαυτοῦ σοφίην,
πολυμαθείην, κακοτεχνίην.

XXII Following Bernays, D. and M. bracket the prefix κατ- in κατελάβομεν, needlessly.

XXII

Men are deceived in the recognition of what is obvious, like Homer who was wisest of all the Greeks. For he was deceived by boys killing lice, who said: what we see and catch we leave behind; what we neither see nor catch we carry away.

XXIII

[[Homer was an astronomer.]]

XXIV

[[Thales practiced astronomy.]]

XXV

Pythagoras son of Mnesarchus pursued inquiry further than all other men and, choosing what he liked from these compositions, made a wisdom of his own: much learning, artful knavery.

XXII In traditional versions of this story Homer, who is blind, dies of chagrin at not guessing the riddle.

XXIII From scholia on *Iliad* XVIII.251: 'Heraclitus calls Homer an astronomer.'

XXIV From Diogenes Laertius: 'Xenophanes and Herodotus express their admiration for Thales <for his practice of astronomy>. Heraclitus also bears witness to him <for this>.'

XXV Pythagoras: see on XVIII.
  inquiry: *historiē*: see on IX.
  much learning: *polymathiē*: see on XVIII.
  artful knavery: *kakotechniē*, the art (*technē*) of doing evil, another coinage of Heraclitus.

XXVI

XXVI (D. 81, M. 18) Philodemus, *Rhetorica* I, coll. 57, 62

[[κατὰ τὸν Ἡράκλειτον κοπίδων ἐστὶν ἀρχηγός.]]

XXVII

XXVII (D. 108, M. 83) Stobaeus III.1.174

ὁκόσων λόγους ἤκουσα οὐδεὶς ἀφικνεῖται ἐς τοῦτο ὥστε γινώσκειν ὅτι σοφόν ἐστι, πάντων κεχωρισμένον.

XXVIII

XXVIII (D. 101, M. 15) Plutarch, *Adversus Coloten* 1118C

ἐδιζησάμην ἐμεωυτόν.

XXIX

XXIX (D. 116, M. 15f = 23e) Stobaeus III.5.6

ἀνθρώποισι πᾶσι μέτεστι γινώσκειν ἐωυτοὺς καὶ σωφρονεῖν.

XXVII I punctuate with Bollack-Wismann. Other editors read ὅτι σοφόν ἐστι πάντων κεχωρισμένον.

XXVI

[[Pythagoras was the prince of imposters.]]   ———

XXVII

Of all those whose accounts I have heard, none has gone so far as this: to recognize what is wise, set apart from all.

XXVIII

I went in search of myself.

XXIX

It belongs to all men to know themselves and to think well.   ———

XXVI   From Philodemus: 'Rhetoric . . . is, in the words of Heraclitus, the prince (*archēgos*, initiator, founder, ring-leader) of imposters'; reference to Pythagoras is not certain.

XXVII   accounts: *logoi*: see on I.
   what is wise: alternate punctuation: 'that the wise is set apart'.
   from all: *pantōn*, ambiguous between 'all men' and 'all things'. For *sophon*, wise, see also XXXVI, LIV, and CXVIII.

XXIX   know themselves: allusion to the Delphic motto *gnōthi seauton* 'Know (lit. recognize) thyself'.
   think well: *sōphronein*, sound thinking, good sense; moderation, self-restraint; cognate with *phronēsis*, thinking, intelligence in III, *phronein* think, act with intelligence in IV and XXXI.

42

XXX

XXX (D. 114, M. 23a) Stobaeus III.1.179

ξὺν νόῳ λέγοντας ἰσχυρίζεσθαι χρὴ τῷ ξυνῷ πάντων, ὅκωσπερ νόμῳ πόλις καὶ πολὺ ἰσχυροτέρως· τρέφονται γὰρ πάντες οἱ ἀνθρώπειοι νόμοι ὑπὸ ἑνὸς τοῦ θείου· κρατεῖ γὰρ τοσοῦτον ὁκόσον ἐθέλει καὶ ἐξαρκεῖ πᾶσι καὶ περιγίνεται.

XXXI

XXXI (D. 113, M. 23d) Stobaeus III.1.179

ξυνόν ἐστι πᾶσι τὸ φρονέειν.

XXXII

XXXII (D. 112, M. 23f) Stobaeus III.1.178

σωφρονεῖν ἀρετὴ μεγίστη καὶ σοφίη, ἀληθέα λέγειν καὶ ποιεῖν κατὰ φύσιν ἐπαΐοντας.

XXXIII

XXXIII (D. 93, M. 14) Plutarch, De Pythiae Oraculis 404D

ὁ ἄναξ οὗ τὸ μαντεῖόν ἐστι τὸ ἐν Δελφοῖς οὔτε λέγει οὔτε κρύπτει ἀλλὰ σημαίνει.

XXXII With Bollack-Wismann I punctuate after σοφίη and not (as with most editors) after μεγίστη.

XXX

Speaking with understanding they must hold fast to what is shared by all, as a city holds to its law, and even more firmly. For all human laws are nourished by a divine one. It prevails as it will and suffices for all and is more than enough.

XXXI

Thinking is shared by all.

XXXII

Thinking well is the greatest excellence and wisdom: to act and speak what is true, perceiving things according to their nature.

XXXIII

The lord whose oracle is in Delphi neither declares nor conceals, but gives a sign.

XXX   **understanding:** *noos*: cf. XVIII.
   shared: *xynos*: see on III.
   by all: *pantōn*: ambiguous gender as in XXVII.
   divine one: *henos tou theiou*, similarly ambiguous between 'the one divine (thing)' and 'the one divine law'.
   suffices for all: *pasi*, same ambiguity: all things? laws? people?
   is more than enough: *periginetai*, is left over, survives intact; prevails over, surpasses. The three terms 'with understanding' (*xyn noōi*), 'what is shared' (*tōi xynōi*) and 'its law' (*tōi nomōi*) are linked by an untranslated word play. For the thought cf. LXV.

XXXI   **Thinking:** *to phroneein*: see on IV.
   shared: *xynon*: see on III.
   by all: *pasi*: 'all things' or 'all men', as in the preceding.

XXXII   **Thinking well:** *sōphronein*: see on XXIX.
   excellence: *aretē*, courage, military prowess; nobility, good breeding, distinction; virtue, moral excellence; alternate punctuation: 'Sound thinking is the greatest excellence, and wisdom is to speak things true and act according to nature by listening < to the *logos* >.'

XXXIII   **The lord** i.e. Apollo.

44

XXXIV (D. 92, M. 75) Plutarch, *De Pythiae Oraculis* 397A

[[Σίβυλλα δὲ μαινομένῳ στόματι καθ᾽ Ἡράκλειτον ἀγέλαστα καὶ ἀκαλλώπιστα καὶ ἀμύριστα φθεγγομένη χιλίων ἐτῶν ἐξικνεῖται τῇ φωνῇ διὰ τὸν θεόν.]]

XXXV

XXXV (D. 45, M. 67) Diogenes Laertius IX.7

ψυχῆς πείρατα ἰὼν οὐκ ἂν ἐξεύροιο πᾶσαν ἐπιπορευόμενος ὁδόν· οὕτω βαθὺν λόγον ἔχει.

XXXVI

XXXVI (D. 50, M. 26) Hippolytus, *Refutatio* IX.9.1

οὐκ ἐμοῦ ἀλλὰ τοῦ λόγου ἀκούσαντας ὁμολογεῖν σοφόν ἐστιν ἓν πάντα εἶναι.

XXXVII

XXXVII (D. 30, M. 51) Clement, *Stromateis* V.103.6

κόσμον τὸν αὐτὸν ἀπάντων οὔτε τις θεῶν οὔτε ἀνθρώπων ἐποίησεν, ἀλλ᾽ ἦν ἀεὶ καὶ ἔστιν καὶ ἔσται πῦρ ἀείζωον, ἁπτόμενον μέτρα καὶ ἀποσβεννύμενον μέτρα.

XXXVI With some misgiving I accept the usual correction εἶναι for εἰδέναι in the MSS.
XXXVII I give the text of Clement. Since Bywater most editors have added τόνδε after κόσμον from an inferior variant found in Simplicius and Plutarch (who do not have τὸν αὐτὸν ἀπάντων).

XXXIV

[[The Sibyl with raving mouth utters things mirthless and unadorned
and unperfumed, and her voice carries through a thousand years
because of the god who speaks through her.]]

XXXV

You will not find out the limits of the soul by going, even if you
travel over every way, so deep is its report.

XXXVI

It is wise, listening not to me but to the report, to agree that all things
are one.

XXXVII

The ordering, the same for all, no god nor man has made, but it ever
was and is and will be fire everliving, kindled in measures and in
measures going out.

XXXIV   From Plutarch: 'The Sibyl with raving mouth, as Heraclitus says . . .'.
   Sibyl, legendary woman who prophesied in trance, possessed by Apollo.

XXXV   **soul:** *psychē,* life-breath, life; ghost, phantom; spirit, soul.
   report: *logos:* see on I; perhaps 'so deep is its measure'.

XXXVI   **wise:** *sophon:* see on XXVII.
   report: *logos:* see on I.
   agree: *homologein,* say the same thing as, agree with, playing here on *logos:* 'to speak in
agreement with the report that says . . .'.

XXXVII   **ordering:** *kosmos,* military array, good order; adornment; world order.
   for all: *hapantōn,* either 'all men' or 'all things', as in XXVII, etc. Alternate version of the
text: 'This ordering no god nor man has made . . .'

XXXVIII

XXXVIII (D. 31A, M. 53A) Clement, *Stromateis* V.104.3

πυρὸς τροπαὶ πρῶτον θάλασσα, θαλάσσης δὲ τὸ μὲν ἥμισυ γῆ, τὸ δὲ ἥμισυ πρηστήρ.

XXXIX

XXXIX (D. 31B, M. 53B) Clement, *Stromateis* V.104.5

θάλασσα διαχέεται καὶ μετρέεται εἰς τὸν αὐτὸν λόγον ὁκοῖος πρόσθεν ἦν ἢ γενέσθαι γῆ.

XL

XL (D. 90, M. 54) Plutarch, *De E apud Delphous* 388D—E

πυρὸς ἀνταμοιβὴ τὰ πάντα καὶ πῦρ ἀπάντων ὅκωσπερ χρυσοῦ χρήματα καὶ χρημάτων χρυσός.

XLI

XLI (D. 76, M. 66e[1]) Plutarch, *De E apud Delphous* 392C

[[ὡς Ἡράκλειτος ἔλεγε, πυρὸς θάνατος ἀέρι γένεσις, καὶ ἀέρος θάνατος ὕδατι γένεσις.]]

XXXIX Here again I give the text of Clement, as corrected from Eusebius. Many editors introduce <γῆ> as subject of the first clause.
XL The MS reading in Plutarch ἀνταμείβεται πάντα, retained by Bywater and revived by Bollack-Wismann, may be correct: but it offers no appreciable difference in sense.

XXXVIII

The reversals of fire: first sea; but of sea half is earth, half lightning storm.

XXXIX

Sea pours out <from earth>, and it measures up to the same amount it was before becoming earth.

XL

All things are requital for fire, and fire for all things, as goods for gold and gold for goods.

XLI

[[The death of fire is birth for air, and the death of air is birth for water.]]

XXXVIII   reversals: *tropē*, reversal, flight in battle, rout; turning around, turning point, esp. of the sun = solstice.
  lightning storm: *prēstēr*, literally 'burner', a violent storm with destructive lightning.

XXXIX   May be continuous with preceding fragment.
  pours out: *diacheetai*, is spread apart, dissolves.
  amount: *logos*: see on I; cf. the sense 'measure' in XXXV. Alternate version of the text: 'Earth dissolves as sea, and it measures up to the same *logos* as was there at first.'

XL   requital: *antamoibē*, exchange; payment; punishment.

XLI   From Plutarch: 'As Heraclitus said ... '

48

XLII

XLIIA (D. 100, M. 64) Plutarch, *Quaestiones Platonicae* 1007D—E

[[περιόδους · ὧν ὁ ἥλιος ἐπιστάτης ὢν καὶ σκοπός, ὁρίζειν καὶ βραβεύειν καὶ ἀναδεικνύναι καὶ ἀναφαίνειν μεταβολὰς καὶ ὥρας αἳ πάντα φέρουσι καθ᾽ Ἡράκλειτον.]]

XLIIB (see M. p. 344) Plutarch, *De Defectu Oraculorum* 416A

[[ἐνιαυτὸς ἀρχὴν ἐν αὐτῷ καὶ τελευτὴν ὁμοῦ τι πάντων ὢν φέρουσιν ὧραι γῆ δὲ φύει περιέχων.]]

XLIIIA

XLIIIA (D. A13, M. 65) Censorinus, *De Die Natali* 18.11

[[est praeterea annus . . . [sc. magnus] . . . cuius anni hiemps summa est cataclysmos, . . . aestas autem ecpyrosis, quod est mundi incendium. nam his alternis temporibus mundus tum ignescere tum exaquescere videtur. hunc Aristarchus putavit esse annorum vertentium IICCCCLXXXIIII, . . . Heraclitus et Linus XDCCC.]]

XLIIIB

XLIIIB (D. A5) Simplicius, *in Physicorum* 23, 38

[[ποιεῖ δὲ (sc. Ἡράκλειτος) καὶ τάξιν τινὰ καὶ χρόνον ὡρισμένον τῆς τοῦ κόσμου μεταβολῆς κατά τινα εἱμαρμένην ἀνάγκην.]]

XLIV

XLIV (D. 94, M. 52) Plutarch, *De Exilio* 604A

Ἥλιος οὐχ ὑπερβήσεται μέτρα · εἰ δὲ μή, Ἐρινύες μιν Δίκης ἐπίκουροι ἐξευρήσουσιν.

XLII

[[The sun is overseer and sentinel of cycles, for determining the changes and the seasons which bring all things to birth.]]

XLIIIA

[[There is a Great Year, whose winter is a great flood and whose summer is a world conflagration. In these alternating periods the world is now going up in flames, now turning to water. This cycle consists of 10,800 years.]]

XLIIIB

[[There is a certain order and fixed time for the change of the cosmos in accordance with some fated necessity.]]

XLIV

The sun will not transgress his measures. If he does, the Furies, ministers of Justice, will find him out.

XLII   From Plutarch: 'the seasons which bring all things to birth, as Heraclitus says'. Reference to the sun may not belong to Heraclitus.

XLIIIA   From Censorinus: 'Heraclitus and Linus <believed this cycle to consist of> 10,800 years.'

XLIIIB   From Simplicius: 'Heraclitus posits a certain order . . .'

XLIV   Justice: *dikē*, personified as daughter of Zeus in Hesiod's *Works and Days*: see on LXIX.

50

XLV

XLV (D. 120, M. 62) Strabo I.1.6

ἠοῦς καὶ ἐσπέρας τέρματα ἡ ἄρκτος καί, ἀντίον τῆς ἄρκτου, οὖρος αἰθρίου Διός.

XLVI

XLVI (D. 99, M. 60) Plutarch (?), *Aqua an ignis utilior* 957A

[['Ηράκλειτος μὲν οὖν εἰ μὴ ἥλιος φησὶν ἦν, εὐφρόνη ἂν ἦν.]]

XLVII

XLVII (D. 3, M. 57) Aetius II.21 (ed. Diels, *Doxographi Graeci* p. 352)

[['Ηράκλειτος εὖρος ποδὸς ἀνθρωπείου (sc. φησὶν τὸν ἥλιον εἶναι.]]

XLVIIIA

XLVIIIA (D. 6, M. 58a) Aristotle, *Meteorologica* II.2 355a13

[[ὁ ἥλιος ... καθάπερ ὁ Ἡράκλειτός φησι, νέος ἐφ' ἡμέρῃ ἐστίν.]]

XLVIIIB

XLVIIIB (M. 58c) Plato, *Republic VI*, 498A

[[οἱ καὶ ἀπτόμενοι (sc. τῆς φιλοσοφίας) μειράκια ὄντα ... πρὸς δὲ τὸ γῆρας ἐκτὸς δή τινων ὀλίγων ἀποσβέννυνται πολὺ μᾶλλον τοῦ Ἡρακλειτείου ἡλίου, ὅσον αὖθις οὐκ ἐξάπτονται.]]

XLVI Another version (in Plutarch and Clement) has the words ἕνεκα τῶν ἄλλων ἄστρων preceding the second clause.

XLV

The limits of Dawn and Evening is the Bear; and, opposite the Bear, the Warder of luminous Zeus.

XLVI

[[If there were no sun, it would be night.]]

XLVII

[[The sun is the size of a human foot.]]

XLVIIIA

[[The sun is new every day.]]

XLVIIIB

[[The sun is extinguished in old age, but rekindled again.]]

XLV limits: *termata*, goal, destination; turning mark for runners in a race; border, limits.
Dawn i.e. the east.
Evening i.e. the west.
The Bear: Ursa Major, the north?
Warder: *ouros*, watchman, warder; boundary, limit; the *ouros* opposite the Bear (*arktos*) must be Arcturus (*Arkt-ouros*), whose risings and settings commonly served to mark the seasons.

XLVI From Plutarch: 'Heraclitus says . . . ' Some versions add 'as far as the other stars are concerned'.

XLVII From Aetius: 'Heraclitus says . . . '

XLVIIIA From Aristotle: 'As Heraclitus says . . . '

XLVIIIB From Plato: 'Those who are kindled <in their interest for philosophy> as boys . . . are, except for a few, extinguished in old age, much more so than the sun of Heraclitus, since they are not rekindled.'

XLIX

XLIX (D. 126, M. 42) Tzetzes, *Scholia ad Exegesin in Iliadem* p. 126

τὰ ψυχρὰ θέρεται, θερμὸν ψύχεται, ὑγρὸν αὐαίνεται, καρφαλέον νοτίζεται.

L

L (D. 12, M. 40a) Arius Didymus fr. 39.2, ed. Diels, *Doxographi Graeci* p. 471, 4

ποταμοῖσι τοῖσιν αὐτοῖσιν ἐμβαίνουσιν ἕτερα καὶ ἕτερα ὕδατα ἐπιρρεῖ.

LI

LI (D. 91, M. 40c[3]) Plutarch, *De E apud Delphous* 392B

[[ποταμῷ γὰρ οὐκ ἔστιν ἐμβῆναι δὶς τῷ αὐτῷ καθ᾽ Ἡράκλειτον· οὐδὲ θνητῆς οὐσίας δὶς ἅψασθαι κατὰ ἕξιν, ἀλλ᾽ ὀξύτητι καὶ τάχει μεταβολῆς σκίδνησι καὶ πάλιν συνάγει, μᾶλλον δὲ οὐδὲ πάλιν οὐδ᾽ ὕστερον ἀλλ ἅμα συνίσταται καὶ ἀπολείπει, καὶ πρόσεισι καὶ ἄπεισιν.]]

LII

LII (D. 84a, M. 56A) Plotinus IV.8.1 (text below)

LIII

LIII (D. 84b, M. 56B) Plotinus (reference above)

[[ὁ μὲν γὰρ Ἡράκλειτος . . . εἰπών . . . μεταβάλλον ἀναπαύεται καὶ κάματός ἐστι τοῖς αὐτοῖς μοχθεῖν καὶ ἄρχεσθαι, εἰκάζειν ἔδωκεν.]]

XLIX

Cold warms up, warm cools off, moist parches, dry dampens.

L

As they step into the same rivers, other and still other waters flow
upon them.

LI

[[One cannot step twice into the same river, nor can one grasp any
mortal substance in a stable condition, but it scatters and again
gathers; it forms and dissolves, and approaches and departs.]]

LII

[[It rests by changing.]]

LIII

[[It is weariness to toil at the same tasks and be always beginning.]]

L   For the context, see note to CXIII.

LI   From Plutarch: 'According to Heraclitus . . . '

LII   From Plotinus: 'Heraclitus left us to guess what he means when he said . . . '

LIII   From Plotinus (continuing LII): 'and when he said . . . '. Alternate rendering: 'It is a
weariness to labor for the same masters and be ruled by them' (Burnet).

LIV

LIV (D. 41, M. 85) Diogenes Laertius IX.1

ἓν τὸ σοφόν· ἐπίστασθαι γνώμην ὅκη †κυβερνῆσαι† πάντα διὰ πάντων.

LV

LV (D. 78, M. 90) Origen, *Contra Celsum* VI. 12

ἦθος γὰρ ἀνθρώπειον οὐκ ἔχει γνώμας, θεῖον δὲ ἔχει.

LVI

LVI (D. 82–3, M. 92b) [Plato], *Hippias Major* 289A–B

[[τὸ τοῦ Ἡρακλείτου εὖ ἔχει, ὡς ἄρα πιθήκων ὁ κάλλιστος αἰσχρὸς ἀνθρώπων γένει συμβάλλειν. ... ἢ οὐ καὶ Ἡράκλειτος αὐτὸ τοῦτο λέγει, ὃν σὺ ἐπάγῃ, ὅτι ἀνθρώπων ὁ σοφώτατος πρὸς θεὸν πίθηκος φανεῖται καὶ σοφίῃ καὶ κάλλει καὶ τοῖς ἄλλοις πᾶσιν;]]

LVII

LVII (D. 79, M. 92a) Origen, *Contra Celsum* VI.12

ἀνὴρ νήπιος ἤκουσε πρὸς δαίμονος ὅκωσπερ παῖς πρὸς ἀνδρός.

LVIII

LVIII (D. 70, M. 92d) Iamblichus, *De Anima*, in Stobaeus II.1.16

[[Ἡράκλειτος παίδων ἀθύρματα νενόμικεν εἶναι τὰ ἀνθρώπινα δοξάσματα.]]

LIV The form ὅκη (as in CVI, D. 117) is a natural emendation for the impossible ὁτέη in the MSS. The plausible readings for κυβερνῆσαι are (1) ἐκυβέρνησε and (2) κυβερνᾶται; but neither seems an obvious correction.

LIV

The wise is one, knowing the plan by which it steers all things
through all.

LV

Human nature has no set purpose, but the divine has.

LVI

[[The most beautiful of apes is ugly in comparison with the race of
man; the wisest of men seems an ape in comparison to a god.]]

LVII

A man is found foolish by a god, as a child by a man.

LVIII

[[Human opinions are toys for children.]]

LIV   wise: *sophon*: see on XXVII.
   plan: *gnōmē*, insight, recognition; thought, opinion, judgment; plan, proposal. Alternate
reading: 'The wise is one thing, namely, to know [lit. master the insight] how all things are
steered through all.'

LV   nature: *ēthos*, character, customary disposition.
   set purpose: *gnōmai*: see preceding note.

LVI   From pseudo-Plato, *Hippias Major*: 'What Heraclitus says is right, that . . . '

LVIII   From Iamblichus: 'Heraclitus believed that . . . '

56

LIX

LIX (D. 104, M. 101) Proclus *in Alcibiades* I, p. 117 Westerink

τίς γὰρ αὐτῶν νόος ἢ φρήν; δήμων ἀοιδοῖσι πείθονται καὶ διδασκάλῳ χρείωνται ὁμίλῳ οὐκ εἰδότες ὅτι 'οἱ πολλοὶ κακοί', ὀλίγοι ἀγαθοί.

LX

LX (D. 87, M. 109) Plutarch, *De Audiendis Poetis* 28D

βλὰξ ἄνθρωπος ἐπὶ παντὶ λόγῳ φιλεῖ ἐπτοῆσθαι.

LXI

LXI (D. 97, M. 22) Plutarch, *An Seni Respublica gerenda sit* 787C

κύνες καὶ βαΰζουσιν ὃν ἂν μὴ γινώσκωσι.

LXII

LXII (D. 39, M. 100) Diogenes Laertius I.88

ἐν Πριήνῃ Βίας ἐγένετο ὁ Τευτάμεω, οὗ πλέων λόγος ἢ τῶν ἄλλων.

LXIII

LXIII (D. 49, M. 98) Theodorus Prodromus, *Epistulae* 1 (Migne p. 1240A)

εἷς μύριοι, ἐὰν ἄριστος ᾖ.

LIX With most editors I accept Diels' conjecture πείθονται for ἕπονται (Clement) or ἠπιόων τε (MSS of Proclus).
LX With Bollack-Wismann, I follow the word order of what seems the more accurate citation. The last two words are inverted in most editions.
LXIII With Bollack-Wismann, I give the text as found in Theodorus and Symmachus. D. and M. combine this with a variant (in Galen and elsewhere) that includes ἐμοί.

LIX

What wit or understanding do they have? They believe the poets of
the people and take the mob as their teacher, not knowing that 'the
many are worthless', good men are few.

LX

A fool loves to get excited on any account.

LXI

Dogs bark at those they do not recognize.

LXII

In Priene lived Bias son of Teutames, who is of more account than the
rest.

LXIII

One man is ten thousand, if he is the best.

LIX   wit: *phrēn*, mind, thought, intelligence, cognate with *phronēsis* and *phronein*: see on
III and IV.
   understanding: *noos*: see on XVIII. The quotation is from Bias, the sage mentioned in
LXII.

LX   loves i.e. tends (cf. X).
   account: *logos*: see on I. Alternate rendering: 'A stupid man tends to get excited at any
report', i.e. at whatever he hears.

LXII   Priene: city near Ephesus.
   Bias: sixth-century statesman and sage, often credited with saying 'most men are worthless' cited in LIX.
   account: *logos*: see on I; here primarily 'esteem, reputation' with a play on Bias' 'saying'.

LXIII   Alternate text: 'One man is ten thousand for me.'

58

LXIV

LXIV (D. 121, M. 105) Strabo XIV.25 with Diogenes Laertius IX.2

ἄξιον Ἐφεσίοις ἡβηδὸν ἀπάγξασθαι πᾶσι καὶ τοῖς ἀνήβοις τὴν
πόλιν καταλιπεῖν, οἵτινες Ἑρμόδωρον ἄνδρα ἑωυτῶν ὀνήιστον
ἐξέβαλον φάντες· ἡμέων μηδὲ εἷς ὀνήιστος ἔστω· εἰ δὲ μή, ἄλλῃ
τε καὶ μετ' ἄλλων.

LXV

LXV (D. 44, M. 103) Diogenes Laertius IX.2

μάχεσθαι χρὴ τὸν δῆμον ὑπὲρ τοῦ νόμου [ὑπὲρ τοῦ γινομένου] ὅκως
ὑπὲρ τείχεος.

LXVI

LXVI (D. 33, M. 104) Clement, *Stromateis* V.115.2

νόμος καὶ βουλῇ πείθεσθαι ἑνός.

LXVII

LXVII (D. 110–11, M. 71 and M. 44) Stobaeus, III.1.176–7

ἀνθρώποις γίνεσθαι ὁκόσα θέλουσιν οὐκ ἄμεινον. νοῦσος ὑγιείην
ἐποίησεν ἡδὺ καὶ ἀγαθόν, λιμὸς κόρον, κάματος ἀνάπαυσιν.

LXV The bracketed words probably represent a mechanical error in copying. I see no
reason to change ὅκως ὑπέρ to ὅκωσπερ with most editors.

LXIV

What the Ephesians deserve is to be hanged to the last man, every one of them, and leave the city to the boys, since they drove out their best man, Hermodorus, saying 'Let no one be the best among us; if he is, let him be so elsewhere and among others.'

LXV

The people must fight for the law as for their city wall.

LXVI

It is law also to obey the counsel of one.

LXVII

It is not better for human beings to get all they want. It is disease that makes health sweet and good, hunger satiety, weariness rest.

LXIV   **Hermodorus:** apparently a contemporary, otherwise unknown. A late legend (perhaps based on this text) made him go to Rome as co-author of the Twelve Tables, the first codification of Roman law.

    best: *onēiston*, most useful, beneficial.

LXV   Cf. XXX.

LXVI   **counsel:** *boulē*, will, intention, plan; advice, counsel; the city council, ruling body in some states.

    of one: *henos*, with usual ambiguity: 'one man' or 'one principle'.

LXVII   Allusion to a proverbial line: 'the sweetest thing is to get what you desire'.

60

LXVIII

LXVIII (D. 102, M. 91) *Scholia Graeca in Homeri Iliadem* ed.
H. Erbse, I (1969), p. 445, on *Iliad* IV.4 (= Porphyry, *Quaestiones Homericae*, p. 69 Shrader)

[[ἅπερ καὶ Ἡράκλειτος λέγει, ὡς τῷ μὲν θεῷ καλὰ πάντα καὶ ἀγαθὰ καὶ δίκαια, ἄνθρωποι δὲ ἃ μὲν ἄδικα ὑπειλήφασιν ἃ δὲ δίκαια.]]

LXIX

LXIX (D. 23, M. 45) Clement, *Stromateis* IV.9.7

Δίκης ὄνομα οὐκ ἂν ᾔδεσαν εἰ ταῦτα μὴ ἦν.

LXX

LXX (D. 61, M. 35) Hippolytus, *Refutatio* IX.10.5

θάλασσα ὕδωρ καθαρώτατον καὶ μιαρώτατον· ἰχθύσι μὲν πότιμον καὶ σωτήριον, ἀνθρώποις δὲ ἄποτον καὶ ὀλέθριον.

LXXI

LXXI (D. 9, M. 37) Aristotle, *Nicomachean Ethics* X.5, 1176a6

[[καθάπερ Ἡράκλειτός φησιν ὄνους σύρματ' ἂν ἑλέσθαι μᾶλλον ἢ χρυσόν.]]

LXVIII M. omits καὶ ἀγαθά (after κάλα πάντα) as unworthy of Heraclitus. But we are probably dealing with a paraphrase, not a quotation.

LXVIII

[[For god all things are fair and good and just, but men have taken some things as unjust, others as just.]]

LXIX

If it were not for these things, they would not have known the name of Justice.

LXX

The sea is the purest and foulest water: for fish drinkable and life-sustaining; for men undrinkable and deadly.

LXXI

[[Asses prefer garbage to gold.]]

LXVIII   From scholia to *Iliad* IV.4: 'As Heraclitus said . . . '

LXIX   **these things:** probably = wrongdoing and punishment.
    Justice: *dikē*, judgment, sentence; trial, lawsuit; justice; just punishment, penalty; personified in Hesiod: see XLIV.

LXXI   From Aristotle: 'As Heraclitus says . . . '

62

LXXII

LXXIIA (D. 13, M. 36a¹) Clement, *Stromateis* I.2.2

ὕες βορβόρῳ ἥδονται μᾶλλον ἢ καθαρῷ ὕδατι.

LXXIIB (D. 37, M. 36c¹) Columella VIII.4.4

[[si modo credimus Ephesio Heraclito qui ait sues caeno, cohortales aves pulvere vel cinere lavari.]]

LXXIII

LXXIII (D. 58, M. 46) Hippolytus, *Refutatio* IX.10.3

οἱ ἰατροὶ τέμνοντες καίοντες [πάντῃ βασανίζοντες κακῶς τοὺς ἀρρωστοῦντας] ἐπαιτιῶνται μηδέν' ἄξιον μισθὸν λαμβάνειν [παρὰ τῶν ἀρρωστούντων] ταῦτα ἐργαζόμενοι †τὰ ἀγαθὰ καὶ τὰς νόσους†.

LXXIV

LXXIV (D. 59, M. 32) Hippolytus, *Refutatio* IX.10.4

γνάφων ὁδὸς εὐθεῖα καὶ σκολιή.

LXXV

LXXV (D. 8, M. 27d¹ = 28c¹) Aristotle, *Nicomachean Ethics* VIII.1, 1155b4)

[[καὶ Ἡράκλειτός <sc. φησιν> τὸ ἀντίξουν συμφέρον καὶ ἐκ τῶν διαφερόντων καλλίστην ἁρμονίαν καὶ πάντα κατ' ἔριν γίνεσθαι.]]

LXXIII I follow the text of Kirk. M. reads ταὐτὰ ἐργαζόμενοι [τὰ ἀγαθὰ] καὶ αἱ νόσοι, following an emendation of Wilamowitz.
LXXIV I follow M., but omit the words μία ἐστὶ καὶ ἡ αὐτή which he assigns to Heraclitus. D. reads γναφείῳ for γνάφων.

LXXII

[[Swine delight in mire more than clean water; chickens bathe in dust.]]

LXXIII

Doctors who cut and burn and torture their patients in every way complain that they do not receive the reward they deserve.

LXXIV

The path of the carding wheels is straight and crooked.

LXXV

[[The counter-thrust brings together, and from tones at variance comes perfect attunement, and all things come to pass through conflict.]]

LXXII   From Clement and Columella (combined): 'Heraclitus says . . . '

LXXIII   A disputed text. For variants see the commentary.

LXXV   From Aristotle: 'Heraclitus says . . . ' The text paraphrases LXXXII, and perhaps also LXXVIII.

64

LXXVI (D. 11, M. 80) [Aristotle], *De Mundo* 6, 401a10

πᾶν ἑρπετὸν πληγῇ νέμεται.

LXXVII

LXXVII (D. 125, M. 31) Theophrastus, *De Vertigine* 9

[[καθάπερ Ἡράκλειτός φησι, καὶ ὁ κυκεὼν διίσταται <μὴ> κινούμενος.]]

LXXVIII

LXXVIII (D. 51, M. 27) Hippolytus, *Refutatio* IX.9.2

οὐ ξυνιᾶσιν ὅκως διαφερόμενον ἑωυτῷ ὁμολογέει· παλίντροπος ἁρμονίη ὅκωσπερ τόξου καὶ λύρης.

LXXIX

LXXIX (D. 48, M. 39) *Etymologicum Magnum*, s.v. βιός

τῷ τόξῳ ὄνομα βίος, ἔργον δὲ θάνατος.

LXXX

LXXX (D. 54, M. 9) Hippolytus, *Refutatio* IX.9.5

ἁρμονίη ἀφανὴς φανερῆς κρείττων.

LXXVI πληγῇ (preserved by Stobaeus) is the usual correction for τὴν γῆν in the MSS of Aristotle.
LXXVIII With D. I give the unaltered text of Hippolytus. M., following Zeller and others, substitutes συμφέρεται for ὁμολογέει, most implausibly. The inevitable Homeric corruption παλίντονος for παλίντροπος appears once in Plutarch (out of three citations), much more often in modern editions.

LXXVI

All beasts are driven by blows.

LXXVII

[[Even the potion separates unless it is stirred.]]

LXXVIII

They do not comprehend how a thing agrees at variance with itself; it is an attunement turning back on itself, like that of the bow and the lyre.

LXXIX

The name of the bow is life; its work is death.

LXXX

The hidden attunement is better than the obvious one.

LXXVI beasts: *herpeton*, creeping thing, used by gods in Homer to refer to mankind.
driven: *nemetai*, pastured.
blows: *plēgē*, probably an allusion to the stroke of Zeus, the thunderbolt by which he rules.

LXXVII From Theophrastus: 'As Heraclitus says . . . '
potion: *kykeōn*, mixture of wine, barley, and cheese, described in *Iliad* XI.639f.

LXXVIII agrees: *homologeei*: see on XXXVI.
at variance: *diapheromenon*, differs from; quarrels with: cf. V.
attunement: *harmoniē*, fitting together; joint, fastening; agreement, compact; musical tuning, scale, tune.
turning back: *palintropos*, an enigmatic variant on the usual *palintonos*, stretching back, epithet of the bow in Homer; probably alludes to solstice (*tropai*) and reversals of fire in XXXVIII.

LXXIX Old word for 'bow' (*biós*) differs from word 'life' (*bíos*) only by the accent, not written in Heraclitus' time.

LXXX attunement: *harmoniē*: see on LXXVIII.
better: *kreittōn*, more powerful, superior; better, preferable.

LXXXI

LXXXIA (D. A22, M. 28c²) Aristotle, *Eudemian Ethics* VII.1, 1235a25

[[καὶ Ἡράκλειτος ἐπιτιμᾷ τῷ ποιήσαντι 'ὡς ἔρις ἔκ τε θεῶν καὶ ἀνθρώπων ἀπόλοιτο' · οὐ γὰρ ἂν εἶναι ἁρμονίαν μὴ ὄντος ὀξέος καὶ βαρέος, οὐδὲ τὰ ζῷα ἄνευ θήλεος καὶ ἄρρενος ἐναντίων ὄντων.]]

LXXXIB (M. 28c⁵) Scholia A to *Iliad* XVIII.107

[[Ἡράκλειτος τὴν τῶν ὄντων φύσιν κατ᾽ ἔριν συνεστάναι νομίζων μέμφεται Ὅμηρον, σύγχυσιν κόσμου δοκῶν αὐτὸν εὔχεσθαι.]]

LXXXII

LXXXII (D. 80, M. 28) Origen, *Contra Celsum* VI.28

εἰδέ<ναι> χρὴ τὸν πόλεμον ἐόντα ξυνὸν καὶ δίκην ἔριν καὶ γινόμενα πάντα κατ᾽ ἔριν καὶ χρεώμενα (?).

LXXXIII

LXXXIII (D. 53, M. 29) Hippolytus, *Refutatio* IX.9.4

πόλεμος πάντων μὲν πατήρ ἐστι, πάντων δὲ βασιλεύς, καὶ τοὺς μὲν θεοὺς ἔδειξε τοὺς δὲ ἀνθρώπους, τοὺς μὲν δούλους ἐποίησε τοὺς δὲ ἐλευθέρους.

LXXXIV

LXXXIV (D. 27, M. 74) Clement, *Stromateis* IV.144.3

ἀνθρώπους μένει ἀποθανόντας ἅσσα οὐκ ἔλπονται οὐδὲ δοκέουσιν.

LXXXII Most editors emend χρεώμενα to χρεών, following an improbable suggestion of Diels.

LXXXI

[[Homer was wrong when he said 'Would that Conflict might vanish from among gods and men!' (*Iliad* XVIII.107). For there would be no attunement without high and low notes nor any animals without male and female, both of which are opposites.]]

LXXXII

One must realize that war is shared and Conflict is Justice, and that all things come to pass (and are ordained?) in accordance with conflict.   /

LXXXIII

War is father of all and king of all; and some he has shown as gods, others men; some he has made slaves, others free.

LXXXIV

What awaits men at death they do not expect or even imagine.

LXXXI   From Aristotle: 'Heraclitus reproaches the poet for saying . . . '
   Conflict: *eris*, strife, personified as a divine power in Hesiod.

LXXXII   **shared:** *xynon*: see on III, and cf. XXX.
   Conflict: see preceding note.
   ordained: text uncertain.

LXXXIV   **expect:** *elpontai*, hope, anticipate: cf. VII.
   imagine: *dokeousi*, believe, decide; suppose, conjecture, guess: cf. IV.

LXXXV

LXXXV (D. 28A, M. 20) Clement, *Stromateis* V.9.3

δοκέοντα ὁ δοκιμώτατος γινώσκει, φυλάσσει.

LXXXVI

LXXXVI (D. 86, M. 12) Plutarch, *Coriolanus* 38 = Clement, *Stromateis* V.88.4

ἀπιστίη διαφυγγάνει μὴ γινώσκεσθαι.

LXXXVII

LXXXVII (D. 28B, M. 19) Clement, *Stromateis* V.9.3

Δίκη καταλήψεται ψευδῶν τέκτονας καὶ μάρτυρας.

LXXXVIII

LXXXVIII (D. 96, M. 76) Strabo XVI.26 = Plutarch, *Quaestiones Conviviales* IV.4.3, etc.

νέκυες κοπρίων ἐκβλητότεροι.

LXXXIX

LXXXIX (D. 21, M. 49) Clement, *Stromateis* III.21.1

θάνατός ἐστιν ὁκόσα ἐγερθέντες ὁρέομεν, ὁκόσα δὲ εὕδοντες ὕπνος.

LXXXVI With Bollack-Wismann, I keep ἀπιστίη in the nominative, the nearly unanimous reading of the MSS both in Plutarch and in Clement. Since Bywater most editors have preferred the dative form ἀπιστίη, which is not transmitted.
LXXXIX M. substitutes ὕπαρ for ὕπνος, needlessly.

LXXXV

The great man is eminent in imagining things, and on this he hangs his reputation for knowing it all.

LXXXVI

Incredibility escapes recognition.

LXXXVII

Justice will catch up with those who invent lies and those who swear to them.

LXXXVIII

Corpses should be thrown out quicker than dung.

LXXXIX

Death is all things we see awake; all we see asleep is sleep.

LXXXV   More literally: 'What the most esteemed man recognizes and defends is <mere> imaginings.'
   eminent: *dokimōtatos*, fully approved, most highly esteemed, with a play on *dokein*, seem, guess.
   imagining things: *dokeonta*, what seems to be so, what is believed: see on *dokeousi* in LXXXIV.
   knowing it all: *ginōskei*, recognize: see note on IV. This text is perhaps continued by LXXXVII.

LXXXVI   **Incredibility**: *apistiē*, untrustworthiness, unreliability; incredulity, lack of confidence. For other construals see commentary.

LXXXVII   Perhaps a continuation of LXXXV.

XC

XC (D. 26, M. 48) Clement, *Stromateis* IV.141.2

ἄνθρωπος ἐν εὐφρόνῃ φάος ἅπτεται ἑαυτῷ [ἀποθανὼν] ἀποσβεσθεὶς ὄψεις, ζῶν δὲ ἅπτεται τεθνεῶτος εὕδων [ἀποσβεσθεὶς ὄψεις] , ἐγρηγορὼς ἅπτεται εὕδοντος.

XCI

XCI (D. 75, M. 1h²) Marcus Aurelius VI.42

[[τοὺς καθεύδοντας οἶμαι ὁ Ἡράκλειτος ἐργάτας εἶναι λέγει καὶ συνεργοὺς τῶν ἐν τῷ κόσμῳ γινομένων.]]

XCII

XCII (D. 62, M. 47) Hippolytus, *Refutatio* IX.10.6

ἀθάνατοι θνητοί, θνητοὶ ἀθάνατοι, ζῶντες τὸν ἐκείνων θάνατον, τὸν δὲ ἐκείνων βίον τεθνεῶτες.

XCIII

XCIII (D. 88, M. 41) Pseudo(?)-Plutarch, *Consolatio ad Apollonium* 106E

ταὐτό τ' ἔνι (?) ζῶν καὶ τεθνηκὸς καὶ τὸ ἐγρηγορὸς καὶ τὸ καθεῦδον καὶ νέον καὶ γηραιόν· τάδε γὰρ μεταπεσόντα ἐκεῖνά ἐστι κἀκεῖνα πάλιν μεταπεσόντα ταῦτα.

XCIV

XCIV (D. 52, M. 93) Hippolytus, *Refutatio* IX.9.4

αἰὼν παῖς ἐστι παίζων, πεσσεύων· παιδὸς ἡ βασιληίη.

XCIII The form τ' ἔνι must be wrong and should probably be bracketed. Some editors exclude πάλιν, needlessly.

XC

A man strikes a light for himself in the night, when his sight is
quenched. Living, he touches the dead in his sleep; waking, he
touches the sleeper.

XCI

[[Men asleep are laborers and co-workers in what takes place in the
world.]]

XCII

Immortals are mortal, mortals immortal, living the others' death, dead
in the others' life.

XCIII

The same ... : living and dead, and the waking and the sleeping, and
young and old. For these transposed are those, and those transposed
again are these.

XCIV

Lifetime is a child at play, moving pieces in a game. Kingship belongs
to the child.

XC   strikes: *haptetai*, touches, is in contact with; sets fire to, kindles, as in XXXVIL.
quenched: *aposbestheis*, extinguished, put out, also of fire in XXXVII; lit. 'the man is
extinguished in regard to his vision'.
touches: *haptetai* again, twice.

XCI   From Marcus Aurelius: 'Heraclitus says, I think ... '

XCIII   Beginning of text is corrupt. Some eds. read 'The same is there ... ' or 'The same
is present in us ... '

XCIV   Lifetime: *aiōn*, vitality, life; lifetime, duration, time; cognate with *aiei*, forever.
moving pieces: *pesseuōn*, playing *pessoi*, a board game perhaps involving dice, like backgammon and modern Greek *tavli*.

XCV

XCVA (D. A19, M. 108b[1]) Plutarch, *De Defectu Oraculorum* 415E

[[ἔτη τριάκοντα ποιοῦσι τὴν γενεὰν καθ᾽ Ἡράκλειτον, ἐν ᾧ χρόνῳ γεννῶντα παρέχει τὸν ἐξ αὐτοῦ γεγεννημένον ὁ γεννήσας.]]

XCVB (D. A19, M. 108b[2]) Censorinus, *De Die Natali* 17.2

[[Hoc enim tempus [sc. annos triginta] *genean* vocari Heraclitus aucto est, quia orbis aetatis in eo sit spatio; orbem autem vocat aetatis dum natura ab sementi humana ad sementim revertitur.]]

XCVI

XCVI (D. 25, M. 97) Clement, *Stromateis* IV.49.2

μόροι μέζονες μέζονας μοίρας λαγχάνουσι.

XCVII

XCVII (D. 29, M. 95) Clement, *Stromateis* V.59.4

αἱρεῦνται ἓν ἀντὶ ἁπάντων οἱ ἄριστοι, κλέος ἀέναον θνητῶν· οἱ δὲ πολλοὶ κεκόρηνται ὅκωσπερ κτήνεα.

XCVIII

XCVIII (D. 20, M. 99) Ibid. III.14.1

γενόμενοι ζώειν ἐθέλουσι μόρους τ᾽ ἔχειν [μᾶλλον δὲ ἀναπαύεσθαι] · καὶ παῖδας καταλείπουσι μόρους γενέσθαι.

XCV

[[A generation is thirty years, in which time the progenitor has engendered one who generates. The cycle of life lies in this interval, when nature returns from human seed-time to seed-time.]]

XCVI

Greater deaths are allotted greater destinies.

XCVII

The best choose one thing in exchange for all, everflowing fame among mortals; but most men have sated themselves like cattle.

XCVIII

Once born they want to live and have their portions; and they leave children behind born to become their dooms.

XCV   From Plutarch and Censorinus, combined: 'According to Heraclitus ... '
  from seed-time to seed-time i.e. from a man's birth to the birth of his son.

XCVI   deaths: *moros*, portion, lot; fate, doom; violent death.
  destinies: *moira*, part, share, fraction; allotment, territory; social status; destiny, Fate.

XCVII   sated: *kekorēntai*, cognate with *koros*, satiety in LXVII, CXX, and CXXIII.

XCVIII   portions: *moroi*: see on XCVI; here 'share of life' with play on 'doom, death'.
  born to become: *genesthai*, to become; last word in sentence echoes first word, *genomenoi*, having been born
  dooms: *moroi* again: see above.

74

XCIX

XCIX (D. 103, M. 34) Porphyry, *Quaestiones Homericae*, on *Iliad*
XIV.200

[[ξυνὸν γὰρ ἀρχὴ καὶ πέρας ἐπὶ κύκλου περιφερείας κατὰ τὸν
Ἡράκλειτον.]]

C

C (D. 24, M. 96) Clement, *Stromateis* IV.16.1

ἀρηϊφάτους θεοὶ τιμῶσι καὶ ἄνθρωποι.

CI

CI (D. 115, M. 112) Stobaeus III.1.180a

ψυχῆς ἐστι λόγος ἑαυτὸν αὔξων.

CII

CII (D. 36, M. 66) Clement, *Stromateis* VI.17.2

ψυχῆσιν θάνατος ὕδωρ γενέσθαι, ὕδατι δὲ θάνατος γῆν γενέσθαι·
ἐκ γῆς δὲ ὕδωρ γίνεται, ἐξ ὕδατος δὲ ψυχή.

CIII

CIII (D. 60, M. 33) Hippolytus, *Refutatio* IX.10.4

ὁδὸς ἄνω κάτω μία καὶ ὡυτή.

CIV

CIV (D. 43, M. 102) Diogenes Laertius IX.2

ὕβριν χρὴ σβεννύναι μᾶλλον ἢ πυρκαϊήν.

XCIX

[[The beginning and the end are shared in the circumference of a circle.]]

C

Gods and men honor those who fall in battle.

CI

To the soul belongs a report that increases itself.

CII

For souls it is death to become water, for water it is death to become earth; out of earth water arises, out of water soul.

CIII

The way up and down is one and the same.

CIV

One must quench violence quicker than a blazing fire.

XCIX   From Porphyry: 'According to Heraclitus . . . '
  end: *peras*, limit, end-point; cf. limits (*peirata*) of soul in XXXIV.
  shared: *xynon*: see on III.

C   who fall in battle: *arēiphatoi*, lit. who are slain by Ares the war god.

CI   report: *logos*: see on I, and sense of measure in XXXIX; for thought cf. XXXV.

CII   souls: *psychai*, see on XXXV.
  become: *genesthai*, with play on 'birth', as in XCVIII; cf. XLI: 'the death of air is birth for water'.

CV

CV (D. 85, M. 70) Plutarch, *Coriolanus* 22.2; cf. Aristotle,
Eudemian Ethics II.7, 1223b22, etc.

θυμῷ μάχεσθαι χαλεπόν· ὃ γὰρ ἂν θέλῃ, ψυχῆς ὠνεῖται.

CVI

CVI (D. 117, M. 69) Stobaeus III.5.7

ἀνὴρ ὁκόταν μεθυσθῇ, ἄγεται ὑπὸ παιδὸς ἀνήβου σφαλλόμενος, οὐκ
ἐπαΐων ὅκη βαίνει, ὑγρὴν τὴν ψυχὴν ἔχων.

CVII

CVII (D. 95, M. 110a[3]) Plutarch, *Quaestiones Conviviales* 644F

[[ἀμαθίην γὰρ ἄμεινον, ὥς φησιν Ἡράκλειτος, κρύπτειν· ἔργον δὲ
ἐν ἀνέσει καὶ παρ' οἶνον.]]

CVIII

CVIII (D. 77, M. 66d[1]) Porphyry, *De Antro Nympharum* 10
(Numenius fr. 30 des Places = fr. 35 Theodinga)

[[ὅθεν καὶ Ἡράκλειτον ψυχῇσι φάναι τέρψιν μὴ θάνατον ὑγρῇσι
γενέσθαι.]]

CIX

CIX (D. 118, M. 68) Stobaeus III.5.8

αὐγὴ ξηρὴ ψυχή, σοφωτάτη καὶ ἀρίστη.

CVIII M. and others follow D. in reading ἦ instead of μή.
CIX With D. and Bollack-Wismann, I keep the full text of Stobaeus, confirmed by a dozen
ancient citations. Most modern editors have been tempted to change αὐγή to αὔη, and then
bracket ξηρή as a gloss.

CV

It is hard to fight against passion; for whatever it wants it buys at the expense of soul.

CVI

A man when drunk is led by a beardless boy, stumbling, not perceiving where he is going, having his soul moist.

CVII

[[It is better to hide one's folly; but that is difficult in one's cups and at ease.]]

CVIII

[[It is delight, not death, for souls to become moist.]]

CIX

A gleam of light is the dry soul, wisest and best.

CV   **passion:** *thymos*, heart, spirit, mind; passion, desire; manly spirit, courage; anger, rage: the last sense is understood here by ancient authors.
    soul i.e. life-spirit or vitality: see on XXXV.

CVII   From Plutarch: 'As Heraclitus says . . . '

CVIII   From Porphyry: 'Hence Heraclitus says . . . '

CIX   **gleam of light:** *augē*, brilliance, ray of sunlight, flare of fire, sheen of metal.

CX

CX (D. 63, M. 73) Hippolytus, *Refutatio* IX.10.6

†ἔνθα δ᾽ ἐόντι† ἐπανίστασθαι καὶ φύλακας γίνεσθαι ἐγερτὶ ζώντων καὶ νεκρῶν.

CXI

CXI (D. 98, M. 72) Plutarch, *De Facie in Orbe Lunae* 943E

[[(τὰς ψυχὰς) ὑπὸ τῆς τυχούσης ἀναθυμιάσεως τρέφεσθαι· καὶ καλῶς Ἡράκλειτος εἶπεν ὅτι αἱ ψυχαὶ ὀσμῶνται καθ᾽ Ἅιδην.]]

CXII

CXII (D. 7, M. 78) Aristotle, *De Sensu* 5, 443a21

[[δοκεῖ δ᾽ ἐνίοις ἡ καπνώδης ἀναθυμίασις εἶναι ὀσμή, οὖσα κοινὴ γῆς τε καὶ ἀέρος ... διὸ καὶ Ἡράκλειτος οὕτως εἴρηκεν, ὡς εἰ πάντα τὰ ὄντα καπνὸς γένοιτο, ῥῖνες ἂν διαγνοῖεν.]]

CXIII

CXIIIA (D. A15) Aristotle, *De Anima* I.2, 405a25 (cf. 404b9)

[[(οὗτοι δὲ λέγουσι τὴν ψυχὴν τὰς ἀρχάς ...) καὶ Ἡράκλειτος δὲ τὴν ἀρχὴν εἶναί φησι ψυχήν, εἴπερ τὴν ἀναθυμίασιν, ἐξ ἧς τἆλλα συνίστησιν· καὶ ἀσωματώτατόν τε καὶ ῥέον ἀεί.]]

CXIIIB (D. 12, M. 40) Arius Didymus fr. 39.2, ed. Diels, *Doxographi Graeci* 471

[[Κλεάνθης ... φησὶν ὅτι Ζήνων τὴν ψυχὴν λέγει αἰσθητικὴν ἀναθυμίασιν καθάπερ Ἡράκλειτος· βουλόμενος γὰρ ἐμφανίσαι (sc. Ἡράκλειτος) ὅτι αἱ ψυχαὶ ἀναθυμιώμεναι νοεραὶ ἀεὶ γίνονται, εἴκασεν αὐτὰς τοῖς ποταμοῖς λέγων οὕτως· ᾽ποταμοῖσι τοῖσιν αὐτοῖσιν ἐμβαίνουσιν ἕτερα καὶ ἕτερα ὕδατα ἐπιρρεῖ᾽. καὶ ψυχαὶ δὲ ἀπὸ τῶν ὑγρῶν ἀναθυμιῶνται.]]

CXIIIB For νοεραί, M. and other editors read νεαραί.

CX

(. . .) to rise up (?) and become wakeful watchers of living men and corpses.

CXI

[[Souls smell things in Hades.]]

CXII

[[If all things turned to smoke, the nostrils would sort them out.]]

CXIII

[[The soul is an exhalation that perceives; it is different from the body, and always flowing.]]

CX   Beginning of the text is corrupt.

   watchers: *phylakes*, guardians; cf. golden race in Hesiod (*Works and Days* 122f.) who after death became spirits and guardians of men.

CXI   From Plutarch: 'Heraclitus was right to say . . . '

CXII   From Aristotle: 'Heraclitus said . . . '

CXIII   From Cleanthes (combined with Aristotle, D. A15): 'Zeno says the soul is a percipient exhalation, like Heraclitus. For Heraclitus, wanting to show that souls as they are exhaled are continually becoming intelligent, likened them to rivers when he said . . . (= fr. L). But souls too steam up out of moisture.'

CXIV

CXIV (D. 119, M. 94) Stobaeus IV.40.23 = Plutarch, *Quaestiones Platonicae* 999E, etc.

ἦθος ἀνθρώπῳ δαίμων.

CXV

CXV (D. 14, M. 87) Clement, *Protrepticus* 22.2

τὰ νομιζόμενα κατ᾽ ἀνθρώπους μυστήρια ἀνιερωστὶ μυοῦνται.

CXVI

CXVI (D. 15, M. 50) Clement, *Protrepticus* 34.5

εἰ μὴ Διονύσῳ πομπὴν ἐποιοῦντο καὶ ὕμνεον ᾆσμα αἰδοίοισιν, ἀναιδέστατα εἴργασται· ὡυτὸς δὲ Ἀίδης καὶ Διόνυσος ὅτεῳ μαίνονται καὶ ληναΐζουσιν.

CXVII

CXVII (D. 5, M. 86) *Theosophia* 68 (Erbse, *Fragmente griechischen Theosophien*, p. 184) plus Origen, *Contra Celsum* VII.62

καθαίρονται δ᾽ ἄλλως αἵματι μιαινόμενοι, ὁκοῖον εἴ τις εἰς πηλὸν ἐμβὰς πηλῷ ἀπονίζοιτο· μαίνεσθαι δ᾽ ἂν δοκέοι εἴ τις μιν ἀνθρώπων ἐπιφράσαιτο οὕτω ποιέοντα. καὶ τοῖς ἀγάλμασι δὲ τουτέοισιν εὔχονται, ὁκοῖον εἴ τις τοῖς δόμοισι λεσχηνεύοιτο, οὔ τι γινώσκων θεοὺς οὐδ᾽ ἥρωας οἵτινές εἰσι.

CXV In what precedes, the words νυκτιπόλοις, μάγοις, βάκχοις, λήναις, μύσταις may also belong to Heraclitus, as Diels thought.

CXIV

Man's character is his fate.

CXV

The mysteries current among men initiate them into impiety.

CXVI

If it were not Dionysus for whom they march in procession and chant the hymn to the phallus, their action would be most shameless. But Hades and Dionysus are the same, him for whom they rave and celebrate Lenaia.

CXVII

They are purified in vain with blood, those polluted with blood, as if someone who stepped in mud should try to wash himself with mud. Anyone who noticed him doing this would think he was mad. And they pray to these images as if they were chatting with houses, not recognizing what gods or even heroes are like.

CXIV character: *ēthos*: see on LV.
  fate: *daimōn*, divinity; fortune for good or evil.

CXV Preceded by 'For whom is Heraclitus prophesying? For nightwandering sorcerers (*magoi*), Bacchoi, Lenai, mystic initiates'; the list may be part of the quotation.

CXVI phallus: *aidoia*, pudenda, genitals.
  Hades: god of the dead.
  Lenaia: festival of Dionysus, probably characterized by frenzied dancing or ritual madness. The phallic hymn and procession belong to a different festival of Dionysus.

CXVII with blood: ritual purification from blood guilt involved use of pig's blood.

82

CXVIII

CXVIII (D. 32, M. 84) Clement, *Stromateis* V.115.1

ἓν τὸ σοφὸν μοῦνον λέγεσθαι οὐκ ἐθέλει καὶ ἐθέλει Ζηνὸς ὄνομα.

CXIX

CXIX (D. 64, M. 79) Hippolytus, *Refutatio* IX.10.7

τάδε πάντα οἰακίζει κεραυνός.

CXX

CXX (D. 65, M. 79 and 55) Hippolytus, *Refutatio* IX.10.7

[[κεραυνὸν τὸ πῦρ λέγων τὸ αἰώνιον. λέγει δὲ καὶ φρόνιμον τοῦτο εἶναι τὸ πῦρ καὶ τῆς διοικήσεως τῶν ὅλων αἴτιον · καλεῖ δὲ αὐτὸ 'χρησμοσύνην καὶ κόρον' · χρησμοσύνη δέ ἐστιν ἡ διακόσμησις κατ' αὐτόν, ἡ δὲ ἐκπύρωσις κόρος.]]

CXXI

CXXI (D. 66, M. 82) Ibid.

πάντα τὸ πῦρ ἐπελθὸν κρινεῖ καὶ καταλήψεται.

CXXII

CXXII (D. 16, M. 81) Clement, *Paedagogus* II.99.5

τὸ μὴ δῦνόν ποτε πῶς ἄν τις λάθοι;

CXIX Reading τάδε for τὰ δέ with Boeder and others.
CXX I give the text of Hippolytus, as in D. M. has transposed the text according to a suggestion of Fränkel.

CXVIII

The wise is one alone, unwilling and willing to be spoken of by the name of Zeus.

CXIX

The thunderbolt pilots all things.

CXX

(Fire is?) need and satiety.

CXXI

Fire coming on will discern and catch up with all things.

CXXII

How will one hide from that which never sets?

CXVIII   The wise is one: *hen to sophon*: identical with initial phrase of LIV; and cf. on XXVII.
of Zeus: *Zēnos* with play on *zēn*, to live.

CXIX   thunderbolt: the weapon of Zeus.
all things: *tade panta*, lit. 'these things, all of them'.

CXX   satiety: *koros* as in LXVII and CXXIII; cf. cognate *kekorēntai* in XCVII. Cited by Hippolytus in his commentary on CXIX: 'By thunderbolt he means the eternal fire. And . . . he calls it Need and Satiety.'

CXXI   discern: *krinei*, separate, select, judge.
catch up with: *katalēpsetai*, catch, grasp, seize, as in LXXXVII.

CXXII   hide from: *lathoi*, escape the notice of.

CXXIII

CXXIII (D. 67, M. 77) Hippolytus, *Refutatio* IX.10.8

ὁ θεὸς ἡμέρη εὐφρόνη, χειμὼν θέρος, πόλεμος εἰρήνη, κόρος λιμός. ἀλλοιοῦται δὲ ὅκωσπερ ὁκόταν συμμιγῇ θυώμασιν ὀνομάζεται καθ᾽ ἡδονὴν ἑκάστου.

CXXIV

CXXIV (D. 10, M. 25) [Aristotle], *De Mundo* 5, 396b20

συλλάψιες· ὅλα καὶ οὐχ ὅλα, συμφερόμενον διαφερόμενον, συνᾷδον διᾷδον, ἐκ πάντων ἓν καὶ ἐξ ἑνὸς πάντα.

CXXV

CXXV (D. 124, M. 107) Theophrastus, *Metaphysica* 15 (p. 16, Ross and Fobes)

[[σάρμα εἰκῇ κεχυμένων ὁ κάλλιστος, φησὶν Ἡράκλειτος, [ὁ] κόσμος.]

CXXIII This is the text of Hippolytus, without his inserted comment (τἀναντία ἅπαντα· οὗτος ὁ νοῦς). Most editors add a word, generally <πῦρ>, as subject for συμμιγῇ.
CXXIV I follow M. and most recent editors in reading συλλάψιες where D. has συνάψιες.
CXXV I give the text of Diels, accepted by Ross and Fobes. M. has κεχυμένον (for κεχυμένων) and he adds <ὡς> before φησίν.

CXXIII

The god: day and night, winter and summer, war and peace, satiety and hunger. It alters, as when mingled with perfumes, it gets named according to the pleasure of each one.

CXXIV

Graspings: wholes and not wholes, convergent divergent, consonant dissonant, from all things one and from one thing all.

CXXV

[[The fairest order in the world is a heap of random sweepings.]]

CXXIII pleasure: *hēdonē*, pleasure; flavor, taste.
  of each one: *hekastou*, ambiguous between 'each person' and 'each perfume'. Some editors introduce 'fire' (after 'as') as subject of last two clauses.

CXXIV Graspings: *syllapsis*, seizing, arresting, catching hold of; combination, comprehending, summing up; biological conception.
  convergent: *sympheromenon*, moving towards; agreeing with, being on friendly terms.
  divergent: *diapheromenon*, moving apart; differing from; quarrelling with: cf. LXXVIII.
  consonant: *synaidon*, accompany in song, sing in agreement with.
  dissonant: *diaidon*, contend against in singing, compete in singing contest; sing apart.

CXXV from Theophrastus: 'Heraclitus says ... '
  The fairest order in the world: *kosmos*, world order, with play on older sense: adornment, ornament.

On reading Heraclitus

It has been noted that every age and philosophical perspective, from
Cratylus to the Neoplatonists and the fathers of the Church, projected
its own meaning and its own preoccupations onto the text of
Heraclitus. This is a familiar enough phenomenon in the history of
ideas: every generation and every school has its own reading of Plato,
Kant, or Marx. But Heraclitus is an acute case. By the ambivalent and
enigmatic quality of his utterance he lends himself as few authors do
to the free play of interpretation. So it has often seemed that the task
of modern scholarship was simply to undo the work of history: to
strip away the various levels of exegesis and distortion deposited by
the centuries, in order to recover the original meaning of the preserved text.

Such is indeed the task of conscientious philology, and I have tried
wherever possible to construe Heraclitus' meaning within the context
of his own time and place. But in principle the effort to recover the
authentic Heraclitus, that is, to attain a uniquely correct interpretation,
is an enterprise that can never succeed. We are not only confronted
with the warning of the onion: if we peel off all the layers of interpretation there may be nothing left, or nothing of any interest. There
is the more fundamental problem that we, good classical scholars that
we are, are also historical beings with a certain perspective, who can
only see what is visible from where we happen to be standing. For
Diels and Burnet, the standpoint was that of the late nineteenth century. For Reinhardt, Snell, and Fränkel it was situated a generation
or two later; and they could also perceive, and criticize, the standpoint of the nineteenth century. For those of us who write in the
latter half of the twentieth century the intellectual atmosphere has
already changed, been enlarged; and what we can see includes not
only new knowledge from our own time but also new perspectives on
the older interpretations. By induction we may be sure that the next
generation, even the next perceptive reader of Heraclitus, will be able
to see something new and different.

Thus our historical sense, our sense for the relativity of human understanding from age to age and the changing conditions for what one can meaningfully perceive or communicate, obliges us to give up the idea of some timeless vantage point from which a uniquely true picture of Heraclitus might be obtained. Any lucid approach will be explicitly hermeneutical; which is only to say that *we* must provide the framework for making sense of Heraclitus, and we had best be aware of what we are doing. Heraclitus' discourse was addressed to other listeners, in another time and place. (And even in the case of the original audience, he was not very optimistic about the chances of being understood.) He will speak to us only insofar as we are able to articulate his meaning in our own terms. The text is there, as a kind of object-language. But it is we who must provide the hermeneutical metalanguage within which today's interpretation can be formulated. The text will not bring forth its own contemporary commentary. And Heraclitus himself is not here either to confirm or correct what we take him to mean.

None of this implies that interpretation is a game with no rules, which anyone can play and in which no mistakes are possible. On the contrary, I shall argue that ancient and modern interpretations of Heraclitus have been profoundly mistaken, in various ways, because they have not provided an appropriate conceptual framework for eliciting the meaning of the text. But beyond the minimum conditions of philological accuracy, there is no higher tribunal to which one can appeal for a judgment between alternative frameworks of interpretation. The hermeneutical circle is constituted by the fact that it is only within the presuppositions of a meaningful framework that we can make sense of a given text; and it is only by its applicability to the text in question that we can justify the choice of a particular framework. From this circle there is no escape. If we do not deliberately construct or select our own interpretative framework, we become unconscious and hence uncritical prisoners of whatever hermeneutical assumptions happen to be 'in the air'.

I shall attempt, then, to articulate the principles that govern the interpretation to be offered here. As my title suggests, I want to emphasize the double significance of Heraclitus' achievement: as a literary artist and as a philosophical thinker of the first rank. I will not defend my view of his philosophical importance; in taking him seriously as a thinker I simply follow the ancient tradition from Plato to Plotinus (not to mention the modern tradition from Hegel to Nietzsche and Heidegger). But his literary artistry, which has been briefly described in section 2 of the General Introduction, calls for more extended discussion, since its contribution to the meaning of his doctrine has been generally neglected. The intimate connection between the linguistic form and the intellectual content of his discourse will be the primary object of my commentary.

In order to elucidate this relationship between literary structure and philosophic thought I make use of three assumptions, two of which are fundamental for my interpretation, while the third is perhaps only a device of expository convenience. The fundamental principles are what I call the *linguistic density* of the individual fragments and the *resonance* between them. The third, more optional principle is a meaningful arrangement for the fragments, as in the ordering imposed here. As was noted earlier, this third principle is itself twofold: (1) I assume that the original order was a meaningful one, and (2) I assume that the order I have chosen is true to Heraclitus' own meaning. Some reasons in favor of the first of these two assumptions were given in the General Introduction. The second assumption cannot be defended by any argument: it is justified only by its utility, to the extent that it makes Heraclitus easier to read and interpret. But this principle of arrangement is not only conjectural and controversial. It also turns out to be dispensable, in the sense that anyone who accepts the other two principles (linguistic density and resonance) may reach the same over-all interpretation of Heraclitus without attaching any particular importance to the order in which the fragments are to be read.

By *linguistic density* I mean the phenomenon by which a multiplicity of ideas are expressed in a single word or phrase. By *resonance* I mean a relationship between fragments by which a single verbal theme or image is echoed from one text to another in such a way that the meaning of each is enriched when they are understood together. These two principles are formally complementary: resonance is one factor making for the density of any particular text; and conversely, it is because of the density of the text that resonance is possible and meaningful. This complementarity can be more precisely expressed in terms of 'sign' and 'signified', if by *sign* we mean the individual occurrence of a word or phrase in a particular text, and by *signified* we mean an idea, image, or verbal theme that may appear in different texts. Then density is a one-many relation between sign and signified; while resonance is a many-one relation between different texts and a single image or theme.[48]

Resonance appears in many different forms. The most explicit

case is a repetition of the very same word, such as the ten occurrences
of *logos* scattered over nine different fragments. With these we connect occurrences of the same theme in cognate words: in the verb
legesthai 'to speak', and also in 'speaking together' or 'agreeing' (*xyn
. . . legontas* in XXX, D. 114; *homologeein* in XXXVI, D. 50, and
LXXVIII, D. 51). Similarly, we find six distinct occurrences of the
term 'shared' or 'common' (*xynon*). Another case is the recurrence
of a single image or theme which may or may not be expressed by
the very same words: sleeping and waking, the bow (LXXVIII and
LXXIX) and the helmsman (LIV and CXIX). Less formal resonance
occurs between words of similar or related meanings, such as War
(*polemos*) and Conflict (*eris*); or the various expressions for seeking,
finding out, hiding, being hard to find. This notion of non-formal
resonance can be extended to the various terms for knowledge, under
standing, wisdom, and intelligence found throughout the fragments
(*gnōsis, noos, sophia, phronēsis*, etc.). At the limit, these diverse
phenomena of resonance, taken together with explicit statements of
identity and connection (such as 'war is shared and conflict is justice'
will serve to link together *all* the major themes of Heraclitus' discourse into a single network of connected thoughts, thus articulating
his general claim that 'all things are one'. It is because of this semanti
role of resonance that the order in which the fragments are read need
not, after all, be decisive for their meaning. The stylistic achievement
of Heraclitus is to have contrived a non-linear expression of conceptu
structure, a hidden fitting-together that is more powerful than the
linear order I have composed. Thus the complex notion of wisdom,
one of his central themes, can be understood by considering the four
texts in which the neuter singular form *sophon* 'wise' occurs (XXVII,
XXXVI, LIV, and CXVIII), without regard to the order in which they
are arranged.

But of course they will in any case be arranged in *some* order. And
whatever that order may be, the phenomenon of resonance (in this
case, between the four occurrences of *sophon*) will give rise to a linea
effect which is like what Anne Lebeck called 'prolepsis', and which
she illustrated in detail for Aeschylus' *Oresteia*, where the linear orde
is independently known.

   The form which repetition or recurrence takes in the *Oresteia* is
   that of proleptic introduction and gradual development. The word
   'prolepsis' here denotes a brief initial statement of several major
   themes *en bloc* . . . In its early occurrences the image is elliptical
   and enigmatic. It is a *griphos* or riddle whose solution is strung out

over the course of the individual drama or the entire trilogy. Significance increases with repetition; the image gains in clarity as the
action moves to a climax. Prolepsis and gradual development of
recurrent imagery, along with the corollary, movement from enigmatic utterance to clear statement, from riddle to solution, dominate the structure of the *Oresteia*.[49]
My arrangement of the fragments is inspired by the assumption that
a similar movement dominates the structure of Heraclitus' own
exposition. Thus I have placed first the most enigmatic reference to
'what is wise' (XXVII), and have reserved for the climax his more
solemn and decisive announcement of 'the wise one alone' (CXVIII).
But however they are arranged, the four fragments on the theme of
sophon will reinforce one another: the earlier occurrences will prepare the reader for the later ones, which in turn will cast some light
back on what precedes. Thus the effect of prolepsis in some form, as
a consequence of resonance over a linear text, is independent of any
particular arrangement of the fragments.

The other principle, of linguistic density within a given text, is
essentially the phenomenon of meaningful ambiguity: the use of lexical and syntactic indeterminacy as a device for saying several things
at once. It will often be convenient to speak of *deliberate* or *intentional* ambiguity. I think these expressions are harmless and justified,
as long as it is clearly understood that there is no external biographical
evidence for imputing such intentions to Heraclitus. For these
expressions simply reflect the fact that we can construe an ambiguity
in the text as meaningful only if *we* perceive it as a sign of the author's
intention to communicate to us some complex thought.

Linguistic density in this sense bears a certain formal resemblance
to the deliberate ambiguity of the Delphic oracle, to which Heraclitus
himself alludes (XXXIII, D. 93). But the semantic structure of the
two cases is fundamentally different. In an oracle like 'If Croesus
makes war on Cyrus, he will destroy a great kingdom', the ambiguity
(namely, whose kingdom?) is certainly calculated. But after the event
there can be no doubt as to what would have been the 'correct'
interpretation. The task of understanding an oracle consists in rejecting various possibilities and selecting the one appropriate message.
With meaningful ambiguity in poetic discourse, however, there can
be no single interpretation that is alone correct: the meaning is essentially multiple and complex. In the process of interpreting a text we
may consider and discard some senses as inappropriate. But we will
be left with an irreducible residue of at least two partially significant

interpretations, two distinct statements to be understood as 'intended' by the author, if the ambiguity itself is artistically meaningful. That is to say, to the stylistic device of polysemy or multivocity on the part of the author must correspond a principle of hermeneutical gener-osity on the part of the reader and commentator.

This principle, which has been taken for granted in literary criti-cism for some time,[50] has unfortunately been neglected in the more austere proceedings of classical scholarship. As a result, a good deal of scholarly effort has been devoted to eliminating multiplicity of meaning and thus impoverishing the semantic content of the text, by defending a single construal to the exclusion of others. In the case of Heraclitus as in that of Aeschylus, the interpreter's task is to preserve the original richness of significance by admitting a plurality of alternative senses — some obvious, others recondite, some superficial, others profound. Such discourse presupposes an art of reading which classical scholars seem to have lost, though they are beginning to re-discover it in recent studies of Aeschylus.[51]

Borrowing a term from contemporary linguistics I shall say that a given text admits several different 'readings', where the readings differ from one another by imposing alternative syntactical combinations on the text or by taking the same word in different senses.[52] I shall first describe my procedure for analyzing linguistic density in general terms, and then illustrate it by an application to the first sentence of Heraclitus' book.

I count as the primary reading for a text the interpretation that seems most natural, most likely to recommend itself 'on first reading'. One or more secondary readings may then be required, either to resolve problems raised by the primary reading (as in the case of our first example below), to take account of equivocal words or construc-tions, to bring out a connection of language or imagery between this text and other fragments. (In the latter case the phenomena of den-sity and resonance will coincide.) In establishing the primary reading it will be important to know not only the linguistic expectations created by earlier literature but also the normal usage of the words in Ionic prose, their 'ordinary' meaning for Heraclitus' original audience. To this end our best guide will be the usage of Herodotus, where the evidence is abundant, of relatively early date, and beautifully analyzed in Powell's *Lexicon to Herodotus*. The only substantial body of sur-viving prose that is older than Herodotus is precisely our material from Heraclitus.[53]

Turning now to the first sentence of the book, we seek a primary reading for the first three words: *tou logou toude* 'this *logos* here'. On the basis of evidence to be presented in the Preliminary Remark on this fragment, we can be sure that an original reader of the book would have understood this phrase as a conventional self-reference, an introduction to the work itself: 'this discourse which I am presenting, and which you are about to read'. But the next two words, *eontos aiei* 'being forever', confront us with a dilemma that has plagued readers since Aristotle and has been the subject of endless dispute among modern commentators – a dispute which, I suggest, can only be resolved if we are prepared to regard ambiguity not as a blemish to be eliminated but as a meaningful stylistic device to be accepted and understood.

What Aristotle noticed, in one of his rare comments on another philosopher's style, was that the word *aiei* 'always, forever' in this opening sentence can be construed either with the words that precede ('this *logos* is forever') or with those that follow ('men always fail to comprehend'). Aristotle offers no opinion on the construction beyond the appropriate remark that such ambiguity makes Heraclitus hard to read (*Rhet.* III.5, 1407b11ff., = DK 22.A4). But modern scholars have felt obliged to take sides, either in favor of the former construction (which was long predominant, and has been defended recently by Gigon, Verdenius, Fränkel, Guthrie, and West), or in favor of the latter (which was urged by Reinhardt, Snell, Kirk, Marcovich, and Bollack-Wismann, among others). What this division of opinion shows is that, as Aristotle observed, there is good reason to take the adverb both ways.

The primary, most natural construal will take *aiei* with what precedes, for two reasons: (1) this construction will become visible first, because what precedes is presented first, and (2) the verb 'is' (*eontos*) is generally used as copula, with some other term as predicate or complement. In Greek as in English, a phrase like 'although this *logos* is . . . ' leads us to expect another word or phrase before the end of the clause – before we 'punctuate' (*diastixai*) as Aristotle put it. (And so in the parallel clause in III, D. 2: 'although the *logos* is . . . shared'. The difference is that in Greek, but not normally in English, these expectations may be mistaken and the verb 'is' turn out itself to constitute the predicate. This possibility will be exploited in our second reading.

On first reading, however, I punctuate after *aiei* and construe: 'this *logos* is forever' (or 'is always'). Now 'being forever', *eontos aiei*, is a standard Homeric phrase for the immortal gods who are 'everlasting'

or who 'live forever'.[54] When the primary senses of *logos* and 'is forever' are combined, they give: 'this discourse is forever alive, is
immortal' — a reading on the face of it so strange that it *obliges* us to
go deeper. But although this first interpretation is puzzling, it is not
necessarily mistaken. On the contrary, its correctness at a deeper level
is confirmed by a phenomenon of resonance: the parallel term
aeizōon 'everliving' is applied to fire in XXXVII (D. 30), together
with the phrase *ēn aei* 'it was forever', in an emphatic (and syntactically ambiguous) triple occurrence of the verb 'to be'. Thus the *logos*
of Heraclitus, though not itself definitely identified as an eternal
principle, is presented from the very beginning in such a way as to
provide a suggestion of everlasting life.

But this idea is at best a *hyponoia* here, a mysterious hint of a
thought not fully expressed. We want something to be said about the
logos that is appropriate to a stretch of discourse; and in this connection the Homeric formula for immortality will not do. Thus our
primary reading collapses under its own weight.

A second reading will take account of the fact that we can punctuate before *aiei* and construe the adverb with what follows: 'men
always fail to comprehend'. This leaves the verb 'is' (*eontos*) without
any predicate or complement in the initial clause: 'although this *logos*
is'. We can make sense of that by appealing to what I have called the
veridical use of the verb, where *esti* or *eon* (Attic *on*) means 'is true,
is so': *ho eōn logos* will be 'the true report', 'an account which states
the facts'.[55] The sentence now becomes 'Although this *logos* is true,
men are forever incapable of understanding it.'

In translating the sentence I have tried to suggest both readings.
But no rendering can do justice to the fact that a reader who wishes
to avoid an arbitrary decision will be left in genuine suspense between
the more natural reading of the first clause 'this *logos* is forever',
which has a proper literary ring to it but leaves us wondering just
what that could mean, and the reading 'this *logos* is true', which is
stylistically more recherché but clear, even banal in its content. When
both readings have a good case to be made for them, it is important
to leave open the possibility that the difficulty of deciding between
them is itself the intended effect. And once we have understood
Heraclitus' thought as a whole, we see why this initial perplexity is
significant. For the *logos* of Heraclitus is not merely his statement: it
is the eternal structure of the world as it manifests itself in discourse.
This will be hinted at in the next words ('men fail to comprehend,
even before they have heard what I have to say'), further indicated

by the diverse usage of *logos* throughout the fragments, and most strikingly in the contrast between 'listening to me' and 'listening to the *logos*' in XXXVI (D. 50).

Thus we have two plausible and instructive readings of the first sentence, corresponding to alternative construals of the adverb *aiei*.[56] And it is the primary, more natural reading ('this *logos* is forever') that is from the point of view of content the deeper and more paradoxical. The reading which is secondary or artificial in stylistic terms ('this *logos* is true') is more unsurprising, even banal in terms of content. So the relation between the surface meaning and the *hyponoia* or 'deeper sense' is itself unstable and complex.

The result is a prose style which fully justifies Heraclitus' reputation as 'the obscure' (*ho skoteinos*). The effect of an initial encounter is preserved for us in the anecdote of Socrates' response, when Euripides asked him what he thought of the book: 'What I understand is excellent, and I think the rest is also. But it takes a Delian diver to get to the bottom of it' (D.L. II.22). An eloquent epigram preserved by Diogenes warns the reader not to peruse the book too rapidly: 'It is a hard road, filled with darkness and gloom; but if an initiate leads you on the way, it becomes brighter than the radiance of the sun.'[57]

I make no claims to reach such dazzling clarity here. But I do believe (with Diels and others) that the longer one reflects upon these fragments, the clearer becomes the unity, complexity, and profundity of the thought they convey.

In conclusion, I want to emphasize that my procedure of recognizing two or more distinct 'readings' is only a hermeneutical device for clarifying the semantic density of the text. Such devices are legitimate and necessary, and they require no apology. But they need not blind us to the fact that there is no natural unit for counting the 'meanings' of a given text. One might reasonably claim that *all* of Heraclitus' fragments have only one single meaning, which is in fact the full semantic structure of his thought as a whole, of which any given phrase is but an incomplete fragment. Our piecemeal 'readings' of particular phrases or sentences are best regarded as workmanlike tools for apprehending and reconstructing this global meaning, as a kind of ladder or crutch to be abandoned once the goal of understanding has been achieved.

Commentary on the fragments

I

Preliminary remark on fragment I

Fragment I is the longest quotation from Heraclitus, and probably the longest piece of surviving Greek prose before the *Histories* of Herodotus, which it antedates by fifty years. It is in turn some fifty years younger than the earliest known prose work, the little book of Anaximander, from which we have one quotation (DK 12.B 1, cited above, p. 18). As this quotation from Anaximander and the nearly contemporary citations from Pherecydes show, and as the fragments of Heraclitus and the long narrative of Herodotus confirm, Ionic prose came into being as a highly developed literary form; for it could from the start draw upon the rich resources of two centuries of written epic and lyric poetry, beginning with the *Iliad* in the eighth century – and of course the *Iliad* in turn could draw upon a long tradition of oral poetry. Thus the high literary level of early Greek prose is not in itself surprising. What is surprising is the extraordinarily dense and personal style of the quotations from Heraclitus.

As we can see from other early samples, Greek prose was at first employed primarily for the publication of Ionian *historiē*: for presenting the results of systematic 'inquiry' or 'research' on a variety of subjects from astronomy to biology, including historical research in connection with the description of lands and peoples (as in the travel book of Hecataeus, a Milesian contemporary of Heraclitus). The old Ionic term *historiē* soon became fixed in its narrow application to 'history' in our sense, because it was this type of investigation that first gave birth to major works of prose literature: the *Histories* of Herodotus and Thucydides. We can form some picture of the earlier Ionian books from what remains of Hecataeus, Anaxagoras and Diogenes of Apollonia, as well as from the older Hippocratic treatises.

From such evidence we know that when Heraclitus begins his

proem with a reference to his own *logos* he is following a literary tradition well established among early prose authors. The oldest surviving
parallel is the preamble to a work of Hecataeus (the *Historiai* or
Genealogiai) which began with these words: 'Hecataeus of Miletus
says as follows. I write these things as they seem to me to be true.
For the reports (*logoi*) of the Greeks are, in my judgment, many and
ridiculous.'[58] The fifth-century treatise of Ion of Chios begins: 'The
starting point of my discourse (*logos*): all things are three, and
nothing more or less than these three' (DK 36.B 1). Other examples
show that such treatises were regularly introduced by a reference to
the *logos* or discourse as such.[59]

   But if this self-reference is a traditional feature in the proem, what
is not traditional at all is the peculiar emphasis on the term *logos* and
the syntactic ambiguities by which it is surrounded (above, p. 93).
The stylistic difficulties here suggest that if Heraclitus' *logos* is from
one point of view the usual Ionian prose 'report', it is also something
quite different. Heraclitus presumably chose to write in prose because
that was the new scientific language of his day and the traditional
idiom of aphoristic wisdom. But whereas the general tendency of
Ionian prose is towards directness and clarity of expression, the distinctive trait of Heraclitus' own style is a more than Delphic delight
in paradox, enigma and equivocation. In this respect, the little book
of Heraclitus will have been a very *atypical* representative of the new
genre. A reader who began by expecting a straightforward report of
scientific research or speculation would be brought up short by the
grammatical dilemma confronting him in the first sentence.

For convenience of reference, I number the three sentences of the
first fragment and consider them one by one.

I (D. 1). 1   Although this account (*logos*) holds forever, men ever fail to comprehend, both before hearing it and once they have heard (or 'when they hear it for
the first time').

Both Aristotle and Sextus tell us this passage came at the beginning
of the book. As we have seen, the initial ambiguity in the syntax of
aiei 'forever' hints at the deeper ambivalence in the status of
Heraclitus' *logos*: it is both his discourse and something more: something universal (all things occur in agreement with it), even eternal
and divine (*eōn aiei*), precisely in virtue of the fact that it is 'common' or 'shared' by all (*xynos* in III, D. 2).

This first sentence sounds the twin themes of *hearing* and *comprehending* that will recur with increasing significance throughout the fragments (II, D. 34; XIV, D. 55; XV, D. 101a; XVI, D. 107; XVII, D. 19; XXVII, D. 108; XXXVI, D. 50, etc.). The complaint that his auditors are unable to comprehend is a natural one on the part of an author who has chosen the language of enigma and equivocation. What is more puzzling is the insistence that men prove uncomprehending not only 'once they have heard my discourse' but *even before*. How can they be expected to understand it in advance? This will make sense only if Heraclitus' *logos* represents a truth that has been there all along: if, like Fire, it always was and is and will be.

Thus the *logos* here cannot be just 'what Heraclitus says', not merely the words he utters or even the meaning of what he has to say, if meaning is understood subjectively as what the speaker has in mind or his intentions in speaking. The *logos* can be his 'meaning' only in the objective sense: the structure which his words intend or point at, which is the structure of the world itself (and not the intensional structure of his *thought* about the world). Only such an objective structure can be 'forever', available for comprehension before any words are uttered. Which is not to say that we can translate *logos* by 'structure' or by 'the objective content of my discourse'. The tension between word and content is essential here, for without it we do not have the instructive paradox of men who are expected to understand a *logos* they have not heard.

I. 2   Although all things come to pass in accordance with this account (*logos*), men are like the untried when they try such words and works as I set forth, distinguishing each according to its nature (*physis*) and telling how it is.

The second sentence begins with a clause in the genitive case that echoes not only the syntax but also the vocabulary of the beginning. The verb *ginesthai* 'become, come to pass', which first expressed men's lack of comprehension, is here applied to all the things that there are (*ginomenōn pantōn*) and that men fail to comprehend. The genitival construction, which first depended upon *axynetoi* 'unable to comprehend', is now connected with *apeiroi* 'lacking in experience'.

The formal parallels between these two sentences suggest that Heraclitus is developing a single point. In both cases the announcement of the *logos* and its universal truth (in the genitival clause) is contrasted with the incompetent response of mankind (in the principal clause). The tension between the two aspects of *logos* — the

actual words of Heraclitus and their everlasting content — is stretched
still further here, where the *logos* as universal law is juxtaposed with
Heraclitus' reference to his own exposition, in the emphatic first person (*hokoiōn egō diēgeumai* 'such as I set forth').

'They are like the untried', 'they resemble men without experience'
is a surprising phrase; for it suggests that in fact men *do* have the
experience in question. And well they might: since it is experience *of
things that occur according to the 'logos'*, and these are *all* things, no
one can be without such experience. But it is difficult for men to
grasp this truth, even when Heraclitus announces it to them directly.
They can make nothing of his words (*epea*), nor of the facts (*erga*)
which he points out, although he 'tells it like it is' and puts each
thing in its place, 'according to its *physis*'.

The word for 'facts', *erga* ('works', 'deeds') has epic overtones: it
may refer to heroic exploits and also to more humble labor, as in
Hesiod's *Works and Days*. The term *physis*, on the other hand, for
the genuine nature or structure of a thing, is the watchword of the
new natural philosophy that radiates from Miletus. By the use of this
characteristic word, which recurs in X (D. 123) and XXXII (D. 112),
as by his use of *historiē* ('inquiry') and *kosmos* (in the sense of
'world order'), Heraclitus expressly claims affinity with the new
scientific tradition, and thus offers his own truth as a supplement or
as a rival to that of the natural philosophers.

I. 3   But other men are oblivious of what they do awake, just as they are forgetful of what they do asleep.

What is striking here is not so much the self-assurance (not to say
arrogance) of the thinker who regards 'other men' as sleepwalkers,
but the almost pathetic epistemic isolation of a man trying to convey
the vision of an obvious and immediate truth to men who stagger
past, unable to *notice what they are doing all day long*, as if it were a
dream they cannot grasp or hold on to. The image of sleep (which will
elsewhere provide a kind of link between life and death) serves here
to give a more drastic expression to the idea of cognitive alienation.
Coming as it does at the very beginning, this paradoxical conception
of the human condition as a state of deepest ignorance in the face of
an immediately accessible truth serves to define the basic framework
within which the specific doctrines must be understood. In particular,
it warns us against an over-hasty interpretation of his relationship to
Ionian science. The *historiē* of men like Anaximander or Hecataeus,

or even Pythagoras and Xenophanes, represents new and technical knowledge, the product of special research, whether derived by watching the stars or by visiting the Thracians and Persians. Such *historiē* is certainly *not* the apprehension of a universal truth of immediate experience, as accessible to men as 'what they do awake'. Hence the attitude of Heraclitus to such science will turn out to be profoundly ambivalent. His own philosophic vision is inspired by the new scientific study of the world, but it is directed towards a truth of an entirely different kind.

Perhaps one may compare Heraclitus' sense of epistemic isolation, and this ambivalent relationship to contemporary scientific knowledge, with the position of Bishop Berkeley in regard to Newtonian physics and optics. Berkeley's sensory idealism depends historically and psychologically upon the new science of his day, and upon careful studies in the geometry of vision. But his philosophical position as such does not logically depend upon any technical knowledge whatsoever. On the contrary, it involves a complete reinterpretation of what all scientific knowledge is about. Berkeley's teaching too involves a truth (from his point of view) closer than hands and feet, which ought to be obvious to every person, but which is in fact devilishly difficult to communicate even to a benevolent reader.

The most crucial disanalogy here — apart from the contrast between the state of the sciences in 500 B.C. and in A.D. 1700 — is the fact that Berkeley's doctrine is concerned with issues that are purely theoretical or cognitive: with the nature of knowledge and what is known. For Heraclitus, questions of cognition are inseparable from questions of action and intention, questions of life and death. The blindness he denounces is that of men who 'do not know what they are doing'. It is the life of mankind that is the subject of his discourse, not the theory of knowledge and perception.

With this proviso, we can say that his proem does characterize human life in epistemic terms, in terms of a well-nigh universal failure to make sense of one's experience. His initial concern is less with the structure of reality than with the extreme difficulty of grasping this structure.

II–III

II (D. 34)   Not comprehending, they hear like the deaf. The saying bears witness to them: absent while present.

III (D. 2)   Although the account (*logos*) is shared, most men live as though their thinking (*phronēsis*) were a private possession.

Since II and III contain elaborate echoes of the proem in diction and in thought, it is natural to suppose they followed on it rather closely. (In the case of III Sextus tells us as much.) Three of the first four words in II are formal repetitions from I: *axynetoi*, *akousantes*, *eoikasi*. The new element is the comparison to the deaf. The paradox 'absent while present' confirms the sense of epistemic isolation. There seems to be an audience there, men listening, but no communication is possible, nothing gets through. These pathetic listeners, who include most men and most of Heraclitus' illustrious predecessors, must be somewhere else, 'off on their own trip'.

III (D. 2) also opens with a phrase from the proem.[60] But instead of 'forever' the *logos* now has as its predicate *xynos* 'common', 'shared'. In its first occurrence this key term is marked by stylistic emphasis, where the mechanism of repetition leads us to expect *aiei*, the epithet of divinity.

On first reading, we understand the *logos* as 'common' because it is shared by all things or events, which take place in accordance with it (I.2). But common *logos* also means 'common consent', 'common cause', as when several powers combine in an agreement or alliance.[61] This is brought out in a later echo of 'listening to the *logos*', when Heraclitus speaks of wisdom on the listeners' part as 'speaking in agreement', *homologein* (XXXVI, D. 50). The notion of 'consensus' or 'agreement' is only latent here; more unmistakable is the notion of the 'common' as the *public*, what belongs to the *community* as a whole, in contrast to what is private. Another overtone of *xynos logos* will emerge in the word play of XXX (D. 114), where *tōi xynōi pantōn* 'what is common to all' presents a phonetic echo of *xyn nooi legontes* 'speaking with understanding'. That 'common' (*xynos*) in III may also suggest the word for understanding or intelligence (*noos*) is made likely by the contrast here between the common *logos* and the private *phronēsis* which men have or claim.[62] I translate *phronēsis* as 'thinking' to preserve the resonance with the cognate verb *phronein*, translated 'think' in IV and elsewhere. The term also means 'intelligence', 'good sense', 'wisdom' in practical decisions. Hence the verb *zōousin* here: it is a question of how men 'live their lives'.

In sum, the *logos* is 'common' because it is (or expresses) a structure that characterizes all things, and is therefore a public possession in principle available to all men, since it is 'given' in the immanent structure of their shared experience.[63] The *logos* is also shared as a principle of agreement between diverse powers, of understanding between speaker and hearer, of public unity and joint action among the members of a political community. The *logos* is all these things because the term signifies not only meaningful speech, but the exercise of intelligence as such, the activity of *nous* or *phronēsis*. The deepest thought of *xynos logos*, more fully expressed in XXX, is that what unites men is their rationality, itself the reflection of the underlying unity of all nature.

I assume that *logos* means not simply language but rational discussion, calculation, and choice: rationality as expressed in speech, in thought, and in action. (All these ideas are connected with the classic use of *logos*, *logizesthai*, *epilegein*, etc., e.g. in Herodotus.) This is rationality as a phenomenal property manifested in intelligent behavior, not Reason as some kind of theoretical entity posited 'behind the phenomena' as cause of rational behavior. The conception of *logos* as a self-subsistent power or principle is foreign to the usage of Heraclitus but essential in the Stoic conception of the divine Reason that rules the universe. (See on V below.)[64]

IV

IV (D. 17)   Most men do not think (*phroneousi*) things in the way that they encounter them, nor do they recognize what they experience, but believe their own opinions.

The first two clauses of IV reformulate the theme of failure to understand; the third introduces the topic of seeming knowledge or guesswork (*dokein*). So far the cognitive condition of mankind has been characterized negatively, as deafness, absence, lack of understanding. The description in more positive terms begins with the comparison to sleep and hence dreaming in I.3, and with the suggestion in III that error involves treating *phronēsis* as if it were something private. (The convergence of these two ideas, privacy and sleep, will come in VI.) The last clause of IV points to a connection between this description of error and an older, half-technical concept of 'appearance' or 'opinion', expressed by cognates of the verb *dokein* 'to seem'. Heraclitus' own use of the concept of 'opinion' is discussed below, on LXXXIV (D. 27)–LXXXV (D. 28A).

The notion of incomprehension is developed by a complex literary device: each clause takes a traditional *topos* or commonplace of

Greek poetic wisdom and stands it on its head. The effect is to present Heraclitus' thesis not simply as a challenge to contemporary *savants*, but as an implicit correction of the wisdom of Homer, Hesiod, and Archilochus.

One of the most famous passages on 'thinking' in Homer is *Odyssey* XVIII.136: 'The mind (*noos*) of men upon the earth is such as the day which the father of gods and men brings upon them.' In context, this means that the fortune and happiness of men is dependent upon the decision of the gods; but the dependence is stated in terms of men's *understanding* of their situation. (And this statement of Odysseus finds its immediate application in the folly of the hearer, Amphinomus, who fails to heed the warning of which these words are part, and which would have saved his life.) Almost the same phrase occurs, with roughly the same meaning, in a fragment of Archilochus (68 Diehl): 'The heart (*thymos*) of mortal men, Glaucos son of Leptines, becomes such as the day which Zeus brings upon them, and their thoughts (*phroneusin*) are such as the deeds (*ergmata*) that they encounter (*enkyreōsin*)', that is, their thought is deter-mined by their situation.[65] The first clause of IV contains, in its two verbs and its comparative structure (*toiauta . . . hokoia* 'in the way that' or 'such . . . as') a clear echo of Archilochus' own words. But Heraclitus echoes Archilochus only to deny what the latter affirms. Men's thinking is *not* in conformity with the reality they encounter — would that it were!

The second clause denies another familiar lesson: learning the hard way, *pathei mathos*. Before becoming the theme of Aeschylus' *Oresteia*, 'knowledge through suffering' was the standard character-ization of the fool who learns too late. In Hesiod's parable of the two roads, one of Justice (*Dikē*) and one of Crime (*Hybris*), the way of Crime is said to be easier at the beginning but disastrous at the end: 'and the fool recognizes this (*egnō*) when he has suffered his punish-ment (*pathōn*), (*Works and Days* 218).[66] Again, Heraclitus alludes to Hesiod's commonplace only to contradict it: experience, even suffer-ing, teaches men nothing at all. They do not have the wit to recognize (*ginōskein*) what is happening to them. The insights that men find in the poetry of Homer, Hesiod, and Archilochus are nothing more than 'believing their own opinions': enough wisdom to satisfy their own folly.

This is our first encounter with the verb *gignōskō* 'to recognize, perceive, know', which occurs in Hesiod's proverb as in Archilochus' own claim to insight.[67] Heraclitus has taken over this verb, with its cognate nouns *gnōmē* and *gnōsis*, as his own term for 'cognition' in a privileged sense, for the insight which men lack and which his own discourse attempts to communicate.

V

V (D. 71–3)   Marcus Aurelius: [Always bear in mind what Heraclitus said ...
And bear in mind the man who forgets where the way leads, and that 'they are at odds with (*diapherontai*) that with which they most constantly associate' (the *logos* which controls all things), and that what they meet with every day seems strange to them, and that one should not act and speak like men asleep.]

(Here I render the fuller context in Marcus; in the translation I gave only what might be a citation from Heraclitus.)

Although this text contains an echo of several fragments (notably of IV), there is no clear trace of literal quotation and hence no basis for detailed commentary. 'They are at odds with that with which they most constantly associate' represents something Heraclitus might have said, and the implicit word play on *diapherontai* is attested elsewhere (CXXIV, D. 10). But Marcus Aurelius is citing from memory, and since his memory is not very accurate there is no way to tell whether he is preserving a genuine fragment or simply developing his own recollection of IV.

In any case, the words in parenthesis, 'the *logos* which controls the universe', represent (even in terminology: *dioikein ta hola*) the Stoic rather than the Heraclitean conception of *logos*.

VI

VI (D. 89)   Plutarch: [Heraclitus says that the world (*kosmos*) of the waking is one and shared but that the sleeping turn aside each into his private world.]

Plutarch is paraphrasing, not quoting verbatim: he uses the ordinary word *koinos* for 'common', where Heraclitus always has *xynos* (5 times in the extant fragments). The absence of any archaic overtones in the sense of *kosmos* here also suggests a post-Platonic phrasing. In general, the rhetoric of the passage is that of Plutarch, not Heraclitus.[68] But I see no reason to doubt that Plutarch is rendering Heraclitus' thought correctly.

VII—X

VII (D. 18)   He who does not expect will not find out the unexpected, for it is trackless and unexplored.

VIII (D. 22)   Seekers of gold dig up much earth and find little.

IX (D. 35)   Men who love wisdom (*philosophoi andres*) must be good inquirers (*histores*) into many things indeed.

X (D. 123)   Nature (*physis*) loves to hide.

I have grouped these four quotations on the basis of their common imagery of searching, finding, being hard to find. Only in one case (IX, D. 35) is there any doubt as to the authenticity of the wording. If genuine, this would be the earliest occurrence of the term *philoso-phos* in Greek. Since the word here has its etymological force ('lover of wisdom' or 'eager for learning new and clever things'), and is paired with the term *histores* that suggests Ionian inquiry (cf. *historiē* in XXV, D. 129), I have ranked this as a quotation. (Clement is gener-ally one of our best sources for literal citations.) If Heraclitus used the term *philosophos*, as I suppose, he may have intended an allusion to the other masters of wisdom, the seven *sophoi* or sages, two of whom (Thales and Bias) are mentioned in the fragments. Thus *philoso-phoi andres* admits a secondary reading: 'men who want to become sages'. Heraclitus himself makes a special use of the concept of *to sophon* 'what is wise'. It would be in character for him to introduce the theme of wisdom in the compound form *philo-sophos*, as the object of ardent desire.[69]

As grouped here, these four quotations deal with the difficulty of cognition from the side of the object. Whereas I—IV describe human incomprehension as a kind of perverse blindness in regard to what is staring us in the face, VII—X recognize that the truth, the character-istic nature of things (*physis*), the prize of wisdom hunted by phil-osophical goldseekers, is not simply there for the taking. Even if the *logos* is common to all, so that the structure of reality is 'given' in everyday experience, recognition comes hard. It requires the right kind of openness on the part of the percipient   what Heraclitus calls 'hope' or 'expectation' (*elpesthai* in VII; compare LXXXIV, D. 27). And it requires inquiry and reflection — digging up a lot of earth and judging it with discretion. The 'gnosis' which Heraclitus has in mind is rational *knowledge*, and it has to be gained by hard work; it is not the miraculous revelation of a moment of grace.

XI–XIII

XI (D. 47)   Let us not concur casually about the most important matters.

XII (D. A23)   Polybius: [It would no longer be fitting to take poets and story-tellers as witnesses for things unknown, as our ancestors did in most cases, citing untrustworthy authorities on disputed points as Heraclitus says.]

XIII (D. 74)   Marcus Aurelius: [We should not act and speak like 'children of our parents', in other words, in the way that has been handed down to us.] [70]

These three texts express a critical attitude towards traditional or current practice and belief; they add little to the more authentic fragments. I print XI as quotation rather than paraphrase only because it occurs in a context (D.L. IX.71–3) with verbatim citations from other authors.

XIV–XVII

XIV (D. 55)   Whatever comes from sight, hearing, learning from experience: this I prefer.

XV (D. 101a)   Polybius: [According to Heraclitus, eyes are surer witnesses than ears.]

XVI (D. 107)   Eyes and ears are poor witnesses for men if their souls (*psychai*) do not understand the language (literally, 'if they have barbarian souls').

XVII (D. 19)   Not knowing how to listen, neither can they speak.

These four statements develop and clarify the thought of VII–X: the usual sources of information are necessary but not sufficient for the cognition that Heraclitus is trying to describe.

XIV seems to insist upon the fact that the truth is not so recondite as it might seem, or as some will pretend: far from requiring any special revelation or abstruse theory, what Heraclitus treasures is something that can be grasped by sight, hearing, and ordinary experience of life (*mathēsis*: compare *mathontes* in IV, D. 17). The preference for eyes over ears has a proverbial ring (as in the Gyges story, Herodotus I.8.2). It expresses not so much an epistemic ranking of the senses as the reliance upon direct experience rather than upon hearsay. This is basic both for Ionian *historiē* (inquiry conceived as finding out for oneself) and for Heraclitus' own attack upon the traditional wisdom of the poets.

But learning from experience involves more than keeping one's eyes and ears open: in order for thinking (*phronein*) to become recognition (*ginōskein*) the soul of the observer must not be 'barbarian', that is, it must know the relevant language. Heraclitus thus develops the double aspect of *logos* indicated in the proem: spoken words, and a universal pattern of experience. The world order speaks to men as a kind of language they must learn to comprehend. Just as the meaning of what is said is actually 'given' in the sounds which the foreigner hears, but cannot understand, so the direct experience of the nature of things will be like the babbling of an unknown tongue for the soul that does not know how to listen.

This is apparently the first time in extant literature that the word *psychē* 'soul' is used for the power of rational thought. (Contrast the 'irrational' psyche described as waking when the body sleeps, in the Pindar fragment cited below, p. 127.) The new concept of the psyche is expressed in terms of the power of articulate speech: rationality is understood as the capacity to participate in the life of language, 'knowing how to listen and how to speak'.

These intimate connections between speech, intelligence, and the *logos* which is 'common to all' appear again in XXX (D. 114), as in III (D. 2), and once more in XXXVI (D. 50).

XVIII–XIX

XVIII (D. 40)   Much learning does not teach understanding (*noos*). For it would have taught Hesiod and Pythagoras, and also Xenophanes and Hecataeus.

XIX (D. 57)   The teacher of most is Hesiod. It is him they know as knowing most, who did not recognize day and night: they are one.

XVIII continues the thought of XVI ('eyes and ears are poor witnesses'), applying it not to the ordinary perception of the man in the street but to the claims of experts: such learning will not give the relevant kind of understanding. That requires something more, something there conceived as speaking the right language and here called *noos* or 'intelligence'. *Noos* (Attic *nous*) is, among other things, the capacity to speak and to listen well. The word can even denote the meaning or intention of what is said. (See Powell's *Lexicon* s.v. *noos*, 3.) This is a specialized development from the more general sense of *noos* as what someone 'has in mind', the character and intentions of men which underlie their words and actions. Thus Odysseus in his

travels 'came to recognize (*egnō*) the *noos* of many men', as the
Odyssey tells us. But like *phronein*, which has the neutral sense of
'thinking' but the laudatory sense of 'thinking well, using good sense',·
the term *noos* also has a normative use. Thus doing something 'with
noos' means doing it in a reasonable way; acting 'without *noos*' means
acting foolishly. The word has its positive sense here, as in XXX (D.
114); cf. LIX (D. 104).

There is no inconsistency between this depreciation of 'learning
many things' and the claim in VIII—X that a great deal of knowledge
and experience is required in the pursuit of wisdom. Heraclitus does
not say that the *polymathiē* is a waste of time, only that it is not
enough: that the mere accumulation of information will not yield
understanding, unless it is accompanied by some fundamental insight.

Four exemplars of learning are named here. Hesiod is the poet of
the remote past, almost two centuries earlier than Heraclitus, whose
didactic poems had come to enjoy the status of revered handbooks
familiar to every educated Greek: the *Theogony* as the authoritative
account of origins, dynasties, and family connections among the gods,
the *Works and Days* as a summa of practical lore, from farming and
astronomy to instruction on unlucky days. As an established expert
on all matters human and divine, Hesiod is a natural target. Pythagoras
may be named next to Hesiod because he, alone among Heraclitus'
recent predecessors, had achieved a kind of legendary prestige within
his own lifetime. Xenophanes and Hecataeus have a narrower claim
to fame: they represent the diffusion of Milesian *historiē* in literary
form.

From our perspective on the history of early Greek philosophy,
gained from Aristotle and the Theophrastean doxography, it is
natural to wonder why we find no mention here of the three Milesians
whom we think of as the creators of the new science: Thales, Anaximander, and Anaximenes. Thales' name will in fact occur in XXIV.
Heraclitus' silence concerning Anaximander and Anaximenes is probably neither the result of ignorance nor a sign of special respect.
Heraclitus (like Plato after him) simply did not think of himself as
addressing the narrow audience that would be familiar with the work
of these men. (They are not mentioned by any extant writer before
Aristotle, and by scarcely anyone later outside of the technical doxographic tradition.) Xenophanes and Hecataeus were influential authors
in their own right and would be known to a wider public.

The attack on Hesiod in XIX provides the first explicit riddle, and
the first clue as to the content of Heraclitus' *logos*: day and night are

one. The point of the riddle is sharpened by the ironical use of three different verbs for 'to know': *epistantai* for the popular intelligence which selects this teacher; *eidenai* for the knowledge they ascribe to him, and Heraclitus' favored term *ginōskein* for the cognition which is denied to Hesiod.

The content of such cognition is expressed here by an unexplained assertion of unity between night and day. This is one Heraclitean riddle about whose solution we can be reasonably certain. It stands first as a kind of emblematic statement for the doctrine of unity or interdependence between opposing powers that constitutes the general pattern and the formal theme for Heraclitus' teaching. It also represents a quite specific insight of an almost technical sort.

Hesiod had conceived Night (*Nyx*) in the manner of early mythic thought, as a positive force which blots out the light of day and the vision of men, as death blots out human life. In Hesiod's view, Night is naturally paired with her opposite number Day, whom she meets at the door of the underworld, one leaving as the other returns from the trip above ground (*Theogony* 748—57). No pattern of opposition seems more firmly grounded in the basic experience of mankind than that between daylight and nocturnal darkness. So no affirmation of the unity of opposites could be more striking nor, at first glance, more paradoxical. But the paradox is only apparent. The natural unit of time, constant throughout the year, is not the day but what the Greeks later called the *nychthēmeron*, the day-and-night interval of twenty-four hours. The astronomers of early Greece had no clocks, but their interest in the calendar made them pay close attention to the changing length of daylight through the year. The discovery of the *nychthēmeron* is just the discovery that the nights get shorter as the days get longer, though the time from noon to noon does not change. The doxography reports, and the fragments of Heraclitus confirm, that considerable attention was paid to the measurement of solstices and equinoxes, and thus to the regular correlation between the visible course of the sun and the relative length of day and night. The knowledge of solstices or *tropai*, as the place where and the time when the sun annually reaches its farthest point to the north and to the south, is as old as Homer and Hesiod; but such matters came under more intensive study in Miletus in the sixth century, probably under Babylonian influence.[71] I have no doubt that these are the 'measures' of the sun referred to below in XLIV (D. 94), where they are said to be enforced by Justice herself. Something similar must be intended by the 'limits of dawn and evening' in XLV (D. 120), over

which Zeus has set his guardian. The word for solstices, *tropai*, occurs
as a cosmological term in XXXVIII (D. 31A). The insight that night
has no positive force but is merely the absence of sunlight, and therefore varies directly with the changing course of the sun, is clearly
expressed in XLVI (D. 99): without the sun it would be night. In this
apparently childish remark lies the solution to our riddle and the real
point of this attack on Hesiod.[72] Far from being separate and irreconcilable powers, day and night are complementary aspects of a single
unit.

This riddle and its solution is a paradigm for the relation between
the *logos* of Heraclitus and the *polymathiē* of Ionian science. The
new science has provided Heraclitus with a much clearer understanding of the relationship between solar motion and length of night-time
than was available to Hesiod. But no amount of *historiē* or astronomical knowledge alone could situate this relationship within a universal pattern of interdependent or co-variant opposition — within
the general framework that we call Heraclitus' 'doctrine of opposites'.
And this doctrine, as expressed in the identification of night and day,
is itself a symbol and a clue for the understanding of human life and
death as a unity, which forms the central insight in what Heraclitus
means by 'wisdom'.

XX

XX (D. 106)   Plutarch: [Heraclitus attacked Hesiod for counting some days as
good, others as bad, because he did not recognize that the nature (*physis*) of
every day is one.]

It is not clear whether this is a separate criticism of Hesiod or a variant
on XIX (D. 57).[73] It seems unlikely that Heraclitus would have
diluted his attack on Hesiod's doctrine of *opposites* — of which Night
and Day are splendid examples — by turning to the conceptually less
interesting contrast between lucky and unlucky days; but the existence of this saying in two independent forms (Plutarch and Seneca)
makes it difficult to reject out of hand. Perhaps the reference is not
to the annual course of the sun and its effect upon the balance of
night and day but rather to the nature of the sun itself as a manifestation of cosmic fire; or to the equivalence between one day and
its successor (see below, p. 225).[74]

XXI

XXI (D. 42) [He said that] Homer deserves to be expelled from the competition and beaten with a staff — and Archilochus too!

This remark presupposes that the poems of Archilochus, like those of Homer, were recited by rhapsodes in public competitions at the festival games (*agōnes*), in connection with athletic contests. (Compare the situation a century later, when Plato names Archilochus and Hesiod with Homer as the standard authors for rhapsodic competition, *Ion* 531A.) Heraclitus takes the wise words of all three 'official' poets — Homer, Archilochus, and Hesiod — as targets for his attack.

As Bollack-Wismann have pointed out (p. 157), XXI can be read as beginning with an invective against Homer in the salty style of Archilochus himself, and then turning the new weapon against its inventor. The patron of the rhapsodes, whose poems were the original subject of recitation, deserves to be punished with his own symbol, the rhapsode's staff or *rhabdos*. But the competitor who would replace him is expelled in turn by the same staff.[75]

XXII

XXII (D. 56) Men are deceived in the recognition of what is obvious, like Homer who was wisest of all the Greeks. For he was deceived by boys killing lice, who said: what we see and catch we leave behind; what we neither see nor catch, we carry away.

This fragment gives the solution to what seems to be a traditional riddle. But it poses its own puzzle: why does Heraclitus find the story significant?

In the *Lives* of Homer that circulated in late antiquity, the riddle of the lice is regularly cited in connection with Homer's death: the poet is usually said to have died of grief at not being able to guess the answer.[76] The later versions emphasize Homer's blindness, and that is probably presupposed by XXII. If so, we have a parallel to II (D. 34): as deafness there represents men's hearing without comprehension, so here the failure to recognize what is clearly visible (*ta phanera*) is compared to Homer's blindness.

Now the story does serve Heraclitus' purpose of showing the wisest of the Greeks to be a fool: he cannot guess a riddle known to children.[77] But the riddle itself should be meaningful. Bollack-

Wismann propose an etymological play here on the word for lice, *phtheir*, phonetically identical with the first syllable of *phtheirō* 'to destroy': what the boys are doing is literally *killing the killers*; and this is what Homer fails to understand. Furthermore, the riddle has the symmetrical form of a double paradox: denying the expected consequence of 'seeing and catching', and then affirming this consequence for *not* seeing and catching. If the play on killing *phtheires* is a clue, we might well be reminded of Euripides' paradox which has the same double form: 'Who knows if life be death, and death be regarded as life below?' (fr. 638 N). Heraclitus himself will offer a paradox of this form, in which mortals and immortals exchange positions with regard to life and death (XCII, D. 62). Of course no one could possibly guess this meaning on a first reading of XXII. But then the device of proleptic statement, or more generally of resonance implies that many dimensions of meaning will not be immediately accessible on our first contact with the text. ('Men fail to comprehend this *logos* when they hear it for the first time.')

The proposed solution becomes even more plausible if we suppose that the riddle of the lice was already associated with the story of Homer's *death*. For then it is natural to understand the 'recognition of what is apparent', in which men are deceived, by reference to Homer's perplexity in the face of his own death. The etymology of lice (*phtheires*) as 'destroyers' thus comes into full play.

Heraclitus' detailed presentation of this riddle, in one of the longest of the fragments, suggests that genuine wisdom is like an enigma, difficult and obvious at the same time, or difficult at first and obvious later. It also suggests that wisdom has something to do with what we see and grasp, but more to do with what we ordinarily do not see and do not grasp.

XXIII–XXIV

XXIII (D. 105)   Scholia on *Iliad* XVIII.251: [Heraclitus calls Homer an astronomer.]

XXIV (D. 38)   Diogenes Laertius: [According to some sources, Thales seems to have been the first to practise astronomy and predict solar eclipses and solstices . . . Heraclitus also bears witness to him.]

There is not much to be made of these bits of doxographical information, except that the names of both Homer and Thales were mentioned in connection with astronomy, perhaps in the same context

(as Marcovich has suggested), just as Heraclitus mentions Hesiod and
Hecataeus together in XVIII (D. 40). Exactly what Heraclitus said
about Thales we can scarcely guess. But the omission of Thales' name
in XVIII (D. 40), where it might easily have stood between Hesiod
and Pythagoras, suggests that the tone was not one of violent hostility;
and that is on the whole confirmed by the context in Diogenes. Probably the reference to Thales reflected his legendary fame as a star-
gazer, as in the story of the eclipse in Herodotus I.74.2: a similar
story seems to have been mentioned by Xenophanes (DK 21.B 19).

The reference to Homer in XXIII is equally uninformative. Its
authenticity has been questioned on the grounds that the scholiasts
who report it assume that *astrology* is meant, as we can see from the
verses they cite. Now there is no trace of such astrology in Greece in
the time of Heraclitus or for a century or two thereafter. But it does
not follow that we should reject the whole reference. The astrological
interpretation with its selection of Homeric verses must be the work
of a Hellenistic commentator. But there would have been nothing for
him to comment on if he had not found some connection between
Homer and astronomy in Heraclitus' own text.[78]

XXV

XXV (D. 129)   Pythagoras son of Mnesarchus pursued inquiry (*historiē*) further
than all other men and, choosing what he liked from these compositions, he made
a wisdom of his own: much learning, artful knavery.

Diels believed XXV was a forgery, because of the reference to written
'compositions' or treatises (*syngraphai*) earlier than Pythagoras,
apparently dealing with scientific research or inquiry. Since its defence
by Reinhardt and Wilamowitz, XXV is now universally recognized as
authentic, but there is still room for doubt as to exactly what 'compositions' are referred to.[79] The word *syngraphai*, like its Attic equivalent *syngrammata*, normally refers to works in prose. The earliest
prose treatises known to us are those of Anaximander and Anaximenes of Miletus and Pherecydes of Syros. As it happens, there was
an ancient tradition associating Pythagoras with Pherecydes, the
author of a strange mythic cosmogony of which some portions have
been preserved.[80] The treatises of Hecataeus, known to Heraclitus as
embodiments of Milesian *polymathiē* (see XVIII), were probably too
recent for him to have in mind as sources for Pythagoras. But there
were no doubt other prose treatises circulating in the neighbourhood

of Miletus, Samos, and Ephesus, of which we know little or nothing.[81]

We can only guess what teachings or exploits of Pythagoras would have provoked Heraclitus' particular indignation. He would probably have been shocked by Pythagoras' claim to recall his previous incarnations, which might have seemed like a caricature of the notion of pre-existence and survival of the psyche which plays a part in Heraclitus' own thought. For all his 'scientific' Ionian background, there was something of the sorcerer and wonder-worker about Pythagoras which was probably inseparable from his enormous prestige in the Greek colonies of South Italy and his considerable reputation throughout the Greek world. Though he was certainly no shaman in the sense of being a primitive witch-doctor, he does seem to have cultivated the role of charismatic leader with superior powers, like bilocation — a man who would be venerated by his followers as more than human, but regarded by outsiders as something of a fraud. That Heraclitus shared the latter view is clear from XXVI, if indeed it refers to Pythagoras.

XXVI

XXVI (D. 81)   Philodemus: [According to Heraclitus <Pythagoras was?> 'the prince of imposters.']

In Philodemus' text the picturesque phrase *kopidōn archēgos* refers to rhetoric, not to Pythagoras. For its application to Pythagoras we have only indirect evidence.[82] The invective certainly fits Pythagoras. There may be a play on *archēgos* (translated here as 'prince') in the sense of 'founder', 'the one who starts things going'. Pythagoras was not only an imposter himself, he founded a school! This corporate relationship between initiator and followers seems to be reflected again in the warning of LXXXVII (D. 28B): Justice will catch up not only with those who invent lies (*pseudōn tektones*) but also with those who swear to them (*martyres*).

XXVII

XXVII (D. 108)   Of all those whose accounts (*logoi*) I have heard, none has got so far as this: to recognize what is wise, set apart from all.[83]

Here for the first time (in my arrangement) Heraclitus begins to disclose the positive content of his doctrine, so far hinted at only by the mysterious assertion of the unity of night and day (in XIX, D. 57). The imagery of the *logos* is now reversed: at first it was Heraclitus' account, or the *logos* as such, to which others must attend (and so again in XXXVI, D. 50); now it is others who do the talking and Heraclitus is cast in the role of listener. But he listens in vain, for it is not in *their* words that he can find a recognition (*ginōskein*) of what he is seeking. This missing content is designated by the neuter form of the word for wise man or sage: *sophon*. Those who passed for wise did not deserve the name: they did not know what wisdom is, and hence were separated from it.

The last words of the sentence present an ambiguity that recurs frequently: the form *pantōn* 'of all' may be read either as masculine (i.e. animate) or neuter (inanimate). The difference is considerable: is the wise separate 'from all men' or 'from all things'? The first reading suggests wisdom as ordinarily conceived, a property men wish to possess, though in fact they fail to attain it. The second seems to posit the 'wise' as a cosmic or divine principle, separate or transcendent like the Intelligence (*nous*) of Anaxagoras (fr. 12) which is 'not mixed with anything else'.

Heraclitus could easily have specified his meaning by adding the word 'men' or 'things' after 'all'. Since he did not choose to eliminate the ambiguity, it is not up to us to do so: the principle of hermeneutical generosity requires us to keep both options open. In this case there is good evidence to support both readings of *pantōn*: (1) that wisdom is inaccessible to men is, in effect, stated by LV–LVIII (D. 78, 82–3, 79, 70); whereas (2) 'the wise' is asserted as a unique divine principle of the universe in CXVIII (D. 32). Since the same ambiguity between masculine and neuter readings of pronouns and quantifier-words will be found again and again, the possibility of two interpretations is not likely to be accidental.

It is significant that, when Heraclitus begins to specify the content of that insight which perception and inquiry alone cannot provide, his characterization is strictly ambivalent between a human property that is rare and difficult and a cosmic power which is unique and remote from all others. For it is precisely this ambiguity or duality between the life of man and the life of the cosmos that structures Heraclitus' entire discourse, as in the duality already noted between *logos* as the utterance of a man and *logos* as the pattern of cosmic process. It is just this duality, this interlocking of man and cosmos expressed by the double value of *logos* and *sophon*, as by the double reading of the pronoun *pantōn*, which constitutes the 'recognition' that other men have missed.

XXVIII

XXVIII (D. 101)   I went in search of myself.

This is as straightforward a paradox as any in Heraclitus. Normally one goes looking for *someone else*. How can I be the object of my own search? This will make sense only if my self is somehow absent, hidden, or difficult to find.[84] Thus XXVIII states, or presupposes, what one might have thought was a distinctly modern reading of the Delphi *gnōthi sauton*: self-knowledge is difficult because a man is divided from himself; he presents a problem for himself to resolve. We are surprisingly close here to the modern or Christian idea that a person may be alienated from his own (true) self.

XXIX

XXIX (D. 116)   It belongs to all men to know (*ginōskein*) themselves and think well (*sōphronein*, keep their thinking sound).

The connection between self-knowledge and *sōphronein* is taken for granted in the archaic conception of wisdom preserved in the sayings of the Sages and inscribed at the entrance to the sixth-century temple of Apollo at Delphi, where *mēden agan* 'nothing too much' was written next to *gnōthi sauton* 'know (recognize) thyself'. Both maxims might reasonably be paraphrased as *sōphronei* 'be of sound mind'.[85]

The pairing of self-recognition and sound thinking is thus traditional; what is unusual in XXIX is the claim that *all men* have a share in this excellence. The Delphic injunction suggests that self-knowledge is difficult, and Heraclitus himself implies as much in XXVIII. So XXIX presents an apparent contradiction both with the Delphic motto and with Heraclitus' own words elsewhere.

The contradiction is not unresolvable; it renews the initial paradox of the *logos* which is there before us, but which we are unable to grasp. Self-knowledge and world-knowledge will in the end converge in this comprehension of the common *logos*. If we interpret XXVIII 'I went in search of myself' as meaning 'I found in myself the universal *logos*, the cosmic law', we ignore the literal sense and the enigmatic technique by which Heraclitus presents his thought. But this is indeed the final implication of what he is saying. Self-knowledge, like understanding the *logos*, belongs to all men by right. But in fact precious few will achieve it.

The formal challenge to the Delphic proverb, the apparent self-contradiction, and the etymological overtones of *sō-phronein* brought out by the parallel to *ginōskein*, should suffice to guarantee the authenticity of XXIX (D. 116) against persistent doubts. These doubts rest only on the questionable judgment that the thought and wording of XXIX are too banal for Heraclitus.[86]

XXX

XXX (D. 114)   Speaking with understanding (*xyn noōi*) they must hold fast to what is shared (*tōi xynōi*) by all, as a city holds to its law (*tōi nomōi*) and even more firmly. For all human laws are nourished by a divine one. It prevails as it will and suffices for all and is more than enough.

The juxtaposition with XXIX (D. 116) is meant to suggest that the subject of XXX is precisely 'all men', whose right to self-knowledge or *sōphronein* is asserted in XXIX. XXX thus specifies what conditions must be satisfied for that right to be realized in fact.

The text contains two examples of the animate-inanimate (masculine-neuter) ambiguity already noted. In the phrase 'common to all', *pantōn* can mean either 'all human beings' or 'all things', precisely as in XXVII (D. 108). Similarly, in 'it suffices for all' *pasi* can be 'for all men' or 'for all things'.[87] There is a comparable ambiguity in the phrase '(nourished) by the divine one', which can be construed either in the neuter, with 'the divine' (*theion*) as a term for the supreme cosmic principle, or as the masculine form agreeing with *nomos*: 'the one divine law'. I suspect that this duality is also deliberate: the single divine principle, 'what is common to all', is and is not willing to be designated as *nomos* 'law'. (For this ambivalence with regard to a particular name, cf. CXVIII, D. 32.)

The community of *logos* is expressed here by the phrase 'holding fast to (or 'strengthening oneself with' *ischyrizesthai*) what is common to all (*tōi xynōi pantōn*)', after the initial word play of 'speaking (together) with understanding' (*xyn noōi legontas*) with its double allusion to the *logos* ('speech') and to 'what is common' (*xyn*). But what is it that can teach understanding (*noos*) in speaking and listening? What cognition can keep one's thinking sound (*sō-phronein*) and prevent it from sinking into the private *phronēsis* (III, D. 2) that has lost contact with what is shared by all? XXIX (D. 116) located the salvaging of one's thought in *self-recognition*, in what might seem to be the most private of cognitions. Yet Heraclitus everywhere insists that soundness and safety lies in what is public: the civic law is as essential as the city wall to the security of those who dwell within (LXV, D. 44). What is the connection between *self*-recognition and this stable reliance upon what is common?

The clue lies in the notion of self-alienation implied in XXVIII: 'I went in search of myself.' The lost or hidden self must be precisely *the common*, in search of which the private self or 'I' must go, in order for one's thinking to be safe and sound. Heraclitus son of Bloson, an individual of Ephesus, went seeking for his own self, and what he found was something common not only to all the citizens of Ephesus but to all men, and not only to all men but to all things whatsoever. Thus did his self-knowing become *sō-phronein*, the salvaging of thinking through understanding (*xyn noōi*), through holding on to 'what is common (*xynōi*) to all'.

We can see why the *nomos*, the public law and moral tradition of a city like Ephesus, should be chosen as an illustration of what produces sound thinking, but why it is only an illustration.[88] It is common, but not common enough: common to all Ephesians but not common to all men and all things. As a result, in the search for soundness of mind one must hold on to something stronger, the source not only of this but of 'all human laws'. The Stoics and other later writers had no hesitation in speaking here of 'divine law' or 'natural law' (as in Lucretius' *lex naturai*). But in the archaic language of Heraclitus the term *nomos* has too human and too social a sound to lend itself to such a locution. Hence Heraclitus hints at, but does not express the notion of a 'divine law' *theios nomos*. Instead he leaves us with a characterization of the common as 'the divine one'.

We can see the syntactic ambiguity between 'all men' and 'all things' in XXX as a formal expression of the view that an individual man, searching for his own self, will come to rest and to rely upon a deeper identity which is that of the universe as a whole. The terms in which this unity is described recall the traditional references to the supreme god, and prepare us for Heraclitus' own introduction of the name of Zeus (in XLV, D. 120; CXVIII, D. 32).[89]

XXXI

XXXI (D. 113)   Thinking (*to phronein*) is shared by all.

We meet once more the ambiguous pronoun *pasi*: shared by all men?
or all things? The first reading simply restates in a weaker form the
thought of XXIX (D. 116: *sō-phronein* belongs to all men), adding
the notion of what is common to all (as in XXX); 'What is "common
to all" is not what all, or almost all, happen to think, but what all
should think, and would, if they had sense' (Vlastos, 347). Yet this
leaves XXXI essentially repetitious, and tends to justify the doubts
of those who would condemn it as inauthentic. But the ambiguity of
pasi (in contrast with the unambiguous *anthrōpoisi pasi* in XXIX) permits a stronger reading, which has been ignored only because it is
perplexing: 'Thinking is common to all *things*.' Taken literally, this
implies something like panpsychism: if all things have some thought
or perception, all things must be alive. This view may seem strange to
some, but it is seriously held by Spinoza and Leibniz in modern
times, and unmistakably held by Empedocles in the fifth century
B.C.: 'For know that all things have thought (*phronēsis*) and a share
of mind (*nōma = noēma*).' (DK 31.B 110, 10; cf. *panta* 'all things' in
B 102–3 and 107.) This stronger meaning saves XXXI from banality
by reinterpreting 'what is shared by all' as a kind of thought or intelligence. And this makes it easier for us to understand how self-
knowledge can lead to the knowledge of what is common to all, since
the universal principle is understood precisely as *thinking*, the activity
of an intelligent psyche. Such panpsychism gives a new dimension to
the ambivalence of Heraclitus' concept of 'the wise', oriented both
towards the human and towards the cosmic. And the strong reading
of XXXI fits well with the doctrine of the limitless psyche in XXXV
(D. 45).

XXXII

XXXII (D. 112)   Thinking well (*sōphronein*) is the greatest excellence and wisdom: to act and speak what is true, perceiving things according to their nature
(*physis*).

This is the most important of the three fragments dealing with thinking (*phronein*) and thinking well (or sound thinking, *sōphronein*) that
are preserved only in the *Anthology of Ethical Sayings* composed by

John Stobaeus, the other two being XXIX (D. 116) and XXXI (D. 113). The authenticity of one or more of these has been questioned.[90] The burden of proof properly falls on those who would deny authenticity, since all three citations are found together with other fragments that are indisputably genuine, and together with *no* fragments that are clearly inauthentic.[91] Since Stobaeus' work is a kind of scrapbook, the documentary value of his testimony varies greatly from case to case, and his reliability at any given point is only as good as that of the source he happens to be following. Now in the two contexts that interest us, in his chapters On Virtue and On Temperance (*sōphrosynē*) in Book III, we find quotations from Heraclitus of great importance and unquestionable authenticity, which in some instances are preserved in no other source. That is the case for XXVII (D. 108), XXX (D. 114), the important double fragment LXVII (D. 110–11), and the description of the drunken man with the wet soul (CVI, D. 117). Since neither context contains any manifest forgeries, the natural presumption (followed by Bywater, Diels, and Bollack-Wismann) is that *all* of the quotations from Heraclitus in these two brief sections of Stobaeus should be authentic.[92] It would really be remarkable if an inferior paraphrase had been handed down to us sandwiched in between XXVII (D. 108), LXVII (D. 110–11) and XXX (D. 114).

To outweigh these circumstantial probabilities, a critic would have to show that the language and thought of XXXII cannot belong to Heraclitus. The interpretation which follows is therefore an implicit defense of the fragment. The question of authenticity is of some importance, since XXXII is the only fragment in which the word *aretē* 'excellence' (or 'virtue') occurs, and the only one to characterize *sōphronein* in a way that goes beyond the Delphic assimilation to self-knowledge in XXIX (D. 116). If XXXII is not his, Heraclitus has nothing really original to say on *sōphrosynē*, the paramount virtue of his age.[93] But if it belongs to Heraclitus, XXXII is his most interesting utterance as a moral philosopher.

The interpretation depends upon the punctuation, which either falls after the third word, *megistē* 'greatest', or after the fifth, *sophiē* 'wisdom'. The former punctuation, given in Stobaeus and most modern editions, allows only two words in praise of *sōphronein* and passes on to speak of *sophiē*. The second punctuation, proposed by Bollack-Wismann, turns the whole fragment into an explication of *sōphronein*. I accept the latter construal, which gives a richer sense.

The first clause, then, states that thinking well or soundness of mind (*sō-phronein*) is the greatest excellence (*aretē*) which a man can have and also the greatest wisdom.[94] We are a long way from the Homeric conception of *aretē* as the warrior's virtue of valor and skill in combat, but we are not far from the Delphic parallel between *sōphronein* and self-knowledge encountered in XXIX (D. 116). The conjunction of *sōphronein* with *aretē*, although post-Homeric, is a familiar theme from early Attic grave inscriptions, which regularly speak of the dead as 'brave (*agathos*) and sensible (*sōphrōn*)' or mention his 'courage (*aretē*) and good sense (*sōphrosynē*)'.[95] In the formula for archaic verse epitaphs *aretē* and *sōphrosynē* preserve their Homeric values, the former designating manly courage and the latter prudence or good sense. But Heraclitus has taken over the traditional formula only to transform its meaning. He has in effect rendered the Homeric notion of *saophrosynē* or good judgment by *sophiē*, so that *aretē* and *sophiē* here represent the two virtues of valor and discretion conjoined in the grave inscriptions; and he has equated both of these with his own conception of sound thinking (*sō-phronein*) modelled on Delphic self-knowledge. Thus Heraclitus does not dissent from praise of valor and good sense; he only insists that these virtues in their highest form are united in thinking well, in salvaging one's thought in the self-knowledge that is also a recognition of what is common to all.

The conception of 'sound thinking' articulated in the first clause by the nouns 'excellence' and 'wisdom', is expressed in the second clause by two infinitives: 'acting and speaking what is true'.[96] Speaking the truth is not a virtue which the Greeks admired without qualification, nor would it always appear to be the course of prudence. One Homeric example of *saophrosynē* describes Telemachus' discretion in not revealing his father's true identity but deliberately accepting Odysseus' disguise as an old beggar (*Od.* XXIII.30). To identify truthful speech as the highest excellence is to take up an uncompromising position on an issue where the traditional Greek attitude was (and is) ambivalent. But this emphasis on 'speaking the true' is what we might expect from the spokesman for a *logos* 'which is (true) forever'; and it echoes Heraclitus' own promise in his prologue to 'tell it like it is'. The terminology of the proem is again suggested by the phrase 'perceiving (or 'noticing' *epaiontes*) things according to their *physis*'. (Cf. I.2: 'distinguishing each according to its nature'.) Accepting the Delphic view of sound thinking as self-knowledge, Heraclitus thus reinterprets it as speech and perception in accordance with the universal *logos*.

On the punctuation adopted here, the two infinitives 'to speak and to act' belong together: in chiastic order 'acting' will echo *aretē* ('manliness') just as 'speaking' echoes *sophiē* ('wisdom').[97] The difficulty with this natural reading is that it implies the phrase 'to act what is true' (*alēthea poiein*), which is not so easy to understand.[98] I have not found a parallel to this expression in Greek. In rhetorical contexts, a fifth-century author may speak of the 'truth of deeds' in contrast to a distorted appearance or a false and partial report, but what he means by 'truth' here is *what really happened*; the contrast is conceived from the point of view of the hearer or spectator (who might be deceived), and not from the point of view of the agent.[99]

Since it is not clear what would be meant by *doing the true*, the reader may be tempted to construe *poiein* with what follows rather than with what precedes. Heraclitus will then speak not of 'acting the true' but of 'acting according to the nature of things (*kata physin*), perceptively (*epaiontes*)', or perhaps 'perceiving things according to their nature, and acting accordingly'. (So roughly DK and Marcovich, p. 96.) These readings are defensible but not obviously correct, as can be seen from the disagreement among the commentators.

Here again I suggest that Heraclitus has cunningly left us in suspense between two constructions (as in the first clause in I.1), to provoke us into some reflection on what 'acting in accordance with (one's knowledge of) the nature of things' might mean, and how that might relate to the other reading 'to speak and act what is true'.

The solution I propose is to give *alēthes* 'true' its etymological value: 'not concealed', 'not hidden in one's heart'.[100] Soundness of thinking will then mean to speak and act the true in the sense of communicating the *logos* in 'words and deeds' (*epea kai erga*, I.2), sharing with others one's perception of how things hang together in unity and are also distinguished in their own nature (*physis*). The man whose thinking is sound will not hide the truth but signify it in his actions as in his words. In this he will imitate the lord of Delphi, who does not hide the truth but shows it with a sign (XXXIII), and whose lesson to mankind is *sōphronein*.

What is distinctive here is the meaning of self-knowledge as recognition of one's true or hidden self, and the connection of this with knowledge of a universal *logos* which distinguishes things 'according to their nature'. More revolutionary still is the cosmic dimension given to *sōphronein* by the claim (in XXXI) that 'thinking' (*phronein*) is common to all, if this is taken to mean that *all things think*. For if *phronein* characterizes the whole universe of things, then sound think-

ing means more than keeping one's wits whole; it means to salvage
what is common, and hence precious, throughout the universe.

XXXIII

XXXIII (D. 93)   The lord whose oracle is in Delphi neither declares nor conceals but gives a sign.

The description does not name Apollo, but identifies the god by rank
(*anax*), function, and locality. (Bollack-Wismann, p. 273, suggest that
this circumlocution is itself an instance of the Pythian style.) The
god's mode of utterance is said to be neither direct statement (*oute
legei*) nor concealment (*oute kryptei*) — which would mean falsehood,
on the interpretation of *alēthea* 'truth' suggested above — but 'signify-
ing', giving a sign (*alla sēmainei*). There is no doubt that Heraclitus is
referring to the Delphic practice of giving advice in indirect form, by
imagery, riddle, and ambiguity, so that it was obvious to a man of
sense that *an oracle required an interpretation.* Even when the surface meaning is clear, it may be necessary to look for a second meaning underneath — as Oedipus discovered to his hurt, when he forgot
to ask *which* man was his father; and likewise Croesus, when he forgot to ask *whose* kingdom he would destroy. Socrates, on the other
hand, shows his wisdom by refusing to take an apparently unambiguous oracle at face value. Instead he asked 'What is the god saying, and
what meaning does he intend by this riddle (*ti pote ainittetai*)?'[101]
'Giving a sign', then, means uttering one thing that in turn signifies
another — what the Greeks called *hyponoia*, a 'hint' or 'allegory'. The
sign may be of different types: image, ambiguous wording, or the
like. The Delphic mode of utterance presents a plurality or complexity of meaning, so that reflection is required, and unusual insight, if
the proper interpretation is to be discovered.

Is the Delphic mode a paradigm for Heraclitus' own riddling style,
as readers since antiquity have supposed? Or is the complexity of
meaning to be located in the nature of things, in the structure of
appearance understood as a *logos*, a kind of meaningful language?[102]
There is much to be said for either view, and we need not choose
between them. One can scarcely miss the Delphic elements in
Heraclitus' own style. But the notion of men who 'listen without
comprehension', who fail to understand because they have 'barbarian
souls', is presented as a characterization of the human condition, not
merely a description of Heraclitus' own readers or auditors. It is

reality itself, or the nature of things, that requires close investigation and readiness to discover the unexpected, 'for it is trackless and unexplored' (VII, D. 18). These two interpretations form the foreground and the background meanings of XXXIII, the obvious sense (applying to Heraclitus' own style) and the *hyponoia* that emerges only upon reflection (applying to the nature of things understood as *logos*). In this way the semantic complexity that is *described* by XXXIII in reference to Apollo is also illustrated by these words in their reference to our double *logos*: the discourse of Heraclitus and the structure of reality. And this parallel between Heraclitus' style and the obscurity of the nature of things, between the difficulty of understanding him and the difficulty in human perception, is not arbitrary: to speak plainly about such a subject would be to falsify it in the telling, for no genuine understanding would be communicated. The only hope of 'getting through' to the audience is to puzzle and provoke them into reflection. Hence the only appropriate mode of explanation is allusive and indirect: Heraclitus is consciously and unavoidably 'obscure'.[103]

The point is not that Heraclitus' paradoxical style is designed to mirror the nature of reality, if this is thought of in the *Tractatus* sense of 'the world', as a structure independent of human understanding. The paradox lies in any attempt to comprehend and formulate this structure in human terms: 'opposites are one, and conflict is justice'. It is not that reality as such is contradictory; what is reflected in the semantic difficulty of interpreting these utterances is the epistemic difficulty of grasping such a structure, the cosmic *logos*, as the underlying unity for our own experience of opposition and contrast.

XXXIV

XXXIV (D. 92)   Plutarch; ['The Sibyl with raving mouth', according to Heraclitus 'utters things mirthless' and unadorned and unperfumed, and her voice carries through a thousand years because of the god <who speaks through her>.]

Here again the problem is to identify just what Heraclitus said about the Sibyl, and to specify what her mode of prophecy is a sign *for*. In both respects we are at a disadvantage by comparison with XXXIII (D. 93), for in that case we can be reasonably certain that Heraclitus' own words have been preserved. In XXXIV Plutarch has so blended the citation into his own text that it is scarcely possible to tell how much is accurate quotation. Some editors would give the whole sentence to Heraclitus; Reinhardt denied him even the mention of the Sibyl! No doubt the truth lies somewhere in between. Heraclitus must have referred to the Sibyl, for otherwise there would be no reason for Plutarch to mention her here, where he is discussing the Delphic Pythia. On the other hand, the calculation of a thousand years is made from Plutarch's point of view, not from that of Heraclitus.[104] Recent editors have agreed that only the words placed within quotation marks above belong to Heraclitus, and the rest to Plutarch.[105] But Plutarch's paraphrase may contain further traces of Heraclitus' thought. Heraclitus is likely to have intended some reference to divine possession or seizure, since the Sibyl is precisely the type of prophetess who, like Cassandra in Aeschylus' *Agamemnon*, bursts into agonized utterance of a vision in her state as *entheos*, invaded by Apollo.[106] If her utterances are 'mirthless' or 'gloomy' (*agelasta*), that is not only because her typical vision is of a coming disaster, but because the Sibylline experience of *enthousiasmos* is itself a form of suffering, a kind of spiritual rape.

This is the earliest reference to the Sibyl in extant literature. It is not clear whether the Sibyl was originally thought of as a unique individual or as a type, whether the word 'Sibyl' is a proper name or a common noun.[107] Later authors spoke of an eighth-century Sibyl named Herophile, from the Ionian city of Erythrae not far from Ephesus, whose oracular wanderings had left a clear trace at Delphi.[108] There is no reason to suppose that the story of Herophile at Delphi need be as old as Heraclitus; but long before his time the institution of ecstatic prophecy had been established at Delphi in the person of a regular priestess, the Pythia. We may think of the Pythia as a kind of sedentary Sibyl, a holy woman who has become a fixed appendage to a particular shrine. Whatever the historical connections may have been between the Pythia and the Sibyl, they represent prophetic phenomena of the same type. In contrast to oracles by signs (from rustling oak leaves, the flight of birds, the liver of the sacrificial victim) and in contrast also to oracle by lots, both the Pythia and the Sibyl are women who serve as 'mediums', who see the future in a trance experience, in the superhuman vision of the god. It is the woman's voice that speaks, but it is Apollo's word that is uttered.

Because of this religious parallel between Pythia and Sibyl, as the same kind of mouthpiece for the same god, it is natural to suppose that Heraclitus himself intended some connection between the oracles of the Delphic god in XXXIII and those of his Ionian proph-

etess in XXXIV. The meaning of XXXIV would then be that just as
the Sibyl's power comes not from herself but from the god, so
Heraclitus' authority is derived not from his own person or opinions
but from the cosmic *logos* in whose name he speaks: 'listen not to me
but to the *logos*' (XXXVI, D. 50).[109]

This view of XXXIV previously seemed attractive to me, and might
just possibly be correct. But the text which is most unmistakably
genuine is the description of the Sibyl as prophesying 'with raving
mouth'. And from what we know about Heraclitus' attitude to madness in CXVI (D. 15) and CXVII (D. 5), as well as his contempt for
drunkenness in CVI (D. 117), it is most unlikely that he would have
cast himself in the role of a prophet whose insight was to be compared to the ecstasy of a woman possessed. It was this correct perception of Heraclitus' deep distaste for Sibylline frenzy which led
Reinhardt to doubt the authenticity of the whole fragment, since
Plutarch presents the quotation from Heraclitus as part of a positive
evaluation.[110] But we can accept Plutarch's quotation while rejecting
his evaluation. In its original context, the contrast between the Sibyl's
madness and her social prestige as spokesman for Apollo may have
been part of Heraclitus' critique of current religious practices, along
the lines of CXV–CXVII (D. 14, 15, D. 5): if one reflects upon the
fact that people accept wisdom from raving lips, one is likely to judge
them as mad as the Sibyl herself.

XXXV

XXXV (D. 45)   You will not find out the limits of the soul (*psychē*) by going,
even if you travel over every way, so deep is its report (*logos*).

'Heraclitus is the first to have given serious thought to, and had something to say about, the soul in man' (*Der Glaube der Hellenen* I
(Berlin, 1931), 375). Wilamowitz's point was that the *psychē* in
Homer is mentioned only when it leaves the body, in death or in syn-
cope: it is the life-breath or animating 'spirit' which departs as a
ghost. So even for Pythagoras the *psychē*, although deathless, belongs
only temporarily and as it were on loan to the individual man. But
with the fuller development of the notion of personality and a more
intimate sense of identity between a man (or woman) and his (or her)
emotional life that found expression in the lyric poetry of the seventh
and sixth centuries, the time was ripe for a new conception of the
psychē as source or center of the human personality. And so we find

in Heraclitus, as Reinhardt said, 'for the first time a psychology worthy of the name'.[111]

But if there is wide agreement on the originality of Heraclitus' view of the psyche, there is less agreement on just what that view is. Some authors give physical accounts of Heraclitus' doctrine which equate the psyche with cosmic fire, or one of its privileged manifestations; but Bruno Snell has proposed an interpretation which emphasizes the psychic as such, the direct intensity of thought or feeling denoted by '*Innerlichkeit*' (inwardness) or 'self-awareness' (*Entdeckung des Geistes*, p. 37).

There is a grain of truth here: the philosopher who said 'I went in search of myself', is one who has reflected upon the nature of his psyche in terms of his living experience. But the fragments show no trace of a Cartesian or Platonic contrast between mind and matter, soul and body.

We have seen that the psyche in XVI is identified as the cognitive or rational element in human beings, and this intellectual conception of the psyche must be emphasized here, since it has been overlooked in several influential studies where the originality of Socrates in this respect has been grossly overstated. Socrates' position in the history of philosophy is secure enough without attributing to him a revolutionary new concept of the psyche as a cognitive principle – a concept which he might have got directly from Heraclitus, but which was probably 'in the air' in fifth-century thought and usage.[112] The concept was a new one, and only after Plato did it come to dominate the earlier view of the psyche as essentially biological, emotional, or non-rational. (The older view survives in Aristotle's conception of the vegetative or nutritive soul, as in Plato's view of the 'irrational' parts of the psyche.) Heraclitus' original readers might have expected an account of the psyche rather more like Pindar's description of 'the image of vitality' which 'sleeps when the limbs are active, but shows to sleeping men in many dreams' a sign of future events (fr. 116 Bowra), or the more mundane view of Semonides, who urges his friend to endure the brevity of life 'by indulging your *psyche* with whatever good things you can get' (fr. 29.13 Diehl, assigned by some to Simonides). In the former case the psyche is thought of as a power of establishing contact with the supernatural in dreams; in the latter case it takes delight in sensual pleasures and 'the good things of life'. Both ideas will be exploited by Heraclitus elsewhere. (For the dream experience see XC, D. 26; for the soul in debauchery, see CVI, D. 117 and the more dubious CVIII, D. 77.) But in his own view the psyche is primarily a principle of rational cognition.

Since Heraclitus is a monist, however, the psyche is also a physical principle. We shall see in commenting on CII (D. 36)—CIX (D. 118) that he identifies the soul not with fire (as is often supposed) but with atmospheric vapor, air or 'exhalation', in the traditional Greek manner.[113]

In the text of XXXV four points call for comment: (1) the 'limits' of the soul, (2) the reference to 'finding out', (3) the 'way' (*hodos*) to be travelled, and (4) the *logos* which the soul has.

(1) On first reading, the mention of 'limits' (*peirata*) to which one travels might recall the Homeric formula for a voyage 'to the ends of the earth' (*Il.* XIV.200 = 301, etc.). So Hesiod speaks of a place where 'the sources and limits (*peirata*)' of earth, Tartarus, sea and heaven are located together (*Theogony* 738 = 809). But Heraclitus denies that anyone can reach the limits of the *psychē*, no matter how far they travel. On second reading, then, this will suggest that the soul is limitless, *apeirōn* in a truer sense than the 'boundless earth'. A reader acquainted with Milesian philosophy may recognize an echo of the Limitless (*apeiron*) of Anaximander or the limitless Air of Anaximenes: the denial of limits involves an allusion to the supreme principle of cosmic structure.

Thus the psyche for Heraclitus plays the role of a 'first principle', a Milesian *archē*; and hence the natural tendency of modern interpreters to identify it with cosmic fire. They are right in principle though wrong in fact. Although the psyche as such is not composed of fire, psyche and fire are alike in playing a double role in Heraclitus' thought. Each one represents a specific physical phenomenon, one elemental form among others. (Thus XXXVII, D. 30 will speak of fire 'going out' — and hence ceasing to be fire — just as CII, D. 36 will speak of 'the death of *psychē*' in the birth of water.) At the same time, both psyche and fire are in some sense universal, all-inclusive. Thus Fire is exchanged for all things, and all things for fire (XL, D. 90). The universality of psyche is expressed here in the denial of limits: wherever you travel, there psyche will be. This is what we must expect, since XXXI (D. 113) was interpreted as a statement of panpsychism. If all things think, then all things are alive. But if all things are alive (*empsycha*), then all must have a share in *psychē*, the life-principle. The soul can travel everywhere, since everything is psychic territory. Perhaps the underlying assumption is that fundamental discontinuity, the emergence of life from non-life, is irrational and unnatural. The doctrine of Thales, that 'all things are full of gods', which Aristotle takes to mean that *psychē* is mingled throughout the universe (*De Anima* I.5, 411a7 = DK 11.A 22), could well apply to Heraclitus: all things are full of soul.

(2) The limitlessness of the psyche is expressed by a phrase that has echoes elsewhere in the fragments: 'you will not find them out'.[114] The verb 'find out' (*exheuriskō*) occurs also in VII (D. 18): he who does not expect the unexpected will not find it out (cf. VIII, D. 22, on 'finding little' gold). In LXXXIV (D. 27) 'the unexpected' will be the fate of men after death. In XLIV (D. 94) the Furies as ministers of Justice (*Dikē*) 'will find out' the Sun, if he oversteps his measures. In LXXXVII (D. 28B) it is Dike herself who will lay hands on liars, as in CXXI (D. 66) fire will 'lay hands on all things'. In these last three fragments, the notions of finding out and catching hold of pretty nearly coincide. Thus the usage of this verb elsewhere in Heraclitus suggests that the limitlessness of the soul is closely connected both with the mystery of death and with notions of cosmic order and personal punishment for wrongdoing. These suggestions are too elusive for us to understand or explicate within the present context. The verbal echoes simply mark this as an instance of proleptic statement, a hint of themes more fully developed elsewhere.

(3) 'By going (on foot), by travelling over every way.' It is natural to think here of 'the way up and down, one and the same' mentioned in CIII (D. 60), and perhaps also of the carding instrument in LXXIV (D. 59), whose path is 'straight and crooked', since the term *hodos* ('way') appears in each case. But the fragment on the carding wheels is too problematic to help us here. I see only two plausible readings for the way travelled in seeking the limits of soul. (i) It can be a very general image for a search that proceeds in vain: 'I looked everywhere'. (ii) It can allude to the course of elemental transformation, with 'the way down' of CIII interpreted as a change to water and earth, 'the way up' as a change to fire.[115] The first reading corresponds to the surface meaning of the text; (ii) suggests a cosmic *hyponoia*.

(4) Finally, what is the deep *logos* which the soul 'has', and which explains our inability to find its end points? On first reading, *logon echei* should mean something like 'it has something to say', 'it has the right (or the capacity) to speak'.[116] Now the possession of rational speech may be a significant overtone here, but this idea cannot explain the adjective 'deep'.

Most authors have rightly assumed that *logos* in XXXV must mean 'measure', as in XXXIX (D. 31B). The limitlessness of the psyche is then to be understood in terms of impenetrable depth. Soundings are

in vain, for no plummet-line will get to the bottom of it. Cf.
Democritus fr. 117: 'we know nothing truly, for truth lies at the
bottom (*en bythōi*)'. It takes a deep diver to discover it, as Socrates
is supposed to have said about the meaning of Heraclitus' book.[117]
So for the soul's *logos*: it is vast, subtle and deep; and intelligence —
not travelling about — is required to find it out.

A *logos* so profound and limitless can scarcely be distinct from the
universal *logos*, according to which all things come to pass. The solution to XXXV thus gives us the fuller explanation for XXVIII (D.
101): by seeking for his own self Heraclitus could find the identity
of the universe, for the *logos* of the soul goes so deep that it coincides
with the *logos* that structures everything in the world. Hence the
error of those men who treat thinking as private, in the face of the
fact that 'the *logos* is common' — common to them and to everything
else (III, D. 2).

XXXVI

XXXVI (D. 50)   It is wise, listening not to me but to the report (*logos*), to
agree <and say> that all things are one.

It seems likely that this sentence, one of the weightiest of all, came
at the end of the introductory section when Heraclitus returns (by a
kind of ring composition) to the theme of the *logos* with which he
began. The following points call for comment: (1) the contrast between 'listening to me' and 'listening to the *logos*', (2) the word play
on *homologein* 'say in agreement', (3) the definition of wisdom, and
(4) the final formula 'all things are one'.

(1) The reference to a *logos* somehow independent of Heraclitus
will be immediately clear if he has just spoken of the 'deep *logos*' of
the soul. The thought will be: listen not to *me* but to the discourse
within your soul, and it will tell you all. If we set aside XXXV (D.
45) and consider only I.2 and III (D. 2), listening to the *logos* will
imply the conception of the world order as a meaningful language
which one hears with more or less comprehension. Heraclitus is after
all a *prophētēs* ('spokesman') for the *logos*: his words are an attempt
to make this larger discourse audible to a few, at least, among the
many who seem deaf.

(2) This thought is developed in *homo-logein* 'to agree', which
carries a phonetic echo of *logos* and an etymological sense of 'speaking together with, saying the same thing'. Knowing how to listen will

enable one to speak intelligently (XVII, D. 19), to hold fast to what is common (XXX, D. 114), by speaking in agreement with the universal *logos* of I.2.

(3) Wisdom or what is wise (*sophon*) consists in just this fitting of the private to the public, the personal to the universal. (See above on *xynos logos* in III.) By its rational structure and its public function in bringing men into a community, language becomes a symbol for the unifying structure of the world which wisdom apprehends.

(4) The sentence which began with a paradoxical contrast between two things that seem identical — listening to Heraclitus and listening to (his) *logos* — culminates in a greater paradox of identification: all things are one. The sense of tension, if not contradiction, is all the greater because *the unity of all things* is here the content that wisdom will put itself in agreement with, whereas in XXVII (D. 108) 'what is wise' is said to be 'set apart from all (things)', *pantōn kechōrismenon*.

This tension between the themes of isolation and community will be fully resolved only in the context of other fragments. (See on LIV, D. 41 and CXVIII, D. 32.) The unity of opposites and the community of the *logos* (with its triple application to discourse, soul, and universe) provide the initial clues for interpreting this extraordinary claim, whose full meaning requires an understanding of Heraclitus' thought as a whole. In that sense, the rest of our commentary will be an exegesis of this proposition: *hen panta einai*.

This is the earliest extant statement of systematic monism, and probably the first such statement ever made in Greece. In textbooks on the history of philosophy, the Milesian thinkers are represented as monists who reduce all things to water, to air, or to the Unlimited. But this view, which ultimately rests upon Aristotle's interpretation of their doctrine in terms of his own concept of the material cause in *Metaphysics* A 3, is anachronistic and misleading, insofar as it imputes to the earliest Greek naturalists a post-Parmenidean notion of some true unity underlying the apparent plurality of things, even when it does not actually assign to them Aristotle's own characteristic concept of the underlying material substratum of change (*hypokeimenon*).[118] There is no good evidence for assigning monism to the Milesians, if this is understood as the claim that 'all things are water' or 'all things are air', that (as Diogenes of Apollonia puts it) earth and sky and sea and air are not really 'different in their own *physis*' but are at bottom one and the same thing.

But the Milesian philosophers *were* monists in a different sense, and their theories must have provided the background for Heraclitus' thesis. What he could draw from them was the double claim (i) that all things are derived from a single *archē* or starting point, and (ii) that as now constituted all things are organized within a single world structure or *kosmos*. And we may add (iii) that Anaximander surely, and Anaximenes probably, thought of the initial principle not only as encompassing (*periechein*), and thus physically unifying the world, bu also as 'steering' and governing it by imposing a rational structure. Aspects (i) and (ii) of Milesian monism seem to be reflected in XXXVII (D. 30); the aspect of cosmic guidance (iii) will emerge in LIV (D. 41).

XXXVII

XXXVII (D. 30)   The ordering (*kosmos*), the same for all, no god nor man has made, but it ever was and is and will be: fire everliving, kindled in measures and in measures going out.

This text, with the two that follow (D. 31A and 31B), gives us our primary information on Heraclitus' cosmological thought and the most natural interpretation of his claim that all things are one. But all three texts are surrounded by thorny problems. What is the relationship between Heraclitus' doctrine and the cosmological theories of his Milesian predecessors? In what sense can a world order be identified with 'everliving fire'? And is Heraclitus here denying the general assumption of a development of the world from some more primitive source?

I have already indicated my answers to these questions in the Introduction. Since my position diverges from the dominant trends in recent scholarship, it will be necessary to support it in some detail. But before entering the precinct of controversy, I want to sketch a preliminary reading of XXXVII that does not raise any of these questions, since it does not presuppose any connection with the doctrines of the Milesians and their successors but takes the term *kosmos* in the context of its early literary usage, without reference to the new, technical sense of 'world' or 'world order'.[119] In the fragments as arranged here, we have had no reference to physical theory (though there is some hint of this in the repeated occurrence of the term *physis*), no mention of the Milesian cosmologists as such (since Thales was apparently paired with Homer, as Pythagoras, Xenophanes and Hecataeus are named with Hesiod), and no reference to cosmology. (The only occurrence so far of the term *kosmos* is in the dubious 'fragment' VI, D. 89.) A reader encountering XXXVII for the first

time might well begin by taking *kosmos* in its normal literary sense
of 'good order', 'adornment', as in the brilliant *toilette* of a woman
of fashion or in the impressive array of disciplined troops.[120]

A '*kosmos*, the same for all' may then be understood either as (1)
a moral or political order, applicable to all men, like the 'divine one'
by which all human laws are nourished in XXX (D. 114); or (2) an
ornament like jewelry, fine clothing, or a work of art. In the long run
this naive reading of XXXVII cannot succeed. But the older, literary
sense of *kosmos* is a natural starting point, since Heraclitus does not
write in a technical language and the new 'cosmological' sense of
kosmos is itself the heir to all these older nuances of the word. The
technical notion of 'world order' will emerge only as a *hyponoia*
brought to the surface by reflection, once it is seen that no good
sense can be made of the idea of 'an adornment the same for all';
and if 'a social order the same for all (men)' does make sense, it is not
easy to understand how such an order could be identified with eternal
fire. It is the formula for eternity ('ever was and is and will be') and
the mention of fire that will force us onto the terrain of natural philosophy.[121]

Before this move to the technical sense of *kosmos* is required, we
are told that 'no god nor man has made the *kosmos*, the same for all'.
Scholars have scratched their heads over this denial that any human
being has made the *kosmos* (why should anybody suppose *that*?) and
have generally dismissed these words as a so-called polar expression,
as if 'neither man nor god' meant simply 'no one at all'. But even the
notion that a *god* has made the world is poorly attested in Greece
before Plato's *Timaeus*. The whole problem here is an artificial one,
created by the mistaken assumption (in turn supported by the mistaken reading *tonde*) that *kosmos* must from the beginning have its
technical sense of 'world order'. For of course if *kosmos* means
'moral (or social) order', or if it means 'ornament', then we naturally
suppose it to be the work of an orderer, whether human or divine.
Thus the sons of Atreus are regularly referred to in the *Iliad* as
'orderers of the host' (*kosmētore laōn*). On our first, naive reading of
XXXVII we see very clearly what Heraclitus is denying, though we
cannot immediately understand why. We are faced with two paradoxes: an array that is not local or particular but 'the same for all';
and an instance of order without an orderer, like a disciplined host
without a commander, a law without a lawgiver, or a work of art
without an artisan. The first paradox is resolved by a shift to the philosophical sense of *kosmos*. The world order is naturally 'common',

the same for all men and for all things: that is just what is meant by a world order. But how can we have an ordered world without a power to set it in order?

By denying that this order is a work of art, Heraclitus implies that it is a work of nature: self-made or self-grown. Thus the cosmological idea begins to emerge, and becomes explicit when the *kosmos* itself is invested with the attributes of divinity: 'it ever was and is and will be'. This is the thought echoed in a famous fragment of Euripides: the student of Ionian science (*historia*) beholds 'the ageless order (*kosmos*) of undying nature (*physis*)' (fr. 910 Nauck = DK 59.A 30). The new philosophical paradox of XXXVII is a denial of any fundamental duality between a generated world order and the eternal source from which it arises or the ruling intelligence by which it is organized. Insofar as the *kosmos* is made, it is self-made; insofar as it is organized, it is self-organized; insofar as it is generated, it is identical with its own eternal source, everliving fire.

XXXVII is built up by wave upon wave of paradox. If the initial problems are resolved by taking *kosmos* in the sense of 'world order' and by the identification of this order with fire, that identification is itself paradoxical, whether we think of fire as an element within the world — for in that case the whole is identified with one of its parts — or whether we think of it as some primordial or transcendent power as the emphasis on its eternal being would suggest. (For then the world is identified with something transmundane!) But the culminating paradox is provided by the last two participles, when this principle of cosmic eternity is said to be regularly *rekindled* and regularly *going out*. What sense can we make of an eternal bonfire going out? And what are the measures according to which it is kindled and extinguished?

So far I have avoided the shoals of controversy, but that is no longer possible. For the question of the measures of fire going out is just the question of whether or not Heraclitus envisaged the world as gradually taking shape from (and eventually reabsorbed into) primordial fire, as the Stoics did after him and in his name. And this double question — the issues of cosmogony and cosmic conflagration, which hang together — stands at the storm center of scholarly dispute. If the Stoics were not actually following Heraclitus, they were certainly following the view indicated by Aristotle and presented in detail by Theophrastus: 'The *kosmos* is generated from fire and is ignited again according to certain periods alternating through all eternity' (D.L. IX.8 = DK 22.A1; see Appendix IIA). Theophrastus' account was accepted in antiquity by all later writers, and by Zeller, Diels, and most modern scholars (though not by Burnet) until the publication of Reinhardt's book on Parmenides in 1916. Since then the tide has turned, and I find myself almost alone today in suggesting that, after all, Theophrastus and the Stoics understood Heraclitus correctly on this point. Although a strong basis was laid by Burnet's presentation of the case, the great success of Reinhardt's argument is due to a new and important insight: not only do the extant fragments not present any detailed statement of cosmogony, but there is good reason to doubt that any lost fragments were more explicit. The doxography of Theophrastus, and the Stoic interpretation that is built upon it, show every sign of relying precisely upon those fragments whose original text has been preserved. So the ancient interpretation has no independent authority.[122] On this point modern scholarship is unanimous. Whatever interpretation we offer must be based upon Heraclitus' words alone, together with whatever we can know of their historical context.

Once this point has been admitted, I believe that the recent denial of cosmogony for Heraclitus will turn out to be a temporary overreaction, an exaggerated by-product of our emancipation from the authority of the Stoic and doxographical interpretations. If we read Heraclitus' words with an ear for their rich allusiveness, we will find that they do not contain a dogmatic denial of cosmogony any more than they contain a full statement of that process. On the contrary, we will find that XXXVII and a dozen other texts are best understood as *presupposing* rather than as denying a genetic account of the order of nature, and as playing fruitfully with the notion that the world will one day go up in smoke. On this point — the primary or pre-eminent sense of 'kindled in measures and in measures going out' — the Stoics did not misunderstand Heraclitus; they distorted his cosmic speculation only by transforming a subtle, poetic vision of the cosmic process into a rigid orthodoxy.

This argument will be pursued in the next sections of the commentary. But I do not share the common view that the question of cosmogony and ecpyrosis is decisive for the understanding of Heraclitus. If we eliminate this cycle of world formation and destruction from his system, the vision of nature will be lacking in completeness and in symmetry, but it will still be essentially the same vision. For the pattern of natural law is the same for macrocosm and for microcosm, for the origins of heaven and earth and their present pattern of transformation: 'kindled in measures and in measures going

out' applies to all of these. The great cosmic cycle is only the
ordinary cycle of natural change and human life writ large. What is
crucial is not the debate about a particular doctrine but the recognition of the *kind of discourse* which Heraclitus presents, and which
separates him from the natural philosophers like Anaxagoras and
Diogenes. This is what Theophrastus and (to a lesser extent) the
Stoics failed to understand, and what Heraclitus himself realized was
so difficult to express. Once we understand his ironical self-distancing
from technical cosmology, and his reinterpretation of all other conceptions in terms of an understanding of human life and death, his
lofty acceptance-but-also-denial of a cosmic cycle will appear as a
natural consequence of his general attitude to Ionian physics.

Before returning to the exegesis of XXXVII, I want to repeat one
very general argument against the currently predominant view, which
holds that by saying the *kosmos* 'forever was and is and will be, everliving fire' Heraclitus meant literally and unambiguously to deny that
the world had emerged from some earlier and simpler state of
affairs.[123] It seems that little thought has been given to how strange,
almost unintelligible, would be the dogmatic rejection of cosmogenesis by an archaic thinker. The instinct to explain things by telling
how they began and how they developed is not only at the basis of
all mythic thought; it also dominates all scientific or philosophic
speculation down to and including Plato's *Timaeus*. 'The principle of
cosmogony was rejected by no one before Aristotle, not even by
Parmenides, and it has perhaps been rejected by no one since, except
under Aristotelian influence. The scientists who write on "the birth
of the solar system" are only giving us the latest version of the creation story.'[124] Aristotle alone broke with this millenial tradition,
and he had a strong motive for doing so. He had abandoned Plato's
realm of imperishable Forms but not Plato's belief that scientific
knowledge requires a fixed and unchanging object. Hence it was
of the greatest importance for him to find an equivalent pattern of
eternal stability within the structure of the natural world. What is
lacking in the case of Heraclitus is any comparable philosophical
motive for espousing such a rare and radical heresy, more than a century before Plato's *Timaeus*.

To return to the identification of *kosmos* and fire: what does this
mean, and why has Heraclitus chosen fire? As indicated in the Introduction, the nearly contemporary theory of Anaximenes provides
the historical background against which Heraclitus' own cosmological monism is to be understood.[125] Our best account of the doc-

trine of Anaximenes comes from Theophrastus, and it seems to contain a fairly close paraphrase of Anaximenes' own words:

He said that the first principle was limitless Air (*aēr*), from which arises what comes into being, what has become, and what will be, and gods and things divine; but other things arise from its offspring. The form of the air is as follows: when it is most uniform it is invisible [sc. as atmospheric air] ; but it is made manifest by cold and heat and moisture and motion. It moves continually; for it would not change as much as it does if it were not in motion. As it thickens or rarefies it appears as different. For when it spreads out into rarer form it becomes fire; winds on the other hand are air as it thickens; from air cloud is produced by compression; and water by still more compression; when further thickened it becomes earth and in its thickest form stones. (Theophrastus in the excerpt of Hippolytus, DK 13.A 7)

The rest of the doxography, and parallels from Anaximander and from Anaxagoras (especially frs. 15 and 16), make clear that this sixth-century monism must be understood in the context of a cosmogony: if the boundless Air is taken as *archē* or starting point, that is just because Anaximenes believes he can explain how, beginning with the nature of air alone, the whole diversity of the world and its structure has evolved, by thickening and thinning in connection with cooling and heating. In this way all things arise from the Air — either directly or 'from its offspring', as the doxography reports.[126]

This genealogical derivation of the world from a single ancestor adapts a pattern that is as old as Hesiod's *Theogony* and will remain standard in the tradition of natural philosophy down to Plato's *Timaeus* (where the Demiurge is called 'father' of the created world at 37C7, but the Forms are father at 50D3, where the Receptacle is mother and the world of becoming is itself 'offspring', *engonos*). In XXXVIII and XXXIX (D. 31A—B) Heraclitus will exploit some aspects of this pattern — and again in LXXXIII (D. 53), where War is called 'father of all things'. But in XXXVII he directly rejects this pattern by insisting upon the eternal pre-existence of the world order as everliving fire.[127] This break with the Milesian scheme has the effect of identifying the world with its eternal source or *archē*, the cosmic order with its divine helmsman or regulator. This is monism with a vengeance. But why is it fire that is selected to represent the 'one'?

A recent writer on the history of science has spoken of 'the air of magic that boils out of the fire: the alchemical feeling that substances

can be changed in unpredictable ways. This is the numinous quality
that seems to make fire a source of life and a living thing to carry us
into a hidden underworld within the material world.'[128] Fire is
indeed a mysterious symbol of life, of superhuman life — despite or
because of the fact that it is the one element in which no animal can
live, and a power that in ancient Greece (as in modern India) often
served to receive human bodies at death. Thus in representing life
and creativity it also represents death and destruction. As an altar
flame consuming the sacrifice, it represents the gods. As fire for
cooking and for warmth in winter it sustains human life. As instrument of the arts, the stolen gift of Prometheus, it points to the divine
element in human activity, the techniques and industry that separate
us from the animals. Fire has many qualities. But it is a most unlikely
choice for a starting point in a literal account of the development of
the world in material terms, since it is not itself a kind of matter, not
a body at all, but a process of transition from one state to another, a
symbol of life and death at once, the very element of paradox.

These are some of the thoughts which Heraclitus' choice of fire
has imposed upon the pattern of cosmic transformation taken over
from Anaximander and Anaximenes. He takes a physical theory as
the background against which his words are to be understood (once
we have been led to interpret *kosmos* as 'world order'); but his
utterance is not itself the statement of a physical theory. Instead, the
paradoxical denial that the *kosmos* has any origin or history at all is
redoubled by the description of an everliving fire that is always going
out. The error of recent interpreters has been to deprive this second
paradox of its sting by refusing to take the words literally, reading
them as a poetic reference to elemental transformations, while con-
struing the first paradox as a literal statement of doctrine. If we take
both statements at face value they indicate that the everliving fire
could equally well be described as ever dying, that it is wholly transitory and always changing, while remaining eternally the same for all.

In order to unravel these puzzles, we must know more about the
measures by which fire is kindled and put out. One clue is provided
in the 'turnings' of fire and the measures of sea in XXXVIII–XXXIX;
another will be found in the measures of the sun in XLIV (D. 94).

XXXVIII–XXXIX

XXXVIII (D. 31A)   The reversals (*tropai*) of fire: first sea; but of sea half is
earth, half lightning storm (*prēstēr*).

XXXIX (D. 31B)   Sea pours out <from earth>, and it measures up to the same amount (*logos*) as it was before becoming earth.[129]

Clement, the only author to cite these two texts, suggests that the first follows closely on XXXVII (D. 30). His citation is compatible with there being no gap between XXXVIII and XXXIX, and many editors treat these as a single fragment. Reinhardt wished to regard all three sentences (XXXVII–XXXIX, D. 30–1) as one continuous text.[130]

If one reads XXXVIII–XXXIX without preconception, but with some knowledge of Ionian natural philosophy, they suggest a cosmogonic development of sea from fire and earth from sea: the very pattern illustrated in the doxography for Anaximenes (above, p. 137) but with Fire in the place of Air. It is just like Heraclitus, after denying that the world order has proceeded from anything else, to turn in the opposite direction and generate the world *as if* his everliving fire was an ordinary Milesian *archē*. This reflects the fact that his own cosmology both is and is not a substitute for the theories of the natural philosophers.

Given what we know about cosmogenesis in the Milesians and Anaxagoras, it takes a certain amount of hermeneutical bias, not to say obstinacy, to read 'first' and 'before' in XXXVIII–XXXIX as if the words did *not* refer to a temporal sequence. The fact that Theophrastus and all later writers, including the Stoics, took them to imply a cosmogony is not in itself a sufficient reason for us to refuse to do so.[131] If recent interpreters have resisted the temptation to recognize some kind of temporal sequence or cycle in XXXVIII–XXXIX, that is because they believed cosmogony was *excluded* by Heraclitus in XXXVII (D. 30). Once we have decided to accept Heraclitus' words in all their diverse, even contradictory suggestiveness, there is no reason to doubt that the two sentences on fire, sea, and earth are intended to *suggest* some process of world formation or transformation, such as we find in the doxography for Anaximenes and frs. 15–16 of Anaxagoras.[132]

Heraclitus does not present us with a prosaic account of how the world took shape. The mysterious occurrence of *prēstēr* here — a lightning storm where we expect an element or a cosmic mass — and the enigmatic reference to sea 'pouring out' and 'being measured' show that he has in mind something rather different from the ordinary Ionian cosmogony. Yet he is clearly playing here with that cosmogonic pattern, just as in the doctrine of fire in XXXVII he is playing with the Milesian notion of an elemental *archē*. The assumption of a temporal sequence is obvious in every phrase of these two sentences, and first of all in the term *tropai* 'reversals'.

In normal literary usage, from Homer to Herodotus, *tropē* has two senses: (1) a rout in battle, when an army turns and runs, and (2) the 'turnings' of the sun at solstice, i.e. the extreme points of sunrise and sunset towards the north in summer and the south in winter, or (2A) the two times of year (in June and December) when the sun reaches these points and begins its movement back in the opposite direction. It is to render both senses that I translate *tropai* as 'reversals'.[133] Since 'the routs of (everliving) fire' is not immediately intelligible, the *prima facie* reading of *pyros tropai* must rely on (2): 'the turning-points of fire', i.e. the extreme points in a periodic movement from something like summer to something like winter.[134] What Heraclitus' words imply is a direct parallel, in poetic terms an identification, between fire and sun. This gives us the clue without which the riddles of XXXVII—XXXIX would remain unintelligible. The measures by which fire is kindled and put out are to be understood as in some sense a re-enactment of the sun's regular course from solstice to solstice. And this link between the annual movements of the sun and the measured death and revival of fire is reaffirmed in the reference in XLIV (D. 94) to the 'measures' of the sun's path as a manifestation of the divine order of the cosmos.

For the sun the *tropai* are the limits in an annual oscillation, marking the seasons of the year. By analogy the *tropai* of fire will not be stages in a graduated sequence but extreme points in some kind of oscillation. This explains why the first 'turning' of fire is not cloud, wind, smoke, or some other item from the atmosphere, as the pattern of Ionian cosmogony would lead us to expect, but sea: the visible mass of water, and thus the opposite of fire, the element that serves precisely to *put it out*. Sea marks the first *tropē* of fire not because fire 'turns into' water by any conceivable physical change, but because water stands at the opposite pole, the extreme 'reversal' which contrasts with fire as winter contrasts with summer, or night with day. In the last analysis, fire and sea are 'one', just as these other opposites are one. But in a more obvious sense, sea represents the death and defeat of fire. Thus the dominant literary meaning of *tropai* as 'routs in battle', which we rejected on first reading, emerges after all as a *hyponoia*.

Such linguistic clues were not understood by the Stoic commentator followed by Clement, who, like Theophrastus and most moderns, misread *tropai* in the light of Aristotle's use of the verb *trepesthai* for 'transformations' and hence must provide some middle term by which fire can 'turn into' sea: 'he means that fire . . . is turned through air into moisture, as seed or semen for the world formation, which he calls "sea".[135] It was left for the moderns to take *tropai* as 'transformations' and at the same time refuse to allow a middle term between fire and water, sun and sea, thus crediting Heraclitus with the strange theory of an elementary transformation from fire to water, and an equally surprising scheme of 'elements' in which the atmosphere — the *aēr* of Anaximenes — is not even represented! Heraclitus' systematic omission of the term *aēr* may well be intentional — something like a deliberate snub. But he cannot have offered a theory of the natural world in which the *atmosphere* was omitted.

If we stick to the text we do not get ensnared in such strange doctrines. After the first reversal of fire as sea we have the reversal of sea (and the second reversal of fire) as 'half earth, half *prēstēr*'. That is, the turning from sea to its opposite takes two equal forms, in turn opposed to one another. The shift from wet to dry, liquid to solid, results in dry land or earth. Here we establish contact with the traditional pattern of cosmogony, in which the emergence of dry land from primeval moisture or sea is a recognized phase.[136] But if for a moment Heraclitus touches base here in standard cosmology, it is only to bound off again in his own direction with the next words. The other turning from sea is back in the initial direction of fire, and what we expect at this point is some representative of the *aēr* or atmosphere, the product of evaporation from the sea which accompanies its drying up. If Heraclitus had been propounding a physical theory he might have written: 'The reversals of sea (or the reversals of fire starting from sea) means that part of the sea moves in the dry (and cold) direction, further away from its starting point in fire, and becomes earth; part moves back towards fire and warmth and becomes atmospheric vapor, clouds, and wind, thus filling the region between earth and celestial fire, and providing nourishment for the fires aloft.' Something of this sort must be what Heraclitus is alluding to, the theory of Anaximenes or some variant on it.[137] But instead of giving any systematic account of the atmosphere, Heraclitus invokes the *prēstēr*.

The identity of this phenomenon is not beyond dispute. Several recent studies have interpreted the *prēstēr* as a tornado or waterspout. But the Greek literary evidence emphasizes a connection with fire from heaven, as in a lightning storm. The word first appears in

Hesiod's *Theogony* as an attribute of winds (*prēstēres anemoi*) between the mention of lightning and thunderbolt, as an instance of celestial flame.[138] Like Aristophanes and Hesiod, Aristotle associates the *prēstēr* with a whirlwind or tornado, but his brief description does not mention a spiral form. He says that *prēstēr* is the name given to a hot or rarified wind drawn down from the clouds, that catches fire: 'for it sets the air on fire (*synekpimprēsi*) and colors it by its conflagration' (*Meteor.* III.1, 371a 15–17). Aristotle thus explains the name by a derivation from *pimprēmi* 'burn, set on fire'.[139] In Xenophon a *prēstēr* is cited as setting a temple on fire (*Historia Graeca* I.3.1). It must then have involved a lightning storm, like the one Aristotle describes as destroying the temple of Artemis at Ephesus with sheets of fire (*Meteor.* 371a 31ff.). When Herodotus speaks of losses to Xerxes' army caused by 'thunder (*brontai*) and *prēstēres* at night' (VII.42.2), he must be referring to a similar storm. Thus the half-dozen mentions of *prēstēres* in extant Greek literature from Hesiod to Aristotle all point to destructive fire from the sky in a great wind storm, perhaps of hurricane force, but not to a tornado or whirlwind.[140] This sense of *prēstēr* as something like sheet lightning is what Heraclitus must have in mind in XXXVIII. It represents fire in the atmosphere, but not a visible return from sea to sky. For in a thunderstorm the bolts of lightning come dramatically *down*. And the ancient texts regularly speak of *prēstēres* as 'falling' (*empesontos* in Xenophon; *epespiptousi* in Herodotus; *kataspōmenon* in Aristotle, etc.).

Of course if Heraclitus were referring to 'a waterspout attended with lightning' (as LSJ renders Burnet's suggestion of a 'fiery waterspout'), then the movement from sea to sky would be vividly exemplified. For in the case of the waterspout a funnel of cloud descends towards the sea and seems to suck the sea up into the sky.[141] Unfortunately, the Greek literary evidence down to the time of Aristotle and Theophrastus (and perhaps beyond) does not point to any necessary or even normal connection between a *prēstēr* and a waterspout, of the sort we find in Lucretius. So this interpretation of Heraclitus' words is quite unsupported.

On any reasonable interpretation, a *prēstēr* is not an element or a cosmic mass, but a devastating discharge of fire from storm clouds: it illustrates the power of cosmic fire as a visual experience. Compare the thunderbolt of Zeus, the *keraunos* which 'steers all things' in CXIX (D. 64).[142] Perhaps there was some connection in Greek experience between the *prēstēr* and the solstitial seasons. But it seems more likely that Heraclitus chose the *prēstēr* as a phenomenon that explodes out of season, not a predictable 'turning' but an expression of the power of opposition, manifesting itself as everliving fire.

On this view, *prēstēr* represents half the sea and infinite power. But on any view these 'measures' seem puzzling. How can one strike a balance between a momentary event like the *prēstēr* and the stable mass of earth?[143] And what will be left of the sea if half changes into earth and half into atmospheric fire? This is a problem for any view that takes *tropai* in XXXVII as transformations, and at the same time insists on regarding the half-and-half measures synchronically, as a ratio between constituents of the world at any given moment.

The most plausible among recent interpretations is that of Kirk. 'Naturally Heraclitus means that one-half of sea *can be regarded* as turning to earth (and replenished by earth), and the other half as turning to *prēstēr* (and replenished by fire); the total remains unchanged as sea.'[144] The assumptions underlying this view (which are widely shared), namely, that the measures of XXXVII—XL are to be understood in terms of simultaneous relationships rather than successive phases, will be examined later. Here I remark only that such a view takes no account of the literal sense of *tropai* and the implied analogy to the course of the sun; that it involves reading a great deal between the lines of XXXVIII; and that it is *prima facie* incompatible with the text of XXXIX (D. 31B), which refers to two distinct temporal stages: before and after the sea becomes earth.

I suggest, therefore, that we understand 'half earth, half *prēstēr*' as an enigmatic reference to long-term tendencies in two opposite directions after the production of sea, a reversal that will eventually destroy the sea by drying and evaporation; the vapors themselves are to be thought of as nourishing celestial fire, in the form of sun, star, and lightning. 'Half-and-half' points (a) to the dual production of earth and atmospheric vapor from the sea, and (b) to the fact that the whole cosmic process unfolds according to rigorous measure and symmetry. This is guess-work; but it is guess-work grounded in the text and in the evidence for early Ionian cosmology.

In the measurement of sea in XXXIX we have a clear statement of (b) and a partial statement of (a): 'sea becomes earth'. But what does it mean to say that 'sea pours out' or 'dissolves' (*diacheetai*)? The last words of XXXIX show that a prior change of sea into earth is presupposed. (Perhaps this is to be understood from 'of sea, half is earth' in XXXVIII; or perhaps something is missing between the two fragments.) Hence there is no need to insert the word 'earth' (*gē*) as subject of 'pours out' (*diacheetai*), as many editors do. With or without this textual change we have a new shift of direction, the reliquefaction of earth as sea, reversing the emergence of dry land.

Now there is some parallel to this in Ionian cosmology.[145] Heraclitus himself says in CII (D. 36) that 'out of earth water is born', and implies that this compensates for the generation of earth which is 'death for water'. In CII we have a process of elemental transformation within the present world order. On my reading of XXXIX, this ordinary cycle of elemental change is an imitation of, or an analogue to, the larger cosmic cycle of formation and reformation of land and sea in XXXVIII and XXXIX. (On the usual reading these two cycles are identical, since the cosmic cycle of XXXVIII—XXXIX is reduced to the elemental exchanges of CII, D. 36.) It would be idle to pretend to a definitive interpretation of such a cryptic text. We cannot tell whether 'sea becoming earth' refers to the well-known Mediterranean phenomena of sinking and rising coastlines — either from deep geological causes (the so-called bradyseism, the slow movement up or down of the earth's crust) or from the silting up of river mouths, as at Ephesus and Miletus — or whether Heraclitus is alluding here to some greater cosmic changes leading up to general conflagration, as Clement says. It may well be that he intends XXXIX to apply ambiguously to both: to visible changes in the relationship between earth and sea and also to the vaster cyclical changes of the cosmos.

Such reversals are conceived as a measured pendulum swing, as in Anaximander's thought of retribution paid 'according to the ordinance of Time'. In emphasizing the equality of exchanges Heraclitus introduces the notion of cosmic order as a pattern of Justice, in which nothing is taken without repayment. (Cf. XL, D. 90 and LXXXII, D. 80.)

The principle of measure, mentioned enigmatically at the end of XXXVII (D. 30), is now clarified as a measure preserved over a sequence of stages, in a temporal progression that returns us to the *status quo ante*.[146] The measures of equality are thus rigorously respected over the long run, no matter how dramatic the reversals may be at any given moment. And since this regularity is expressed by the term *logos* in XXXIX, it is thematically connected with the *logos* of I.2, 'in accordance with which all things come to pass'.

XL

XL (D. 90)   All things are requital for fire, and fire for all things, as goods for gold and gold for goods.

By its echo of XXXVII the mention of fire suggests a cosmic application, which is confirmed by the reference to 'all things'. Heraclitus is again playing with the pattern of Ionian cosmology and the element theory of Anaximenes. But the substitution of fire for air does not leave the rest of the theory as it was. Fire represents a process of destruction, and only in this sense can one imagine everything 'turning to fire'. In return, the only thing that naturally arises from fire is smoke and ashes. If fire is chosen as a model for physical transformation, to replace the Milesian model of evaporation and condensation, it will intuitively prefigure the annihilation of nature, the devastation of the world order, as fire in warfare prefigures the burning of the ships, the destruction of the crops and fruit trees, the sack and pillage of a town. This only makes it more paradoxical that fire in XXXVII should represent a world order that is eternal.

Hence I believe the Stoics (and other ancient readers before them) must have been right to think that the imagery of fire for Heraclitus presages some cosmic conflagration or ecpyrosis. And they were right too to think that, in this dimension, the eternity of the *kosmos* can only consist in the recurrence of the same phases, the eternal repetition of cosmic 'reversals' between opposites, whether as oscillations between fire and flood, in the polar catastrophes of Great Summer and Great Winter, or between Fire itself and the world order, as in the Stoic cycle.[147] I doubt that Heraclitus had much more to say about the details of this world cycle than what we read in XXXVII–XXXIX. (But see below on XLII and XLIII.) He was content to suggest a cycle in which fire occupies a dominant position at the end as at the beginning; for in a circle the two coincide (XCIX, D. 103). So much followed from the notions of cosmic symmetry he had accepted from the Milesians (and which he may have applied even more rigorously than they did) once he had chosen fire as his starting point. The vicissitudes of the cycle will then appear as the ever-recurring extinction and rekindling of the eternal flame.

Heraclitus' cosmic cycle was probably a development from Milesian views; it exerted in turn a decisive influence on Empedocles and, later, on the Stoics.[148] Unlike these philosophers, Heraclitus was interested not in propounding but in *using* physical theories to project a vision of cosmic order and an understanding of human life and death. That is why the question whether or not Heraclitus envisaged a world conflagration, although a great subject of scholarly debate, is not a crucial issue in understanding his thought. (The best of all modern interpreters of Heraclitus, Karl Reinhardt, was in my view passionately mistaken on this very question.) But it is crucial for giving a natural sense to the text of XL.

If we attend to the words and imagery of XL, three points emerge.

(1) Fire possesses a unique and universal value, like gold in a land that has never heard of silver. The imagery of gold suggests the gift of princes and exceptional offerings to the gods.[149] The essential point is that fire is worth 'all the rest' (*ta panta*). This is an echo, and an interpretation, of the unity of 'all things' in XXXVI (D. 50). It establishes a parallel to the sun, who is worth all the other stars (XLVI, D. 99), to the outstanding man of LXIII (D. 49: 'one is ten thousand, if he is the best'), and above all to the aim of superior men (XCVII, D. 29) who choose everlasting fame: 'one thing in exchange for all'.

(2) The polar movement between 'fire, all things' and 'all things, fire' finds a parallel in CXXIV (D. 10): 'from all things one and from one thing all'. The primary application must be to the cosmic cycle that leads from primordial fire to the creation of sea and land and all things — and back again. But this does not exclude the implication that similar exchanges between cosmic fire and other things — the elements, or the cosmic masses — are going on all the time. (The pattern of Ionian cosmogony is designed to serve as a paradigm for understanding the world as it is.) The universal exchange for fire is, in one sense, a fact of human experience: we see all sorts of things going up in flames. But the reverse process, the generation of all things *from* fire, is not a fact of observation at all. It is a pure requirement of theory, a consequence of the principle of symmetry. In this respect Heraclitus' doctrine is equally dogmatic, equally devoid of empirical support, whether it is taken as a claim about continuing processes of nature or as a thesis about cosmogony. If anything, the cosmogonic thesis has an epistemological advantage over the doctrine of a continuous emergence of all things from fire, since at least the former cannot be *falsified* by empirical observation, as the latter clearly seems to be.

(3) The exchange between fire and all things is expressed by the term 'requital' (*antamoibē*) which suggests some principle of compensation or retribution: *antamoibē* may imply reward or punishment, or both at once. The term is perhaps an echo of Anaximander's phrase

about elemental principles 'paying the penalty and making retribution to one another'. Now the alternating aggression and punishment of opposites in Anaximander seems to be a continuous process going on within the world, at present, but a pattern realized 'according to the ordering of time', that is, in a sequence or cycle. There is no need to suppose that Heraclitus is referring only to one cycle, from fire to world and back again. Like Anaximander, he has in mind all possible cycles that illustrate a 'reversal' between poles: day and night, summer and winter, rain and dry weather, youth and old age, life and death. But if the reciprocal exchange between fire and all things is taken as a paradigm for such cycles, as fire itself is taken as a paradigm for the world order in XXXVII (D. 30), then the most natural interpretation of this paradigm — and the primary interpretation of cosmic fire going out and being rekindled in XXXVII — is a pattern of cosmogonic emergence of all things from fire balanced by a similar process in reverse, of the sort sketched in XXXVIII—XXXIX.

Excursus I: On traditional interpretations of the cosmic cycle

Since my interpretation of XXXVII—XL flies in the face of dominant trends in recent scholarship on Heraclitus, I shall here review three of the most influential interpretations, beginning with that of Zeller. My aim is not to evaluate these interpretations as a whole but to examine the assumptions on which they are based, in particular the insistence upon understanding Heraclitus' pattern of cosmic order in terms of synchronic (simultaneous) rather than diachronic (periodic) structure. The reader who is not interested in the history of Heraclitean scholarship may skip ahead to the discussion of the next fragment on p. 153.

For Zeller, the fundamental principle of Heraclitus' thought is the doctrine of universal flux, the continuous change and transformation of all things. This doctrine Zeller found of course in Aristotle, in the doxography, and above all in Plato's account. But he also found it in the fragments on the river (L—LI, D. 12 and D. 91), in the assertion of the unity of day and night (XIX, D. 57), the interchange of living and dead, sleeping and waking, young and old (XCIII, D. 88), and in other texts.[150] Zeller understood this doctrine as an explicitly metaphysical thesis, the derivation of all phenomenal things as transitory appearances of a single entity, 'which engenders them all and takes them all back into itself, and which is the only thing to remain and preserve itself in restless change' (p. 796). From this metaphysical principle Heraclitus derived his physical doctrine that everything is fire by a kind of imaginative intuition, perceiving fire as the natural expression of motion and life (p. 809). Fire for Heraclitus is not an immutable substance or element but the being which is continually undergoing change, passing into all material entities, penetrating all parts of the universe and taking on a different form in each. It is not simply visible fire but heat in general and dry exhalation (*anathymiasis*) in particular (pp. 814f.); not simply phenomenal fire but cosmic fire, *Urfeuer*, the universal being which forms both the source and the substance of all things (pp. 817—19).[151]

It is in this connection that Zeller interprets XL: 'all things are exchanged for fire, and fire for all things' (p. 819); he understands this as a derivation of all things from a single principle or *Urstoff*, without reference to cosmogony or to any other temporal process. If he nevertheless ascribes a cosmogony to Heraclitus it is on the basis of XXXVIII (D. 31A) alone, with its mention of the *tropai* or 'turnings' of fire to sea, earth, and *prēstēr*. Schleiermacher and others had taken this as a reference to the cycle of transformations of elements within the present world order; if Zeller feels obliged to reject that interpretation it is not because of anything he finds in the text of Heraclitus, but solely because 'we have no reason to mistrust the assertion of Clement, according to whom the fragment referred to the formation of the world' (p. 847, n. 2). Zeller is a good enough historian to eliminate the more obviously Stoic features of Clement's commentary, but he follows that commentary in taking *tropai* to mean 'transformations'. Hence he reads XXXVIII as saying that primordial Fire first changes into water or 'sea', from which in turn arises the solid earth and the hot and fleeting *prēstēr* (*Glutwind*, flaming wind). In treating XXXIX (D. 31B), Zeller again follows Clement in seeing the return of earth to sea as the first stage of the reverse process that leads to the conflagration (p. 865 with n. 3). As for this final stage, he finds it directly asserted in CXXI (D. 66) 'the fire coming on will judge all things' and notes that it is fully confirmed by statements in Aristotle and all later authors.[152] But neither cosmogony nor conflagration is central in Zeller's account. The basic physical doctrine is the cycle of elemental transformations within the present world order, a cycle which he finds in XL and again in the statement about the upward and downward path: the closer any body approaches to the fiery condition, the higher it rises; the farther it departs from this condition, the lower it sinks. But the transformation moves in a circle, since once the material reaches the condition of earth, at the farthest remove from its original state, it turns back through the intermediate stages and returns to its fiery starting point (pp. 854f.).

The first remarkable feature in Zeller's interpretation is the central role he assigns to the doctrine of flux, understood as a physical cycle of elemental transformation. (Here Zeller follows Plato's account at *Timaeus* 49Bff. – as many others have done in assigning an elemental cycle to Heraclitus. The evidence for such a cycle in the fragments is, in effect, limited to CII, D. 36, unless one accepts the authenticity of XLI, D. 76.) The other remarkable feature is the extent to which his argument for cosmogony and ecpyrosis depends upon the authority of Clement, Aristotle, and other secondary sources. If XXXVIII–XXXIX are interpreted by him in this light, it is because 'we have no reason to mistrust Clement', and not because of any close analysis of the text and its pre-Socratic parallels, as has been attempted here. The only other fragment he cites in support of ecpyrosis is the judgment of all things by fire in CXXI (D. 66). If the authenticity of CXXI can be called into question, if the authority of Clement, Aristotle and the doxography can be successfully challenged, and if the text of these two or three fragments can be shown to bear another sense, Zeller's whole case for cosmogony and ecpyrosis must collapse.

This sapping operation will be the work of Burnet, completed by Reinhardt. Burnet starts from a different fundamental insight: not the doctrine of flux but the unity of opposites. 'The truth hitherto ignored [sc. by Heraclitus' predecessors] is that the many apparently independent and conflicting things we know are really one, and that, on the other hand, this one is also many. The "strife of opposites" is really an "attunement" (*harmonia*) . . . Wisdom is . . . a perception of the underlying unity of the warring opposites' (Burnet, p. 143). This leads Heraclitus 'to seek out a new primary substance'. His principle of fire 'was something on the same level as the "Air" of Anaximenes', but chosen to represent a certain view of unity and stability within a process of constant change. 'The quantity of fire in a flame burning steadily seems to remain the same, the flame seems to be what we call a "thing". And yet the substance of it is continually changing. It is always passing away in smoke, and its place is always being taken by fresh matter from the fuel that feeds it.'[153] Thus Burnet returns to Zeller's own starting point but from a different point of view: the essential feature of the process of transformation is that the *structure* and *pattern* of things remains constant. 'How is it that, in spite of this constant flux, things appear relatively stable? The answer of Herakleitos was that it is owing to the observance of the "measures", in virtue of which the aggregate bulk of each form of matter in the long run remains the same, though its substance is constantly changing' (p. 150). In this connection Burnet cites the measures according to which everliving fire is kindled and extinguished (XXXVII, D. 30), the exchange of all things for fire and fire for all things (XL, D. 90), and the measures which the sun will not exceed (XLIV, D. 94).

Before turning to Burnet's attack on cosmogony and ecpyrosis, I must point out that, despite his illuminating account of the symbolism of fire and river in terms of a *structured pattern of change* rather than a metaphysical unity 'behind' or 'underneath' the appearances, his version of the doctrine of measures cannot easily be accommodated to Heraclitus' text. In trying to make sense of the extinction and rekindling of an everliving fire, a reference to 'the aggregate bulk of each form of matter in the long run' does not appear, at first sight, to offer a plausible solution. (If Burnet's version has come to seem natural, that is only because it has been repeated by so many interpreters, beginning with Reinhardt.) And the measures which the sun will not overstep must mark its path in the sky, charted daily or over the course of a year. Only in the *logos* by which sea is measured in XXXIX (D. 31B) do we have any reference to the bulk of some form of matter, but the equality there is explicitly said to be not constantly maintained but *restored* to what it was at some previous time (before it became earth, according to the text accepted by Burnet himself). In both cases, then, where the meaning is clear, the measures represent a symmetry or equality maintained by a periodic recurrence. Here the temporal dimension is not negligible — as it may be when one talks of things 'remaining the same in the long run' — but *essential*: for Heraclitus as for Anaximander the measures of justice are recognizable only as 'an ordering of time'. And a diachronic interpretation for the first case also, that is, for the measures by which cosmic fire is put out and rekindled, is suggested not only by the parallel between fire and sun introduced with the term *tropai*, but also by the common-sense observation that a fire is not ordinarily kindled and extinguished *at the same time*.

The three passages just discussed are the only ones in which the terms *metra* or *metreisthai* ('measures', 'to measure') occur, but there are several in which *logos* may convey this sense. Thus we have two statements referring to the *logos* of the soul, first of all in XXXV (D. 45): one cannot find the 'limits of psyche' because it has such a deep *logos*. And there is also the somewhat dubious fragment CI (D. 115): 'To the soul belongs the *logos* which augments itself.' In neither text is the meaning of *logos* crystal clear, but it cannot be found in any preservation of 'the aggregate bulk of each form of matter in the long run'. If there is any reference to bulk at all (which is not obvious), it must be to a magnitude that *increases* or whose limits cannot be discovered. And even if, as I believe, the *logos* of I.2 'according to which all things come to pass' is also intended as a suggestion of measure, that statement is too cryptic to tell us what kind of measure is involved.

There are, however, some texts and testimonia that refer unambiguously to measure or equality preserved over time. That is so for the cycles and seasons mentioned in XLII (D. 100), the Great Year in XLIII (DK A 13 and A 5), the extinction and renewal of the sun each day (XLVIII, D. 6), and the generational measure of thirty years as a return from childhood to childhood (XCV, DK A 19; and compare XCVIII, D. 20). Succession rather than simultaneity is also suggested by the identification of deity with 'day and night, winter and summer, war and peace, satiety and hunger' (CXXIII, D. 67). It is again a diachronic rather than a synchronic pattern that emerges from the 'transposition' (*metapesonta*) and equivalence between 'living and dead, waking and sleeping, young and old' (XCIII, D. 88). So it is reasonable to assume that it is successive stages in time, rather than some mysterious identity at every moment, that is implied by the equation of mortals and immortals, 'living the other's death, dead in the other's life' in XCII (D. 62).[154] Similarly, when we hear that 'the beginning and end are common' in a circle (XCIX, D. 103), there is reason to think of a cycle of periodic recurrence. All the more so for CII (D. 36): 'for souls it is death to be born as water, for water it is death to become earth; out of earth water comes to be, out of water soul'. Here the terminology of birth and death makes clear that we are dealing with a cycle of successive stages, where equivalence is expressed as recurrence. It may or may not follow from such a pattern of transformation that, in Burnet's words, 'the aggregate bulk of each form of matter in the long run remains the same'; but that is most certainly not what CII (D. 36) *says*.[155]

In sum, the notion of periodicity, of measure and equality preserved by regular recurrence over time — whether a single day, a lifetime, or a Great Year — is a central theme in the fragments. If there is *one* notion of measure that predominates in Heraclitus' thought, it is this one; in fact, this is the *only* notion of measure clearly illustrated in the texts.

Now the unity or harmony of opposites can also be exemplified in states or processes envisioned at a single moment, as in the case of the bow (LXXVIII, D. 51), where the archer's arms and the parts of his instrument are stretched in opposite directions at the instant of maximum tension, just before the arrow is released. In that case the unity and balance of opposites is realized by their simultaneous operation, their momentary co-presence.[156] Heraclitus' doctrine of *harmoniē*, the equilibrium and fitting-together of opposites, is not reducible to the theme of periodicity or recurrence. But, I submit, the doctrine of measure is so reducible. In every case where the notion of measure or *quantitative* equality is clearly applicable in the fragments, the only unmistakable applications are to cycles of succession and recurrence. And that even holds for the one case where what is measured seems to be the bulk of a form of matter (XXXIX, D. 31B).

This point is of primary importance, since Burnet's case against the cosmic cycle of world formation and conflagration in Heraclitus depends very largely upon the claim that 'it is inconsistent with the central idea of his system, the thought that possessed his whole mind' (pp. 158f.). According to Burnet, that thought is 'the perception of the underlying unity of the warring opposites' (ibid. p. 143); and he has interpreted this unity in exclusively synchronic terms (in the light of the bow image as reinforced by Plato's contrast between Heraclitus and Empedocles, p. 144), so that the harmony of opposites, and the measures that preserve it, are *identified* with a simultaneous condition of equality, rather than with some periodic restoration of the balance. As a result, when Burnet comes to discuss the phenomena of periodicity which he recognizes within Heraclitus' thought, he is obliged to describe these as an *exception* to the doctrine of fixed measures![157] A cosmic cycle of conflagration followed by recurrent world formation is 'inconsistent with the central idea' of Heraclitus' system only if this idea is construed in terms of momentary rather than diachronic balance. There is no inconsistency if the *kosmos* which is 'the same for all' is conceived as a pattern spread out over time, like a sine curve in wave theory: a fixed cycle of transformations between polar extremes. The evidence from the fragments in favor of such a diachronic view is, I hope to have shown, overwhelming. Simultaneous equality, as in the drawn bow, is a particular case of the unity of opposites. It is not the pattern of cosmic order as such.

When Burnet comes to discuss XL he again finds an argument *against* the conflagration. 'When gold is given in exchange for wares and wares for gold, the sum or "measure" of each remains constant, though they change owners. All the wares and gold do not come into the same hands. In the same way, when anything becomes fire, something of equal amount must cease to be fire, if the "exchange" is to be a just one.'[158] Since this argument has exerted a considerable influence, we must look a little more closely at its logic. It infers that if the cosmic process reached a point where all things were absorbed into fire, or had not yet emerged from it, then by analogy there would have to be a market situation with *only* gold and no merchandise (or with all of both confusedly in the same hands). But of course there is normally no such situation. Therefore Heraclitus cannot have used the market simile to express a cosmic development into and out of fire.

Now this argument is cogent only if we add a premiss to the effect that (i) Heraclitus intended the market simile to be applicable to cosmic fire in every respect, or (ii) the relevant respect is just the continuity of exchanges based upon a permanent distinction between coins and merchandise. Now the first premiss is absurd: no philosopher can use a simile or comparison that is apt in *every* respect. And the second premiss, though not absurd, is quite arbitrary: it guarantees the desired conclusion by begging the question at issue. Hence this interpretation of XL provides an argument only if we need none, that is to say, only if we are already convinced that the point being made is just that the rules of cosmic exchange exclude a passage of all things into fire. Those who are not convinced will find the meaning of the simile elsewhere, in the equivalence established between fire and all things, and in the formal parallel to CXXIV (D. 10): 'from all things one and from one thing all'. Together, these two points guarantee that the measures of cosmic order will be preserved even in the case of the most radical change conceivable: the total extinction of cosmic fire or its rekindling at the cost of everything else.

It was Karl Reinhardt who created the modern study of the pre-Socratics by insisting that archaic thinkers like Heraclitus and Parmenides could only be understood by careful study of their own words, not by taking over the interpretations worked out from a later point of view by Aristotle and Theophrastus. For Heraclitus Reinhardt went further and showed how different views of his thought are projected according to the philosophical interests and presuppositions of each author who quotes him. It was easy enough for Reinhardt to undermine Zeller's position on the ecpyrosis by pointing out how largely it depended upon Clement's interpretation, whereas this interpretation in turn can be shown to derive from some Stoic commentator.[159] In addition, Reinhardt deprived Zeller's interpretation of its most picturesque support within the text by rejecting as a Stoic or Christian paraphrase the reference to judgment by fire in CXXI (D. 66). This passage will be considered in its place. For the moment we look at Reinhardt's interpretation of the concept of measure, which determines his understanding of XL.

Reinhardt begins by suggesting that if the measures of cosmic fire in XXXVII (D. 30) are to be interpreted in terms of world formation and conflagration, they must mean that each world period 'takes the same length of time, represents the same development, as all the others'. (*Parmenides* pp. 176f. This is not entirely accurate. As we have seen, the doctrine of measures preserved over time means that even the most radical extremes, fire alone and all things in the universe, are in some sense equivalent or of equal value, so that the measures of equilibrium are preserved by a regular oscillation from one pole to the other.) Against this over-specific interpretation of XXXVII (D. 30), Reinhardt offers two objections. First, 'no Heraclitus was needed to teach that: that was the concept of *diakosmos* from the very beginning, as taught by the old Milesians'.[160] Reinhardt's second objection is: 'How can such a sense be hiding in such words? *Metra* must rather mean the quantity of matter (*Stoffmasse*) transformed by being burnt up and extinguished', since this is the sense expressed by the verb *metreitai* ('is measured') in the following context (XXXIX, D. 31B). 'The measure of the sea remains the same, while the material is continually changing . . . the water flows by, but the river remains always the same (L, D. 12). The sun is new every day, and yet will in all eternity never transgress its measures (XLIV, D. 94) . . . Thus the *pyros tropai* too, the transformations of fire, are not alternating periods but a continual transition between material opposites' (ibid. 177). 'Earth is only transformed fire, fire is transformed earth, as the dead are only the living deceased, the living are dead reawakened to life . . . the inner unity, the *tauton*, the "invisible harmony" (LXXX, D. 54) becomes visible only through duality, contradiction, and eternal exchange' (p. 179). It is in this context that Reinhardt cites, without further commentary, the exchange of fire for all things in XL.

It will not detract from Reinhardt's great services to the interpretation of Heraclitus if we note that, on the question of 'measures', his view is largely identical with that of Burnet. In his eagerness to deny the doctrine of world periods, he is even prepared to overlook the importance of periodicity and to interpret the concept of measures exclusively in terms of the relative proportion of cosmic masses and the like *at the present moment*.[161]

Agreeing with Zeller, Burnet, and Reinhardt on so many points, I must also agree that Heraclitus' conception of the universal structure of things can be illustrated by instantaneous or momentary phenomena, like the tension of the drawn bow, or by processes spread out in time that are not necessarily cyclical or periodic, like the flowing of water in a river and the tuning or playing of a lyre. But I insist that the most systematic expression of cosmic structure in the fragments refers to processes of a cyclical character, like the pattern that unifies day and night. And I see no reason why Heraclitus should have failed to find this same pattern of symmetry and balance in the Milesian doctrine of world formation, as long as it is completed by the reverse process of a return to the starting point. The unity of primordial fire and differentiated world is simply the unity of day and night written in the largest possible letters, like the unity of summer and winter within the rhythmic structure of a great or greatest year. That he did in fact play with this tremendous pattern, like Anaximander, like Empedocles, and like a modern cosmologist (but perhaps with more irony), seems to me established not because we can trust Clement's interpretation, but because we can trust the direct and vivid sense of the words and imagery of the fragments.

It would be tedious to prolong the polemic by considering in detail the recent reformulations of the Burnet-Reinhardt view by Kirk and Vlastos. I would in conclusion only ask how, if cosmogony is to be excluded, the equivalence between fire and *all things* is to be understood. (This is the same as to ask: in what sense are all things 'reversals of fire'?) Within the cosmogonic pattern the answer is easy and obvious. Without it, any answer must be arbitrary and contrived. If the chronological priority of fire is denied, then the only priority left for it is symbolical and perhaps metaphysical. But there is no *physical* sense in which it is true to say that all things are exchanged for fire, but false to say that all things are exchanged for water or for earth.[162]

XLI

XLI (D. 76)   Plutarch: [As Heraclitus said, the death of fire is birth for air and the death of air is birth for water.]

The authenticity of this, one of the most familiar of all quotations from Heraclitus, was challenged long ago by Zeller and has often been denied since.[163]

On the question of authenticity, we cannot arrive at any definite conclusion. But there is a more important and less controversial point to be noted: that Heraclitus spoke of a cyclical pattern of elemental transformation in terms of birth and death. For that is precisely the point which this text has in common with CII.

Since my commentary on XLI—XLIII will be more concerned with problems of documentation and the reliability of our sources than with the interpretation of Heraclitus' own text, I have grouped this discussion as Excursus II. The questions at issue may be of little interest for the general reader. The commentary proper resumes on p. 158.

Excursus II: On the documentary basis for XLI—XLIII

As a verbatim quotation of XLI, the only plausible candidate is the text of Plutarch given above. The version of Maximus of Tyre, 'Fire lives the death of earth and air lives the death of fire; water lives the death of air, earth that of water', although preferred by Bywater and given first place by Diels, is obviously a free variant, imitating the language of XCII (D. 62), which Maximus has just cited.[164] Hence Maximus is alone in speaking of *life* and death here, where Plutarch and Marcus Aurelius speak of birth and death, as in CII (D. 36). Also, his version of the cycle is asymmetrical, and the leap from earth to fire has no parallel either in other fragments or in other early theories. Any judicious comparison of the candidates for XLI will lead to the elimination of this version.[165] Much the same can be said for the citation in Marcus Aurelius. Unlike Maximus, Marcus knows Heraclitus well; but he quotes from memory, and his verbal memory is not particularly good. It is doubtful whether any of the numerous citations from Heraclitus in Marcus' *Notebooks* gives us the original text. The quotation here is continued by V (D. 71–9), where we can recognize a vague paraphrase of IV (D. 17, from Clement). There is no reason to suppose that Marcus' version of XLI is closer to the original.

So we are left with Plutarch's text, and with the special problems surrounding quotations in Plutarch. Plutarch is a man of vast erudition, with a special fondness for Heraclitus. One of his lost works was entitled 'What were Heraclitus' doctrines?' (Lamprias Catalogue no. 205, in the Teubner *Moralia* VII, ed. F.H. Sandbach, p. 9.) Over 60 citations or clear allusions to Heraclitus have been counted in his extant works, covering some 30 of the 126 fragments in Diels' original numbering.[166] In the surviving literature of antiquity, only Clement of Alexandria displays a comparable knowledge of Heraclitus' text.[167] But Plutarch is an accomplished stylist, who can blend Heraclitus' words into his own text or even imitate the archaic manner in developing a 'quotation' along his own lines (as in reference to the Sibyl in XXXIV, D. 92). Furthermore, Plutarch relied upon his memory, which was fortunately very good; he 'did not verify his quotations, or did so rarely, by looking up the passage in his texts'.[168] As a result, when we rely upon Plutarch for the best or only citation of a fragment, there is always some reason to doubt whether we have an exact quotation.[169]

In the case of XLI, Plutarch himself seems to have regarded this as a faithful rendering, since he cites a shorter and freer version elsewhere.[170] The parallels in Marcus and Maximus show that the doctrine was well known and regularly ascribed to Heraclitus. Unfortunately, this is no proof of authenticity. The form of XLI seems to be more Stoic than Heraclitean, in view of the mention of 'air' in all three versions: Plutarch, Marcus, and Maximus. As Zeller pointed out, *aēr* is conspicuously absent from XXXVIII–XXXIX and CII (D. 36). Even the Theophrastean doxography does not mention *aēr*, but speaks only of 'exhalation' (*anathymiaseis*) from earth and sea. Now we know that the Stoics adopted the canonical four elements from Aristotle; and we have a Stoic commentary on XXXVIII that inserts *aēr* between fire and earth. (See p. 314, n. 135.) It is easy to suppose that Plutarch and our later authorities for XLI are reproducing not an original text but a Stoic paraphrase. And the Stoic text in turn will have been a natural, but misleading extrapolation from CII (D. 36), with fire and air taking the place of 'souls'. Such is now the prevailing view.[171]

I previously argued against this view on the grounds that it was supported by unjustified assumptions.[172] The concept of elemental *aēr* was not discovered by the Stoics; it is an essential concept in Milesian meteorology, and there would be nothing *anachronistic* in a reference to the air in Heraclitus. On the contrary, it is the absence of air in XXXVIII–XXXIX and CII (D. 36) which is surprising and requires some explanation. Furthermore, there is something absurd about the three-element theory foisted upon Heraclitus by Zeller and Burnet. Such a view cannot give any plausible account of evaporation, wind formation, or the production of rain and lightning from the clouds — precisely the range of natural phenomena in which Ionian speculation took a special interest, and which best illustrates Heraclitus' own saying: 'cold warms up, warm cools off, moist parches dry dampens' (XLIX, D. 126). According to the three-element theory, these atmospheric phenomena could be defined and distinguished from one another only by some kind of mixture of water (or sea) and fire, some combination of these elements in distinct proportions. But there is no trace of any such doctrine either in the fragments or in the Theophrastean doxography. The theory of elemental mixture or compounds (and in this sense, the very notion of element) seems to have been an invention of Parmenides, developed by his successors. In the absence of such a theory, the early cosmologists had to explain each phenomenon separately, in terms of its causal source and consequences. There is no room for the reduction of many stages to three, or for the elimination of atmospheric phenomena in favor of fire and sea. Heraclitus may have had his own reasons for omitting any mention of *aēr*; and CII (D. 36) can be explained without resorting to a theory of three elements. The latter is a creation of Zeller, a misbegotten product of the Theophrastean doxography, a result of reading XXXVIII and CII as if they were presented as the complete statement of a systematic cosmology.[173]

Thus the reasons often given for rejecting XLI are bad ones. But the fact that a claim has been supported by poor arguments does not show that the claim itself is false. There are also good reasons for suspicion here. There is the lack of a uniform text underlying the different variants (Plutarch, Maximus, Marcus), the absence of *aēr* elsewhere while it is present in every variant of XLI, and the natural explanation of this discrepancy in the Stoic exegesis which introduces the four elements into Heraclitus' cosmology, an exegesis so ancient and widespread by Plutarch's time that he could easily confuse it with a memory of Heraclitus' own words.

XLII

XLIIA (D. 100)   Plutarch: [The sun is overseer and sentinel <of cycles> for determining . . . changes and 'seasons which bear all things' according to Heraclitus.]

XLIIB   Plutarch: [The year contains in itself beginning and end together of 'all things which seasons bear and earth brings forth'.]

Here we face the problem of Plutarch quotations in an extreme form. In XLIIB (*De Defectu Oraculorum* 416A) Heraclitus' name is not cited, and this passage was not listed by Diels among the fragments. But Heraclitus has just been mentioned twice in the context, first for his view of a human generation as thirty years (XCVA = D. A19) and then in connection with the (explicitly Stoic) doctrine of conflagration (*De Defectu Orac.* 415F). In XLIIA, from *Platonic Questions*, Plutarch is discussing Plato's view of time in the *Timaeus* as astral motion, ordered and measured by regular cycles or periods. 'And of these [viz. measure and limits and cycles] is the sun overseer and sentinel, for defining and arbitrating and revealing and displaying changes and "seasons which bear all things" according to Heraclitus; the sun turns out to be collaborator with the first and sovereign god not in small or petty matters but in the greatest and most decisive' (*Plat. Quest.* 1007D–E, after Cherniss). Thus in both passages the seasons are mentioned in connection with other periods, beginning with the human lifetime and its recurrence from generation to generation, passing through the various astronomical cycles, including what Plato calls the 'Perfect Year' when planets, sun, and moon will return to the same relative position (*Timaeus* 39D), and culminating in the cosmic cycle of conflagration and renewal, as recognized by the Stoics (*De Defectu Orac.* 415F). This is a witches' brew of erudition and speculation, and it is hard to see what we can safely extract for Heraclitus.

Reinhardt connected these passages with two other groups of testimonies, on the length of the human generation (XCV, D. A19) and on the length of the astronomical Magnus Annus (XLIII, D. A13).[174] He proposed, in effect, that some lost Heraclitean text indicated a proportional relationship between (1) the annual cycle of the seasons, whose measure would be 3 seasons of 4 months each, with 30 days to a month, i.e. $3 \times 4 \times 30 = 360$; (2) the cycle of human life as 30 years, as a 'month' each of whose days is a year, and (3) the Great Year of 10,800 (= 360×30) solar years, each of whose 'days' is a human generation.

Since the word 'season' (*hōrē*) also means 'hour' or 'interval of time', Heraclitus' phrase 'the seasons which bear all things' (or perhaps 'all things which the seasons bring') would then refer to this whole system of proportional cycles.[175]

I find this reconstruction persuasive, since it brings together bits of information that would otherwise be disjointed and almost unintelligible, and it presents the whole as a genuine *kosmos*, a marvelous structuring of natural change by fixed measures of recurrence, understood according to the seasonal pattern of the year. Still, the phrase about what the seasons bring is the only thing expressly ascribed to Heraclitus in XLII, and that is not much. So it is understandable that not all commentators accept Reinhardt's interpretation.[176]

One aspect of Plutarch's context in XLIIA that Reinhardt did not explore is the role of the sun as regent for the cosmic monarch and overseer of astral cycles. This is so obviously a theme which Plutarch derives from Stoic and Hellenistic sources that it might seem pointless to trace it to Heraclitus. (Cf. von Arnim I, 499, 502, etc.) But here too the Stoics may be following rather than leading. The parallel between sun and cosmic fire is attested in the *tropai* of XXXVII (D. 30); it is alluded to again in CXXII (D. 16): 'how will one escape from that which never sets?' If the divine ruling principle is a kind of superior sun, then the sun is a kind of inferior cosmic god. The notion of the sun as regent of the universe is attested in the *Cratylus* where Plato is giving a cosmological etymology for 'justice' (*to dikaion*). The principle of cosmic justice is first represented by the sun, which 'administers all things' (*epitropeuein ta onta*, 413 B5), but a moment later identified with fire (413 C2). The term for 'administer', *epitropeuein*, means literally 'to rule in another's name', 'to rule as governor or viceroy'. It is a good Ionic form and *could* have been used by Heraclitus.[177]

Plato's text shows that the Heracliteans of the late fifth (or early fourth) century were familiar with the notion of the sun as representative or viceroy of cosmic fire. It is another and bolder step to conclude that the idea goes back to Heraclitus himself.[178] If we take this step, we can provide a neat counterpart to the relation between the sun and Justice asserted in XLIV (D. 94): the sun maintains cosmic justice by watching over the course of the other stars, but (like some Persian satrap under surveillance by the King) his own path from solstice to solstice is guarded by Dike herself and the Furies.

XLIII

XLIIIA (D. A13)   Censorinus: [There is a <Great> Year . . . whose winter is a great flood (*cataclysmos*) and whose summer is an *ecpyrosis*, that is, a world conflagration. For it is thought that in these alternating periods the world is now going up in flames, now turning to water. Heraclitus and Linus <believed this cycle to consist of> 10,800 years.]

XLIIIB (D. A5)   Simplicius: [Heraclitus posits a certain order (*taxis*) and fixed time for the change of the cosmos according to some fated necessity (*heimarmenē anankē*.]

Here again we must wade into the swamp of the doxographical tradition in order to retrieve some information about what Heraclitus said. We begin with XLIIIB, which is free of Stoic contamination.

Simplicius' source is Theophrastus (fr. 1, Diels, *Doxographi Graeci* p. 475). This is guaranteed by verbal parallels in independent versions of the doxography. Thus Diogenes Laertius: 'The cosmos is generated from fire and again ignited according to certain alternating cycles throughout eternity; and this occurs according to fate (*kath' heimarmenēn*).'[179] In Diogenes the abstract word for 'fate' replaces the adjectival form 'fated necessity' in Simplicius. The latter probably reproduces Theophrastus' own text. The original connection also shows through in Aetius: 'Heraclitus [held that] all things occur according to fate, which is the same as necessity.'[180]

So, according to Theophrastus, Heraclitus spoke of the 'fated necessity' of a periodic change in the world order, involving the generation of all things from fire and their eventual dissolution into fire again. In this respect, the only thing new in the Stoic version is the term 'ecpyrosis' for the conflagration.

I have argued that in recognizing allusions to such a cycle in the fragments Theophrastus was essentially right. We must now ask whether (a) he is also right in saying that Heraclitus posited 'a definite time' for the change, and (b) whether he is correct in speaking of 'fated necessity'. There is no direct evidence, but the indirect evidence supports an affirmative response to (b). The term 'necessity' is attested in a similar connection for Empedocles (fr. 115); and the cosmic application, implicit in Empedocles, is explicit in the almost contemporary fragment of Leucippus: 'nothing happens at random, but all things take place for some reason (*logos*) and by necessity (*anankē*)' (DK 80.B 2). The same term occurs in Heraclitean imitations in the treatise *On Regimen*, where 'necessity' is paralleled by expressions for Fate: 'everything occurs by divine necessity (*anankē*) . . . each thing fulfills its allotted destiny (*peprōmenē moira*).'[181] There is thus no reason to doubt Theophrastus when he asserts that Heraclitus used similar language.

We are left with question (a), whether Theophrastus is also to be credited when he reports a definite time for the cosmic change. This is ambiguous. It can mean either (a.1) that Heraclitus asserted that the cycle lasted a definite time, without saying how long, or (a.2) that he specified a definite temporal interval. Now on (a.1) the report is unproblematic, even trivial: *if* Heraclitus spoke of a cosmic cycle, he certainly thought of it as fixed and definite: that would follow naturally from the importance he assigns to 'measures'. But (a.2) is more interesting: if we follow Theophrastus on *this* point, we must combine his information with the doxography from Censorinus, which tells us just what that temporal measure is supposed to be.

Censorinus' source is not Theophrastus but some Stoic author, perhaps Diogenes of Babylonia, a pupil of Chrysippus, active in the first half of the second century B.C.[182] By this time the Stoics had been interpreting Heraclitus according to their own lights for at least a century. Was one of them prepared to go further and furnish a number for the cosmic cycle lacking in Heraclitus' text?

Nothing in the preserved fragments would lead us to expect a definite number like 10,800 years: the only *number* given for a cosmic change is a rough one: half and half (in XXXVIII, D. 31A). But the number 10,800 is indirectly confirmed by the much better attested number 30 for a generation (XCV, D. A19). For 10,800 is 30 × 360: it represents a 'year' in which each 'day' is a generation. Since the number 30 is almost certainly genuine, the number 10,800 is likely to be so as well. Or are we to suppose that some Stoic commentator invented a cosmic number to fit Heraclitus' own number for a generation? Anything is possible here; but the doubt just expressed seems to carry scepticism a bit too far. Most scholars have felt, with reason, that the two numbers stand or fall together; and nearly all have accepted both as authentic.[183] What they have not all seen, however, is that if we accept the number 10,800 for Heraclitus' great year, we can scarcely separate it from Theophrastus' report about a 'definite time' for cosmic change. If the number 10,800 is genuine, that must be what Theophrastus is referring to.

Conclusions on XLII—XLIII

Thus the implications of the phrase 'all things which the seasons bring to birth' in XLII are considerably enriched, if we accept as Heraclitean the number 10,800 given in XLIIIA and combine it with the figure of 30 years for a human generation (XCV, D. A19). For what emerges is a set of proportional relations linking together the seasons in the narrow sense, determined by the annual course of the sun (XLIV, D. 94), with the succession of human generations, the cycle of elemental transformations, and some vast expanse of time: a great year in which each day is the length of a human generation. We cannot dismiss as a Stoic distortion this interpretation of the number 10,800 in terms of a great year, with a summer of cosmic fire and a winter of cosmic flood. For that becomes, in effect, the report of Theophrastus, or a natural inference from it, given the additional information about a 'great year' of 10,800 ordinary years. For to call the larger cycle a year is to imply that it has seasons. And the great summer will of course be hot (and, in Greece, dry), while the winter will be wet and cold.[184]

The passage in Plato's *Timaeus* (39D) which contains the earliest reference to a Great Year in extant literature says that it is the time when the sun, moon and planets all return to the same relative position, despite all their intervening 'reversals' (*tropai*). The passage in Censorinus just before XLIIIA similarly defines the Great Year in astronomical terms; and goes on to speak of the summer of ecpyrosis and the winter of cosmic flood. Reinhardt protested that the great year of the astronomers and the cosmic cycle of flood and conflagration 'are the most widely separate things that can be found in the world', since the former is a matter of exact calculation and the latter a wild astrological phantasy 'which mocks all calculation and is not even of Greek origin' but imported from Babylon (*Parmenides*, p. 184). But here Reinhardt was mistaken. We now know that the technique of exact astronomical calculation was itself imported from Babylon. And we know from Renaissance figures like Kepler that wild 'Pythagorean' speculation about cosmic harmonies and mystic numbers can be combined with — can even directly contribute to — major achievements in exact science. Indeed, the growth of astronomy in Babylon was itself a response to the superstitious interest in eclipses as omens of disaster. So Heraclitus, like some Stoics and many other thinkers after him, may well have entertained the notion of a vast cycle conceived in precise astronomical terms but interpreted as a wholly speculative pattern of decline and renewal for the cosmos.

Reinhardt rightly insisted upon the close connection between the great year and the cycle of human generations. But this systematic parallel between macrocosm and microcosm, between day, month, year, generation, and cosmic year has consequences which Reinhardt was unwilling to face. Just as one day-and-night yields to another, its equal or equivalent (XX, D. 106), and as one cycle of the moon is repeated in the following month, one circle of seasons renewed by the next year, even so is the life of man repeated in the next generation, when a man's son is reaching his full powers as the father's life declines. (See on XCIII–XCVIII.) When this pattern is extended to a cosmic year, it implies that the cycle of vitality and decline, waxing and waning, 'kindling and going out', will be repeated by a successor, as a father by his son. The notion of a single *logos* or numerical ratio applying throughout, a single *kosmos* or ordering 'the same for all', implies that the present world order is like a living being, an 'everliving fire' whose survival takes the form of replacement and renewal by an equivalent successor. Some such idea of successive worlds was probably older than Heraclitus. What is distinctive of his thought is the rigour with which the parallel between day, year, life, and cosmos is pursued, and reflected in a system of numerical proportions.[185]

Our information is too scanty to tell whether Heraclitus identified the 'winter' of the great year with a cosmic cataclysm, a destruction by flood. (Some pre-Socratic theorist must have done so: see n. 184.) It is quite possible that Heraclitus' own reference to the Magnus Annus of 10,800 years was carefully ambiguous between a cycle of cosmic disasters short of world destruction (as in Plato's version in the *Timaeus*) and a larger cycle of cosmogony and ecpyrosis.

XLIV

XLIV (D. 94)   The sun will not transgress his measures. If he does, the Furies, ministers of Justice (*Dikē*), will find him out.

The text poses two questions: (1) what are the measures of the sun? and (2) why is Justice involved?

(1) The measures which the sun will not 'overstep' (*hyperbesetai*) must be his visible path through the sky which varies with the season of the year, as the Greeks (and before them the Babylonians) knew very well. They laid out their maps according to the direction both of the *summer* sunrise and sunset and also of the *winter* sunrise and

sunset; in between they defined due east and due west as the 'equinoctial rising' and the 'equinoctial setting'.[186] Thus the annual variations in the sun's path were taken as a basis for establishing what we call the points of the compass. And the same variations serve to define the four fixed points in a scientific calendar: summer and winter solstices (*tropai*), with spring and autumn equinoxes. When star charts are drawn to plot the sun's course through the zodiac, the annual variations in the visible path are correlated with stages in its invisible path among the constellations; points of solstice and equinox mark off the astronomical seasons as four sections of this course. When the geometry of the celestial sphere is fully understood, the two equinoctial points will be determined by the intersection of the ecliptic (the sun's annual path) with the celestial equator. It is unlikely that Heraclitus was familiar with this last conception. Although the theory of the celestial sphere seems to have begun in sixth-century Miletus, we do not know whether it reached this degree of geometrical clarity before the time of Oenopides in the middle of the fifth century.[187] But anyone like Heraclitus, who had access to the astronomical knowledge available in Miletus and Samos at the end of the sixth century, must have been familiar with the correlations between the annual changes in the sun's visible path and its less conspicuous course among the stars. It was the latter, after all, that permitted the astronomers and calendar-makers to mark off the progress of the seasons on a day-to-day basis — directly, once the zodiac was in use, and indirectly earlier, by reference to such events as the rising and setting of Arcturus just before or just after the sun.

Now for Heraclitus 'the invisible fitting-together (*harmoniē*) is better than the visible' (LXXX, D. 54). So if, initially, the measures of the sun are represented by its path in the sky on any given day, these measures must also be traced in the pattern of annual variation from solstice (*tropē*) to solstice and back again. The measures of the sun are ultimately the measures of the solar year. The imaginary situation of the sun's overstepping these measures might be realized by a deviation from its course on any given day. But the more dramatic, and humanly more meaningful transgression would be for the sun to continue, in the winter, to rise later and farther to the south, and finally fail to rise altogether. This fear of the sun *going out* as the days grow shorter seems to have played a great role in archaic religions. It accounts for so many festivals (including Christmas) in the vicinity of the winter solstice, mostly festivals of celebration once the days have begun to lengthen again as the sun rises further to the north. Thus we celebrate our own 'new year' shortly after this reversal of direction. In Mediterranean lands the shortening of the nights towards the summer solstice is less dramatic than in northern Europe. But in modern Greece at any rate, St John's Day (24 June) is traditionally celebrated with bonfires as in the north, and associated with the solstice. Some villagers observe the custom of rising 'early on this day in order to see the sun turning like a "windmill or a wheel", as they say'.[188]

(2) The cosmic guarantee against the primitive fear of the sun's failure to rise (or, in summer, to set) is appropriately expressed by Heraclitus in the strongest imagery of Greek religion, where the Furies (*Erinyes*) represent relentless, primitive vengeance against moral and ritual transgression. But the mention of Dike indicates that the order in question is not one of blind vengeance. Dike represents the enlightened principle of the Justice of Zeus, his daughter by Themis or 'law', whose sisters are named Lawfulness (*Eunomiē*) and Peace (*Eirēnē*) in the standard genealogy (*Theogony* 901f.).

It was Anaximander who first articulated this notion of justice and fate as a cosmic reparation between opposing powers 'according to the ordering of time'. (See text above, p. 18). The role assigned to Dike by Heraclitus in XLIV is a personified expression of Anaximander's concept of cosmic justice, insofar as both authors see the regularity of nature as exemplified in the order of the seasons.

For other references to Justice, see on LXIX (D. 23), LXXXII (D. 80), LXXXVII (D. 28B); compare XL (D. 90), CXXI (D. 66), and CXXII (D. 16).

XLV

XLV (D. 120)   The limits (*termata*) of Dawn and Evening <is> the Bear; and opposite the Bear, the Warder of luminous Zeus.

I interpret this as a commentary on XLIV. But there are some points that must be taken account of in any interpretation.

(1) 'Dawn and evening', the first two words in the Greek sentence, have a double sense: (*a*) the beginning and end of day, and (*b*) the directions of east (sunrise) and west (sunset).

(2) *Termata* ('limits') means the goal of a race or the completion of a journey; the stone or pillar around which runners or chariots turn before heading back to their starting point; and, by extension, the borders or limits of a region.

(3) 'The Bear' (*arktos*) must designate Ursa Major, our Big Dipper or Great Bear, a general mark for the celestial pole and hence for the north.[189]

(4) The Warder (*ouros*) opposite the Bear (*arktos*) can only be the star Arcturus (Gr. *Arkt-ouros*), described as the Bear-watcher (*arkto-phylax*) in the astronomical poem of Aratus (*Phainomena* 92).[190]

Now the risings and settings of Arcturus are a familiar signal of the seasons as early as Hesiod. In *Works and Days* 566 and 610, the evening and dawn risings of Arcturus (its 'limits of dawn and evening') correspond to the beginning of spring and fall, that is, roughly to the equinoxes.[191] But in XLV Arcturus appears not as a seasonal sign but as the mythical guardian set by Zeus to watch the Bear. The unusual epithet 'luminous' or 'bright' (*aithrios*) can be a reference to his traditional role as sky-god and weather-god (since *aithriē* means 'clear sky', 'good weather'), but also a reinterpretation of Zeus as celestial fire in the upper sky (*aithēr*).

So much is clear. What follows is my own best guess at unravelling the knot of the riddle.

Dawn and Evening stand not merely for east and west but for sunrise and sunset, and hence as marks for the course of the sun. The Bear, or celestial pole, is the point or region *around which the sun turns* in its daily course. On first reading, taking *termata* as turning-point for the sun each day, it is only the Bear (and not the Bear-watcher) whose presence here is explained. Hence I propose a strong punctuation after 'Bear'.

On second reading, however, the *termata* may be understood as the 'limits' or extreme points for sunrise and sunset over the year, that is, as the *tropai* or solstitial points which mark the annual course of the sun. These risings and settings are at best alluded to in the enigmatic 'limits (*termata*) of dawn and evening'. How far the reader is willing to credit Heraclitus with this allusion is likely to depend on whether he has been convinced by my interpretation of XLIV.

What then of 'the Warder of luminous Zeus, opposite the Bear'? I read this second clause as a distinct thought. Opposite the Bear (and revolving around it, like the Sun) stands Arcturus, the star which in Hesiod gives the signal for spring and fall. If Arcturus is presented here as guardian of the Bear, it is because the Bear stands for the pole, and hence for the fixed regularity of solar and astral cycles. Its stellar guardian will preserve the measures of cosmic justice after the sun has set. (Compare the watcher 'that never sets' in CXXII, D. 16). Just as 'luminous Zeus' here corresponds to Dike in XLIV, so Arcturus appears in the role of the Furies as celestial policeman. Once the sun has set, the daily and annual ordinances of bright Zeus are represented by the clockwork regularity of the fixed stars.

XLVI–XLVIII

XLVI (D. 99)   Plutarch: [Heraclitus says 'if there were no sun it would be night.']

XLVII (D. 3)   Aetius: [Heraclitus says the sun is the size of a human foot.]

XLVIIIA (D. 6)   Aristotle: [As Heraclitus says, the sun is new (or young) every day.]

XLVIIIB   Plato: [The sun of Heraclitus . . . is extinguished in old age . . . but rekindled again.]

These four texts present two sets of contrasting elements in the description of the sun. (1) It grows old and is extinguished every night; but it regains its youth and vitality when rekindled every morning. (2) It is a small and insignificant portion of the universe, no bigger than it appears or about the size of a human foot, but also the cause of day and night, whose light exceeds that of the moon and all the stars together. The first antithesis is presupposed by Plato's text, and confirmed by the post-Aristotelian doxography.[192] The second antithesis is not formulated as such in any extant testimony, but it makes a meaningful pair out of what are otherwise two isolated comments.

The commentators have debated whether or not Heraclitus' remark about the size of the sun is to be taken literally. My view is that he is exploiting, without endorsing or criticizing, the natural assumption that the sun is just the size it appears.[193] Scientific specu- lation on the size of the sun was provoked by the geometric model for the heavens proposed by Anaximander and his successors. The earliest attested estimate, ascribed to Anaxagoras (DK 59.A 42.8), that the sun exceeds the Peloponnesus in size, must have seemed phantastically large at the time. A century later the diffusion of Ionian science had transformed the situation for an educated man. Aristotle takes for granted the belief that the sun is 'larger than the inhabited earth' (De Anima 428b4). But Heraclitus was living in the age when serious estimates of stellar distances and magnitudes were just beginning, when they were weakly grounded and known only to

an enlightened few. In referring to the sun going out and being rekindled Heraclitus again makes use of a naive point of view. It may
be helpful to cite here a contemporary picture of a peasant mentality
that still sees the world as most men will have seen it in Heraclitus'
day. Solzhenitsyn reports or imagines the following conversation between his hero, Ivan Denisovich Shukhov, and an educated officer.

'Listen, captain, where according to that science of yours does
the old moon go when it's through?'

'Where does it go? What ignorance! It simply isn't visible any
more!'

Shukhov shook his head and laughed:

'Well, if it's not visible, how do you know it's there?'

'So, according to you,' said the captain, astonished, 'we get a
new moon every month?'

'What's so strange about that? People are born every day, why
shouldn't there be a new moon every four weeks?'

'Pfui!' The captain spat. 'I've never met such a dumb sailor as
you. So where do you think the old moon goes?'

'That's what I'm asking you — where?' Shukhov grinned.

'Well, where does it go, tell me?'

Shukhov sighed and said, hardly lisping:

'At home they used to say that God broke up the old moon for
stars.'

'What savages!' The captain laughed. 'I've never heard such a
thing! Do you believe in God, Shukhov?'

'Why not?' Shukhov replied, surprised. 'When you hear Him
thunder, you can't help believing in Him.'

'And why do you think God does that, then?'

'Does what?'

'Break the moon up into stars?'

'Well, don't you understand?' Shukhov shrugged his shoulders.
'The stars fall down from time to time and it's necessary to fill the
gaps.' (*One Day in the Life of Ivan Denisovich*, tr. G. Aitken (New
York, 1971), p. 111)

It is a view of the world something like this that Heraclitus is presupposing. I see no reason to believe that he uncritically accepted the
naive view of the sun and stars, any more than the popular view of
the Furies or some myth about Zeus setting Arcturus as a watchman
over the stellar Bear. He makes use of traditional belief and imagery
for his own purposes, in this case probably to stress the paradoxical
contrast between the sun's relatively small appearance and its indis-

pensable function in the cosmos, and certainly to suggest a pattern
of periodic extinctions and rekindling that is both an example and a
paradigm for the measured lighting and quenching of cosmic fire (in
XXXVII, D. 30). The remark about the dependence of daylight on
the sun was probably intended to point to the union of day and night
(XIX, D. 57).

In XLIV (D. 94) the sun is presented as an anthropomorphic being
pursuing his daily path. In XLVIII the sun is again animate, passing
from youth to age; but its vitality is there conceived as fire, kindled
and quenched. When we turn to the Theophrastean doxography, we
find this imagery of kindling and quenching taken literally in a quasi-
mechanical explanation of the sun, moon, and stars, according to
which these phenomena are produced by the gathering and igniting
of bright exhalations in certain celestial bowls or basins (*skaphai*). If
we could accept Theophrastus' report as reliable, we would have a
rather detailed account of astronomical and meteorological theories.
But these doctrines are so different from the allusive and ambivalent
manner of Heraclitus in the preserved fragments that I do not think
we can rely upon them for an understanding of his thought. For this
material see Appendix IIA.

XLIX

XLIX (D. 126)   Cold warms up, warm cools off, moist parches, dry dampens.

Heraclitus here describes qualitative changes between physical
opposites in the language of felt experience rather than scientific
observation.[194] The verb *theretai* 'warm up' can be used of a person
warming himself by the fire. The word for 'cools off', *psychetai*,
suggests an application to human souls (*psychai*). This presentation
of the cold and the hot as if they were living beings reflects
Heraclitus' view of the underlying identity between the psyche and
the physical elements. (See below on CII, D. 36.) When Heraclitus
speaks of the cosmos as a *living* fire, we must take him at his word.

The conception of elemental opposites illustrated here comes from
Miletus; it is found again in the fragments of Anaxagoras and other
fifth-century writers, before being incorporated into the canonical
doctrine of Aristotle (for whom the four elementary bodies are
defined by one member from each of the two pairs: hot-cold, wet-
dry). What Heraclitus expresses, then, is not so much his own thought
as a common presupposition of Greek natural philosophy from Anaxi-

mander to Aristotle and beyond.[195] It is precisely this notion of
pervasive physical change that the Eleatics rejected as false (Melissus
fr. 8.3), while the physicists took it for granted as an obvious truth
of experience (Diogenes fr. 2). Plato has this in mind when he speaks
of a doctrine of continual change and becoming that is held by
Protagoras and Heraclitus and Empedocles 'and by all the wise men
except Parmenides' (*Theaetetus* 152E) and which he finds in the
Heraclitean image of the river, where 'everything moves on and
nothing stands still' (*Cratylus* 402 A8). On Plato's reading, the
choice of the opposites cold-warm and moist-dry is merely a traditional scheme for expressing the thesis of radical flux.

In its historical context, however, it is precisely the change of
opposites into one another that connects this sentence with the fragment of Anaximander and with the tradition illustrated in Anaxagoras and Melissus. And it is this archaic notion of the opposites as
opponents or adversaries that underlies Heraclitus' own conception
of War as father and king of all (LXXXIII, D. 53). The four opposites
mentioned here, and the processes they structure, point to the
domain of meteorology, with its processes of evaporation and precipitation, drought and rainfall, changes in temperature and humidity
We are reminded of Aristotle's description of the atmospheric cycle
in Heraclitean language:

> Now this cycle <of evaporation and precipitation> occurs in
> imitation of the circle described by the sun. For as the sun passes
> laterally back and forth, this cycle moves up and down. One must
> think of it as a river flowing in a circle up and down, common to
> air and to water. (*Meteor*. I.9, 346b35–347a3)

For Heraclitus too these daily and seasonal changes may be
regarded as a cosmic river, whose flux is structured by a system of
which the opposites are the coordinates, and whose balance is maintained by its periodicity.

L

L (D. 12)   As they step into the same rivers, other and still other waters flow
upon them.

This fragment is cited by Cleanthes in a comparison of Heraclitus'
and Zeno's views of the soul. But the text itself contains no reference
to the psyche. For Cleanthes' interpretation see CXIIIB.

The wording offers several oddities. There is the plural form of 'rivers': why is one river not enough? And there are four consecutive dative forms: *potamoisin toisin autoisin embainousin*, which can in principle be construed in either of two ways: (1) 'into the same rivers, as they step', as in my translation, or (2) 'into rivers, as the same [men] step'. This ambiguity would have been avoided if either bathers or rivers had been referred to in the singular. Thus the two oddities of the sentence in fact coincide.

Since elsewhere Heraclitus makes deliberate use of syntactical ambiguity, it is possible that both constructions are intended here.[196] If so, the ambiguity serves to emphasize a parallel between the identity of the human bathers and that of the rivers; and this parallel would suggest that the men too remain the same only as a constant pattern imposed on incessant flow. This is a 'Heraclitean' thought familiar from Plato.

> Mortal nature seeks . . . to be forever and to be immortal. But it can only do so by . . . leaving something else new behind in place of the old . . . as when a man is called the same from childhood to old age. He is called the same despite the fact that he does not have the same hair and flesh and bones and blood and all the body, but he loses them and is always becoming new. And similarly for the soul: his dispositions and habits, opinions, desires, pleasures, pains, fears, none of these remains the same, but some are coming-to-be, others are lost. (*Symposium* 207D)

I take it that Plato is here sympathetically developing a Heraclitean insight.

A second reason for the repeated dative forms would be more properly stylistic: to suggest the incessant movement of the river water by the rhythm and assonance of the four words ending in *-oisin* or *ousin*, reinforced by the more explicit repetition in 'other and other waters'. (Thus the sentence structure imitates the river: the dative forms suggest the disappearance of water downstream, whereas the neuter plural subject *hetera kai hetera hydata* represents the oncoming waters from upstream.) Finally, the use of plural forms throughout implies generality: Heraclitus is referring not just to the Cayster or Maeander but to all rivers; not to a given moment or bather but to all moments and all men.

This is the only statement on the river whose wording is unmistakably Heraclitean. It does *not* deny the continuing identity of the rivers, but takes this for granted. (For the denial that we can step into the same river twice, see LI.) Hence the point here concerns neither the irreversibility of the flow of time, the uniqueness of an individual

event or experience, nor the general instability of things. What is
emphasized is that the structure and hence the identity of a given
river remains fixed, despite or even because its substance is constantly
changing. And if the parallel mentioned above is pressed, something
similar is indicated about the structure and identity of individual
human beings. Taken generally, the thought expressed by the river
image reinforces that of the flame: the preservation of structure
within a process of flux, where a unitary form is maintained while its
material embodiment or 'filling' is constantly lost and replaced.[197]

LI

LI (D. 91)   Plutarch: [According to Heraclitus one cannot step twice into the
same river, nor can one grasp any mortal substance in a stable condition, but by
the intensity and the rapidity of change it scatters and again gathers. Or rather,
not again nor later but at the same time it forms and dissolves, and approaches
and departs.]

It is curious that the most celebrated and in a sense the most profound saying of Heraclitus, that you cannot step twice into the same
river, is not unmistakably attested in his own words. It was already
a famous saying in Plato's time; and even before Plato, Cratylus must
have been familiar with the paradox, since he tried to cap it with one
of his own. Cratylus denied that you could even step in the river *once*,
since you are changing too.[198]

Thus the statement seems to go back to Heraclitus himself. But
Plato does not give a verbatim quotation: 'Heraclitus says, doesn't he,
that all things move on and nothing stands still, and comparing
things to the stream of a river he said that you cannot step twice into
the same river' (*Cratylus* 402A). Like the formula *panta rhei* 'all
things flow', which occurs later in the dialogue, the remark about
the river seems to be paraphrase rather than quotation.[199] The
citation from Plutarch in LI is similar to Plato's except for the
impersonal form. This is probably as close as we can get to Heraclitus'
own wording, unless we assume with several recent editors that the
famous statement is simply a free rendering of L (D. 12). (Kirk (pp.
374f., 381), Marcovich (p. 206). Cf. Reinhardt, *Parmenides*, p.
207n.)

But if it is strange that Heraclitus should have expressed himself
twice in such similar terms, it seems even stranger that Cratylus or
some anonymous predecessor should have invented this formula,
which would have been enough to assure Heraclitus' immortality

even if all his other words were lost. Hence I prefer to regard 'One cannot step twice' as an independent fragment, perhaps designed to complete L (D. 12) by drawing an even more radical conclusion: since new waters are ever flowing in, it is in fact *not* possible to step into the same river twice. Or, more plausibly, the formula of LI may have been stated first, with L following as its justification: 'One can never bathe twice in the same river. For as one steps into [what is supposed to be] the same rivers, new waters are flowing on.'²⁰⁰

What follows in Plutarch is a long description of the fleeting character of mortal existence, along the lines of the passage from the *Symposium*. In the context of several citations from Heraclitus comes a series of phrases describing the transitory character of human existence: 'It scatters and again gathers. (Or rather, not again nor later but at the same time) it forms and dissolves, and approaches and departs.' The words in parenthesis are pretty clearly a Plutarchean interpolation, inspired by Plato's contrast between Heraclitus and Empedocles in the *Sophist* (242D–E). But the three pairs of contrasting verbs are intended to suggest Heraclitus' taste for antithesis; and any pair – or even all three – might reflect Heraclitus' text. The last pair ('it approaches and departs') would fit the river image perfectly; the other two suggest processes of cosmology or meteorology. All three pairs have had their advocates among modern scholars; no one pair has imposed itself as obviously authentic.²⁰¹ Our best course is to admit uncertainty and turn to more reliable information.

LII–LIII

LII–LIII (D. 84)   Plotinus: [Heraclitus left us to guess what he meant when he said . . . 'it rests by changing' and 'it is weariness to toil at the same tasks and be ⟨always?⟩ beginning'.]

These two brief citations do not give us a firm grip on the text of Heraclitus. Plotinus is quoting from memory, and we have no way of telling how far his memory reflects his own reading of Heraclitus or some more traditional account.²⁰² Plotinus takes both sentences to refer to the soul in its blessed condition before the fall into the body; we are free to take them otherwise.

'It rests by changing' can be read as an impersonal construction with no definite subject, like 'rest comes through change'. But the connection between 'rest' (*anapauesthai*) in LII and 'weariness' ⟨*kamatos*⟩ in LIII, reinforced by the occurrence of these terms as a

pair in LXVII (D. 111), suggests that the two citations belong
together. And the interpretation of the second sentence is more
difficult.

The traditional rendering (from Burnet and Diels to Marcovich)
takes the dative *tois autois* as referring to the masters for whom one
labors and by whom one is ruled: 'it is weariness to toil for and be
ruled by the same' (Kirk). This translation is not impossible; but
neither is it the natural sense of the words. As Bollack-Wismann have
pointed out, the dative with *mochthein* normally indicates the
object of toil or cause of suffering, not the person for whom one
labors. Hence we expect a translation like 'to labor at the same tasks'
or 'to suffer from the same ills'. The difficulty then is to understand
archesthai, which can mean 'to begin' as well as 'to be ruled'. I prefer
the former sense: it is weariness 'to be (always) beginning': never to
get to the end of the job but toil continually at the same work and
thus never find rest by changing.

LIV

LIV (D. 41)   The wise is one, knowing the plan (*gnōmē*) by which it steers all
things through all (*or*: how all things are steered through all).

LIV brings to a close the section on cosmology, so far as I have been
able to reconstruct it. (The texts dealing with the soul will be considered below in the section on death and human destiny, LXXXIV–
CXIV.) Thus, after a long introduction (I–XXXIV), we have some
twenty fragments 'on the universe', *peri tou pantos* (XXXV–LIV),
including one on the *logos* of the soul (XXXV), whose full meaning
will not be clear until later. In my reconstruction, the cosmological
section begins with a reference to the soul and closes here in LIV
with an anticipation of the doctrine of the cosmic god, to be developed in the 'theological' sections of the work.[203]

There is a textual problem in LIV, which must affect the translation but does not alter the general interpretation. Two Greek words
are transmitted in garbled form, and no emendation is entirely satisfactory. The first word is either a relative pronoun ('which' or 'by
which') or relative adverb ('in which way', 'how'); the second word is
a form of the verb *kybernaō* 'to steer', 'control', or 'govern'. I follow
Gigon and Kirk in reading the first word as *hokē* (or *hokēi*) 'how'.[204]
The second word can be restored either as *ekybernēse* 'it steers' (with
the tenseless aorist, as often in Heraclitus: see XXVIII, D. 101; LVII,

D. 79; and LXXXIII, D. 53); or as *kybernatai* '(things) are steered'.
There is something to be said for both readings, and no clear grounds
for choice between them.[205] In translating one must choose; but in
view of the textual uncertainty I have rendered both possibilities.

This is the third of four fragments that define *sophon* or to *sophon*:
'what is wise'. In XXVII (D. 108) the goal of inquiry is 'to recognize
(*ginōskein*) what is wise, separated from all'. In XXXVI (D. 50) the
same words *sophon esti* appear more inconspicuously: 'it is wise,
listening to the *logos*, to say in agreement (*homologein*) that all
things are one'. In the second case, then, what is *sophon* is proposed
as a norm for human speaking and thinking. By contrast the fourth
occurrence of *sophon* in CXVIII (D. 32) clearly refers to a wisdom
that is unique, divine, and beyond the reach of men. The *sophon* of
XXVII (D. 108) admits, as we saw, both human and cosmic readings.

The 'wise one' of LIV (D. 41) is, I suggest, similarly ambiguous
between the two conceptions of wisdom, human and divine. The
opening words *hen to sophon* emphasize the unitary character of
wisdom, in contrast with *polymathia*, 'the learning of many things',
which Heraclitus holds up as a reproach to his predecessors. This
unique wisdom consists in knowledge or rather in mastery, for that
is the original sense of *epistasthai*: to stand over an activity as 'expert'
or 'the one in charge'.[206] Wisdom here is mastery of a *gnōmē*, a form
of knowledge and a plan of action. The noun *gnōmē* occurs only here
and in LV (D. 78, where Heraclitus denies that human nature can
have or keep such 'insight'). But the cognate verb *ginōskein* is regularly used by Heraclitus for the penetrating form of cognition which
most men lack and which his discourse aims to provide.[207] This cosmic *gnōmē* corresponds to the universal *logos* of I.2 (and cf. XXXVI,
D. 50). The order of the universe is here understood as a work of
cognition and intention, an act of 'steering all things through all'.
The concept of the cosmos thus leads — by an inference that remains
implicit — to the idea of the cosmic god, ordering the regularity of
the sun and stars, the daylight and the seasons, by an act of cosmic
intelligence.[208] The new Zeus of the philosophers, 'the wise one
alone' of CXVIII, is regularly pictured as captain or pilot of the universe. This principle, which Heraclitus elsewhere names 'thunderbolt'
(CXIX, D. 64) or 'luminous Zeus' (XLV, D. 120), is not named in
our fragment; but its role is indicated by the expression *kybernan
panta* 'steering all things'. The cognition and the plan will be that of
the universal helmsman, who knows where his course lies and how to
direct his ship along it (*gnōmē hokē kybernan*).

The parallel to XXXVI (D. 50), where *sophon* is offered as a norm for human understanding, suggests a weaker reading for LIV. The 'wise one' may be the human insight into this cosmic plan (*epistasthai gnōmēn*). The stronger reading emerges only when we give *epistasthai* its full archaic value 'to master', 'have at one's command'. For only the captain is master of the art of steering.

The double reading is reflected in the distribution of the two phrases *sophon esti* and *hen to sophon*. The former applies to human insight in XXXVI, the latter to divine wisdom in CXVIII. When the former appears in XXVII and the latter here in LIV, both senses are admissible.

This symmetry reflects an ambivalence in Heraclitus' conception of humanity and divinity. LV–LVIII show his reluctance to speak of human beings as wise; and in this he anticipates Socrates. But the traditional Greek conception of *sophia*, enshrined in the legends of the 'Seven Wise Men', defined *sophos* as an attribute of men: of poets, craftsmen, statesmen, and moral teachers. Heraclitus himself recognizes this when he speaks mockingly of Homer as 'the wisest (*sophō-teros*) of all the Greeks' (XXII, D. 56), and when he implies that Pythagoras with all his learning had acquired a reputation for wisdom (*sophiē*, in XXV, D. 129). Xenophanes used the term *sophiē* of his own accomplishments (fr. 2, 12 and 14). The four fragments in which *sophon* occurs suggest an attempt on Heraclitus' part to appropriate the term 'wise' to a new use, to designate the goal of his own thinking and his message to men. In this sense Reinhardt was right when he said that 'Heraclitus' principle, what corresponds in his case to the *apeiron* of Anaximander and the *on* ['being'] of Parmenides, is not fire but *to sophon*' (*Parmenides*, p. 205). The ambiguity in this conception of wisdom is deep and essential, and it cannot be resolved by distinguishing two different senses of *sophon*, as some have proposed. The notion of wisdom is so elevated that even the name of Zeus is scarcely appropriate for it; but it is this same notion that Heraclitus wants to claim as his own achievement and to offer as a norm for human thinking in general.

LV

LV (D. 78)   Human nature (*ēthos*) has no set purpose (*gnōmai*), but the divine has.

By translating *gnōmē* as 'set purpose' I have short-circuited the interpretation of LV in order to render the predominant thought. Initially, *gnōmē* here as in LIV must be understood in the ordinary sense of cognition (opinion, judgment) or intention (plan, purpose) — what a person 'has in mind' either as a belief concerning the facts or as an aim for action. The word has overtones of public deliberations, where each orator will speak his 'mind', until one 'opinion' prevails; and so in a legal debate ending in a judicial 'opinion' or verdict. The term also applies to memorable sayings or advice, the 'gnomic' aphorisms of the Wise Men.

It is therefore paradoxical to deny opinions and intentions to human nature — the life of men is largely made of such stuff. The term for human nature or character (*ēthos*), which indicates a pattern of habitual behavior and the corresponding state of mind (as in CXIV, D. 119), gives us no useful clue for resolving the paradox. A better hint is provided by the cosmic connotations of *gnōmē* in LIV; but the plural form here makes it unnatural to limit the term to some privileged insight into the cosmic plan.

The key to understanding LV seems to lie in the stronger reading of *echei* as 'holds on to', 'keeps in control'.[209] The utterance is puzzling only if we take *echei* in the weak sense of 'has', or 'possesses'. Men do in fact have judgments and plans . . . but not for long. New waters flow over them; their grip is relaxed; their nature and their habits cannot retain their thoughts and intentions. Beyond the traditional Greek contrast between divine knowledge and human folly,[210] LV is a comment on the ambiguity of *wisdom* implied in LIV. The character and experience of men, the thoughts and purposes they have in mind, are partial constituents of the cosmic order: their own *gnōmai* can be seen as transient aspects of the supreme *gnōmē* which is the structure of the universe understood as cognition.

LVI–LVIII

LVI (D. 82–3)   Pseudo-Plato, *Hippias Major*: [What Heraclitus says is right, that the most beautiful of apes is ugly in comparison with the race of men . . . Or doesn't Heraclitus, whom you cite, say just this, that the wisest of men seems an ape in comparison to a god, both in wisdom and in beauty and in all the rest?]

LVII (D. 79)   A man is found foolish by a god (*daimōn*) as a child by a man.

LVIII (D. 70)   Iamblichus: [Heraclitus thought that human opinions are toys for children.]

Of these three closely related sayings, only LVII (D. 79) is stylistically recognizable as a literal quotation. LVIII is a late and derivative
echo. The passage from the *Hippias Major* (LVI) is more difficult to
assess. It compares man to an ape rather than a child, and in respect
of beauty as well as wisdom. Since the reference to beauty is motivated by the topic of the dialogue and could in turn have led to the
mention of the ape, some editors regard this not as an independent
citation but an imaginative paraphrase of LVII.[211] But it is at least
equally plausible to read the passage as reflecting a remark quite
different from LVII:

> Doesn't Heraclitus say that the wisest of men is an ape in com-
> parison to god, as the most beautiful ape is ugly in comparison to
> a man?

On this reading both LVI and LVII will have the form of a geometric proportion, which Hermann Fränkel recognized as a characteristic 'thought pattern' in Heraclitus. Both illustrate the formula: as *X*
stands to man (in respect of wisdom or beauty), so man stands to
god.[212] Although no other fragment shows this schematic form,
several similes have implicitly the same structure: as the sleeper is to
the waking man, so the waking man to one who has insight (I.3, etc.);
as the deaf is to a man of ordinary hearing, so the latter to one who
comprehends the *logos* (II, D. 34).[213] As Fränkel suggests, Heraclitus
uses these ratios or analogies in order to project the conception which
is strange to his audience (the divine wisdom, or the human share in
it) by extrapolation from a familiar contrast (child-man, ape-human,
sleeping-waking, deaf-hearing) — while implying that the usual contrast becomes negligible in comparison with the third term: divinity
or the wise (*to sophon*).

The first two words of LVII, *anēr nēpios* 'man (is found) foolish',
can also mean 'man, a child'; and thus they express the complete
thought in advance, compressed in a tight form that the rest of the
sentence will unfold. The third word *ēkouse*, translated 'is found',
means literally 'has heard', that is 'has heard himself called (foolish)',
according to a common idiom. Given the recurrent theme of perceiving or hearing (the *logos*), this idiom is likely to have been chosen
with malice aforethought: in wisdom and capacity for *hearing*, man
is a mere infant. The last phrase of the clause is also double-tongued:
pros daimonos means (1) '(so spoken of) by a god', and also (2) '(a
mere babe) in relation to a god'.

LIX

LIX (D. 104)   What wit (*phrēn*) or understanding (*noos*) do they have? They believe the poets of the people and take the mob as their teacher, not knowing that 'the many are worthless', good men are few.

There may be some specific or local reference here, as in the sarcastic attack on the Ephesians in LXIV (D. 121). But the comparison with XIX (D. 57), where Hesiod was described as 'teacher of most men', suggests Heraclitus has the mass of mankind in view. The slight incoherence in speaking of most men as taking the mob as their teacher is meaningful: they have in effect no leaders, the poets *of the people* (or 'of the peoples', with a curious plural form *dēmōn*) being merely a reflection of popular ignorance. The mob is both teacher and pupil, leader and follower at once.

The term *noos* here recalls the understanding that distinguishes wisdom from mere accumulation of knowledge (XVIII, D. 40), the comprehension of 'what is common to all' (XXX, D. 114). The word *phrēn* 'wit' or 'mind' echoes the theme of 'thinking' (*phronein*) and especially 'sound thinking', 'good sense' (*sō-phronein*).

The final contrast of the many and the few probably looks ahead to the praise of Bias in LXII (D. 39).

LX–LXI

LX (D. 87)   A fool loves to get excited on any account (*or* 'at every word', *logos*).

LXI (D. 97)   Dogs bark at those they do not recognize.

The juxtaposition of these two fragments is intended to suggest a simile or ratio: as dogs react to strangers, so do foolish men to every *logos*. (For the pattern, compare VIII (D. 22) with IX (D. 35): as gold-seekers must dig up a lot of dirt, so lovers of wisdom must wade through a mass of inquiry.) The clue to LXI is given by the term 'recognize' (*ginōskōsi*) with its special sense: the recognition of the *logos*, the cosmic structure.[214] Thus the fool or 'stupid human being' (*blax anthrōpos*) in LX stands for men generally in their incapacity to comprehend. The expressive term *blax* seems to have meant 'dull' or 'sluggish', as well as 'fool' or 'imbecile'. (In the form *vlakas*, with the general flavor of 'you idiot', it remains a popular term of abuse in Modern Greek.) There may be a pointed contrast between the sluggishness of human nature and the ease (literally, the desire: *philei*) with which it is aroused. It is because men in general are asleep on their feet that they become so suddenly alarmed by the challenge of a *logos*. The verb rendered 'get excited', *eptoēsthai*, literally 'set aflutter', can mean either 'terrified, dismayed', or 'agitated, aroused'; both senses are apt.

I assume a play on *logos*: (1) word, statement ('whatever you say to these fools, they lose their heads!'), and (2) the specifically Heraclitean *logos* that involves measure or ratio, as in the pattern illustrated by LX—LXI and more schematically by LVII (D. 79). Such a ratio is a small-scale exemplification of the cosmic measures 'according to which all things come to pass'. Thus the fool who gets excited or alarmed over every bit of news, is (like the dog who barks at a strange face) a figure for the man who comprehends neither Heraclitus' discourse nor the cosmic pattern it reflects, but will be roused to some inappropriate response — alarm, disgust, or sheer irritation — by his own failure to recognize what he is confronted with.

LXII

LXII (D. 39)   In Priene lived Bias son of Teutames, who is of more account (*logos*) than the rest.

Here again there must be a play on *logos*. The surface meaning is 'esteem' or 'renown'. But Heraclitus seems to have shown his own esteem for Bias by quoting his famous *logos* or saying (above, LIX, D. 104): the fame of the sage is inseparable from that of his 'word'. It is possible that here, as in LXI, we are expected to recall the deeper sense of *logos* as well. The word play will then contain some hint of the cosmic pattern expressed in geometric proportions — for there is after all only *one* order. And on what term could one play more meaningfully than on *logos* itself, the word for language and for cosmic structure?

In pursuing this clue, we can start from the fact that Bias is regarded with exceptional favor; as Diogenes says in quoting LXII, 'even Heraclitus who was so hard to please praised him particularly' (I.88). Bias was a leading citizen of the Ionian city of Priene (not far from Ephesus), who lived a generation or two before Heraclitus. The justice of Priene, represented by Bias, was proverbial in his own lifetime.[215] Herodotus praises him for the good advice he gave to the Ionians after their conquest by Cyrus: to combine forces and settle in the west, in Sardinia (I.170.1). As the popular legend of the Seven Wise Men took shape, Bias was one of the four (with Thales, Solon, and Pittacus) whose names appeared on all the different lists. Among the sayings associated with his name, Aristotle quotes the celebrated line 'power will reveal the man' (*archē andra deixei*), and the cautious counsel 'love your friends as if they are to become your enemies, and hate your enemies as if they are to become your friends'.[216] The view underlying both these sayings is expressed in the aphorism Diogenes ascribes to him: 'most men are worthless (or 'vile', *kakoi*)'.[217]

If it is indeed this saying that is quoted in LIX and alluded to here, it is natural to connect Heraclitus' high regard for Bias with the judgment there expressed. No doubt Heraclitus shared Bias' harsh judgment of the common run of men. The sharpest statement of this is XCVII (D. 29), where we find something more than an aristocrat's contempt for the mob. While the many 'sate themselves like cattle', the saving grace of the excellent few is precisely their choice of ever-living glory, 'one thing in exchange for all'. (Cf. XL, D. 90, and the parallels cited above, p. 000.) The opposition in LXII between the single individual Bias, who by his justice and wisdom merited an esteem (*logos*) so much greater than the rest as to appear semi-divine, and the mass of mankind as characterized in his saying (*logos*) — this antithesis exemplifies in human terms that proportion (*logos*) between the one and the many, between fire and all the rest, that structures the order of the universe.

And in fact Bias achieved, in the most literal sense, 'ever-renewed fame among mortals' (*kleos aenaon thnētōn*), according to the terms of XCVII (D. 29). Not only was he widely remembered as wise judge and councillor, but his city dedicated a shrine in his honor, the Teutameion, making him the object of a hero cult after his death.[218] The fact that the shrine bore the name of his father may account for the emphatic position of the patronymic in the center of LXII. (Contrast the absence of a patronymic in the favorable reference to Hermodorus in LXIV, D. 121.)

LXIII

LXIII (D. 49)   One (man) is ten thousand, if he is the best.

The opposition suggested in LXII is expressed here in numerical terms. In Greek 'ten thousand' (*myrioi*) is regularly used to mean 'countless', 'innumerable'.

As Bollack-Wismann have pointed out, of the two citations that
preserve the essential clause 'if he is best', neither one includes the
personal reference 'for me'. (See texts 98 (a) and (c) in Marcovich,
pp. 515f.) The alternative form 'one is ten thousand for me' was
proverbial by Cicero's time and came to be assigned to Heraclitus.
(Marcovich texts 98 (b), (e) and (e¹).) Modern editors have been ill-
advised to combine the two versions in a composite text that is not
represented in any ancient source. The result is not only methodo-
logically unsound; it trivializes the thought of LXIII by expressing
the cosmic ratio as a personal opinion.

LXIV

LXIV (D. 121)   What the Ephesians deserve is to be hanged to the last man,
every one of them, and leave the city to the boys, since they drove out their best
man, Hermodorus, saying 'Let no one be the best among us; if he is, let him be so
elsewhere and among others.'

Nothing more is actually known of Hermodorus. It is natural to
assume (as later authors do) that Heraclitus is referring to a contemporary event. Strabo, Pliny, and the jurist Pomponius report that
after his exile Hermodorus went to Rome to help the decemvirs com-
pose (or interpret) the Twelve Tables, the fundamental document of
early Roman law. Pliny even says there was a public statue dedicated
to him in the forum. Although it may explain the statue, the story
itself is not credible: the Twelve Tables were not published until 449
B.C., which is a generation too late for a contemporary of Heraclitus.
But the legend shows that LXIV was well known in Rome; it is quoted
in Latin by Cicero.[219]
    Hermodorus and Bias are the only two persons mentioned by
Heraclitus with praise; although their destinies were different, their
qualities must have been similar in his eyes. The shame of the
Ephesians is just that they, unlike the men of Priene, were unable to
profit from their most profitable citizen. The rare word *onēistos*
'best', which here occurs twice, is cognate with the verb *oninēmi* 'to
profit or benefit (someone)'; it must have been chosen to bring out
the irrational character of the Ephesians' action. They are deliberately
doing harm to themselves by depriving their city of its most valuable
asset.[220] And Heraclitus' formulation of this point is even more
subtle: if the Ephesians applied their principle recursively ('let no
one of us be the best'), they would end by expelling every citizen to

the last man, and thus deliberately give themselves 'what they deserve'.

The motive which Heraclitus attributes to his fellow citizens is a paradigm of human folly, for the principle they appeal to — let no one among us be the *one* who excels — is a rejection of the cosmic proportion that balances one thing (fire, gold, everlasting glory) against everything else. The egalitarian hostility towards unique excellence is more than a political mistake: it ignores the role which unity plays in the structure of the world as in the safety of the city. In the polis this principle of intelligent unity (*hen to sophon*) is represented both by the 'shared' order of the law (in XXX, D. 114, and LXV, D. 44), and by the human capacity to grasp the common interest and enforce the requirements of justice. Heraclitus' political tastes were no doubt conservative, but that is not the issue here. What he depicts is the self-destructive action of a community that rejects the leadership of its ablest citizens.[221]

This long sentence is structured by antithesis and implicit proportionality. The basic contrast between *one* man who has been driven out (despite his merits), and *all* who are left (and who, if they got what they deserve, would all hang) is reinforced by the suggestion that it is they who ought 'to leave the city'. The secondary contrast opposes the *useful* man to those whose action is self-destructive. Their *uselessness* is expressed by a familiar proportion in a new form: as citizens the grown men of Ephesus are even worse than boys!

LXV–LXVI

LXV (D. 44)   The people (*dēmos*) must fight for the law as for their city wall.

LXVI (D. 33)   It is law also to obey the counsel (*boulē*) of one.

These two references to the law (*nomos*) echo the thought of XXX (D. 114): the dependence of human laws on a 'divine one'. In CIV (D. 43) Heraclitus will compare violence or lawlessness (*hybris*) to a house on fire. In LXV the image of the defenders on the city wall defines the same threat, the need for law as a basis for civic life and the only protection of the weak against the strong. In emphasizing the rational necessity (*chrē*) *for the common people* (*dēmos*) to preserve the law, Heraclitus appeals not to divine sanction or traditional obligations but to a recognition of their own vital interests.

We know nothing of the precise political situation in Ephesus, per-

haps under moderate democracy established by the Persians immediately after the disastrous Ionian revolt of 499—494 B.C.[222] But we
can understand the ideological background in terms of Solon's
analysis of a political crisis in Athens about a century earlier:

Thus the public evil comes home to every man,
The gates of his courtyard will no longer hold it out,
It leaps over the high wall and finds him in every case,
Even if he flees inside, to hide in the nook of his chamber.
These things does my heart bid me to teach the Athenians,
How the greatest evils to the city are the gift of Lawlessness
    (*Dysnomiē*);
While Lawfulness (*Eunomiē*) makes everything orderly and right,
And she frequently fetters the feet of those who are unjust.
Lawfulness smoothes what is rough, puts a stop to excess (*koros*)
    and makes dim the deed of violence (*hybris*).
It withers the flowers that bloom from disaster and folly (*atē*).
It makes crooked judgments (*dikai*) straight, and humbles the
    work of arrogant pride.
And it puts an end to acts of civil strife. (fr. 3.26—37 Diehl)

Heraclitus must have approved of the political principles of Solon, his
emphasis on the rule of law and his conception of social justice as a
measure (*metron*) or balance between unequal parties. The conflict
between the rich and the poor, of the sort that Solon confronted, is
probably alluded to in Heraclitus' antithesis of 'satiety' or excess
(*koros*) and 'need' (*chresmosynē* in CXX, D. 65) or 'hunger' (*limos*
in LXVII, D. 111).[223] Solon's image of the public disaster that leaps
over the walls of a man's house to seek him out in the privacy of his
bedroom illustrates perfectly (and probably influenced) Heraclitus'
conception of the law which is 'common to all' and whose preservation
is as vital as the city wall which protects the inhabitants from pillage
and massacre.

Heraclitus goes beyond Solon in grounding this interest in law and
civic concord upon a cosmic basis in 'the divine one'. And this reliance
upon the one leads Heraclitus to emphasize the role of the outstanding individual in a way that is not theoretically articulated in Solon's
political poetry, but exemplified in his career as statesman and lawgiver. Heraclitus has, in effect, expanded Solon's political theory to
include Solon's own practice of enlightened leadership, which is here
articulated as a principle of universal unity. His reminder that it is
also law 'to obey the counsel (*boulē*) of one' is an echo of the 'wise
one' of LIV (D. 41), where the term *boulē* ('plan, advice') here is

paralleled by the *gnōmē* ('insight, judgment') that controls the cosmos. The most familiar of all the overtones of the phrase 'the *boulē* of one' is 'the plan of Zeus' (*Dios boulē*) announced in the proem to the *Iliad*, the plan and power of the supreme deity that dominates the entire epic.[224]

Several features of LXVI (D. 33) call for comment. *Boulē* here may signify (1) deliberation and (2) the council, as a constitutional body exercising some executive power, both in oligarchies and in democracies. Perhaps the thought is as follows. It is law to obey the Boule, the city council. But the role of the Boule is to deliberate, to make intelligent plans for the interests of the community. If such wise counsel (*boulē*) is offered by a single man, it is no less the expression of what is common and lawful.

The final word *henos* 'of one' presents the grammatical ambiguity that is Heraclitus' stylistic signature. If this form is construed as masculine, the phrase means 'the advice of one man'; taken as neuter, it gives us 'the plan of one (principle)'. The political application presupposes the former reading, the cosmic allusion the latter. The sentence can thus be read as an elliptical résumé of Heraclitus' political theory: law is what is common (XXX, LXV); what is common is thinking (XXXI); sound thinking is wisdom (XXXII); wisdom is the one (CXVIII) and the recognition of the cosmic plan (LIV). Hence it is law to follow this unified plan, even when it is represented by the wisdom of a single man.

LXVII

LXVII (D. 110–11) It is not better for human beings to get all they want. It is disease that has made health sweet and good, hunger satiety, weariness rest.

These two sentences provide the point of connection between what has been called Heraclitus' 'ethics', that is to say his view of human folly and wisdom, and the doctrine of opposites which is generally recognized as his central thought. I shall first argue that the two sentences are to be read together.[225]

There is a familiar rhetorical device in early Greek poetry and prose, strangely dubbed a 'Priamel', which is illustrated in a poem of Sappho that begins 'some say a troop of cavalry is the fairest thing, some say foot-soldiers, others a fleet of ships . . . but I say it is whatever one loves' (fr. 16 Lobel-Page). One of the best known examples of this scheme is an elegiac couplet cited by Aristotle as the Delian inscription:[226]

The fairest is what is most just, the best of all is health;

But the sweetest thing of all is to obtain what one loves (*erai*).

Aristotle tells us these verses were inscribed in the propylaeum to the shrine of Leto in Delos; they thus formed a kind of Ionian sister to the inscription 'Know thyself' at the entrance to Apollo's temple in Delphi. The same couplet is preserved, almost in the same words, in the verses of Theognis (255f.). A prose version of the second verse is also found among the sayings ascribed to Thales: 'The sweetest thing is to obtain what you desire (*epithymeis*).'[227] Whether Heraclitus knew this sentiment as a saying of Thales or, more likely, as an inscription at Delos, the first sentence of LXVII seems intended precisely as a denial of this familiar adage: 'It is *not* better for men to get whatever they want.' Now the traditional formula contains the word 'sweetest' (*hēdiston* or, in Theognis, *terpnotaton*). And this thought is continued in Heraclitus' second sentence: 'It is disease that has made health *sweet* and good.' Hence it is only when the two sentences are taken as a unit that their polemical reference to the conventional word of wisdom is fully expressed.

The three pairs of opposites, each consisting of one positive term (health, satiety, rest) and one negative (disease, hunger, weariness), are thus introduced in a denial that what is good (or 'better') for human beings is getting what they want. The three pairs illustrate a common pattern of strong contrast between positive and negative terms, with some kind of causal dependency of the former on the latter. In each case it is opposition that is obvious, while reflection is required to perceive the causal link that explains why it is not better for human beings to get everything they desire.

In rejecting the traditional aphorism Heraclitus points to a unity which conventional wisdom ignores. What passes for wisdom is a form of folly deeply grounded in the structure of desire itself. The negative experiences of disease, weariness, and hunger are necessary conditions for the enjoyment of health, rest, and satiety. The first pair of contraries differs from the other two in that disease is not a physical pre-condition for health in the way that exertion and hunger are directly required for resting and satisfying one's appetite. But it is only the contrast with sickness that permits us to recognize health as something 'sweet and good'. Thus it would not be better, it would not even be good, for human beings to get all they want. The structure of desire is irrational in that it is potentially self-destructive; if we got everything we desired, nothing would be desirable. Just as the wish for an end to strife would, if fulfilled, destroy the cosmic order that depends upon opposition (LXXXI, D. A22), so the wish that all human desires be satisfied would, if fulfilled, destroy the order of human life by eliminating desire and depriving us of our conception of what is good and precious.[228]

According to the insight of LXVII human desire is inevitably imprisoned within the structure of opposition. The opposites appear as limitations on the human condition, natural deficiencies in the human point of view. (Hence the opening word is *anthrōpois*: 'for human beings'.) From this irrationality there is no escape except through wisdom: dominating what is unreasonable by comprehending it in a larger unity. And the first step is to recognize the positive contribution made by the negative term in the link that unites them. For then these oppositions can be seen for what they are, as a mirror of the universal pattern manifest in the alternate kindling and quenching of cosmic fire. So the unity in opposition is not only the constitutive feature of our mode of being as human animals, where need and gratification, hope and fear, joy and grief are bound together. A similar structure will recur at other levels: to link (by antithesis) human experience to that of different animals (LXX–LXXII), to link the fate of mortals to that of immortals (XCII, D. 62), and to link cosmic powers to one another (as in the unity of night and day, XIX, D. 57).

LXVIII

LXVIII (D. 102)   Scholia to *Iliad*: [Heraclitus says that for god all things are fair and good and just, but men have taken some things as unjust, others as just.]

As Bywater recognized, and Wilamowitz and others have pointed out since, the wording here is that of some anonymous Homeric commentator, perhaps a Stoic, and we cannot know how well it reflects what Heraclitus said.[229] The second clause can be seen as an extension of the thought of LXVII to the moral distinctions between just and unjust, right and wrong. Heraclitus cannot have meant, as the scholiast's wording might suggest, that the distinction is man-made in the sense of being arbitrary or groundless. This is excluded by the doctrine of XXX (D. 114) that human laws and moral codes (*nomoi*) are the expression of cosmic order. The authentically Heraclitean thought (known from LXIX, and imperfectly expressed in the present text) is that men cannot define justice except by specifying its violation: the city determines what is just by making laws that prohibit and punish actions recognized as unjust. The conceptual point is a general one. As Socrates (or Plato) said, the knowledge of opposites is one and the same. But justice is a peculiarly 'negative virtue' in that instances of injustice are more striking.

Less clear is the statement that such moral distinctions are cancelled or non-existent from the divine point of view. It is difficult to extract from this a thought that is uncontaminated by Platonic or Stoic conceptions of providence and universal harmony. But we do know that Heraclitus conceived of a hidden fitting-together of opposites in which conflict and justice would coincide (LXXVIII–LXXXII). It is only in this perspective that he could have asserted that 'for god all things are fair and good and just'. It is not that the human distinctions cease to have validity – for the only validity they ever had was validity *for men*. The distinction between rest and weariness will not disappear from the point of view of divine wisdom; wisdom will recognize this distinction for what it is: an essential feature of the human condition.[230] And the same must be true for the distinction between right and wrong. Its validity for human society is not in question. But this antithesis, like any other, is contained within a total order that is itself designated as just – and then the term 'just' is used in such a way that nothing can actually be unjust. Notice that there is still some *meaning* attached to the term 'unjust' at the level of cosmic order, although here the term has no true application. The violation of justice in this sense would have to be, *per impossibile*, the violation of the world order, as in the contrary to-fact hypothesis of the sun diverging from his ordained path. Even for a god *this* would not be just and fair and good!

We must separate two questions that are confounded in the wording of LXVIII: (1) the general question whether it is valid and necessary for men in society to distinguish between right and wrong, to have *some* moral or legal code, and (2) the specific question whether in any given society (sixth-century Ephesus, or twentieth-century America) this distinction is correctly drawn. Heraclitus' doctrine of opposites is properly concerned only with the former question: *all* human laws are nourished by the divine (XXX, D. 114). But from a recognition that some established and generally respected system of *nomos* or 'law' is required for any society to survive, it is possible to argue that whatever distinctions are in fact recognized ought to be respected. This conservative reasoning (which is roughly that of Protagoras and Herodotus, and later of Hobbes) may have tempted

Heraclitus. But it is not clear that he yielded to it in his defense of *nomos*. In questions of religious cult and belief he was anything but a conservative.

LXIX

LXIX (D. 23)   If it were not for these things, they would not have known the name of Justice (*Dikē*).

'They' here are human beings generally and Greeks in particular (since the fragment plays upon the sense of *dikē* in Greek). 'These things' probably refer to acts of injustice (*adikia*), violations of the law, with their resulting penalties and punishment.[231] Heraclitus seems to be alluding to the old, but not obsolete use of *dikē* for the decision or 'indication' of a judge.[232] The *dikē* may be either (1) the decision itself, characterized as 'straight' or 'crooked' if the judge is thought to have 'pointed' in the right direction or deviated from the true course of judgment, or (2) the punishment or compensation decided upon, as in the phrase *didonai dikēn* 'to pay the penalty', literally 'to give what was indicated (as compensation)'. And *dikē* also comes to be used (3) for the lawsuit or the trial itself. Thus the word properly designates 'justice' as the principle for settling legal disputes, the principle personified by Hesiod as daughter of Zeus, who watches over lawsuits and reports to her father when the ruling princes 'judge crooked sentences (*dikas*)' (*Works and Days* 256–64; cf. 219–24). Although the term also comes to mean lawful conduct and the virtue of justice, the original connections with lawcourts and punishment remain prominent. So when *Dikē* is invoked as guarantor of the sun's course in XLIV (D. 94), the point is that the sun would be found out and punished if he were to transgress his lawful measures.

The thought of LXIX seems then to be the conceptual dependence of justice upon the existence of injustice and legal disputes. But the thought is expressed not in terms of concepts but in terms of the name by which Justice is known. If there were no judgments and penalties, men could not know or understand the word *dikē* that denotes them. But then they would not know the name of Justice.

LXX–LXXII

LXX (D. 61)   The sea is the purest and foulest water: for fishes drinkable and life-sustaining; for men undrinkable and deadly.

LXXI (D. 9)   Aristotle: [As Heraclitus says, 'Asses prefer garbage (*syrmata*, sweepings? chaff?) to gold.']

LXXII (D. 13 and 37)   Clement and Columella: [Heraclitus says that 'swine delight in mire rather than clean water'; chickens bathe in dust.]

These three fragments, only the first of which is preserved in Heraclitus' own words, contrast the needs or preferences of mankind with those of another species: fishes, donkeys, pigs, perhaps also chickens and cows.[233] The relationship between opposites here thus differs from that in LXVII–LXIX, where the terms (health-sickness, justice-injustice, and the like) were both defined within the framework of human experience. Here the human point of view is restricted to one member of an opposing pair. (The reference to men is explicit in LXX, implicit in the other two.)

We may safely reject the moralizing interpretation of LXXI and LXXII, which construes the inter-species comparison as a rhetorical device for assimilating the preferences of most men to the taste of asses and pigs.[234] This moral judgment is expressed in XCVII (D. 29), where two forms of *human* life are contrasted, one of which is compared to that of beasts. But the striking element in LXXI and LXXII is precisely the concrete description of animal behavior. There is an old and fairly constant tradition which utilizes such descriptions to make a point about inter-species relativism. The most elaborate statement is that which Plato puts in the mouth of Protagoras.

I know many things which are unprofitable to human beings, both food and drink and medicine and much more, and others which are profitable. And some which are neither profitable nor unprofitable to human beings, but to horses; and some to oxen only; others to dogs. But some are good for none of these, but for trees. And some are good for the roots of trees, but bad for the buds, like manure . . . Thus olive oil is very bad for all plants and quite inimical to the hair of all animals except man, but it is an aid to human hair and to the whole body. So complex and varied is the good, that even in this case what is good for the external use of the human body is quite bad for internal use. And hence all doctors forbid sick persons to take olive oil in their food, except in very slight quantities. (*Protagoras* 334A–C)

This is a Platonic development of the thought expressed in LXX. There are echoes both in an early and in a late treatise of the Hippocratic Corpus.[235] Finally, a sceptic like Sextus will include both the Heraclitean examples of sea water (LXX) and pigs bathing in the mire

(LXXII) and Plato's point about olive oil among the standard arguments for suspending judgment. The argument is designed to show that 'the same objects do not produce the same impressions (*phantasiai*) because of the difference between animals'.[236] Sextus' point is that 'we can say how the object is regarded by us, but not how it is in nature', since we cannot sit in judgment between our own impressions and those of the other animals (I.59).

Thus Sextus finds the same thought in LXXII as in LXX. And this inter-species comparison is also the point of LXXI according to Aristotle, our only source in this case: 'The pleasure of a horse and a dog is different from that of a man.'

I assume, then, that we may treat LXX—LXXII as a group, though it is only in the first instance that we have the assurance of an authentic text.

The thought of LXX is built upon an observation so familiar as to escape ordinary notice. Despite the necessity for human life of an adequate supply of water, the most conspicuous form of water for those who inhabit a coastal town, namely the sea, is not only useless for this purpose but actually dangerous. For other forms of life, however, the sea is not a threat but a home; for them, sea water is truly water, the element of life.

Thus we are both right and wrong to perceive the sea as water. For it is water in physical or cosmic terms. (Cf. XXXVIII—XXXIX, D. 31.) But it cannot *function* as water for the vital needs of men. This is a limitation on human nature, however, not a defect of the sea. Its virtue as water is manifest in the life of fishes.

This thought is articulated by three pairs of contrasting adjectives, each with its own resonance. The physiological contrast between man and fish is mentioned in second place, as comment on the first pair of terms, more suggestive and more obscure: the sea is 'water, purest and foulest'. The meaning of this initial opposition cannot be restricted to the physiological contrast that follows: the first pair of opposites is not subordinated to the contrast between men and fishes. There is an exclusively human dimension in which the sea is both pure and foul. It serves in certain rites of purification as the universal cleanser (as in *Iliad* 1.314f.); but it is defiled or polluted (*miaros*) by all the garbage of harbor and ships, by excrement and carcasses of man and beast. This contrast (and union) of the clean and the foul, the pure and the polluted, is recalled in the reference to swine in LXXII, for whom mire is better than clean (*katharos*) water, and in the comparison of purification by blood to washing with mud in CXVII (D. 5).

The contrast between men and fish is expressed in the third pair of adjectives as an opposition between life and death: the sea is both preserver (*sōtērion*) and destroyer (*olethrion*). Beyond the basic opposition of drinkable-undrinkable, Heraclitus thus hints at a broader antithesis: the sea, so necessary for the life of fish, is a constant threat and often a tomb for men who sail upon it.

There were probably similar overtones in the original text of LXXI and LXXII. Thus the pure-impure contrast is alluded to in LXXII; in LXXI the mention of gold may have been intended to invoke its symbolic value (cf. VIII, D. 22 and XL, D. 90); just as the word for 'garbage' or 'sweepings' (*syrmata*) may be echoed in the description of the cosmos as a heap of sweepings (*sarma*) in CXXV (D. 124). Without a full and literal text, however, it would be idle to pursue such hints.

In LXXI and LXXII the contrast is a matter of natural preference or pleasure (pigs in mud, asses in garbage or the like), whereas in LXX it is a question of life and death.[237] But in all three cases we have the opposition between a negative and a positive term: an object of pursuit (*haireton*) and one of avoidance (*pheukton*). And the point in each case is that what has negative value for human beings (sea water, mud, garbage) is a positive term of desire, delight, or vitality for another kind of creature. There is surely something here about the underlying unity of opposites, but the thought is not so vague, naive, or confused as it is often made to appear.[238] There is no reason to make Heraclitus conclude that life and death are the same because the sea can be source of both, or that delight and disgust are identical because both reactions might be provoked by the same object in different subjects. The trivial reading of Heraclitus' doctrine here is that there is no accounting for tastes. The fallacious reading is that because one man's meat is another man's poison there is no difference between meat and poison. The confused reading is that all things are inherently contradictory.[239] If we wish to ascribe an intelligent doctrine to Heraclitus in some coherent connection with LXVII–LXIX, these texts provide the basis for a valid generalization: in an opposed pair the negative term, as defined by human needs and desires, is never wholly negative. Just as in LXVII–LXIX a term like hunger was noted as a necessary condition or point of contrast for the positive experience of satiety, so here the negative term for human beings is revealed as a positive term for another form of life.

It is this positive interpretation of the principle of negativity that has made the thought of Heraclitus so congenial to Hegel and his followers. For there is indeed something like an anticipation of Hegelian dialectic in Heraclitus' treatment of the opposites. In the examples just considered, this dialectic of opposites is focussed on the partiality of the human perspective. (See the great summary statement in CXXIV, D. 10: 'graspings: wholes and not wholes'.) It is not that we are mistaken in preferring sweet drinking water and clean baths, any more than we are wrong to prefer health to sickness and satiety to hunger. But the doctrine of opposites is, among other things, an attempt to attain a larger vision by recognizing the life-enhancing function of the negative term, and hence comprehending the positive value of the antithesis itself.

LXXIII

LXXIII (D. 58) Doctors who cut and burn [and torture their patients in every way] complain that they do not receive the reward they deserve [from the patients], acting as they do.[240]

Despite the textual uncertainty, this sentence clearly points to the positive or beneficial aspects of something generally perceived as negative and destructive. In a phrase that seems to have become pro-verbial, Heraclitus refers to the paradoxical harm-for-the-sake-of-benefit exemplified in the fearsome medical practice of cutting and cautery: *temnein kai kaiein*, 'the twin horrors of pre-anaesthetic sur-gery'.[241] The primary point is that doctors do (or at least seek to do) *good* to their patients by inflicting what is in an obvious sense grave damage or harm. Such suffering, normally regarded as an evil to be avoided (*pheukton*), is accepted by sick men as a benefit (*haireton*). Both positive and negative terms are here defined by reference to human needs and experience, as in LXVII–LXIX. But the 'unity of opposites' (that is, the positive value of the negative term) is seen from a new point of view. There is an implicit contrast between what is beneficial for the healthy man and what is beneficial for the sick, and hence a structural parallel to the inter-species comparisons of LXX–LXXII.

What is perplexing, and obscured by textual difficulties, is Hera-clitus' reference to the doctors' reward. On one reading, doctors demand a fee when in fact they deserve nothing. This version ascribes the negative evaluation of surgery to Heraclitus himself, which is un-likely on philosophical grounds. The reading accepted here makes the doctors complain that they do not get the fee they deserve. This is better attested in the tradition (as Kirk has shown), and gives an excellent sense. The patients, suffering the torments of the damned at the hands of their 'benefactors', are unwilling to pay the exorbitant fee requested. The doctors are unsatisfied with what they get, and insist upon the high value of their services. This 'strife' between doctors and patients neatly reflects the opposition between harm and benefit inherent in such cures.

The worst puzzle is the last phrase in the Greek text: *ta agatha kai tas nosous* 'the good [consequences] and the diseases'. I follow Kirk in regarding this as a corrupt gloss.[242] Ending LXXIII with the emphatic phrase 'acting as they do' (*tauta ergazomenoi*) leaves it suspended between the neutral comment 'they claim high fees for what they do' and the malicious one: 'they have the cheek to claim such fees for torturing their patients!'.

LXXIV

LXXIV (D. 59)   The path of the carding wheels is straight and crooked.

This text of LXXIV is in doubt, and its interpretation has been the subject of controversy quite out of proportion to the philosophical issues at stake.

The first problem is to identify the instrument Heraclitus is referring to, and to see in what sense its path is both straight and crooked (or twisted, *skoliē*). The word for the instrument or for its user, translated here as 'carding wheels', seems to be corrupt in the manuscripts and has been emended in two or three different ways.[243]

Such textual diversity shows how uncertain any interpretation must be. I follow Marcovich in assuming some reference here to a circular carding instrument set with thorns or spikes, for Herodotus tells us that such an instrument was used by Croesus for inflicting a painful death.[244] Since the torture instrument is referred to by the name from carding (*knaphos*), it must have been related to some equipment used in the operation by which hairs of raw wool, after an initial washing, are combed, disentangled, and regularized so that they are ready for spinning into thread. Carding proper (*knaptein*) in the sense assumed here is a more elaborate alternative to the process of combing the wool by hand (*xainein*).[245]

The ancient sources speak of thorns, spines or spikes (*akanthai*) set in a circular roller (*gnaphos* or *knaphos*); and the passage in Herodotus suggests an instrument large and strong enough for a man

to be broken on, as on the rack. We do not know the form of the
ancient instrument. I shall describe instead a modern instrument
which serves the same purpose and illustrates Heraclitus' point rather
vividly. This is a machine now used for carding in Andritsaina, a
mountain village of the western Peloponnese. Today its frame is made
of steel and it is driven by electricity; but perhaps the principle is
simple enough to reproduce the general practice of antiquity. The
striking feature of this contemporary carding machine is that it consists of a fixed half-drum, roughly semicircular in shape, around
which are set a number of movable rollers, of two alternating sizes,
each of which is furnished with metal spikes or teeth. (Note that
Marcovich's text restores *gnaphōn* in the plural for paleographical
reasons; but the plural form requires some explanation.) The rough
wool is fed into the machine at one end of the drum and, as the
rollers turn, it passes under a large roller and then over a small one,
and then again under the next large one, and so on over and under
the wheels until it emerges fully combed at the other end of the
drum. There is a direct, intuitive sense in which the path of the wool
through this machine is both straight and crooked: its mean course
around the drum is a smooth curve, like a semi-circle, but its actual
path is continually up and down, over and under the successive rollers,
in a serpentine or zig-zag movement.

It would be foolish to claim that this modern machine is a replica
of the instrument Heraclitus had in mind. But his carding wheels
might have worked in this way, turned by hand, perhaps, or by water
power like a mill.[246] I cannot imagine a simpler machine that would
both fit the ancient texts and illustrate Heraclitus' point. In any case,
our machine requires no fancy screw or *cochlias* (as Hippolytus
assumes in his citation of LXXIV, probably on the basis of some
more sophisticated device for pressing cloth rather than carding). All
that is needed is a source of rotary motion, as in a mill for grinding
grain. Whether driven by water power or by hand, it would not
require much adjustment to transform this equipment into a fearful
instrument of torture — though the man would of course be dragged
over the rollers and not, like the wool, between them.

Assuming some such literal sense for LXXIV, what is its philosophic point? The text is cited by Hippolytus following LXXIII (D.
58) which (on his interpretation) shows that good and evil or medical
treatment and disease come to the same thing; and he next cites CIII
(D. 60): 'The way up and down, one and the same.' The term *hodos*,
'way' or 'path', occurs both in LXXIV and in CIII.[247] Modern

interpreters have taken this as one more example of how 'what are conventionally counted as irreconcilable opposites are found to inhere at one and the same moment in the same activity', or in the same object.[248] Such an attribution of contrary predicates to the same subject led some to suppose that Heraclitus had, in effect, intended to deny the principle of contradiction.[249] Strictly speaking, he cannot have done so, since the principle itself was not formulated before the poem of Parmenides, and then only indirectly; the first explicit formulation (in terms of the incompatibility of contraries) is in Plato's *Republic*. But that is not the point in any case. Of course it is no contradiction to assert that the path of wool through the carding machine (whatever its exact construction) is straight in one respect but crooked in another. But that is also not a very interesting proof that these opposites are 'one and the same'. What it shows is that they are essentially *connected* — within the structure of a unified, purposeful activity.[250] In my model, the straightening of the fibres is ingeniously effected by a circuitous course of the machine. (And this will be true for any carding process that justifies the description as 'straight and crooked'.) In this perspective, the unity of the opposites is their necessary co-presence as cause and effect within a single intelligent activity. And this process is motivated by the contrast between the initially twisted and finally straight condition of the fibres.

So interpreted, the figure of the carding instrument points to a different aspect of the doctrine of opposites, illustrated by the drawn bow in LXXVIII (D. 51): the functional unity of opposing tendencies within a purposeful human activity. But the occurrence here of the word 'path' (*hodos*), echoed in CIII (D. 60) for the 'way up and down', may also point to a larger unity of opposites within the process of cosmic change.

In this generalized version of the doctrine illustrated by the archer's bow and the process of carding, the positive-negative contrast seems to be lost from view. In fact, it will be represented in LXXVIII by the pairing of the bow and the lyre, as here by the contrast between twisted and straightened wool. Furthermore the positive-negative opposition is directly preserved by the connotations of the terms 'straight' (*euthus*, Ionic *ithus*) and 'crooked' (*skolios*). We have seen these as opposed characterizations of *dikē*, the judgment rendered by a prince or law court. But *dikē* suggests punishment, and that idea may be in the background here if Heraclitus was familiar with the carding wheel as an instrument of torture used by his Lydian neigh-

bors, the former rulers of Ephesus. At the most allusive but also
most meaningful level, this brief text can be understood as a comment
on the order of nature and the course of human life. Irrational, cruel,
and needlessly destructive as it often appears, this 'twisted' course of
events is pilotted according to a wise pattern that is — like the course
of the elements and the seasonal variations in the sun's path — ultimately to be seen as 'straight' and just.

LXXV

LXXV (D. 8)   Aristotle: [Heraclitus says 'the counter-thrust brings together',
and from tones at variance comes the finest attunement (*harmonia*), and 'all
things come to pass through conflict'.]

There is now general agreement that (as Bywater had already supposed) this text is a reminiscence rather than a direct quotation. But
Aristotle's memory was a remarkable one, and the last clause ('all
things come to pass according to strife') is a literal, though partial,
citation of LXXXII (D. 80). Similarly the first clause, though not
elsewhere attested, seems to be a faithful reflection of something in
Heraclitus' text, as the presence of the Ionic word *antixoun* indicates.
(So rightly Kirk, p. 220.) It is only the second clause, 'from notes at
variance (i.e. differing and quarreling, *diapherontōn*) comes the finest
harmonia', whose accuracy is subject to doubt. Recent authors,
beginning with Gigon, have assumed that this is a paraphrase of
LXXVIII (D. 51); and Marcovich (p. 124) has plausibly suggested that
Aristotle was influenced here by the memory of a Platonic phrase,
offered (at *Symposium* 187A) as an exegesis of LXXVIII: 'from high
and low notes that were previously at variance . . . when they later
come to an agreement, a *harmonia* is produced'.
     That leaves us with the initial antithesis, *antixoun sympheron*, as a
possible quotation not otherwise preserved. My rendering suggests
the literal image: pressure in the opposite direction has the paradoxical
effect of bringing things together, as in the case of the bow, where
the movement of the hands apart brings the two ends of the bow
closer to one another. This thought recurs in the pairing of 'convergent, divergent' (*sympheromenon diapheromenon*) in CXXIV (D. 10).
But the two terms also have a figurative sense: 'the hindrance is a
benefit', 'opposition is profitable'. This gives an explicit statement of
the thought implicit in LXVII—LXXIV: in the perspective of wisdom,
the negative term will always have a positive value.

LXXVI–LXXVII

LXXVI (D. 11)   All beasts are driven <to pasture> by blows.

LXXVII (D. 125)   Theophrastus: [As Heraclitus says, even the potion separates unless it is stirred.]

These two texts emphasize the beneficial role of motion and compulsion, in overcoming the natural tendency of a mixed drink to separate and of cattle or flocks to stand still or to wander off in the wrong direction. The unity and stability of the mixture depends on its being disturbed and agitated; the safety of the herds is preserved and their appetites satisfied, as it were against their will. Compare LII (D. 84A): 'it rests by changing'.

Beyond this first level of meaning we may recognize 'signals' (*sēmata*) of a deeper view. The violence illustrated in LXXVI and LXXVII probably alludes to the guidance by which the general order of things is maintained. The commentators have noted that the word *plēgē* for the herdsman's blow invokes an old poetic theme 'the stroke of Zeus', which applies literally to the thunderbolt and figuratively to the power and decisive action of Zeus in human affairs.[251] The application to human life is indicated by the term *herpeta* 'creeping things' for animals or beasts, in another Homeric echo of the phrase for human beings, most miserable 'of all the things that breathe and creep upon the earth'.[252] In the image it is the cattle on their way to pasture, in the figurative allusion it is ourselves that receive the herdsman's stroke.

There is probably another *hyponoia*, implied in the stirring movement by which the unity of the potion is preserved in LXXVII. This may serve as an image for the celestial rotation of sun and stars by which cosmic order is maintained, and which is itself the residue of a primordial vortex or whirlpool (*dinē*) from which this order was generated. The rotary motion of the heavens, which plays a central part in the cosmology of Anaxagoras, was later satirized by Aristophanes in his description of Whirl (*Dinos*) as driving out Zeus and stealing his throne (*Clouds* 380f.; cf. 828). It must have figured conspicuously in the system of turning wheels (*kykloi*) that composed the original cosmos of Anaximander; and it will be such a motion that Xenophanes has in mind when he speaks of his greatest god as 'effortlessly shaking all things by the intention of his mind' (fr. 25). So the motion of the drink whose name means 'stirring' or 'churning' (*kykeōn*, from the verb *kykaō*), and whose consistency depends upon the continuation of this motion, is an apt figure for the cosmic rotation.[253]

LXXVIII

LXXVIII (D. 51)   They do not comprehend how a thing agrees at variance with itself: <it is> an attunement (or 'fitting together', *harmoniē*) turning back <on itself>, like that of the bow and the lyre.

The philosophical interpretation of LXXVIII has been obstructed by needless controversy over three textual and philological problems, which must be briefly dealt with before the content can be discussed.

(1) The manuscripts of Hippolytus have the reading *homologeein*, a trivial miswriting of *homologeei*: 'it (that is, the universal arrangement or any particular instance of it, speaking as a *logos*) agrees with itself'.[254] Zeller, insensitive to the imagery and flexibility of Heraclitus' language, proposed that we 'correct' this admirable text on the basis of no paleographical evidence whatsoever, in order to conform with a free paraphrase in Plato's *Symposium* 187A, in the speech of Eryximachus quoted above, where instead of *homologeein* Plato writes *sympheresthai*, obviously on the basis of the *sympheromenon-diapheromenon* contrast in CXXIV (D. 10: 'convergent divergent'). It is one of the strangest phenomena in Heraclitean scholarship that this indefensible alteration of an unexceptional text transmitted by our most reliable ancient source — an alteration based upon nothing more than an inexact quotation in an after-dinner speech — has been accepted by a whole generation of recent editors from Gigon and Walzer to Marcovich. But in thus 'emending' the text they are certainly ill-advised.[255] With Diels-Kranz and Bollack-Wismann, we may keep the text of Hippolytus with complete confidence.

(2) For *palintropos* 'back-turning' as epithet of *harmoniē* in Hippolytus, Plutarch (who cites this fragment three times) once substitutes the Homeric epithet for the bow: *palintonos* 'back-stretched' or 'back-bending'. This misquotation is a natural one, since the expression *palintona toxa* 'back-bending bow' is familiar to everyone brought up on Homer. And that it is a misquotation is guaranteed by the fact that Plutarch confirms Hippolytus' reading in two out of three cases.[256] Hippolytus is our best source; and his reading is also the *lectio difficilior*, as Wilamowitz pointed out. It is predominant in Plutarch, our only other reliable authority for this fragment. And this

phrase *palintropos harmoniē* turns out to have a definite philosophic importance. So here again we can accept Hippolytus' text without the shadow of a scholarly doubt.

(3) The last preliminary problem concerns not the text but the meaning of *harmoniē*, a term which occurs at least twice in Heraclitus (here and in D. 54; in LXXV, D. 8, it may not represent an independent citation). The original sense and development of the term are fairly clear. *Harmoniē* is derived from a root (represented in the verbs *arariskō* and *harmozō*) meaning 'to join' or 'to fit together'; it is used by Homer, Herodotus, and some later authors to mean a joint or seam or a 'fitting together', as in works of carpentry or shipbuilding (*Od.* V. 248, 261; Hdt. II.96.2). But from the beginning the word is also used figuratively, for 'agreements' or 'compacts' between hostile men (*Il.* XXII.255), and hence for the personified power of 'Reconciliation', the child of Ares and Aphrodite in Hesiod (*Theogony* 937). So Empedocles could employ *Harmoniē* as another name for *Philotēs* or Aphrodite, his counterpart to Strife or Conflict, the principle of proportion and agreement which creates a harmonious unity out of potentially hostile powers.[257] Another figurative use is for the tuning of a musical instrument, the 'fitting together' of different strings to produce the desired scale or key. This musical application is well attested in Pindar, where the term occurs three times in the semi-technical sense of 'scale', 'mode', or 'musical composition'.[258] Both musical and wider metaphorical values of the word are combined in the Pythagorean view that opposing powers of the cosmos are held together by a principle of *harmonia*, an 'adjustment' or 'reconciliation' that takes the form of a musical 'octave' (Philolaus fr. 6). The Pythagorean doctrine of the music of the spheres, presupposed in Plato's Myth of Er and reported by Aristotle (*De Caelo* II.9), seems to be implicit in Philolaus' notion of *harmonia* and might go back to the founder of the school.[259]

Thus we have a triple range of meaning for *harmoniē*: physical fitting together of parts, as in carpentry; military or social agreement between potential opponents as in a truce or a civic order; and musical attunement of strings and tones. The half-musical, half-political sense of 'concord' or 'harmony' which predominates in the later history of the term had not been established as a fixed usage for *harmoniē* in the time of Heraclitus.[260] But that usage is nothing more than a simplified fusion of two of the three archaic senses of the term just surveyed.

On the view of Heraclitus' verbal technique which I have proposed, we expect to find *harmoniē* used in all available senses: as a physical fitting together of parts, as a principle of reconciliation between opponents, and as a pattern of musical attunement. These three senses are combined in the new, specifically Heraclitean notion of the structure or fitting together of the cosmic order as a unity produced from conflict.[261]

Now for a literal exegesis. I consider the phrases one by one, and then survey the thought of the fragment as a whole.

The opening words *ou xyniasin* 'They do not comprehend' take us back to the theme of the proem: 'men ever fail to comprehend this *logos*' (I.1); 'uncomprehending (*axynetoi*), even when they have heard they are like the deaf' (II, D. 34). The syllable *xyn-* echoes or anticipates the term *xynos*, 'what is shared' or 'common': the *logos* is shared (*xynos*), but men treat their thinking (*phronēsis*) as though it were private (III, D. 2). The uncomprehending are precisely those who do not grasp what is common (*xynon*); speaking with understanding (*xyn nooi*) means holding fast to what is shared (*tōi xynōi*) by all things (XXX, D. 114). LXXVIII tells us just what this common structure is: the *logos* 'according to which all things come to pass' is here articulated as the agreement or 'fitting together' of a system of tension and opposition.

'They do not comprehend how a thing at variance with itself (*diapheromenon heōutōi*) speaks in agreement (*homologeei*).' It is difference or conflict that is obvious; what men do not see is the unifying structure. (Compare XIX, D. 57 on the unity of day and night.) The term for opposition, *diapheromenon*, has an etymological sense of 'moving apart', 'diverging', hence 'differing'; but the syntax with the dative singles out the notion of hostility as predominant. The principle of agreement-in-conflict is expressed in neuter form, as in CXXIV (D. 10): *sympheromenon diapheromenon* 'it moves together and it moves apart' ('convergent divergent') and *synaidon diaidon* 'it sings together and it sings apart' ('consonant dissonant'). In both cases we have a strangely personified neuter, which there sings and here quarrels and 'speaks in agreement' with itself. (Compare the neuter in LII, D. 84A: 'it rests by changing'.) The force of the neuter is one of generalization: this pattern applies to the universe as a whole and to every organized portion thereof.

The term for agreement, *homologeein*, must echo or anticipate XXXVI (D. 50, which Hippolytus has just quoted): wisdom consists in *listening to the logos* and *saying in agreement* (*homologein*) that all things are one. This term thus connects LXXVIII both with the initial theme of *logos* and the culminating assertion of unity, as well as with that notion of wisdom that is grounded in the recognition of unity. (Cf. LIV, D. 41.)

This implicit personification of the cosmic pattern, as a *logos* that while quarrelling agrees with itself, lapses after the word *homologeei*. In its place we have an image involving two comparisons: 'a *harmonië*, turning back on itself, like that of the bow and the lyre'. In this image one aspect is clear and two are obscure. What is clear is the notion of *harmonië* for the lyre, since the term immediately denotes the stringing or tuning of the instrument, and a 'tune' which the lyre may play. The double enigma lies in (1) '*harmonië* of the bow', where *harmonië* cannot have the same sense, and (2) the epithet *palintropos* 'back-turning', which has no obvious point, but is emphatically placed at the very center of the fragment.

Consider first the '*harmonië* of the bow'. Taken by itself, the phrase is unproblematic: *harmonië* means the physical fitting together or construction of the bow. The riddle lies in the conjunction of the two comparisons: how is a single pattern illustrated both by the *harmonië* of the bow and by that of the lyre?

We can avoid the paradox by taking *harmonië* in the same sense twice: structure of the bow, structure of the lyre. But this is not very plausible for the lyre, given the musical connotations of *harmonië*. (Both Plato and Aristotle understood the musical sense here, as will be seen.) In fact, this is one of those 'solutions' to Heraclitus' riddles that simplify the text by impoverishing its range of meaning – in this case, by eliminating the semantic tension between two senses of *harmonië*: the structure (and function) of the bow, the tuning (and playing) of the lyre. The music of Apollo's favorite instrument and the death-dealing power of his customary weapon must be taken *together* as an expression of the 'joining' that characterizes the universal pattern of things.

But the two images can also be understood separately. The best commentary on the 'fitting' of the bow – the fitting of the string to the bow-arms and the fitting of an arrow to the string – is still that of Lewis Campbell (who took his inspiration from Plato's remark at *Republic* 439B): 'As the arrow leaves the string, the hands are pulling opposite ways to each other, and to the different parts of the bow.'[262] A single rational intention (in the most literal sense of *intendere*: aiming at a target) is realized by a system in which physical tensions in opposite directions serve both as instance and as symbol for the general principle of opposition. The opposing forces 'speak as one' in the flight of the arrow. In the lyre, however, while the thought of the tense strings, perhaps even of the curving arms, continues the idea of *harmoniē* of the bow, the predominant notion is the distinctly musical thought rendered in CXXIV (D. 10): *synaidon diaidon* 'consonant dissonant', or, as Aristotle puts it, 'from tones at variance comes the finest *harmoniē*'.[263] Whether 'the *harmoniē* of the lyre' means a scale, a mode, or a melody, it is in any case a unity produced from diversity which, but for the musician's skill in *tuning* (and plucking) *the strings*, would easily fall apart into dissonance or cacophony. And the diversity is essential. If the strings stood in mechanical agreement, or if the musician plucked only one string with constant tension, no music could result.

This leaves us with the enigmatic epithet *palintropos*, in its dominating position at the center. Some editors have sought to avoid (rather than resolve) this riddle by preferring the textual variant *palintonos* 'back-stretched', a regular, almost ornamental epithet of the bow. Its occurrence here would not be surprising, just as it is no surprise to find this as a variant in some ancient citations. But in fact Heraclitus seems deliberately to have chosen *palintropos* as an unexpected substitute for the familiar epithet, and he has left us to wonder why.[264] What is the point to this less banal and less perspicuous epithet? For although *palintropos* 'back-turning' has roughly the same sense as *palintonos* 'back-stretched', it does not apply so neatly here, precisely because (since it omits the root of *-tonos*, *teinein*) it does not refer directly to the stretching or tuning of strings.

The solution to this puzzle is obvious, once we grasp the allusive nature of Heraclitus' style and his systematic use of resonance. By Homeric reminiscence, *palintropos* immediately suggests *palintonos* (as the variant citations show). Hence the former term is richer, since by association it includes the latter as well. But it adds something more in the notion of *-tropos*. This is the clue to the significance of the whole fragment as a description of cosmic structure and unity. For the epithet 'back-turning' provides a direct allusion to the 'turnings' or 'reversals' (*tropai*) of fire in XXXVIII (D. 31A), and hence to their more familiar parallel, the seasonal turning back of the sun in summer and winter. (See above on XLIV, D. 94.) By this perplexing use here of a compound in *-tropos* 'turning', Heraclitus recalls that other riddle about the 'turnings' of fire. And he recalls its solution as well, in the annual pattern of reversals of the sun when it reaches its *termata* or limits (XLV, D. 120), north in summer, south in winter, the slow seasonal pendulum swing of the sun back and forth, the *palintropos harmoniē* by which the diversity and uniformity of the life cycle of nature is guaranteed.

With the phrase *palintropos harmoniē* Heraclitus thus forges the link between his doctrine of opposites and his cosmology. The notion of a *harmoniē* or fitting together serves to connect the anthropocentric doctrine of opposites outlined in LXVII–LXXIII with the wider notion of the cosmic *logos* (echoed here in *homo-logeei*) and with the notion of the *kosmos* itself, the world ordering represented by the measures of fire, as exemplified in the alternation of day and night and in the annual cycle of the sun. It is appropriate that this link between various kinds of opposition be articulated by the very notion of 'joining' or 'fitting together' (*harmoniē*). This concept is more vividly illustrated by the drawn bow, more richly and subtly by the tuning and playing of the lyre, and most completely by the conjunction of the two: the twin attributes of 'the lord whose oracle is in Delphi', whose 'sign' in this case is a pair of instruments related to one another as war to peace. (For the appearance of war and peace between the 'cosmic' terms *day and night, winter and summer* and the 'human' opposites *satiety and hunger*, see CXXIII, D. 67.)

The mediating concept which makes possible the generalized doctrine of opposites, and which therefore provides the key to understanding the unity of Heraclitus' system, is precisely this notion of *harmoniē* as an intelligent structure or purposeful activity, a unified whole whose essential parts (or stages or tendencies) are related to one another by polar contrast.[265] Although this notion is most clearly exhibited in products of human art or in activities such as archery and music, carding wool and stirring the *kykeōn* drink, it also applies to the understanding of (that is, the comprehension of unified structure within) such natural phenomena as night and day, summer and winter, and the cycle of elementary transformations. The concept of *harmoniē* as a unity composed of conflicting parts is thus the model for an understanding of the world ordering as a unified whole. And it is the comprehension of this pattern in all its applications that constitutes wisdom. For it is this structure that is common (*xynon*) to all things. And this pattern, or its recognition, is what Heraclitus designates as *gnōmē*, the plan or intention by which all things are steered through all (LIV, D. 41).

LXXIX

LXXIX (D. 48)   The name of the bow is life; its work is death.

This is one of three fragments in which Heraclitus' interest in words and word play manifests itself in the mention of a particular name.[266] The concern with the truth and falsity of names, with 'etymology' understood as a search for the deeper significance hidden in words and naming, is characteristic of archaic thought generally, not only in Greece. But it is particularly striking in the literature and philosophy of the early fifth century. We find a comparable interest in Parmenides, though with a different philosophic bias. In the Eleatic conception of language, names typically express a false or mistaken view of reality.[267] Heraclitus is closer to the standard archaic view reflected in Aeschylus, that names are 'truly' given (*etētymōs, alēthōs*) and hence that there are truths expressed in them for whoever knows how to read the meaning.[268] This view gives rise to the allegorical interpretation of divine names that is developed in the *Cratylus* and even more systematically by the Stoics. It is probably no accident that three out of four of the references to naming in Heraclitus concern the designation of divine powers (Zeus, Dike, and 'the god' of CXXIII, D. 67). But the truths hidden in divine names or familiar words are for Heraclitus only a special case of the epistemic situation: the truth is continually speaking to men, like a *logos* or discourse, but they cannot grasp the *hyponoia*, the underlying thought or meaning.

LXXIX is the only instance where Heraclitus refers to a name that is not that of a deity. But the bow is important in its own right, as weapon and symbol of Apollo, in addition to the special use that Heraclitus makes of it in LXXVIII. Now at the surface level our text presents a paradoxical opposition between the old name for the bow (*biós*), which in the unaccented written form was indistinguishable from the ordinary word for life (*bíos*), and the actual use of the instrument in hunting and warfare. This opposition is expressed by a verbal antithesis (*onoma* versus *ergon*) that prefigures the sophistic contrast between 'in word' (*logos*) and 'in deed' (*ergon*). A superficial judgment would thus conclude that the bow had been ill-named. But that judgment implies the error of taking the opposition of life and death as irreducible, by failing to see 'how it agrees in variance with itself'. The life-signifying name for the instrument of death points to some reconciliation between the opponents, some fitting together as in the unity of Day and Night (XIX, D. 57).

The connections of the bow with death and destruction are obvious enough. But how can it also stand for life, or for some union of the two? One might think of the use of the bow in hunting, where the death of animals sustains the life of the killers. But probably more is meant here, some deeper connection between life and death such as is indicated in XCII (D. 62) and XCIII (D. 88). Taken alone, LXXIX can only stand as a *griphos*, a riddle in which the name of the bow hints at some larger meaning that we cannot yet make out.

LXXX

LXXX (D. 54)   The hidden attunement (*harmonië*) is better than the obvious one.

This is one of the shortest and most beautifully designed of the fragments. Out of four Greek words (*harmonië aphanēs phanerēs kreittōn*) two are presented as epithets of *harmonië*, while the third is construed as epithet of the same noun elliptically understood (in the genitive). Two of these three adjectives are formally related as positive and privative: *phaneros, aphanēs* 'apparent, unapparent' or 'obvious, hidden'. By placing these terms in central position, Heraclitus has exhibited the unifying role of opposition within the verbal structure of this brief sentence. And by affirming that the negative term is superior to the positive, he has expressed in a formal way the dialectical re-evaluation of the negative principle that characterizes so much of what he has to say about the opposites.

Any exegesis of LXXX must be speculative, since the sentence itself does not specify what is meant by the hidden *harmonië*. But a literal reading poses no real problems, as long as we avoid the trap of supposing that Heraclitus intends his words to be taken in only one sense. The range of meaning for *harmonië* is too wide for any one rendering to be adequate. As partial translations we might offer 'Sweeter than heard harmonies are those unheard' (after Keats), or 'Hidden structure is more powerful than visible structure' (after Bronowski). If we give up the attempt to render *harmonië*, the rest can be translated literally as: '*Harmonië* which does not appear clearly is superior to that which is clear and apparent.' The adjective *kreittōn* is again polysemous, meaning 'stronger, more powerful', but also 'better, more desirable'. The latter will presumably be the natural sense on first reading; the physical or political notion ('stronger', 'dominant') brings with it a deeper interpretation. For once we take

kreittōn in this sense, it suggests a verbal allusion to the 'divine one'
mentioned in XXX (D. 114), which 'prevails (*kratei*) as it will and
suffices for all'. The universal *harmoniē* or fitting together and the
divine unity that structures the world are only different modes of
designating the same principle.

The phrase 'hidden structure', *harmoniē aphanēs*, might thus be
taken as a general title for Heraclitus' philosophical thought.[269] And
it is no accident that the same title may describe his mode of
expression, where the immediate 'surface' meaning is often less
significant than the latent intention carried by allusion, enigma, and
resonance.

What is the contrasting notion of *phanerē harmoniē*, the 'visible
structure' or 'plain attunement'? In the musical sense, the manifest
harmoniē must be the tune, the fitting together of notes produced by
the musician and apprehended by the audience. On this reading LXXX
states that the less conspicuous attunement (between human or cosmic opposites) is finer and more powerful than the harmonies of the
lyre. But if *harmoniē* is taken physically, as the construction of a bow
or any work of plastic art, then the thought becomes: no joiner builds
as well as the pilot of the universe. No work of art achieves a unity
and fitting together as strong as the natural *kosmos* which most men
fail to see.

These musical and structural senses of *harmoniē* are combined in
the Pythagorean notion of the *harmoniē* of the heavens, the cosmic
music ordered by the basic ratios of 2:1, 3:2, 4:3. Now the music of
the heavens, according to the Pythagoreans, is something we cannot
hear. In this sense it is *aphanēs*, hidden. In view of Heraclitus' conspicuous antipathy for Pythagoras, it is not likely that the *harmoniē*
he has in mind in LXXX is just the one defined in the Pythagorean
doctrine — even if we could be sure that the doctrine in question was
known at this time.[270] But just as Heraclitus' doctrine of the psyche
and its destiny after death can only be understood as a modification
and development of Pythagorean ideas, so perhaps his conception of
an all-pervasive *harmoniē* is best seen as a response to Pythagoras'
own conception of the world in terms of the musical numbers. The
ratios 2:1, 3:2, and 4:3 will represent the underlying, non-apparent
fitting together of strings and instrument that permits the musician
to produce tones that are *perceived* as consonant or concordant.

Thus the connection between measures, cosmic order, and the pattern of opposites and their agreement, could have been suggested to

Heraclitus by a Pythagorean concept of musical *harmonia* in numerical
terms, presented as a key to the structure of the heavens. Now the
notion of cosmic measures goes back to Miletus.[271] But Heraclitus'
own conception of this order in terms of *logos* and *harmoniē* is more
directly intelligible as a generalization of the Pythagorean notion of
the musical ratios, where these are conceived as a principle of 'attunement' by which opposing principles are reconciled and set in order, as
Philolaus says (DK 44.B 6). Philolaus comes later, of course, and it is
possible that his own conception of a cosmic *harmonia* joining the
opposites by musical proportion is itself derived from Heraclitus. It is
my guess that the line of influence goes in the opposite direction, and
that Philolaus here preserves an old Pythagorean view utilized by
Heraclitus.

LXXXI

LXXXIA (D. A22)   Aristotle: [Heraclitus reproaches the poet for the verse
'Would that Conflict might vanish from among gods and men!' (*Iliad* XVIII.107).
For there would be no attunement (*harmonia*) without high and low notes nor
any animals without male and female, both of which are opposites.]

LXXXIB   Scholia A to *Iliad* XVIII.107: [Heraclitus, who believes that the
nature of things was constructed according to conflict (*eris*), finds fault with
Homer <for this verse>, on the grounds that he is praying for the destruction of
the cosmos.]

There is only one point here that clearly goes beyond a summary of
doctrines better preserved in other quotations, namely, that Heraclitus
introduced his own apotheosis of strife and warfare by a rejection of
the prayer uttered by Achilles in his great speech of regret over the
quarrel with Agamemnon. This attack on Homer, which must be connected with Heraclitus' own view of war in LXXXII–LXXXIII, is the
counterpart to his criticism of Hesiod for failing to recognize the
unity of night and day. Homer and Hesiod, the pre-eminent wise men
and teachers of the Greeks, represent the general folly of mankind in
failing to perceive the 'unapparent *harmoniē*' in which the tension
between opposing powers is as indispensable as their reconciliation
within a larger unity. The thought here is probably connected with
the riddle of XXII (D. 56) where Homer like other men is 'deceived
in the recognition of what is apparent'. For to *recognize* the apparent
is precisely to see it within the framework of the hidden fitting
together.

LXXXII

LXXXII (D. 80)   One must realize that war is shared and Conflict is Justice, and that all things come to pass (and are ordained?) in accordance with conflict.

In this and the next fragment (LXXXIII, D. 53) Heraclitus formulates his doctrine of opposition as an explicit theme, under the title of War (*polemos*) and Conflict (*eris*). LXXXII may be read as a further statement of the thought of LXXVIII, the insight that Homer and most men cannot grasp: how anything at variance with itself is also in agreement. Four clauses represent four different answers to the question 'What is it that most men do not comprehend?'

(1) 'One must realize that War is common (*xynos*, shared).' Heraclitus pursues his polemic against Homer (cf. LXXXI) by adapting the poet's own words; and since the quotation is also familiar from Archilochus there may be a side-thrust in this direction as well.[272] Homer had said: 'Enyalios (i.e. Ares) is common (*xynos*), and the killer gets killed' (*Il.* XVIII.309). The passage occurs just 200 lines after Achilles' curse on strife, which was prompted by the death of Patroclus. This time it is Hector, Patroclus' killer, who is speaking and who is, in effect, predicting his own death. Archilochus repeats the sentiment with emphasis: 'truly, Ares is common (*xynos*) to men' (fr. 38 Diehl). The sense of 'truly' (*etētymon*) may be echoed here by Heraclitus' use of the participle *eonta*: 'war is really common'. But in place of the familiar thought that the fortunes of war are shared by both sides and that the victor today may be vanquished tomorrow, Heraclitus takes *xynos* 'common' in his own sense of 'universal', 'all-pervading', 'unifying' (above, pp. 101f.), and thus gives the words of the poets a deeper meaning they themselves did not comprehend. The symmetrical confrontation of the two sides in battle now becomes a *figura* for the shifting but reciprocal balance between opposites in human life and in the natural world, for the structure designated *harmoniē* in LXXVIII (D. 51). The imagery of the bow and the lyre is thus supplemented by that of two champions or two armies facing one another. The description of this combat as *xynos* hints at the principle which unites and reconciles the warriors, not by an open truce or agreement but by a more obscure *harmoniē* in 'the divine one', the structure that is 'common to all things' and binds them together, as the law of the city is a common bond for all the citizens (XXX, D. 114).

(2) 'Conflict is Justice' or 'justice is strife'. The word order does not permit us to distinguish subject and predicate; it makes no difference, since Heraclitus is in effect identifying the two terms. This

identification is at first sight utterly perverse. For in the tradition of
moral thinking represented by Hesiod and Solon, the notions of conflict and violence are systematically opposed to those of law and justice.[273] In an innovation that might be seen as an earlier response to
Homer's curse on *eris*, Hesiod had distinguished 'good conflict' or
creative competition from evil strife that leads to warfare, lawlessness,
and crime.[274]

It is a natural consequence of Heraclitus' monism that he should
reject Hesiod's distinction between good and bad strife. But the provocative character of his assertion is best appreciated if we think of
him as accepting the distinction for the sake of the argument, and
then equating *evil* Eris with the principle of justice.

The point of this paradoxical equivalence can be understood only
if we bear in mind that warfare has become a figure for opposition in
general: only at the cosmic level can Conflict and Justice be reconciled
and seen as one. In human terms, the relationship between strife and
'straight judgments' is as Solon and Hesiod have depicted it: it is
quarrelling that makes Justice necessary, and it is the function of wise
judgment to eliminate violence from the community. But just as war
has been generalized for the opposition that structures all things, so
Heraclitus (following Anaximander) has taken Justice in the widest
possible sense, as the pattern of order and reciprocity in the cycle of
the seasons, the principle of regularity that oversees 'the measures of
the sun'. (See on XLIV, D. 94.) In this larger order, the principle of
just requital and compensation (*dikē* and *antamoibē*) coincides with
the principle of tension and opposition, for these are alternative
descriptions of a single, all-embracing structure.

In the fragment of Anaximander *adikia*, 'injustice', denotes the
victory of one opposing power over another. Hence Heraclitus' identification of conflict with Justice can be seen as a deliberate correction.
Thus Vlastos wrote:

> Two of the fundamental ideas in Anaximander — that there is
> strife among the elements, and that a just order is nevertheless
> preserved — are reasserted in a form which universalizes both of
> them and thereby resolves the opposition between them: what is
> a 'nevertheless' in Anaximander, becomes a 'therefore' in Heraclitus.
> The result is that no part of nature *can* 'over-step its measures' . . .
> and not . . . that long-term excess is punished . . . which is . . . what
> Anaximander had taught . . . There can be no excess at all, long-
> term or short-term either. ('On Heraclitus', in Furley and Allen, p.
> 419)

Since *dikē* is regularly thought of as a balance of crime and punishment, Heraclitus' extension of this notion to a cosmic system of opposition and 'reversals' (*tropai*) might have been made even without Anaximander's phrase about injustice and retribution. But the general dependence of Heraclitus' thought on Milesian cosmology is so clear, and the conception of the elementary opposites so similar, that it is natural to suspect some allusion to Anaximander's words in the juxtaposition here of Conflict and Justice. Still, the polemical thrust of this identification is probably directed less against the recondite text of Anaximander than against the mainstream of Greek thought represented by Homer, Hesiod, Archilochus, and Solon.

Polemical intent aside, Vlastos is clearly right to insist that Heraclitus' conception of cosmic justice goes beyond that of Anaximander, since he construes *dikē* not merely as compensation for crime or excess but as a total pattern that includes both punishment and crime itself, as necessary ingredients of the world order. We have here the cosmic analogue to LXIX (D. 23): 'If it were not for these things, they would not have known the name of Dike.'

(3) 'All things come to pass (*ginomena*) in accordance with conflict.' The stylistic echo of the proem ('all things come to pass in accordance with this *logos*') serves to define the central role of opposition. When *logos* is understood not merely as the discourse of Heraclitus but as the structure he describes, this structure is seen as one of antithesis, tension, conflict.

The word *ginomena*, 'come to pass', can also mean 'come into being', 'be born'. This vivid sense of birth, perhaps latent here, becomes explicit in LXXXIII, where war is described in mythic terms as 'father of all'.

(4) 'And (all things) are ordained (?) in accordance with conflict.' Unfortunately the last word of LXXXII (*chreōmena* in the manuscript) is almost certainly corrupt. I have kept this reading with only the faintest hope that this might be possible Greek for 'are ordained (as by an oracle)', 'are established as right and necessary', with the sense of the participle oriented by the opening word of the fragment (*chrē*), as Bollack-Wismann suggest. But the text is too uncertain to support any interpretation that will not stand on its own feet.[275]

LXXXIII

LXXXIII (D. 53)　War is father of all and king of all; and some he has shown as gods, others men; some he has made slaves, others free.

The doctrine of opposition is here restated in even more dramatic and more puzzling form. How can war, the typical cause of death and destruction, be universal father responsible for birth and life? And if it is clear how warfare can account for the distinction between free men and slaves (since it was common practice to enslave the population of a conquered city), in what sense does it fix a distinction between men and gods?

The resolution of both puzzles turns on the ambiguity between war in the literal sense and Heraclitus' use of the term for a universal principle of opposition. It is the second notion that is personified here in the phrase 'father of all and king of all', echoing the Homeric formula for Zeus: 'father of men and gods'. The term *pantōn* 'of all' is ambiguous (as elsewhere) between personal and neuter form, so that War is presented as father not only of gods and men like Zeus, but of 'all things that come to pass' (*ginomena panta* in LXXXII); and the phrase 'king of all (persons, or things)' is not formulaic, hence even more emphatic here.[276] Thus War figures not merely as a substitute for Zeus but as a kind of super-Zeus, like 'the divine one' of XXX (D. 114). An assimilation to Zeus is also suggested by the verb *edeixe* 'he has shown some as gods, some as men', which recalls the typical signal of Zeus' governance, when he gives an omen on high 'showing a sign' of his favor or ill-will.[277] This personification of the chief cosmic principle, in terms of imagery normally associated with the king of the gods, prepares and explains the announcement that 'the wise one alone is unwilling and willing to be called by the name of Zeus' (CXVIII, D. 32).

As long as War is understood in this general sense there is no difficulty in seeing how it is responsible for mortality and divinity, slavery and freedom, since it is (by definition) the decisive plan or causal factor in everything that comes to pass. It remains to be seen whether another coherent interpretation can be given by taking *polemos* literally throughout, as ordinary combat. There is no problem with the freedom-slavery distinction on this reading. But what sense can we make of war 'showing' or 'designating' gods as well as men? Gigon thought that the reference must be to death in battle: those who survive remain men; those who fall are raised to the condition of deity.[278] Insofar as this question concerns the fate of human beings after death, it will be dealt with below (on XCII, D. 62; XCVI, D. 25; C, D. 24; and especially CIX, D. 118).

By contrast with LXXXII, the apotheosis of War in LXXXIII is distinguished by its vivid personification and sharper focussing on the

destiny of mankind. The human condition is defined by a double set
of oppositions: the internal antithesis between free and servile status
(the most radical contrast conceivable in ancient society); and the
external contrast between men and gods, as in the traditional conception of human beings as mortal earthlings. The parallel may suggest
that just as freedom and slavery are alternative, sometimes successive,
conditions for the same beings, so humanity and divinity are alternative, even alternating states which — like day and night, war and peace,
life and death — define by their opposition and succession the full
dimensions of human existence. (Recall 'war is common': the killer
gets killed, and he who conquers one day may be vanquished the
next.) It is just such an equivalence-in-succession that we find in
XCII (D. 62): mortals are immortals, immortals mortals.

Before turning to texts dealing with the afterlife, we may sum up
the doctrine articulated in LXVII–LXXXIII. These fragments list
pairs of opposition of different kinds which are all in some sense
anthropocentric, in that the opposing terms correspond to two contrasting human experiences (LXVII and LXXIII), two states or concepts governing human life (justice and injustice in LXVIII–LXIX,
slave and free in LXXXIII), the contrast between a human response
and that of another species (LXX–LXXII), some tension characteriz-
ing a human activity (LXXIV–LXXIX), or an opposition between
the human and the divine (as in LXVIII, LXXXIII; cf. the human lack
of insight in LV–LVIII). Other fragments present a different range of
oppositions more properly described as *cosmic*, in that the relevant
contrast does not depend in any essential way upon the existence of
human beings: night and day in XIX and CXXIII, cold-warm and
moist-dry in XLIX, fire-sea, sea-earth and sea-*prēstēr* in XXXVIII–
XXXIX, winter-summer in CXXIII. The 'cosmic' fragments are full
of cosmic antitheses; and nearly all of these may be thought of as
manifestations of the kindling and quenching of universal fire
(XXXVII, D. 30).

Now it would be tedious to attempt a catalogue of all examples of
polar contrast or opposition: there is scarcely a text of Heraclitus
that would not have to be included. The pattern of antithesis structures his whole work, just as it structures the reality he is trying to
describe. In this sense the doctrine of opposites, like the thesis of
unity which is its counterpart, is coextensive with Heraclitus' thought
as a whole. Perhaps the only generalization which applies in every
case is that the opposition between the terms is obvious, whereas
some insight is required to grasp the *harmoniē* binding them together.

And this insight will generally involve recognition of a positive role for what is *prima facie* a negative term. At the very least, the negative term functions as a point of contrast by reference to which the positive contrary is made conceptually definite and distinct; but the link between the two is never *merely* conceptual.

My distinction between anthropocentric and cosmic oppositions is somewhat artificial, since by allusion or direct juxtaposition (as in CXXIII, D. 67) Heraclitus will insist upon the connections between these two sets of terms. But the distinction has the merit of focussing attention upon the crucial antithesis between life and death, formulated in the riddle of the bow (LXXIX) and developed in the theory of the psyche. This topic of life and death lies at the very point of contact or fitting together of the cosmic and anthropocentric dimensions in Heraclitus' thought.

LXXXIV–LXXXVII

LXXXIV (D. 27)   What awaits men at death they do not expect or even imagine

LXXXV (D. 28A)   The great man is eminent in imagining things, and on this he hangs his reputation for knowing it all.

LXXXVI (D. 86)   Incredibility escapes recognition.

LXXXVII (D. 28B)   Justice will catch up with those who invent lies and those who swear to them.

LXXXIV announces a new doctrine of human destiny after death: it raises the curtain on what we might call Heraclitus' eschatology, the doctrine of the end or endlessness of human life. But for the moment the curtain rises on a bare stage. It is only with the parallel between death and sleep in LXXXIX and XC that Heraclitus gives us some hint of his own conception of what awaits us when we die.

The two verbs that express men's ignorance in LXXXIV, *elpontai* and *dokeousin*, are suggestive but ambiguous: *elpontai* '(what) they expect' can also mean '(what) they hope for'. Is the fate in store for us better than our fondest hopes or worse than our grimmest expectations? The point of LXXXIV is that *we do not know*; and the choice of words is not designed to give us any further clues.[279] The verb *elpontai* may recall another remark: 'He who does not expect will not find out the unexpected (*anelpiston*), for it is trackless and unexplored' (VII, D. 18). This echo would indicate that the inquiry or search for wisdom will not be complete until it has resolved the riddle of death.

The verb *dokeousin*, 'they do not imagine', contains another echo of the fragments on human ignorance: most men 'do not recognize (*ginōskousin*) what they experience, but they believe their own opinions' (*heōutoisi dokeousi* in IV, D. 17). The self-delusion of men in the face of death is of a piece with the complacent failure of insight that characterizes their life throughout.

The theme of 'seeming', 'imagination' or 'opinion' represented by the verb *dokein* provides the historical root for the metaphysical distinction between appearance and reality. This distinction was first systematically drawn in the poem of Parmenides, where divine cognition (*noein*) and truth are contrasted with mortal opinions (*doxai*) 'in which there is no true trust (*pistis*)'. But before Parmenides, and before Heraclitus, Xenophanes had denied that a man can have clear vision or certain knowledge of the most important matters and insisted that we must be satisfied with guesswork (*dokos*, fr. 34) or with opinions like unto truth (*dedoxasthō*, fr. 35). Thus *dokein* in LXXXIV invokes the notion of a typically human and typically fallible type of cognition.[280] This same notion of *dokein* or guesswork is taken up and played upon in LXXXV, where the eminence of the man who enjoys public recognition and approval (*ho dokimōtatos*) is contrasted with the shabby credentials of what he himself recognizes and accepts: *dokeonta*, mere seeming or imagining.[281]

The thematic resonance of *dokeousin* in LXXXIV and LXXXV, together with the context of the second quotation in Clement, suggests that LXXXV also implies some reference to the mystery of the afterlife. (This would be confirmed if LXXXV was directly followed by LXXXVII in Heraclitus' text, as many editors have thought.) If so, the great man of general esteem will be some supposed expert on the afterlife, like Pythagoras.

There is not much to be made of the brief and enigmatic LXXXVI. I include it in this context because of the play on *ginōskein* (a possible echo of LXXXV) and because our sources (Plutarch and Clement) both take *apistiē* 'incredulity' or 'incredibility' in a sense relevant to the mysteries of death and afterlife. For Plutarch the reference is to *ta theia*, 'divine (or supernatural) matters': it is because the truth in these matters is so strange and difficult to credit that they succeed in escaping our recognition.[282]

Finally, LXXXVII announces that Justice will catch up with

inventors of lies and those who testify on their behalf.[283] The role of Dike here in regard to human transgressors recalls that of XLIV (D. 94), where she (with her ministers, the Furies) watches to see that the sun does not exceed his measures. The parallel between cosmic order and the human situation is what we have come to expect. What is more surprising is the focus on lies and false testimony as the crimes calling out for punishment. This is the only reference in the fragments to falsehood as such, as distinct from ignorance and lack of understanding. The closest parallel to this charge of fabricating lies is the accusation of 'artful knavery' and 'imposture' directed at Pythagoras (XXV–XXVI, D. 129 and 81). Hence it is natural to suppose that it is not the poets and wise men generally but Pythagoras and his like, the solemn mystifiers and specialists on the fate of the soul after death, whom Heraclitus has in mind here.[284]

We are left wondering how Dike will take retribution. Heraclitus is relying upon the traditional Greek feeling that 'for great wrongdoings (*adikēmata*) there are great punishments sent by the gods' (Hdt. II.120.5). But our text does not tell us whether punishment will come in this life or the next.

LXXXVIII

LXXXVIII (D. 96)   Corpses should be thrown out quicker than dung.

No utterance of Heraclitus is better calculated to offend the normal religious sensitivities of an ancient Greek than this contempt for the cult of the dead, as every reader of the *Antigone* will recognize. The shock effect of this aphorism made it one of the best known throughout antiquity.[285] Even Heraclitus' mockery of purification rites and temple worship does not touch such deep feelings of piety as this attack on the usual forms of ritual respect for the dead. Older than the cults of the city and closer to every human being's sense of his own vulnerability, the mourning and burial of a kinsman represents the most fundamental stratum of ancient religion. If Heraclitus chooses to mock it in this extravagant way, that may be because he touches here on the nerve center of his own preoccupations, because he wishes to provoke us into an appreciation of the radical insight which his predecessors have missed. Ordinary cult practice and abstruse doctrine on the afterlife are equally remote from true understanding.

Behind its provocative character, the statement itself remains enig-

matic. Perhaps there is some allusion to the return of the dead body
to the earth and its contribution, by way of its own decay, to the
renewal of life from the soil. Still, the comparison is scarcely flatter-
ing. It suggests that what awaits men at death is what awaits their
excrement and the offal of their farm animals. For Heraclitus any
other sense to death and any other continuation of life must be concerned not with the corpse but with the element that has abandoned
it: the psyche or life-spirit.[286]

LXXXIX

LXXXIX (D. 21)   Death is all things we see awake; all we see asleep is sleep.

I have placed this carefully constructed sentence at the climax of
Heraclitus' riddling, the darkest moment following on a succession of
other mysteries (war distinguishing gods and men, justice apprehending liars, the surprise of death, corpses thrown out like dung) that
have not yet been resolved. The sentence opens with the promise of
a decisive clarification, a definition of death ('Death is . . . '), whose
scope is surprisingly general: 'all we can see'. But the restriction to
'when we are awake' is puzzling, and the next clause frustrates any
hope of clear information. Since sleep and waking are opposite states,
if what we see awake is *death*, then what we see asleep should be *life*
— or so the symmetry of the clauses leads us to expect. But when we
reach the last word, we find not 'life' but 'sleep'.

Does Heraclitus mean after all to identify life with the private,
half-conscious, phantom experience of the dream world? Apparently
not, and that is why the sentence does not end as symmetry would
require. Why then does he deliberately arouse our expectations in
this misleading way?

Until we know what life is, we cannot understand the definition of
death: what does it exclude? And since much of what we see awake is
alive in the ordinary sense, in what extraordinary sense does death
include this visible realm of living plants and animals?

XC

XC (D. 26)   A man strikes (*haptetai*) a light for himself in the night, when his
sight is quenched. Living, he touches (*haptetai*) the dead in his sleep; waking, he
touches (*haptetai*) the sleeper.

Here the word play on *haptetai* and *aposbestheis*, the two terms for the kindling and quenching of 'everliving fire' in XXXVII (D. 30), offers an initial clue for drawing together the cosmology and anthropology of Heraclitus into a unified vision of life and death: it is the phenomena of sleep and dreaming that may initiate us into these mysteries.[287]

We have seen that one aspect of what awaits men at death can be understood by attending to the fate of corpses which, like dung, are reabsorbed into new life and vegetation by regression to more elementary forms. As Eliot put it, the earth is flesh, fur and faeces. Human beings, like plants and animals, are 'everliving' in as much as their bodies pass into the unending cycle of elemental transformation, which is a cycle of life. This emergence of all bodily forms from the perishing of what has gone before seems to provide the most plausible reference for the enigmatic statement in LXXXIX that 'death is all things we see awake': the death of old structures and organisms that have yielded to something new.

The second part of LXXXIX ('everything we see asleep') refers to the dream experience and thus to a different mode of transformation. In XC Heraclitus pursues his reflection upon sleep, the twin of death, as a partial revelation of the limitlessness of the psyche, that deep *logos* that will not permit us to find the ends of the soul, 'even if you travel over every path' (XXXV, D. 45). The description of our psychic experience in terms of quenching and kindling suggests that the soul must have its own mode of exemplifying the cycle of everliving fire, its own mode of survival and revival where life and death will somehow alternate like sleeping and waking. Hints of such a view are given here in the play on *haptesthai* ('lighting' and 'grasping') and in other stylistic peculiarities of XC.

The first sentence seems to be a straightforward description of lamplighting at dusk. But there is the dramatic generality of the opening words (*anthrōpos en euphronēi* 'human being in (the) night') a most unusual construction in the phrase 'strikes (*haptetai*) a light for himself', and an implicit suggestion that some other light is being replaced.[288] Above all, there is the curious wording of *aposbestheis opseis*, which literally says that he, the man and not his eyes, has been extinguished like a lamp. The fall of night is thus depicted as a kind of death, a quenching of personal fire.[289]

These hints are more fully worked out in the next sentence, where the sense of *haptetai* shifts from 'kindles' to 'touches, grasps': 'Living, he touches the dead in his sleep.' It is difficult to see how this can refer to anything but the dream experience of the psyche, in Pindar's phrase the 'phantom of life' (*aiōnos eidōlon*), which 'sleeps when the limbs are active but shows to sleeping men in many dreams' the vision of things not seen by day.[290] Unlike Pindar, Heraclitus refuses to admit a more penetrating psychic life in dreams: in sleep 'all we see is sleep'. At nightfall we have lost our contact with the daylight, the fire that is *shared*. So each one is obliged to strike a light 'for himself'. (Compare VI, D. 89, on sleep as a turning-away from what is common.) The experience of nightfall is one of isolation, where the individual, in his own person, reflects the quenching of diurnal fire. Like the lighting of the lamp, the dream experience is a weaker counterpart for the lucid fire of the day. The juxtaposition of XC and LXXXIX suggests a contrast between this private encounter with the dead in the flickering light of sleep and the more public vision of death that is given in all our waking hours.

'Waking (literally 'having awakened'), he touches the sleeper.' With its own form of ring structure, XC ends by a return to the point from which it began its descent into the darker regions of the psyche. How does the waking man grasp the sleeper? Presumably not as one man awake touches another man asleep, but rather by the contact of memory and physical continuity between the awakened sleeper and his own former self in sleep. The riddle lies less in the statement itself than in its studied parallelism with what precedes. Why should the waking continuity with the dream self be assimilated to the dream experience of contact with the dead? And why are both experiences presented as formal parallels to the lighting of a lamp at nightfall?

We are surrounded by a thicket of riddles, but a pattern begins to emerge: a sequence of psychic stages linked to one another by a thread of quenchings and lightings and ending by a cyclical return to the starting point. The failure of ordinary visual experience at nightfall is compensated by the lighting of a lamp. Our waking consciousness is in turn 'put out' in sleep, but we kindle for ourselves a new lamp, and thus make contact with the realm of the dead — a realm which is 'touched' but not entered, since the sleeper is still alive. The final stage, when the sleeper awakes, is a return to the initial daytime state, but now 'in touch' with all that precedes.

Every stage but the last one represents an increase of darkness and death over daylight and life — a kind of psychic descent into the underworld. In this respect the pattern of night-time, sleeping and waking parallels the elemental stages outlined in CII (D. 36), which represent the 'death' of *psyche* into inert forms and its rebirth from these elements. Since some parallel to a physical or cosmic cycle is strongly suggested by the terminology of 'quenching' and 'kindling', there has been a temptation to interpret XC in elemental terms, as when Kirk speaks of the soul in sleep 'approaching the completely watery state which means its *thanatos*' or death.[291] But no physical doctrine is stated in XC; and there is no clear basis in the fragments for a stage-by-stage correlation of waking and sleeping with the elemental cycle of CII (D. 36).

Neither CII nor XC says anything about a destiny of the psyche that rises above its normal waking state, whose vision was equated with death in LXXXIX. In this sense the whole range of ordinary human experience, asleep or awake, can be seen as so many different stages in a cycle of death. Where then is true life to be found? This question can only be answered from other fragments: XCII, XCIII, and CIX (D. 118).

XCI

XCI (D. 75)   Marcus Aurelius: [Heraclitus says, I think, that men asleep are laborers and co-workers in what takes place in the world.]

The emperor in his meditations cites from memory, without great concern for accuracy. Hence XCI is at best a free paraphrase, and some editors count it only as a reminiscence of I.3: 'men are forgetful of (do not notice) what they do asleep' (so Marcovich, p. 10). It seems more likely that Marcus here, like Plutarch in VI (D. 89), is recalling some statement on the sleeper otherwise lost, so that XCI would form a pendant to VI: in sleep a man turns away from the common world of the waking, but he is never altogether 'out of touch'. But the indication here is too vague to add anything substantial to our understanding of Heraclitus' conception of sleep.

XCII

XCII (D. 62)   Immortals <are> mortal, mortals immortal, living the others' death, dead in the others' life.

This is in point of form Heraclitus' masterpiece, the most perfectly symmetrical of all the fragments. The first two clauses of two words each (with copula unexpressed in Greek) are mirror images, identical but for the word order: a-b-b-a. The third and fourth clauses involve more complex inversions: to the participle 'living' in the third clause corresponds the noun 'life' in the fourth; and conversely for 'death' in the former and 'dead' in the latter. The symmetry is again reinforced by chiastic order: participle, noun phrase; noun phrase, participle. The two-to-two, four-to-four structuring of these twelve words points to some tight pattern of unity between life and death whose exact content is not easy to make out.

The interpretation poses two distinct problems: what is Heraclitus' own meaning here? and what is the place of this utterance in the Greek tradition of speculation about the afterlife? It is only the first question which directly concerns us; the second problem will be briefly touched on.

XCII asserts some equivalence between mortals and immortals by an interchange of death and life; it is the mode of interchange that is problematic. As a starting point for literal exegesis we may assume that the mortals and immortals mentioned here are the same as in the usual notion of men and gods, who are distinguished by War in LXXXIII (D. 53). Since the terms 'men' and 'mortals', 'gods' and 'immortals' are practically synonymous in Greek, it would be arbitrary to take them otherwise here unless we have some special reason to do so. Hence on a first interpretation we assign 'death' and 'dying' only to mortal men. The second half of XCII then says: 'they (the gods) live our death; we are dead in their life'. On this, which I will call the weak reading, there is no reference to the death of the gods. The thought is: 'we mortal men are immortal in that our death is really a new kind of (divine) life; they, the gods, are mortal not because they die but because their life is derived from *our* death'.

A stronger interpretation will reverse the roles of men and gods, as the symmetry of the clauses seems to require. But first we develop the implications of the weaker reading, in which immortals are defined as beings whose life is nourished by our death. What beings are these? The initial reference must be to elemental bodies or powers — water, earth, and the funerary fire — into which our bodies, and perhaps our psyches also, pass after death. But the beings who live from our death should include also new forms of life that spring up from the earth: the grass, the budding plants and trees, the flowers of Greek autumn and spring, as well as those worms and other animals believed to be born from the soil. Now these beings are themselves mortal. So to pursue this thought will bring us to the second, stronger interpretation, where mortals and immortals change places with one another.

In other respects also the weaker reading pushes us in the same direction. For instance, if the death of mortals is life for immortals, then the latter will include elemental water, since (according to CII, D. 36) what is death for the (human) psyche is birth for water. Hence water is one of the 'immortals' who live from our death. But by the same token water is a 'mortal', since its death is the birth of earth (CII, D. 36). Or if we think of the death of mortals here in terms of the 'extinction' of night-time and sleeping in XC (D. 26), then the immortals will be represented by successive psychic states that come to life as our normal consciousness is quenched in darkness and sleep. Included among these 'immortals' will be the nocturnal psyche and the dead whom we encounter in dreams. So once again we end up with the stronger reading: the immortals turn out to include not only the mortals but the dead.

I conclude that no weak reading, which preserves the traditional dichotomy between mortals and immortals, can stand as a complete interpretation of XCII. And a strict equivalence between the two classes is strongly suggested by the formal reversibility of the first four words, where it makes no difference which term we take as subject, which as predicate. If we take the first pair of terms as affirming that mortals are immortal, the second will affirm that immortals are mortal, and conversely. But if it makes no difference which term is subject, then it makes no difference which term serves as antecedent for the possessive pronoun 'their' (*ekeinōn*) in the two following clauses. The weaker reading construes the two occurrences of this pronoun in two different ways: the immortal gods live *our* death, the death of mortals; whereas we mortals are dead in *their* life, in the life of the gods. On the strong reading, accepting full equivalence, we reverse the antecedents and have:

Mortals live the death of immortals.[292]

Immortals are dead in the life of mortals.

For the ordinary Greek view of the gods these claims are extraordinarily shocking — scarcely less so than the contempt which Heraclitus expresses for the ritual regard for the dead. In early poetry and myth, freedom from death is the essential characteristic of the gods: mortality is what separates the human condition from the divine. By asserting the mortality of the gods in XCII, Heraclitus breaks completely with traditional Greek piety. This heretical doctrine finds some curious echoes in the literature of the fifth and fourth centuries, as we shall see. But before considering these parallels, we must pursue one step further the interpretation of XCII within the context of Heraclitus' own thought.

For a full interpretation, the strong reading requires two theses which reinforce one another and which may be seen as complementary aspects of a single claim: (1) the reversibility of the process of death, by analogy with sleeping and waking, day and night, summer and winter, and (2) the complete relativization or generalization of the notion of death, conceived as any change of state in which something old gives way before something drastically new. Hence it will not be a metaphor to speak of the death of water (for instance, in evaporation) or of the death of day at nightfall, any more than it is metaphorical to speak of the dying out of spring vegetation in the long drought of Greek summer. Human death — the death of each of us, and of those dear to us — will have to be understood as a phenomenon of precisely the same sort, a change of state within the total life cycle of nature. This thought will be developed in XCIII.

We may now note some historical parallels to this paradoxical view. Since the basic axiom of traditional Greek piety is that the gods are immortal, to speak of their death is the gravest sort of blasphemy.[293] In the case of the one god, Dionysus, whose death was recounted in a myth of the classical period, the evidence is too obscure and complicated to be discussed here. What is clear is that Herodotus, when he refers to a comparable Egyptian myth concerning Osiris (whom he identified with Dionysus), is always careful to hedge his report with something like mystic silence: 'who it is they mourn on this occasion, it is not pious (*hosion*) for me to say'.[294] But if to speak of the death of a single god is an act of sacrilege, what are we to say of the general pronouncement that 'immortals are mortal'? As Wilamowitz observed, at Athens Heraclitus would have been put to death for impiety.

I do not know of any true parallel in the classical period to this insistence upon the mortality of the immortals. Empedocles does speak of powers 'swiftly growing mortal (*thnēta*) which had previously learned to be immortal (*athanata*)' (fr. 35.14). Empedocles may be echoing Heraclitus, but his context is cosmogonic and allegorical: he is referring to the formation of mortal compounds from the combination of elemental principles, under the influence of Love. Thus, although there is a genuine affinity of doctrine, the esoteric verses of Empedocles have nothing like the provocative force of XCII. It seems unlikely that any pious Greek was scandalized by this passage.

On the other hand the converse assertion, that a mortal can become a god, is announced by Empedocles in another poem, his *Katharmoi* or 'Purifications', in terms that must have been regarded as provocative: 'I greet you, I an immortal god, mortal no longer.'[295] To find a

parallel to this extraordinary pronouncement in the classical period
we must look to the mystic promise preserved on two of the gold
tablets from Thurii in South Italy, buried with a body in the grave:
'Fortunate and most blessed, you will be a god instead of a mortal.'[296]

Now the claim that a mortal may become a god, however presump-
tuous it may sound in the fifth century, has at least a mythic precedent in the story of Heracles' acceptance among the Olympians. The
related thesis, that this human life is in reality the death of a higher
being, is much more esoteric. Again we find a hint of such a view in
the *Purifications* of Empedocles, where the body is described as an
'alien garment of flesh' (fr. 126) and birth seems to be referred to as
the unwelcome arrival in an unfamiliar place, to be greeted by
funereal cries and lamentation (fr. 118; cf. 119 and 125). Even closer
parallels to XCII can be found in Attic literature:

Who knows if life be death, but death in turn
be recognized below as life? (Euripides, fr. 638 Nauck)

Plato quotes these Euripidean verses in the *Gorgias* (492E) as evidence
for the view that 'perhaps we are truly dead'; and he speaks in this
connection of a doctrine that regards the body (*sōma*) as the tomb
(*sēma*) of the soul.

This is not the place to discuss the origins and ramifications of this
non-standard view of the human psyche; my point was simply to illustrate the affinity of language between XCII and certain mystic doctrines associated with the so-called Orphic, more accurately
Pythagorean, tradition. But it does not follow from the fact that
Heraclitus uses the language of this tradition that he accepts the view
of the psyche which it implies. The monistic tendency of his own
thought is really incompatible with the doctrine of an individual
psyche migrating from body to body. Heraclitus makes use of this
mystic language in part for its shock effect, to suggest the drastic
novelty of his own insight into the unity of life and death, the radically
'unexpected' truth that awaits men beyond the grave.

XCIII

XCIII (D. 88)   The same . . . : living and dead, and the waking and the sleeping,
and young and old. For these transposed are those, and those transposed again
are these.[297]

As a basis for the interpretation for XCIII, I recall the two complementary principles enunciated above: (1) the reversibility of the pro-

cess of death, by analogy with the alternation of sleeping and waking and with the return of the seasons of the year, and (2) the generalization of the notion of death, conceived as any change of state in which something old gives way before something radically new. The first thesis, implied by XCII, is here stated explicitly. The corresponding generalization or relativization of the concept of death, which seems implicit in both XCII and XCIII, is more directly documented by CII (D. 36), if we take the reference to the 'death' of water and earth quite literally. Both the literal interpretation of CII and the generalized notion of death are entailed by the panpsychism I have attributed to Heraclitus on the basis of XXXI (D. 113) and XXXV (D. 45). (By the usual hermeneutical circle, this attribution is now confirmed by its application to XCII, XCIII, and CII.) And of course *some* unity between life and death, including some positive evaluation of the negative term, follows from Heraclitus' central conception of the *harmoniē* or fitting together of opposites, as was seen in the discussion of LXXVIII (D. 51) and LXXIX (D. 48). What remains to be shown is how these various doctrines are connected in a coherent view of life-beyond-death for the human being or for the psyche.

It is natural to begin by a comparison with the Pythagorean doctrine of transmigration, for this must have served as point of departure for Heraclitus' own view of the afterlife. The Pythagorean doctrine satisfies my principle of reversibility by positing a process of rebirth (in a new body) as the converse of dying (when the psyche leaves its previous body). It also involves a relativization of the notion of death, insofar as birth and death are both interpreted as a change of state for the psyche rather than as radical coming-to-be and passing-away. To this extent, there is a genuine affinity between Heraclitus' thought and the mystic view of the soul, which justifies the affinity of language already noted. But the Pythagorean doctrine implies a basic disparity between the destiny of the deathless psyche and that of the mortal body, and hence a fundamental dualism between the realms of the animate (or deathless) and inanimate (or mortal). It is precisely here that Heraclitus' view diverges in virtue of his monism, which in this context means his panpsychism, and his extension of the notion of death to any radical change of state. The statement of CII (D. 36), that the psyche which dies is reborn as water and the water which dies is reborn as earth, can be seen as a generalization of the doctrine of transmigration for the whole cycle of elemental transformations, in which every stage is simultaneously a death and a rebirth. (Thus Heraclitus has extended the Pythagorean cycle of re-

birth to the general Milesian conception of elemental coming-to-be
and passing-away expressed in the fragment of Anaximander.) Since
the Pythagoreans themselves had emphasized the continuity between
different forms of life — human, animal, vegetable — their view could
be formulated by Plato as the claim that 'all nature is akin' (*Meno*
81C9). The panpsychism of Heraclitus is perhaps best understood
as an insistence upon taking this claim literally, together with a will-
ingness to draw the most radical consequences from it for the interpretation of human destiny. As XCIII indicates by the parallel to
waking and sleeping, youth and age, and the claim that all these are
'the same', the alternation of psychic death and rebirth in a new
form, by which the dead become the living and 'these are transposed
as those', is then only a special case of the general law of nature with
its rhythmic alternation between opposite poles, as in the mutual
succession of night and day, the annual *tropai* of the sun and seasons.
This was perfectly understood by Plato, who introduces the doctrine
of the rebirth of souls from the dead in the *Phaedo* as a conclusion
from the more general theory concerning 'all animals and plants and
all things that have a coming-to-be (*genesis*)', a theory which argues
in impeccable Heraclitean form that in every case 'they come to be as
opposites from opposites, and in no other way' (*Phaedo* 70D–E).

Now the natural objection to this generalized view of immortality
and the reversibility of death — an objection which the mystic doctrine of reincarnation seeks to avoid — is that it is always something
new that is reborn, and not the same entity as before. Just as yesterday and tomorrow are not the same day, and last summer and next
summer are not the same season, so it will never be the same man
who, after growing old, becomes young again, nor will it be the same
human being who can hope to be reborn after his death. And therefore, this objection runs, there is a crucial disanalogy between these
cases and phenomena like sleeping and waking, where the psyche
undergoes a fundamental change of state but remains one and the
same throughout. The analogy articulated in XCIII thus fails to take
account of the central feature of personal identity, the fact of psychophysical continuity established both by memory and by bodily persistence between the man awake and his former self asleep, as between
the waking man now and his earlier waking state. But there is no comparable identity or continuity between the man living and the man
dead (except for the persistence of his bodily components in their
slow return to the elements), and none at all between the old man
and some future state of youth. Consequently, the principle of rever-

sibility posited by the analogy to sleep fails utterly in the case of death and aging. Any hope of survival or revival which rests upon this analogy must be fallacious, and can offer no real consolation either for our individual death or for our experience of diminution in old age.

This objection is a crucial one, and the answer to it will bring out more clearly the radical nature of Heraclitus' thought about life and death. For his answer must take the form of a fundamental denial of the notions of personal and psychic identity as ordinarily conceived. I think there is no doubt that Heraclitus would confidently reject the charge of fallacy and would insist that the alleged disanalogy is a snare and a delusion. In reality, neither our bodies nor our psyches are, in the strict sense, ever one and the same from one moment to the next: they are continually undergoing radical transformation, dying and being reborn again at every instant. Once more Plato has rendered Heraclitus' thought with complete fidelity, in the passage already cited from the *Symposium* (207D–208B, above, p. 167). But let the old riddler speak for himself.

'As they step into the same rivers, other and still other waters flow upon them' (L, D. 12). The identity of the river is one of form and physical continuity, but not of material identity or preservation of the same content. And as the reference to men stepping in makes clear, this coexistence of continuity with massive change is understood in terms of the human experience of a world that is fundamentally stable but never really the same. If you look for strict identity, 'you cannot step twice into the same river'.[298] That is to say, the lack of identity between one day or one summer and the next is exactly paralleled by the lack of identity between one moment of our experience and another moment of our experience of 'the same thing'. Even in the case of personal continuity between the sleeping and waking man, between the dream self and the everyday self, the relationship is one of psychic contiguity or contact, not strict identity: the waking 'touches' (*haptetai*) the sleeping in memory, as the living sleeper touches the dead in dreaming (XC, D. 26). Thus there is just as much, and just as little, unity and identity between a man and his dreams, between a man and his past self and past experience, as between a man and his offspring (see XCV and XCVIII below), or between a man and his lasting fame (XCVII); and just as much and as little identity between one elemental form and its successor, or between the river today and the river tomorrow.

Still, the objection has not been fully answered. For if we understand (as I think we must) the Heraclitean river-of-flux doctrine in the way that has just been indicated, the objector may respond as follows. Even if there is no such thing as absolute identity over time for individual persons or objects, nevertheless there are different grades of relative identity. In the case of persons, there is first the phenomenon of physical continuity (from time to time and from place to place) for a body of the same general form, with massive overlap of the same material constituents from one interval to the next — the kind of identity over time which human beings share with physical objects such as stones or trees, and which lasts beyond their death as long as the body remains more or less intact. And there is also the fact of psychological continuity with the same self in the past and in the future. This psychic continuity, which we tend to think of as distinctly human (though it must be shared to some extent by other animals as well) connects me with my past self not only by explicit memories but also by the entire pattern of habits, skills, preferences, nostalgias, phobias, and recurrent moods — by the entire pattern of my personality as a legacy from childhood and adolescence, down to my delightful or irritating experiences of yesterday or of five minutes ago. On the other hand, this same psychic continuity connects me with my future self not only by the persistence, more or less unchanged, of this elaborate pattern from the past, but also by the constant projection of myself into the future, by way of hopes and fears for tomorrow, by long- and short-run plans for actions, ambitions for future achievements and rewards, forboding of future losses (including the death of those dear to me, and also my own death), a whole range of prepared responses for coming contingencies of all sorts. Now the importance of the first concept, the thought of physical or bodily continuity beyond death, is reflected in all the immense variety of ancient funeral cult and grave adornment, but most strikingly in the Egyptian practice of mummification, designed precisely to preserve the recognizable form of an individual body. On the other hand, the psychic continuity beyond death is presupposed, in some sense, by all concern with the future of one's fame and of one's family, including perhaps the concern for one's own burial — as if one were to be among the spectators — and for future remembrance in the regular tending of one's grave. But in this perspective the most striking expression of a concern for future psychic continuity, corresponding in principle to the practice of mummification for the preservation of bodily identity, is the Pythagorean doctrine of a recollection of previous existences, with the corresponding importance in the eschatology of the South Italian gold tablets of the promise of a drink from the waters of Memory, the cool drink from the lake of Mnemosyne in the world below, that will permit the dead to retain the essential psychic contact with his personal past in the future state that awaits him.[299]

Such is our ordinary, pre-philosophic concept of personal identity or individual survival in its double form, bodily and psychic. Quite distinct is our notion of generic or specific identity, as when one horse or one tree is replaced by another, or when parents are replaced by children who become parents in turn in successive generations. It is this notion of generic survival, or replacement in kind, that is exemplified by the sequence of days and of seasons, and in a different way also by the waters that are continually being replaced within a given river.[300]

Finally, there is a third, and again different notion of replacement or survival in which the principle of generic identity or likeness of kind is given up, as when plants are consumed by animals, or when dung and corpses are reabsorbed into the earth and the elements, or when one element such as water yields to another element such as earth, according to Heraclitus' own doctrine. Here there is a certain notion of physical continuity from one state to the next, and a regular sequence of stages, but no sense in which any likeness of kind or definite form is preserved.[301]

Our objection against Heraclitus' view of the interchange of living and dead, young and old in XCIII can now be reformulated as the claim that he systematically blurs the distinction between these three kinds of 'survival', characterized by (1) some preservation of psychic or bodily individuality, (2) the maintenance or recurrence of the same generic form, and (3) regularity in the sequence of changes, with some continuity between stages but no preservation of individual or even generic identity. What men ordinarily desire is individual survival in the first sense, which is promised to them in some measure by the various grave cults of antiquity, and even by the dismal Homeric picture of the *psychai* as phantoms of men in the world below, but which finds its most perfect fulfillment in the mystic promise of future bliss (whether pagan or Christian). It is the second form, generic survival or replacement by another individual of the same kind, which is represented in the desire for offspring and in the practice of naming a male child after the grandfather or some other older relative. However, if Heraclitus' generalization of the notion of death is taken seriously, so that the death of water and the birth of earth are to be regarded as strictly parallel to the death and birth of an individual human being, this has the effect of reducing the first two forms of survival to the third. But the third form of continuity in change is *mere transformatio:* the production of something new with the annihilation of what has gone before, so that neither individual survival nor likeness of kind is maintained.

To this natural objection I believe the true Heraclitean response will be: 'You have entirely misunderstood my doctrine. Yes, I do reduce all sorts of change and survival to one type, but it is to the second and not to the third: to likeness of kind and identity of structure, which the river illustrates by preserving its form while all the individuating matter has been replaced: the river as a concrete individual is ever dying and being reborn, as "other and again other waters" are ever pouring in. And this identity of pattern holds generally for nature as a whole: it includes the constant structure of the year, within which the seasons change, as well as the constant unit of the night-and-day, within which the relative length of the night and of the day will vary according to the seasons. So even if (as I am willing to grant) Anaximander or some other theorist was right to suppose that the formation of the world will be balanced in time by its destruction, so that the ruling principle of fire will eventually consume all things in a regular exchange between itself as fire and itself as cosmos, even so the unity of the whole pattern will be preserved, within which all the parts must change and recur with likeness of kind. In short, the only identical *individual* is the cosmic process as a whole, with its cycle of recurrence over the longest year, whatever time and pattern this cycle of transformations may take; but its unity of structure is guaranteed by the regular recurrence of the *same forms*, by likeness of kind, as defined by the permanent tension and rhythmic alternation between opposites at every level: from individual birth and death to the daily lighting and quenching of the sun; from the birth and death of the elements to the eternal kindling and extinction of cosmic fire. This is the sense of personal identity and personal survival which I have come to recognize: the unity of all things in the wise one alone, which I found when I set out in search of myself.'

Thus it is the recognition of this common pattern in the part and the whole, this universal law of polar tension and the regular pendulum swing back and forth between opposites, the endless recurrence of 'everliving fire' in the same forms, which provides the only consolation there is or could be for human aging and death. Perhaps the greatest surprise that awaits us at our death is that things will not be very different, since we are and always have been familiar with the experience of continually dying and continually being reborn.

XCIV

XCIV (D. 52)   Lifetime (*aiōn*) is a child at play, moving pieces in a game. Kingship belongs to the child.

My own solution to this most enigmatic of Heraclitean riddles is indicated by the translation of *pesseuōn* as 'moving pieces in a game', where this is understood as an echo of 'things transposed' (*metapesonta*) in XCIII (D. 88). What was there said to be moved back and forth was 'living and dead, and the waking and the sleeping, and young and old'. Such reversals constitute the very principle of cosmic order. More specifically, these three pairs define the structure of human experience as an alternating pattern of being kindled and going out. On my view the fundamental thought is not the childlike and random movements of the game (as some interpreters have supposed) but the fact that these moves follow a definite rule, so that after one side plays it is the other's turn, and after the victory is reached the play must start over from the beginning. The rules of the *pessoi*-game thus imitate the alternating measures of cosmic fire.

My interpretation assumes a continuity of thought and imagery between XCIII (D. 88) and XCIV (D. 52). This continuity would be guaranteed if we could be sure that the game of *pessoi* envisaged in XCIV involved the use of dice, like modern *tavli* or backgammon (as Marcovich suggests, p. 494). For the verb *metapesein* for 'transpositions' in XCIII has the literal sense of 'fall out otherwise' and could immediately suggest the fall of a die. But whether or not we bring dice into this game the verb *metapesein* will remain relevant to XCIV, since it is a synonym of other verbs (*metatithenai* and *metaballein*) that typically describe moving pieces on a board.[302]

If we agree, then, to take the back-and-forth movement of XCIII (with its cosmic and human applications) as a clue for understanding the *pessoi*-game in XCIV, we are left with three puzzles to unravel:

(1) Why is the player named *aiōn* 'lifetime'?
(2) Why is he called 'a child at play' (*pais paizōn*)?
(3) Why is the child described as a king?

Any answer to (2) is likely to seem conjectural; the first and third puzzles admit of rather straightforward solutions.

(1) *Aiōn* has the sense 'vitality', '(human) life', as when Pindar calls the soul 'the image of [the man's] *aiōn*' (fr. 116 Bowra). On this sense is based the standard usage of the word for 'lifetime', 'duration (of a life)', which, under the influence of the cognate adverb *aiei* ('always', 'forever') eventually makes *aiōn* a synonym for 'time' (*chronos*). Finally, in Plato's *Timaeus* and thereafter, *aiōn* acquires the technical sense of timeless 'eternity' as contrasted with temporal duration. This later technical sense is irrelevant here. But the whole range of other meanings, from human lifetime to larger temporal periods, are all properly suggested by the name of the player whose game includes both the movements of human life and death and the back-and-forth reversals of the cosmos.

(3) It is obvious why the player possesses 'kingship', since the game is a cosmic one, and the player must be lord of the universe, like the pilot who 'steers all things' according to LIV (D. 41) and CXIX (D. 64). Now the only other text where this ruling principle is called 'king' is LXXXIII (D. 53), where War is 'father of all and king of all', appointing some as gods, others as men, some slave, others free. If we bear in mind the equation-by-transposition of mortals and immortals in XCII, we see that the games played by Lifetime and by War have the same structure. Just as the bow, whose work is death, is named 'life' (*bios*), so the king of conflict and destruction can be called 'lifetime' (*aiōn*).

(2) The hardest question is why the king, designated 'father' in LXXXIII (D. 53), appears here as a child at play, 'playing the child'. The triple occurrence of the stem 'child' (*pais, paizōn, paidos*) does not seem fully explained by the fact that *pessoi* is a children's game.

At the risk of yielding to free association, I propose some connection with the theme of father-son transpositions in the cycle of generations developed in XCV (D. A19) and XCVIII (D.20).[303] The 'everlasting child' (taking *aiōn pais* together, with a play on *aei ōn* or *aeizōōn* 'everliving', as in XXXVII, D. 30) remains forever youthful, even infantile, throughout his 'lifetime', playing his endless game and maintaining his eternal kingship by a series of births and deaths across the generations, by the endless *begetting of children*. The father thus sees the 'kingship' — the initiative, the first move in the game — pass to his son, who becomes a father in turn and is confronted with the same game.

Also possible here is the commentators' suggestion of arbitrary or random movement, as in the cast of the dice: a truly *childish* game not guided by mature intelligence or reasonable plan. This would present a paradoxical counterpart to the insistence elsewhere on the *wisdom* of the cosmic principle that is more than a match for Zeus (CXVIII, D. 32). This notion of a witless or arbitrary ruler might be understood as a parallel to CXXV (D. 124): as the finest *kosmos* or adornment is produced by random sweepings, so the wise balance of the universe emerges from the thoughtless movements of a child at play.

XCV

XCVA (D. A19)   Plutarch: [A generation is thirty years according to Heraclitus, in which time the progenitor has engendered one who generates.]

XCVB (D. A19)   Censorinus: [Heraclitus is the authority for calling thirty years a generation, because the cycle of life lies in this interval. He calls the cycle of life <the interval> until nature returns from human seed-time to seed-time.]

There has been some confusion over the literal meaning of this state-ment, a confusion which goes back to an ancient variant and which, despite its careful correction by Fränkel and Kirk, has not been eliminated from the most recent commentaries.[304] The confusion lies in counting the generational period of thirty years from the birth of the grandfather to the birth of his grandson, i.e. as a cycle of *two* generations by any normal count, instead of from a father's begetting of a son to the son's becoming a father in turn. It is the latter interval, from one begetting to the next, that is described by both Plutarch and Censorinus; and the period of thirty years corresponds to a natural cycle of human generations, as will be seen in a moment. There is no reason to take seriously the other interpretation, even though the mistake is as old as Philo.[305]

The error is a natural one, since the text reflected in Plutarch describes the father-son relationship as repeated indefinitely, so that the father becomes the grandfather as the son begets in turn. Thus a man becomes a grandfather thirty years *after he becomes a father.* From this mention of the third generation some ancient author, per-haps Philo himself, drew the biologically correct but humanly un-interesting observation that thirty years is *the earliest age at which one can become a grandfather!* Since no Greek male was the father of a legitimate child at the age of 15, this theoretical doubling of the time required for puberty is quite irrelevant to the thought of XCV. A generation is the interval between parents and children, not be-tween grandparents and grandchildren.

Thirty years may seem an arbitrary number, but there is good evidence for the social and historical reality of this figure, which scholars sometimes use as a basis for calculating dates from genealogical lists. Thus it is Hesiod's advice that a man should marry around the age of thirty (*Works and Days* 696f.); and three centuries later Plato specifies that the age of marriage should be between 25 and 35, or 30 and 35.[306] In a careful anthropological study of one of the most archaic societies of Greece today, the semi-nomadic Sarakatsani shepherds of the Zagori mountains in northwest Greece, J.K. Campbell reports that the sons are normally married at about the age of 30.[307] Now in a traditional society, where marriage is quite deliberately undertaken in view of procreation, a man who marries around the age of thirty can generally expect to become a father within a year. Of course the first child may not be a son. But if it is, and if the son marries in turn at thirty, the situation described by Heraclitus will be realized. Hesiod and Plato indicate that this happened quite often in ancient Greece, as it does today (or did yesterday, since the study relates to 1945–55) among the Sarakatsani, where 58 out of 123 sons married at the age of 30 of 31, and most of the others married within a year or two of that age.

The human significance of this period, where the son assumes in turn the role of father, can be seen in Campbell's description of a concretely observed society.

> Although the late date of marriage of brothers is not unconnected with the duty of first discharging obligations towards the sisters before a man acquires a family of his own, it is not a simple correlation. It is also related to the balance of power between father and son. If a man marries at the age of 30 and his first son is born a year later, this son will in turn reach the age of 30 when his father is in his early sixties, an age at which he becomes physically incapable of the strenuous life that the executive head of a shepherd family necessarily leads . . . He must, then, bow to the inevitable, arrange the marriage of his son and in a short time (at the birth of his first grandchild) hand over control; for, as we have stressed, it is not compatible with the values of this community for a married man with a child to be still under parental control and not master in his own house. But fathers do not normally hand over control until they have to. (*Honour, Family, and Patronage*, pp. 83f.)

The life and values of contemporary Sarakatsani shepherds are not those of the citizens of Ephesus in 500 B.C. But in the rude conditions

of existence for their joint families, they illustrate in a very striking
way the succession of power and vitality, the exchange between age
and youth, father and son, in the endless, repetitive game played by
Lifetime (*aiōn*).

For the connections between this human cycle of 30 years and the
cosmic cycle of 10,800 years in the 'great year', see above on XLIII
(D. A13 and A5). The conflict and succession of generations is the
central human instance of the pattern of opposition and exchange between the old and the new, between life and death: the pattern of
renewal by destruction and recurrence. The father dies, and is replaced
by his son, who buries his father but continues his life, biologically
and also ritually in the tendence of his grave. 'Mortals are immortal,
immortals mortal.'[308]

XCVI

XCVI (D. 25)   Greater deaths (*moroi*) are allotted greater destinies (*moirai*).

Formally speaking, this is another gem of artful construction in
miniature. Of the five words of XCVI, the first four begin with the
same letter. The first and fourth are cognates and near-synonyms
(*moroi, moirai*), masculine and feminine noun-formations from the
root of *meiromai* 'to receive as one's share'; here they correspond
syntactically as subject and object of the verb. The second and third
words represent the same adjective, structured syntactically by agreement with the corresponding noun (*mezones, mezonas*). Thus the
syntactic pattern is a-a-b-b, but in meaning and morphology it is
a^1-b-b-a^2. The tight antiphonal symmetry is relieved by the longer
and phonetically unrelated final word *lanchanousi*, whose meaning is
closely akin to the root of *moros* and *moira*: '(receive as) one's share
or portion'. At first sight the fragment is a mystifying tautology:
'greater portions have allotted to them greater shares'.

Though etymologically sound, this trivial reading cannot suffice.
The meaning of *moros* as 'portion' or 'lot' survives only in a few technical uses; from Homer on, the term acquires the literary sense of
'doom' or 'violent death'.[309] The cognate *moira* does have a wide
range of uses in which the etymological value is preserved: 'part',
'share', 'fraction', hence 'allotted region', 'territory', or 'share of
esteem', 'social class'. But *moira* in poetry characteristically refers to
the personal fate of a man, his allotted share of life delimited by the
moment of death. Thus Moira is personified as goddess (after Homer,

goddesses) of Fate, where 'fate' is understood in reference to death. Taking the words in this literary sense we get as a second reading: 'the magnitude of one's death determines the magnitude of one's destiny or share of life'.

There are two natural interpretations of this statement, neither of them entirely satisfactory. There may be an allusion here to the mystic promise of something beyond the grave, a fate 'far better for the initiated' or purified souls than for the others, who suffer punishment or 'lie in the mire'.[310] Such an allusion comes as a surprise, for the Heraclitean doctrine of survival seems to point to a single destiny of elemental psychic recurrence for all alike. The only hint so far of possible differences in destinies beyond the grave lies in the threat that Justice will lay hands on those who fabricate lies or testify to them (LXXXVII, D. 28B); and the lies in question seem to relate to the fate of the soul after death. It is not clear how this conception of justice, with the hint there of punishment and here of reward, can find a place within the monistic pattern of Heraclitus' thought. This is, perhaps, the most difficult problem for the interpretation of his philosophy as a coherent system. I return to it in the commentary on CIX.

There is a second, less mysterious interpretation, which poses similar problems for Heraclitus' monism but which does explain how one's destiny can be determined by one's death or *moros*. This view, which interprets the greater destinies by reference to the traditional Greek glorification of an heroic death in battle, has been accepted by Diels and many other commentators, since it appears to be confirmed by Heraclitus' own remarks about the pursuit of glory (in XCVII, D. 29) and the honor bestowed on those who die in battle (in C, D. 24). The glory won by risking one's life in single combat is the theme of the *Iliad*; and Tyrtaeus speaks in similar terms of the warrior who defends his city in the hoplite phalanx. Great is the share of honor for him who dies fighting in the forefront: he is lamented 'by young men and old alike; the whole city mourns him with terrible grief. His tomb and his children are pointed out among men, and his children's children and his race thereafter. Never will his noble fame (*kleos*) perish, nor his name, but even when he lies under the earth he becomes immortal (*athanatos*), he whom furious Ares destroys as he excells in bravery, standing firm in combat, fighting for the sake of his land and his children' (Tyrtaeus, fr. 9. 23—34; cf. frs. 6—7).

Now Heraclitus is not one to follow the poets or to take the mob as his master. But he has chosen his terms in such a way as to suggest this traditional glorification of the hero's death.[311] The classical exaltation of military death, echoed in Horace's ode *pro patria mori*, is part of the fundamental ideology of civic solidarity on which the city-state depended for its very existence. And Heraclitus has expressed his own endorsement of such a view in other texts, as when he speaks of 'holding fast to what is shared by all' (XXX, D. 114) and 'fighting for the law as for the city wall' (LXV, D. 44).

Both mystic and military interpretations are surely relevant, but neither can render the full content of this tantalizing sentence. The initial appearance of tautology, reinforced by the extraordinary formal symmetry, strongly suggests that the greater rewards are somehow immanent in the quality of the death as such.

XCVII–XCVIII

XCVII (D. 29)   The best choose one thing in exchange for all, everflowing fame among mortals; but most men have sated themselves like cattle.

XCVIII (D. 20)   Once born they want to live and have their portions (*moroi*); and they leave children behind born to become their dooms (*moroi*).

These two fragments belong together on thematic grounds; both deal with the ends men choose in living. And there is a formal reason for combining them. The understood subject of XCVIII is almost certainly *hoi polloi* 'most people', mentioned in the last clause of XCVII; so that it is plausible to read the former as a direct continuation of the latter. Taken as a continuous text, XCVII–XCVIII provide a commentary on XCVI, recalled here by the word play on *moros*.

XCVII–XCVIII give us two opposing conceptions of life and immortality: the choice of the noblest (*hoi aristoi*), like Achilles in love with imperishable fame (*kleos*); in contrast to the desires and satisfaction of 'most men', who are compared to cattle or beasts of burden (*ktēnea*). The terms of heroic choice recall the cosmic value of fire which, like gold, serves as payment for all things (XL, D. 90): 'one thing in exchange for all'. The choice of the cattle-men is described in terms of 'satiety' *koros*. (For this theme compare LXVII, D. 111; CXX, D. 65; and CXXIII, D. 67.) If my arrangement is correct, this *same* choice of beast-like satisfaction is described in XCVIII by reference to the sequence of generations. The cycle of generations is here reinterpreted as a cycle of births (*ginomena . . . genesthai*) equivalent to so many deaths (*moroi*: both terms repeated in each clause of XCVIII).[312]

Achilles is the paradigmatic hero precisely because, when confronted with a clear choice between long life (*aiōn*) or undying fame (*kleos*) to be paid for by an early death, he unhesitatingly pursues the course of honor and death in combat.[313] Heraclitus has generalized this choice as an option between two forms of death and survival: a flaming ardor for 'one thing in exchange for all', or the animal satisfactions of a portion of life continued across the generations by procreation. The latter course is not only common to cattle and sheep; it is in a larger sense the pattern of death and immortality for all things, in the river of everflowing change and recurrence. The former, distinctively human choice is exemplified by (but scarcely limited to) the continuous stream of glory which flows from a heroic death in battle.

The stylistic detail of XCVII–XCVIII merits attention. We have seen how 'one thing in exchange for all' in XCVII establishes a formal parallel between the aim of a noble life and the omnivalent principle of fire. The phrase which follows immediately, 'everflowing fame among (literally, of) mortals', is marked by a curious syntactic ambiguity and a famous literary parallel. In his encomium on the glorious dead of Thermopylae, Simonides spoke of 'the tomb which is an altar . . . a funeral offering which all-conquering time will not efface', and of Leonidas 'who left behind a great adornment of excellence (*aretās kosmon*) and everflowing fame (*aenaon te kleos*)'.[314] Leonidas and his men would furnish a splendid example of what Heraclitus meant by the choice of 'the best' or 'the noblest ones' (*hoi aristoi*).

The syntactic ambiguity (pointed out by Bollack-Wismann) lies in the construction of the phrase 'everflowing fame of mortals' with the preceding clause. The natural reading is to take this phrase as spelling out the 'one thing' which the best will choose 'in exchange for all'. But that construction (which must be included in the total meaning of XCVII) makes the genitive *thnētōn* 'of mortals' curiously superfluous, not to say clumsy. The use of the genitive seems to be motivated by its formal parallel with the preceding *pantōn* '(in place) of all things'. That parallel suggests that 'the best' are related to 'mortals' as 'the one' (or glory, or fire) is related to 'all things', so that these noblest ones become themselves 'the ever renewed glory' which is produced from, and worth the price of, the totality of 'mortal beings'. Thus taking 'everflowing fame' in apposition with the subject (*hoi aristoi*) rather than with the object of choice, we see these heroes as eternally rejuvenated from among the dying ('out of the mortals', with the partitive construction), since it is precisely by such deaths that *mortals become immortal* — at least in the traditional sense illustrated in Tyrtaeus and Simonides, and perhaps in another sense yet to be specified.

The composition of XCVIII contains a ring effect, suggesting a cycle of recurrence, produced by the repetition of the same verb as first and last word in the sentence: *genomenoi . . . genesthai.* This repetition is my excuse for rendering the verb twice, first 'born (as children)' and then 'become (dooms)'. The double occurrence of *moroi* also highlights the multivocity of this term, which was implicit in XCVI. In its first occurrence here 'to have (one's) *moros*' seems to mean 'to get one's share of life', to obtain one's place in the sun. But from XCVI and the literary use of *moros* elsewhere, we know that these portions of life are really 'dooms' or 'deaths'. In their animal pursuit of satiety (*koros*), by trying to get their share of life most men gain their share of death. Instead of leaving behind like Leonidas 'an adornment of excellence and everlasting fame', they leave behind children who will contest their power and control their property, first occupying their portions of life and then following them into the grave.[315]

XCIX

XCIX (D. 103)   Porphyry: [According to Heraclitus, the beginning and the end (*peras*) are shared in the circumference of a circle.]

This is one of those remarks which, like CIII (D. 60: 'the way up and down is one and the same') might be equally appropriate in other Heraclitean contexts: to mark the diurnal recurrence of the sun (from darkness to darkness), the cycle of the year, the cosmic seasons, the transformations of elements into one another, and so on. I connect it here with the cycle of generations seen as a cycle of mortality, in order to mark the pattern of ring composition (*genomenoi . . . genesthai*) in XCVIII, and hence to characterize the cyclical form of immortality-through-dying defined in XCVI–XCVIII. (On my arrangement, Heraclitus reverts to the nobler form of immortality in C, thus returning by a larger ring structure to the thesis posed in XCVI and the first sentence of XCVII.) In this symmetrical pattern of periodic recurrence the immortality of mankind does not differ in principle from that of beasts or even elements, as we have seen, since they too 'have their shares (*moroi*)' in the universal life of nature.

This generational cycle, in which like is regularly replaced by like, offers a mundane equivalent to that 'terrible, grievous wheel' of rebirth from which the mystic initiate hoped to escape.[316] For Heraclitus there is no escape. But there must be some alternative destiny represented by the choice of glory in XCVII (D. 29). Our understanding of his psychology and eschatology will not be complete until we can make sense of this nobler destiny within the context of Heraclitus' monism.

There are two linguistic features of Porphyry's citation in XCIX which suggest literal authenticity, and which might offer a preliminary clue for the solution of our problem. One is the term *peras* for the end point or limit of the circle.[317] The only other occurrence of this word in the fragments is in the statement on the *logos* of the soul, so deep that we cannot find its limits (*peirata*) even if we travel over every path (XXXV, D. 45). So the endless cycle of XCIX may allude to another endlessness of the psyche, based on its own *logos* which need not be cyclical in the same sense. The second hint of verbal accuracy in XCIX is the old Ionic form *xynos* for 'shared', 'common'. The use of this thematic term should be a hint that the circle in question is precisely the common pattern of cosmic order. But the concept of 'what is common' has two dimensions: objectively, it is the universal structure of unity, symmetry and recurrence; subjectively, it is the apprehension of this structure. Thus 'thinking is shared (*xynos*) by all' (XXXI, D. 113), and men of understanding (*noos*) 'hold fast to what is shared by all', in their thought as in their speech and action (XXX, D. 114). If the soul has its own mode of endlessness, that must consist precisely in the firm grasp of cosmic order by which the few with understanding are distinguished from the many, who exemplify but do not comprehend the universal pattern.

C

C (D. 24)   Gods and men honor those who fall in battle (*arēiphatoi*, 'those who are slain by Ares').

One commentary on C has already been provided by Tyrtaeus' description of the extraordinary honors that men heap upon the grave and memory of him 'whom Ares has destroyed' (above, p. 232). What C adds to this traditional thought is honor from the gods as well. If we translate this according to the 'transpositions' of XCII and XCIII, we can say: honor among the dead as well as among the living, honors in the larger fate of the psyche and not only at the grave and in the memory of men.

The parallel between gods and men recalls LXXXIII (D. 53), where war, as king of all, appoints 'some as gods, others as men'. It seems likely that the exceptional status of those who die *sur le champ d'honneur* is somehow connected with the fact that the god Ares who destroys them can himself be identified with King Polemos, the universal power of conflict and opposition.

This link to LXXXIII makes of C more than a banal restatement of traditional Greek respect for those who die in battle. But it does not yet explain how the special honors *given by the gods* are to be integrated within a general theory of the psyche and its destiny.[318]

CI

CI (D. 115)   To the soul (*psychē*) belongs a report (*logos*) that increases itself.

This statement would be of great interest for the theory of the psyche if we could be sure that it comes from Heraclitus. Unfortunately, the language is not distinctive enough to guarantee authenticity; and the textual attestation is weak.[319] There is a suspicious resemblance to the definition of *psychē* which Aristotle cites (and refutes) as 'the number which moves itself'.[320] However, since there is a reference to the *logos* of soul in XXXV (D. 45), and since the notion that the *psychē* grows or feeds itself with the body is attested in Hippocratic writings,[321] it is just possible that CI is after all a quotation from Heraclitus.

With all due caution, then, I conjecture (1) that the self-augmenting power of the psyche is part of what is meant by the 'deep *logos*' of the soul in XXXV (D. 45), and (2) that this power of self-expansion is manifested in the exhalation or 'boiling up' of heated vapor. (See CXIII below, and commentary on CII.) Heraclitus would thus conceive the psyche as Homer conceived wrath, 'which increases like smoke within the breasts of men' (*Iliad* XVIII.110). This expanding *logos* of the soul would be something quite different from the *logos* or measure of the sea, which remains constant despite its transformations (XXXIX, D. 31B).

CII

CII (D. 36)   For souls (*psychai*) it is death to become (be born as) water, for water it is death to become earth; out of earth water arises (is born), out of water soul (*psychē*).

In another example of ring composition CII ends where it began, with the word *psyche*. The shift from the plural (*psychai*) to the singular prevents the repetition from being too mechanical; but this shift is probably motivated by a difference in connotation. The plural form at the beginning suggests the soul or life-breath of individual men, which, in popular belief, abandons the body at death and passes as a phantom to the world below. But the singular form points to *psyche* as a constituent of the natural order, like earth or water. (Compare the generic singular in XXXV, D. 45.) Heraclitus thus replaces the Homeric picture of the descent of human *psychai* into the underworld with his own account of the elemental 'way down' to water and earth, after which the same stages are repeated in reverse order as a 'way up'. As we have seen, the language of birth and death seems to allude here to a mystical cycle of rebirth, as in the Pythagorean doctrine.

Only the transition *downward* to water and earth is described as death (as well as birth); the return upwards is described only as birth or becoming.[322] Given the careful symmetry of this and similar fragments, the strong asymmetry here is scarcely accidental. Insofar as the ways up and down are 'one and the same' (CIII, D. 60), every birth can also be described as a death. But there is another sense in which the way down is more truly the path of mortality, the quenching of fire, whereas the way up is in this same sense the path of life and rekindling. We thus have a foothold, within Heraclitean psychophysics, for the dualism required by a distinguished destiny for noble deaths.

There is an obvious parallel between the sequence of stages here and the passage from sea to earth and back again described in XXXVIII and XXXIX (D. 31A and B). What is new (besides the substitution of 'water' for 'sea') is the description of these transitions in terms of death and birth, and the presence of *psyche* at beginning and end of the series. These two points are connected. For Heraclitus everything is a form of life, and there can be no fundamental discontinuity between the realm of the psyche and the realm of elemental transformation. CII makes this clear by integrating the psyche within a series of physical transformations.

What physical form does Heraclitus associate with the soul? CII says only that psyche passes into, and reappears out of, water. From this it has been generally inferred, on the strength of the parallel with XXXVIII–XXXIX, that the psyche must be identified with the principle of fire whose 'reversals' are described in those fragments.

The inference is surely a curious one, given the evidence before us. For fire vanishes into smoke and ashes, but not into water. And if fire can burst forth from many things, water is not one of them. What we expect to find emerging from and returning to watery form is some type of vapor, steam, cloud, or air, the product of water by evaporation and the source of rain or moisture by condensation. That this is what Heraclitus has in mind here is confirmed by the other texts that speak of psyche as alternatively 'moist' (CVI, D. 117; CVIII, D. 77) and 'dry' (CIX, D. 118). For of course air, wind and vapor may in fact be either dry or humid; whereas this contrast makes no sense if applied to fire or flame. Hence psyche changes to water by precipitation or condensing, just as water changes to earth by further condensation. The relevant parallel is to the series of elemental transformations ascribed to Anaximenes and attested for Anaxagoras: *psychē* here occupies the place of *aēr*, wind and cloud in the standard sequence.[323] By his substitution of 'soul' for 'air', Heraclitus has reshaped the element physics of Milesian cosmology as a doctrine focussed on the human principle of life and mortality.

As proxy for the elemental power of the atmosphere, psyche in CII corresponds somehow to the *prēstēr* or lightning storm of XXXVIII (D. 31A), which emerges from sea in what appears to be an upward path of elemental change. This suggests not that psyche and *prēstēr* are physically identical but that there must be some analogy between the human soul and the flash of lightning in the sky. The force of this analogy will be brought out in CIX (D. 118).

As was noted, most modern commentators have interpreted the parallel between CII and XXXVIII—XXXIX as showing that Heraclitus identified the soul with elemental fire. This mistake follows directly from the assumption that in both cases Heraclitus is expounding a theory of three (and only three) elemental forms. But this assumption, for which there is no ancient authority, is without any basis in the texts except precisely as a misreading of XXXVIII and CII, taking them both as the expression of a complete theory of elemental transformation. The misreading, which goes back as far as Zeller, is itself the result of an erroneous conception of Heraclitus as a prosaic cosmologist or *physikos*.[324] Zeller took over this misconception from Aristotle and Theophrastus; but neither one committed the modern mistake of identifying psyche as fire in Heraclitus. Aristotle described the soul as a vaporous 'exhalation' (*anathymiasis*), which means something like smoke of steam or mist (CXIIIA below). The Theophrastean doxography in Diogenes is silent on this point; but in the remote echoes of this doxography in Aetius and Philo the soul is defined respectively as *anathymiasis* and *pneuma* ('breath, wind').[325] So the Stoics attributed to Heraclitus the view that 'souls steam up (are exhaled, *anathymiōntai*) from moisture' (CXIIIB). The respectable ancient evidence is thus unanimous in confirming the natural interpretation of CII, with the psyche understood as a kind of atmospheric vapor emerging from water.

It is in fact the prevalent view in early thought, in Greece as elsewhere, that the 'soul' or spirit of a man is a kind of vital breath, inhaled from birth (or from the moment of creation, in the case of Adam) and 'expired' at death. Thus an interlocutor of Socrates reports that most men will suppose that, when the psyche leaves the body at death, 'it is scattered like wind (*pneuma*) or smoke' (*Phaedo* 70A). It was just this commonplace view of the soul as an atmospheric substance like breath that was developed in quasi-scientific form in the school of Ionian natural philosophy from Anaximenes to Diogenes of Apollonia.[326]

The cyclical movement of CII parallels the movement between light and darkness, waking and sleeping in XC (D. 26), as well as the cycle of generations in XCV (D. A19) and XCVII–XCVIII (D. 29 and 20); it contains no hint of any higher psychic path such as will be suggested in CIX–CXII.

CIII

CIII (D. 60)   The way up and down is one and the same.

CIII calls out for some context which it does not provide. I have placed it here as a comment on the cyclical destiny of the psyche which is at the same time a passage through higher and lower elemental forms.[327] Both psychological and elemental interpretations of CIII are well entrenched in the ancient commentary.[328] And there is no need to choose between them, since elements and psyche are so many different phases or aspects of a single reality, the kindling and quenching of cosmic fire.

There is a still simpler, more literal interpretation (proposed by Calogero and developed by Kirk, p. 112) which takes the statement to mean only that every uphill path can equally well be described as downhill, depending upon where one is standing; just as it is one and the same road that runs from Philadelphia to New York and from

New York to Philadelphia. This literal reading of CIII is presupposed
by both the psychological and elemental interpretations.

CIV

CIV (D. 43)   One must quench violence (*hybris*) quicker than a blazing fire.

CIV is the only fragment where fire is presented in negative terms, as
a purely destructive force.[329] This may simply reflect the fact that
Heraclitus is exploiting the familiar literary conceit 'to quench
hybris'.[330] But perhaps there is more at stake.

In form this fragment recalls two others: LXXXVIII (D. 96)
'Corpses *are more to be thrown out* than dung', and XXX (D. 114)
'One must hold fast to what is shared by all, as a city holds to its law,
and *even more firmly.*' This common comparative pattern suggests
that, beyond the traditional warning against *hybris*, CIV is designed
to express a more distinctly Heraclitean thought. As an enemy attack
on the city wall threatens all the inhabitants of the city, so a house
on fire threatens the whole neighborhood with destruction. And just
as the defense of the civic law is seen (in LXV, D. 44) to be as vital as
the defense of the wall, so here the suppression of *hybris* — the suppression of that violence which disregards the law and endangers the
community — is seen to be more urgent than the quenching of a fire
raging out of control. In alluding to the dangerous power of fire,
Heraclitus thus implicitly qualifies his praise for the principle of war
and conflict when it appears as wanton violence. Like strife, fire
itself can become purely destructive if it threatens civic unity and the
common interests of all (*to xynon pantōn* in XXX).

The formal parallel to the aphorism on corpses suggests that there
may also be some hidden connection between the fire of *hybris* and
the destiny of the soul. This hint will be pursued in the commentary
on CV.

CV

CV (D. 85)   It is hard to fight against passion (*thymos*); for whatever it wants
it buys at the expense of soul (*psychē*).

As Reinhardt remarked, CV seems to presuppose a customary phrase
about 'buying something with the *psychē*' where the meaning is 'pay-

ing for it with one's life', as in the purchase of freedom or glory.[331]
But this sense of the phrase leads to paradox. For to pay with one's
life for something noble (as in the decision of Achilles to avenge
Patroclus) is an action we expect Heraclitus to approve of. Why should
one struggle against *thymos* if the consequences of yielding to it are
so noble? And how can this threat to one's life explain why resistance
is so difficult?

The beginning of an answer might be found if Heraclitus is alluding
precisely to the anger (*thymos*) of Achilles, which was paid for by
the death of Patroclus. (See the reference to Achilles' refusal to
'quench his wrath' at *Iliad* IX.678.) But this line of thought is ruled
out by most commentators, who take *thymos* not as 'anger' but as
'desire' or 'appetite' generally, what Plato and Aristotle call *epithymia*
On this view, the loss of psyche is a result of sensual indulgence, as in
drink: 'the gratification of desire implies the exchange of dry soul-
fire for moisture', said Burnet, referring for support to CVI (D. 117),
CVIII (D. 77), and CIX (D. 118).[332]

This modern view must be mistaken, however, for it flies in the
face of the classical understanding of *thymos* as 'manly spirit' or
'anger', to be sharply distinguished from sensual appetite (*epithymia*),
as in the tripartite psychology of Plato's *Republic*. When Aristotle
and Plutarch cite CV they always take *thymos* in this sense, just as
Plato does in the two passages where he apparently echoes our text.[33]
We could believe that the ancients misunderstood Heraclitus here only
if we had some reason to suppose that the sense of *thymos* in his
Ionic dialect differed substantially from the Attic usage familiar to
Plato and later writers. But the opposite is the case, as we can see
from Herodotus. Although he does show some trace of the older,
wider use of the word in Homer (where *thymos* could mean 'heart' or
'spirit' in general, the organ of mind and intelligence as well as desire),
in most instances Herodotus' use of *thymos* corresponds closely to
that of Plato.[334]

I conclude that our ancient sources understood Heraclitus perfectly
when they took *thymos* to mean 'anger'. The picture of aggressive
rage as a difficult adversary to fight against is vivid and striking; and
hence the success of Heraclitus' phrase. The imagery of combat would
be much less apposite if we took *thymos* as sensual desire.

This leaves us with the question how yielding to anger is to be connected with loss of psyche. And (beyond a possible allusion to the
death of Patroclus) the answer must depend upon the Heraclitean
view of psyche as a kind of breath or vapor. (See above on CII, D.

36.) Anger and psyche are thus related by the fact that both can be understood in terms of *anathymiasis*, the boiling up of some sort of steaming vapor.[335] Anger is so difficult to resist precisely because its expression, the passionate act of self-affirmation in righteous rage or indignation, resembles so closely the principle of vitality as such, the fiery affirmation of one's own life. But just as fire and strife must be quenched when they threaten the common good (CIV, D. 43), so the spirit of anger can lead to crime and destruction if allowed to rage unchecked. As Democritus said (in what is a continuation rather than a negation of Heraclitus' thought), 'although it is hard to fight against anger (*thymos*), it is the task of a man to prevail over it, if he has good sense' (fr. 236).

The tendency of anger to lead to acts of *hybris* or wanton violence explains how it works its will 'at the expense of *psychē*', by damage to the agent's own vital interests and to the life of others in an outburst of destructive rage. But Heraclitus' thought should probably also be spelled out in psychophysical terms: we must prevent the fire of wrath and *hybris* from consuming our own life-breath. Yielding to irrational anger may thus be seen as a kind of suicide by self-conflagration. This would imply that there is another 'death' for the psyche, distinct from but comparable to the dissolution into water: an excess of unthinking ardor that wastes the psyche in vain, instead of risking it deliberately in a noble cause.

It may be raised as an objection to this view that it spoils the neat one-to-one correlation between different stages on the elemental way up and down and some linear scale of nobler and baser destinies for the soul: it now turns out that not every passage of the psyche into a more fiery condition will be a 'greater share', a fate which a wise hero might choose. On this reading of CV, fire can be a force of irrational destruction in the soul as well as in the city. But what the psychophysical theory loses in simplicity it gains in subtlety and realism. For a man of spirit, anger is indeed a greater temptation than drink or sensuality, just because its ardor resembles that of courage and nobility of soul. Thus the wrathful man will see his own motivation in terms of honor or justice even when pursuing a course of blind destruction.

I note, by way of anticipation, that there need be no contradiction between this conception of anger as irrational ardor of the psyche and CIX (D. 118); for the latter distinguishes the wisest and best soul by its dryness and clarity, not by its heat.

CVI

CVI (D. 117)   A man when drunk is led by a beardless boy, stumbling, not perceiving where he is going, having his soul (*psychē*) moist.

CVI may almost do without a commentary: the reader scarcely needs reminding that the joke about the man who has drenched his soul with drink is also to be taken literally, as a reference to psychic dissolution or partial 'death' into the watery element (CII, D. 36). I note only the resonance here with the language of other fragments. The man led by a beardless (*anēbos*) boy recalls the Ephesians of LXIV (D. 121), who should be 'hanged to a man (*hēbēdon*) and leave their city to the boys (*anēboi*)': those citizens stumble like drunken men, and a drunkard is worse than a child. So likewise the verb *epaiōn* ('not) perceiving (where he goes') echoes by inversion the definition of temperance or 'sound thinking', *sōphronein* in XXXII (D. 112): 'to act and speak . . . perceiving (*epaiontes*) things according to their nature'. As Bollack-Wismann point out, the participial constructions develop a kind of causal analysis in three stages: the man has lost control of his body, because he has lost his perception, because the lucidity of his psyche has been weakened by fluids.[336]

CVII

CVII (D. 95)   Plutarch: [As Heraclitus says, it is better to hide one's folly (*amathiē*), but that is difficult in one's cups and at ease.]

Bywater and Burnet accepted the reference to drinking as Heraclitean if so, CVII would be appropriate here after CVI. But if (as most editors have supposed) the mention of wine is due solely to Plutarch's own adaptation of the saying, it will be difficult to give any definite point or context to CVII, which then reduces to a three-word saying of proverbial form: '[it is] better to hide [one's] folly'. It is true that the term for 'folly', *amathiē*, echoes by negation the kind of 'learning from experience' (*mathēsis*) that most men lack (IV, D. 17) and for which Heraclitus has a high regard (XIV, D. 55). The notion of 'hiding' also recurs in X (D. 123), where *physis* or the nature of things is said to love to hide itself, and in LXXXVI (D. 86), where incredibility or incredulity (*apistiē*) escapes being recognized. But I do not see how such verbal resonance sheds any light on CVII.

CVIII

CVIII (D. 77)   Porphyry: [Hence Heraclitus said it was delight, not death, for souls to become moist.]

Porphyry is following an allegory of Numenius, a neo-Pythagorean philosopher of the second century A.D. Although this passage is often cited as a 'fragment' of Numenius, it is in fact a paraphrase by Porphyry which may have only the most tenuous connection with Heraclitus' own words. Hence some commentators would disregard CVIII entirely, as an unreliable echo of other fragments.[337] However, Numenius' version of XCII (D. 62), preserved by Porphyry in the very next sentence, does retain some of Heraclitus' original wording.[338] So it is also possible that the old poetic word *terpsis* 'delight', which occurs once in Herodotus, may represent Heraclitus' own description for the experience of the soul's becoming moist. (The fact that Numenius offers an allegorical exegesis of *terpsis*, as 'the fall of the souls into generation', suggests that the word itself is part of the text he is commenting on.) This fits well with, but does not substantially add to, the idea of the soul moistening itself with drink attested in CVI (D. 117).[339]

CIX

CIX (D. 118)   A gleam of light is the dry soul, wisest and best.

The transformations and deformations of CIX make one of the stranger stories in the twisted course of Heraclitean scholarship. Before discussing its meaning we must deal with an old problem concerning the text.

It is as certain as anything of this sort can be that the first three words of Heraclitus' sentence were *augē xērē psychē* 'gleam of light, dry, soul', with the adjective 'dry' placed ambiguously between the two nouns. That is the form in which the quotation is found in no less than six of our ancient authorities: Musonius, Stobaeus, Philo, Plutarch, Galen and Hermias.[340] The accuracy of this version is confirmed by the fact that only this ambiguous position for the adjective can explain the existence of three ancient variants: (1) one in which the ambiguity is avoided by placing the adjective after *psychē* so that it must be construed 'dry soul' and not 'dry beam of light';[341] (2) one in which the wording is altered in the opposite sense, so that the only possible reading is 'dry beam of light';[342] and finally (3) a late and shortened version reflecting the construal in (1), but where all mention of *augē* 'gleam' has been omitted, and we are left with the phrase 'dry soul' as subject of the sentence.[343]

The Renaissance editor Stephanus (Henri Estienne), followed by Bywater and by many editors since, thought that the chief variants could be explained by positing the comparatively rare word *auē* (*psychē*) 'dry (soul)' as the Heraclitean original, and then taking *augē* 'gleam' as a corruption for this unfamiliar form. But the form *auē* is simply unattested in the ancient and medieval tradition of CIX, down to the fourteenth century, whereas *augē* is given in eleven ancient works by nine different authors, including three of our best sources for Heraclitus' text: Plutarch, Clement, and Stobaeus.[344] There is no sound paleographical basis for altering the text. An emendation would be justified only if the text as transmitted did not make good sense. But, as we shall see, it makes excellent sense.[345]

The textual question resolved, we are faced with the syntactical ambiguity from which the variants arose. Since CIX consists of two feminine nouns (*augē* and *psychē*) and three feminine adjectives ('dry', 'wisest', and 'best'), and the last two adjectives can be construed only with *psychē*, it is natural to try taking the first adjective with *augē*. This gives us the equation 'a dry beam of light, the wisest and best soul'. This construction is attested in two ancient sources, and it accounts for Ficino's Latin version *lux sicca, anima sapientissima*. But the difficulty is that if 'a dry light' might make some sense in Latin or English, a dry *augē* seems to make very little sense. For *augē* is normally used for the rays of the sun, the flash of lightning, the glare of fire, the sheen of gold or brass, even for the rays or brilliance of the eyes; it is regularly a *visual* phenomenon in which dryness or moisture seems to play no part.

Hence Plutarch and Clement, the two ancient authors best acquainted with Heraclitus' riddling style, both realized that the full meaning of CIX required taking 'dry' with 'soul', as counterpart to 'moist soul' in CVI (D. 117); and both adjusted their quotations to make this clear.[346]

It would be agreeable to my general scheme of interpretation to find some significance in this syntactical ambiguity, and to offer a reading of CIX according to both constructions. And at least one ancient author, Porphyry, thought he could make sense of the phrase 'dry *augē*'.[347] But in this case I do not see that the ambiguity enriches our understanding of CIX enough to be worth attending to. Hence I consider only the reading that construes *xērē* 'dry' as attributive with 'soul' (as in the best ancient tradition) and takes *augē* 'gleam' as the predicate. We thus have two statements with a single subject: (1) dry *psychē* is a beam of light, and (2) dry *psychē* is wisest and best.[348]

This gives a new dimension to Heraclitus' doctrine of the soul: just as moisture weakens the soul so that it may perish into water, so dryness strengthens and improves it to the point where it may be *purified as light* (not fire). Looking back to XC (D. 26), we see that the conception of the psyche in terms of light was probably anticipated in the riddle about the man who lights a lamp (*phaos*, light) for himself in the night. But the lamp there was a nocturnal substitute for the truer life of the psyche in the light of day; and it is of course daylight that is suggested by the term *augē* in CIX. Now *augē* can refer to any gleam or radiance, including the flare of fire or the glistening of bright metal. But the poetic associations of the word connect it with the light of the sun as a figure for life itself, as in the Homeric phrase 'to see the rays (*augai*) of the sun', meaning 'to be alive' (*Il.* XVI.188; cf. *Il.* I.88, *Od.* XI.498, etc.). The radiance of the sunlit sky thus stands traditionally for life; it is the innovation of Heraclitus to identify this physically with the finest state of the psyche.

This conception is deeply rooted both in the language of early Greek poetry and in the theories of pre-Socratic philosophy. In poetic terms CIX defines the best condition of the psyche as a kind of *aithēr*, not fire as such but the clear and luminous upper sky, as contrasted with the murky and moist lower *aēr*, comprising haze, mist, and cloud.[349] This atmospheric contrast between translucent and opaque, dry and damp, is preserved in the Ionian cosmology of Diogenes and directly applied to the psyche: our soul and that of animals, the principle 'by which they all live and see and hear, and have the rest of their perception or intelligence (*noēsis*)', is composed of air, but a form of air that is 'hotter than the air outside in which we live, but much colder than that by the sun' (Diogenes, fr. 5). According to Theophrastus, Diogenes held that a man 'thinks well (*phronein*) with air that is pure and dry; for the juice or moisture (*ikmas*) disturbs his intelligence (*nous*); hence in sleep and drunkenness and when one is full of food, one thinks less well. And there is a sign that moisture removes intelligence in the fact that the other animals are not as smart; for they breathe the air from the earth and eat wetter food.'[350]

Now the doctrine of Diogenes belongs to a later period in the fifth century, and it might have been influenced by Heraclitus' remarks about moisture in the soul. More probably, however, it represents a direct development from the old Milesian school tradition: from the doctrine of Anaximenes that constituted Heraclitus' own point of departure. If so, the moist-dry contrast in Heraclitus' psychophysics is not original; he takes it for granted as the theory current in 'scientific' circles of his own time and place. What is distinctly Heraclitean is the enrichment of this physical doctrine with figurative and poetic overtones: the drunkard with a wet soul, and the dry soul as lucid as sunshine. These images serve not merely as an ornament of style but as the symbolic expression for a rigorous correlation between physical and moral-intellectual states of the psyche. As we proceed downwards, we have in elemental terms the physical death of psyche into water (CII, D. 36), in psychological terms the visual 'quenching' of a man in darkness followed by the quenching of his consciousness in sleep (XC, D. 26), in psychophysical terms the moistening of the soul in drunkenness (CVI, D. 117) and perhaps in sensual pleasure generally (CVIII, D. 77), corresponding to the cattle-death of men who seek satiety and procreation (XCVII–XCVIII, D. 29 and 20). In all probability, the discharge of semen in intercourse was conceived as the waste of life-spirit into liquid form. By contrast, the rational clarity of the best men who choose 'one thing in exchange for all' represents the polar opposite to this dissolution into water and darkness: the dry state of the soul, which is (or is like) a beam of light.

Before summing up the implications of this doctrine for Heraclitus' ideas on death and immortality, it will be useful to clarify my interpretation by a contrast with the common view that the psyche for Heraclitus is a form of fire. This view goes back to Zeller and Burnet, but it is best stated by Kirk in an article on Heraclitus' conception of death. Kirk is attempting to show how there can be alternative destinies for the soul after death, and in particular how it can be advantageous to die in battle (cf. C, D. 24). Although 'it is death to souls to become water' (CII, D. 36),

> not all souls suffer this 'death' on the death of the body. Some retain their fiery character and rejoin the mass of pure fire in the world; and since dryness, i.e. greater fieriness, was in life held to be the condition of wisdom and excellence, it follows that those souls which remain fiery and do not undergo the death of becoming water are the souls of the virtuous, and that the association with pure fire is the after-life which Heraclitus seems to promise [in XCVI, D. 25; CX, D. 63; CXI, D. 98; taken together with LXXXIV, D. 27 and XCII, D. 62] . . .

If, then, when the body dies the soul either becomes water or remains fiery, and becomes more fiery still, what is the factor that determines the issue? Clearly, the composition of the soul at the moment of death; the soul in life contains varying proportions of fire and moisture, according as it is wise or foolish, percipient or unpercipient; if the amount of water at the moment of death exceeds the amount of fire, presumably the soul as a whole suffers the 'death' of turning to water: but if the soul is predominantly 'dry', then it escapes the 'death' of becoming water and joins the world-mass of fire.[351]
On this basis Kirk can explain the advantages of death in battle, which lie in the suddenness rather than in the violence of the end, 'so that the soul at the moment of death is in its normal [i.e. healthy, robust] condition, and has not been debilitated and moistened by the experience of sickness' (and, we may add, of old age). This will not guarantee a fiery destiny for a soul that is depraved; 'it only insures that its fate should depend solely on *ēthos*', that is on its character. (Cf. CXIV, D. 119.) 'Other things being equal, however, it is better to die in battle, especially because this is normally a noble activity which, unless cowardice be shown, tends to increase the fire in the soul.'[352]

I agree with Kirk on the need to reconstruct for Heraclitus a kind of 'identity theory' of body and mind, in which stages of physical change and states of moral psychology are not merely put in one-to-one correspondence but are conceived as aspects of a single reality: wisdom and excellence simply *are* the dry condition of the psyche. Furthermore, we agree that this psychophysical theory must, as in the case of Empedocles, take account of different destinies after death for the noble and the base, the wise and the foolish. We differ, however, in regard to the physical constitution of the psyche in a living man, and hence in regard to the 'greater destiny' for a noble soul after death.

I see no evidence in the fragments to support the view that 'the soul in life contains varying proportions of fire and moisture as it is wise or foolish'.[353] The fragments do not speak of psyche as a mixture but as a single entity or substance or elemental principle that can be *either* dry *or* wet. Nothing whatsoever is said about it being fiery. On the contrary, our interpretation of CV (D. 85) suggests that psyche can actually be consumed by too much heat or 'boiling' (above, p. 243). All of this fits perfectly with a conception of psyche as an atmospheric principle like breath or air, produced from water by evaporation or 'exhalation' (*anathymiasis*), tending upwards and aspiring to the condition of the luminous sky or upper air (*aithēr*), but not to the condition of fire as such.

Now the distance between Kirk's view and mine can be diminished if we think of celestial fire — the fire of the sun and the stars — simply as atmospheric air or exhalation become dry and luminous (like the best and wisest psyche of CIX), and hence rational and orderly in such a way as to account for the regularity of the celestial motions. To the periodic measures of the sun, as a visible expression of order in nature, would correspond the physical substance of celestial light, as the highest manifestation of cosmic fire. We recall that the doxog-, raphy ascribes to Heraclitus an account of the celestial bodies as flames produced by a gathering of bright and pure exhalation (*anathy-miaseis*) from earth and sea: the moon is in an impure region nearer the earth, while the sun's light and heat are more intense since 'it lies in a translucent (*diaugēs*) and unmixed region', presumably a region of pure, dry radiance, unadulterated by mist and moisture from below.[354] If there is a kernel of truth in this report, it indicates that the matter of the best and wisest souls must itself constitute the effulgence of the heavenly bodies, or their celestial source and environ-ment.

On this view, there must be some distinction between celestial fire or light, as the highest destiny for the soul, and terrestrial flame here below. They are both forms of fire, but the status of the fiery element in our immediate vicinity is ambivalent, since it may (like wrath and *hybris*) manifest itself in a raging, destructive conflagration. Being burnt to death in a city on fire can no more guarantee a 'greater fate' for the soul than dying in a quarrel kindled by unreasoning fury. By contrast a death in battle would be sanctified symbolically, as a death bestowed by Ares the War-King, and also physically and morally, since it would guarantee that the ardor of the psyche would not be wasted in wanton violence but expended in the rational defense of the city and its *nomos*, in 'holding fast to what is shared by all' (XXX, D. 114). Such a death will naturally be honored by men and also by gods, that is, by the elements and powers of the cosmos. For it guarantees the passage of the psyche upwards in a rational direction, towards the lucid sky of 'luminous (*aithrios*) Zeus' (XLV, D. 120). Those outstanding men who choose 'one thing in exchange for all' know what they are choosing. Whether philosophers or not, they know in effect 'what the wise is, set apart from all' (XXVII, D. 108). They recognize, in choosing the gleam of light that is the 'ever-renewed glory of mortals', both the fire exchanged for all things and 'the wise one alone': the wisdom that governs the universe and the sun that never sets (CXXII, D. 16). The task of the philosopher is only to make explicit, to articulate in discourse (*logos*), the pattern exemplified in the life and death of such men.

On this view of psyche as an atmospheric substance intermediate between water and fire, roughly in the position of air or breath (*pneuma*), it can of course be moist; but if it actually turns to water — if it liquefies or condenses — it 'dies', that is, it ceases to be psyche (CII, D. 36). And similarly, although the life-breath may be dry and hot and suffused with light, perhaps it cannot be inflamed as celestial fire without 'dying', without ceasing to be psyche as such. This is a point on which the fragments leave us in doubt, and perhaps for good reason. Heraclitus wants to conceive the psyche as a particular physical form; but he also describes the cosmic fire itself as 'ever-living' and implies that every form of 'kindling' is a form of life. What he probably meant, therefore, but what would be difficult to say (since *psychē* means 'life') is that the passage of psyche into celestial fire might be both the death of psyche and at the same time its attainment of the highest form of life. This is, perhaps, the ultimate paradox expressed in the statement that mortals and immortals live one another's death and are dead in one another's life (XCII, D. 62).

We now see Heraclitus' answer to the question about what awaits men at their death. All men's bodies will take the downward path of dissolution into earth and water. The *psychai* of most men may follow a similar course, or else remain in atmospheric form and be reintegrated into the *psychai* of other living things. But the souls of those men who have nobly lived and nobly died will move upwards to the form of fire constituted by celestial light. How much individuality can be assigned even to the best souls in such an afterlife is not clear (and will depend upon an interpretation of the next three, very difficult fragments). But it is also not clear why *individual* survival — a continuation of personal identity or self-awareness — should be important for Heraclitus in the long run. Whether we speak of the higher destiny of psyche in physical terms, as the radiant sky, or in psychological terms as an effort of sound thinking (*sō-phronein*), there seems to be no ground or motive for the conservation of the person or psyche as such, as a particular physical and mental form.

It is true that wisdom, or the search for wisdom in sound thinking (*sōphronein*), begins with self-knowledge (XXIX, D. 116); and Heraclitus went in search of himself (XXVIII, D. 101). But what he found within his own psyche was a *logos* deep enough to be co-extensive with the universe (XXXV, D. 45). So the true recognition of one's self is a discovery not of what is private and personal but of what is 'shared by all': the unity of all nature which is the deep *logos*, the deepest structure of the self. And this unity is discovered in thinking, *phronein*, which is 'common to all' (XXXI, D. 113), and common not only because for Heraclitus all things think but because it is precisely in thought, when it is in sound condition — as in the case of the dry soul — that one can embrace the structure of the whole universe.

In *sōphronein*, which is the greatest excellence and wisdom (XXXII, D. 112), one can, by putting one's own words and deeds into agreement with the cosmic *logos*, succeed to some degree in knowing or mastering the intention, the rational plan (*gnōmē*) by which all things are governed (LIV, D. 41). For Heraclitus there can be no higher human destiny than this, which surely requires knowledge and rational perception, but need not involve anything specifically personal or individual. And the higher (as well as lower) fates of the psyche after death may be incompatible with any awareness of a personal self, as they seem to be incompatible with the corresponding physical existence of an individual psyche, as a particular vaporous bubbling up of breath or air.

But if everything that goes up must come down again, since there is no transmundane realm, no escape from the cosmic cycle (even if this cycle includes the eventual destruction and renewal of the cosmos as such, and particularly if it does so), one might question the coherence of this conception of the soul's path upwards to celestial light or fire as a 'greater destiny' (XCVI, D. 25). For if the soul that dies into water and earth will eventually be reborn as soul, and so likewise everything else will eventually be exchanged for fire and back again (XL, D. 90), where is there any ultimate difference of principle between the nobler and the baser fate, where in the long run is there any advantage allotted to wiser lives or better deaths?

This is the specifically Heraclitean form of a general question that any monistic system of ethics must face. And Heraclitus would surely have answered like Spinoza: the beatitude which rewards a life of excellence is the quality of that life itself; in his own words 'man's character is his fate', his *daimōn* for good fortune or for bad. Since we are forever dying and being reborn in body and in psyche, both asleep and awake, the change at the moment of physical death, when the psyche departs and the body is left behind like excrement, is less fundamental than it might seem. The immediate destiny of the psyche beyond the grave will be simply an extrapolation of its condition during the life of the person. Whether it rises to more lucid form or dissolves into the lower elements or (perhaps) hovers as breath and atmosphere until it is inhaled into the new lives of children or animals, will depend upon the kind of life it has lived and the manner in which it confronts death. In the long run it makes no difference, perhaps, because in the long run there is no personal identity, no continuation of the individual psyche as such. What properly concerns us is only the course of one's own life, its share of lucidity and the soundness of its thinking, and the prolongation of this course in the direction taken by the psyche at death. Beyond this immediate prolongation the individual as such cannot see, and need not look. There can be no personal interest in what happens in the long run.[355]

We have, then, a system with no place for personal immortality through all time, in the Christian or even in the Pythagorean sense. It might be called a meaningful conception of the afterlife with no place for personal immortality at all. (And the same holds for Aristotle's view of the soul, though he speaks less often of what awaits us when we die.) 'Salvation' for Heraclitus is *sō-phronein*, to save one's thinking by recognizing one's own self in the structure of the whole. This is, perhaps, to lose one's self but to find something better: the unity of all things in the wise one.

This all-embracing unity of the living and the dead, of dying and being reborn, being kindled and being put out, is familiar to us all in elemental exchange, in respiration and excretion, in sleeping and waking, in the experience of nightfall and sunrise, winter and spring. It is this familiar pattern of experience that permits us to 'grasp the dead while alive' (XC, D. 26), but which we do not comprehend as such, and hence 'do not think such things as we encounter nor recognize what we experience' (IV, D. 17). This universal structure of living-through-dying, the deep *logos* of the soul which makes it (in one sense) co-extensive with the cosmos, is the very *logos* according to which 'all things come to pass', that is, according to which 'all things are born' (*panta ginomena*, I.2). In another sense, the psyche is only one elemental form among others, a bubble that bursts and is forgotten in the continual steaming up of new vapors from the waters ever flowing on in the river of the cosmos. But insofar as it is able to grasp the identity between its own *logos* and that of the universe, insofar as a man comes to salvage his thinking by recognizing what he encounters in his experience, by holding fast in cognition and in action to *what is shared by all*, to this extent the psyche can 'travel over every path' without limit (XXXV, D. 45) and can come to realize its unity with the cosmos as a whole, in the everliving fire forever kindled and forever put out. As Pascal put it, in almost Heraclitean word play: 'par l'espace, l'universe me comprend et m'engloutit comme un point; par la pensée je le comprends'.[356] It was in a similar spirit that Spinoza described scientific knowledge and rational proof as 'the eyes of the mind, by which it sees and observes things', and by which 'we feel and experience that we are eternal'.[357] For Heraclitus, as for Spinoza, this experience of eternity, far from being a matter of personal survival, consists rather in the overcoming of everything personal, partial, and particular, in the recognition and full acceptance of what is common to all.

CX

CX (D. 63)   . . . to rise up (?) and become wakeful watchers of living men and corpses.

Hippolytus, our source for CX, sees a reference here to the resurrection of the body on Judgement Day and to the God responsible for resurrection. The beginning of the quotation is unintelligible, and no satisfactory restoration has been found.[358] We can be sure only of some mention of a 'rising' or 'standing up'. Hippolytus' remark and the Hesiodic parallel to be considered immediately both indicate that this rising must concern the fate of men — at least of some men — after death.

Any key to the meaning must lie in the comparison with Hesiod's myth of the metals, where the golden race of men, who 'lived like gods' and 'died as if overcome by sleep', are said after death (literally, 'after the earth had covered them over') to have been made 'divinities (spirits, *daimones*) by the counsels of mighty Zeus, noble ones upon the earth, guardians of mortal men' (*Works and Days* 121–3). It is presumably these same spirits of the golden race that Hesiod later describes as 'thirty thousand upon the fruitful earth, Zeus' immortal guardians of mortal men; who watch over judgments (*dikai*) and evil deeds, clothed in mist (*aēr*), travelling everywhere over the earth' (ibid. 252–5). That Heraclitus is deliberately alluding to this passage is confirmed not only by the use of the term *phylakes* for 'watchers' or 'guardians' but also by the fuller expression 'watchers of living men and corpses', an intriguing variant on Hesiod's repeated formula: 'watchers of mortal men'.

The Hesiodic passage is full of ideas and phrases that lend themselves to reinterpretation along Heraclitean lines. These men of the
Golden Age are mortals who become immortal (*athanatoi*, verse 253),
whose death is like a sleep (verse 116) but who are 'reawakened' as
guardians. (The reference to 'waking' is explicit in CX, but implicit in
Hesiod's simile.) Their chief concern is to see justice done; and the
second mention of these guardians introduces Hesiod's apotheosis of
Dike herself as daughter of Zeus (verse 256). By implication, it would
seem that for Heraclitus too these guardians must serve as ministers
of Justice for human life and death, just as the Furies do for the
movement of the sun (XLIV, D. 94).

Pursuing this clue, let us see what the analogy can tell us of Heraclitus' view of the afterlife. Does CX refer to all men or only a chosen
few? And does it refer to their fate after death, as Hippolytus sup-
poses?

The Hesiodic parallel would clearly point to an afterlife for superior
men, since Hesiod is speaking of the golden race, the finest men of all
time, who become *phylakes* only after their death. Even without the
passage in Hesiod we would be safe in referring CX to the *psychai* of
outstanding men rather than to their bodies, in view of Heraclitus'
contempt for corpses (LXXXVIII, D. 96) and the fact that the body
will not naturally 'rise' but must pursue its elemental return into
earth. (Note that if the mention of *aēr* in Hesiod's passage is relevant
at all, it confirms my account of the soul as an atmospheric principle.)
CX seems, then, to refer to 'greater destinies' allotted to the psyche in
exceptional cases. This destiny is a state of wakefulness that lies
somehow *above the earth* (this is indicated by 'rising' as well as by
the Hesiodic parallel). Finally, this wakeful watching enforces justice
on 'living ones and corpses'. This striking phrase seems to be chosen
not only for its grim realism but also for its ambiguity. It may mean
'the living and the dead' (as most translators render it); but it may
also mean (if we remember that for Heraclitus corpses are worse than
dung) 'living things and inert beings like dumb earth'. This broader
reading would suggest that the watching in question extends to elemental as well as human affairs, thus reinforcing the cosmic surveillance carried out by the Furies.

To go further is to speculate, but some speculation may be in order.
If these guardians are ministers of cosmic justice, we must connect
them with the judgments of Dike (in LXXXVII, D. 28B) and fire (in
CXXI, D. 66), as well as with the inescapable vigilance of the sun that
never sets (CXXII, D. 16). But these guardians must also have some
place within the natural world, and I have suggested that they be con-

ceived as privileged *psychai*, in or above the atmosphere. More exactly
they should correspond to the wisest and best souls, dry and clear as
a beam of light (*augē*). On this assumption, the souls who have died
heroic deaths or lived lives of excellence and lucidity will rise up as
guardians in the upper atmosphere, mingling with celestial light and
astral fire. They will appropriately perform the function of celestial
watchman traditionally assigned to the sun. (See below on CXXII,
D. 16.) For they will in effect *be* the sun, or at least the sunlight, and
perhaps the stars as well.

It is more difficult to say how the guardians of CX, provisionally
identified with the light-souls of CIX, are related to other forms of
celestial fire, for example to the *prēstēr* or lightning storm of
XXXVIII (D. 31A). The fragments are silent here. My own guess is
that the watchful role of select souls is represented by the whole
range of fiery phenomena in the sky, including the fearsome flash of
prēstēr and thunderbolt, as expressions of the power that 'pilots all
things' (CXIX, D. 64). What appearance could be more fitting for
these guardian spirits than the luminous signals which are the traditional instruments of the wrath and justice of the highest god?

CXI–CXII

CXI (D. 98)   Plutarch: [(After death, the purified souls that rise to the moon)
are nourished by the exhalation (*anathymiasis*) which reaches them, and Heraclitus
was right to say that souls (*psychai*) smell things in Hades.]

CXII (D. 7)   Aristotle: [It seems to some that the smoky exhalation, which is
common to earth and air, is smell . . . That is why Heraclitus said what he did,
that if all things turned to smoke the nostrils would sort them out.]

Neither of these texts is a definite quotation; if the language of
Heraclitus is preserved at all, it may be in the phrase 'souls smell
things in Hades' (CXI). I place the two passages together in the hope
that, obscure to the point of unintelligibility if taken separately, they
may clarify one another by juxtaposition. In its own context, each
statement implies a causal link between exhalation and the sense of
smell.[359] This seems to have been a standard view in Greek theories
of smell, as Aristotle observes.[360]

What is unusual in CXII is the suggestion that everything might
become smoke, so that smell would be the only useful form of perception. Reinhardt interpreted this as a mere conceptual possibility
or literary conceit, like the contrary-to-fact conditionals of XLVI
(D. 99) and CXVI (D. 15) (*Parmenides*, p. 180, n. 2). The smoke of

CXII would then be only a figure for the underlying unity in which our nostrils would detect superficial differences. Kirk and others have assimilated this to the one-in-many idea illustrated by incense in CXXIII (D. 67). But the conditional of CXII is potential, not counterfactual. Things do become smoke; and the possibility of *everything* going up in smoke is paralleled by the thought of fire 'catching up' with all things in CXXI (D. 66). Reinhardt's ingenious reading of CXII is designed to avoid this obvious parallel, since he wished to eliminate any allusion to cosmic conflagration or judgment by fire from the fragments. Leaving aside this issue, I suggest we take the imagery of CXII literally and ask: what kind of fire might turn all things to smoke?

There are two plausible possibilities: the altar flame and the funeral pyre. The former points to the imagery of incense in CXXIII (D. 67); but then CXII gives us no information beyond what we could derive from CXXIII alone.[361] But if the fire is a funeral pyre, then 'turning to smoke' alludes to the fate of men after death, and the exhalation here will be directly linked to that of CXI (D. 98), which is inhaled by souls who 'smell things in Hades'.[362]

The question then is: how much information can these remarks about smell and exhalation give us concerning Heraclitus' conception of the afterlife? I first propose an answer that is independent of the elaborate myth in Plutarch's context for CXI; I then consider the possibility of other Heraclitean elements in this myth.

A minimal meaning for CXI is provided by the popular etymology for 'Hades' (Greek *Aidēs*, since the initial aspirate does not occur in the Ionic dialect of Heraclitus): *a-idēs* means 'invisible'.[363] 'Souls smell things in the invisible realm' then means: souls use another sense to perceive what they cannot see. (This confirms the link with CXII: the differences which become invisible if all things turn to smoke will still be perceptible to smell.) But the normal connotations of 'Hades' also involve the fate of the psyche after death. As the living man kindles a new light for himself when he is 'quenched in his vision' (XC, D. 26), so the psyche of a dead man replaces the light of life by another form of perception. And since smell is connected with smoke and cloudy exhalation, there should be some contrast between these souls and the best and wisest who, as a beam of light (*augē*), have affinities rather with the upper, clearer sky and the brighter sense of vision. The souls that smell in Hades and that are associated with smoke are likely to be the breath or *pneuma*-souls of most men, circulating in the lower, murkier atmosphere when they leave the body at death. Only the exceptional (and driest) souls will soar aloft to look down as guardians on the world below. On this reading, the souls, smoke, and smell of CXI–CXII refer to the ordinary souls of ordinary men, whose bodies will (in some cases) have been burnt to smoke, and whose souls and bodies thus suffer similar fates after death, in contrast to the select souls of CIX (D. 118) and CX (D. 63), whose destiny leads them up towards celestial light, while their body pursues its own elemental course below.

It is fascinating, though rather unprofitable, to consider how far Plutarch's myth in *The Face on the Moon* (from which CXI is taken) preserves authentic traces of Heraclitus' own eschatology. An extended discussion would be out of place, because we must *first* reconstruct that eschatology before knowing how to recognize traces of it in Plutarch's tale. Plutarch's myth of the soul's journey through the atmosphere to a region beginning at the moon, and then upwards to a purer condition in the sun, is predominantly Platonic in inspiration, with a liberal admixture of Aristotelian, Stoic, and other ingredients. There is no general method for sifting out the Heraclitean component. I simply note the following points as relevant to an evaluation of CXI.

The quotation is prepared by an identification of Hades with the region between earth and moon.[364] Just before our quotation this region, 'the gentlest part of the air', is described as 'the meadows of Hades' (943C). CXI refers to the purified souls who have travelled through this upper air and reached the moon: 'in appearance resembling a ray of light (*aktis*) but in respect of their nature . . . resembling the *aithēr* about the moon, they [sc. these souls] get from it both tension and strength as edged instruments get a temper, for what laxness and diffuseness they still have is strengthened and becomes firm and translucent (*diauges*). In consequence they are nourished by any exhalation that reaches them, and Heraclitus was right in saying: "Souls employ the sense of smell in Hades" ' (943D–E, tr. Cherniss). The point of the quotation is that smell serves these refined beings in place of more substantial food.[365] While waiting in their lunar or lower habitation for the final purification that will take them on to the sun, these spirits are not inactive. Among other beneficial roles, these *daimones* serve as 'guardians (*phylakes*) and chastisers of acts of injustice' on earth, 'and they flash forth (*epilampousin*) as saviors manifest in war and on sea' (944D, after Cherniss).

If I am correct in locating the souls of the dead in the atmosphere and upper sky, Plutarch's account of Hades is largely Heraclitean. Only he has blurred the distinction I draw between ordinary souls in the lower air, who must rely upon smell, and the select souls that rise higher and take the form of light. Plutarch has combined the atmospheric souls of CXI–CXII with the higher destiny depicted in CIX (D. 118) and CX (D. 63), because the fundamental distinction in his myth is not between lower and upper atmosphere but between a moon-destiny and a sun-destiny, corresponding to the Platonic distinction between a compound soul (*psyche*) and the purified intellect (*nous*).

CXIII

CXIIIA (D. A15)   Aristotle: [(Many thinkers, above all those who considered the cognitive powers of the psyche, identified it with their first principles or *archai*.) And Heraclitus too says the first principle is <the same as> soul, since he identifies it with the exhalation (*anathymiasis*) from which he produces all the rest. And <he says it is> most incorporeal and always flowing.]

CXIIIB (D. 12)   Cleanthes cited by Arius Didymus: [Zeno says the soul is a percipient exhalation, like Heraclitus. For the latter, wanting to show that souls as they are exhaled (*anathymiōmenai*) are continually becoming intelligent (*noerai*), likened them to rivers when he said: 'As they step into the same rivers, other and still others waters flow upon them' (L). But souls too steam up (or 'are exhaled', *anathymiōntai*) from moisture.]

The literal quotation in CXIIIB has already been discussed (L, D. 12); here we are concerned only with the context from Cleanthes and the parallel in Aristotle.[366]

Aristotle and Cleanthes agree in describing Heraclitus' psyche as an *anathymiasis* or 'exhalation'. But what is this? The Latin *exhalatio* (which has provided the established translation since Lucretius and Cicero) has the etymological sense of 'breathing out'; whereas the Greek term rather connotes 'billowing up' and typically applies to smoke or steam. The uncompounded form of the verb (*thymiasthai*) is commonly used for burning incense or causing smoke. The prefix (*ana-*) emphasizes upward motion, so that the rarer compound *anathymiasthai* has the sense 'steam up, rise in fume or vapor' (LSJ). There is no doubt, then, that Aristotle and Cleanthes ascribe to Heraclitus the view presented here, that the psyche is essentially not fire but an atmospheric principle like air, breath, or vapor. Both authors add the information that this psychic exhalation is percipient or cognitive.[367] This information must be correct, as we can see from Heraclitus' own remarks on the psyche as well as from the Ionian doctrine of *aēr* as developed by Diogenes.[368]

More problematic is Cleanthes' comment that 'souls steam up from

moisture'. I take this to be a paraphrase of CII (D. 36) 'out of water
psyche arises (*ginetai*)'. But *anathymiasis* may also be used for vapors
or gas produced from food and liquids within the body.[369] In the
context preceding CXIIIB, sperm is described as 'a fragment of the
psyche', a mixture of breath (*pneuma*) and moisture, which after
conception develops as embryo from moisture in the womb.[370]
Other Stoic sources speak of the soul as *pneuma* nourished by blood
in the body, and some commentators would understand Cleanthes'
words here in just this sense: souls are exhaled by evaporation from
the blood or from the internal river of humors in the body.[371]

This Stoic doctrine is a natural development of Heraclitus' view.
(Compare the similar doctrine of vital *pneuma* or 'animal spirits' in
Aristotle's biology.) But I see no reason to attribute this or any other
physiological doctrine to Heraclitus himself.[372] The *anathymiasis*
referred to by Aristotle in CXIIIA is clearly cosmic or elemental: it
is 'the exhalation from which he (sc. Heraclitus) derives everything
else'.[373]

I conclude by mentioning, without attempting to resolve, some
curious difficulties in understanding Cleanthes' exegesis in CXIIIB.
Even if we grant his dubious assumption that the Heraclitean river is
an image for the soul, it is strange that he believes this text was
intended 'to show that souls as they are exhaled are always becoming
intelligent (*noerai*)'.[374] Perhaps Cleanthes simply took for granted
that the rivers were fluids within the body, so that their 'waters'
could be interpreted as exhalations or vapors; such vapors, as *pneuma*,
will be perceptive and intelligent according to the Stoic theory of
pneuma. But the only safe conclusion is that Cleanthes allowed himself great freedom in reading Stoic doctrines into Heraclitean
texts.[375]

CXIV

CXIV (D. 119)   Man's character is his fate (literally, his *daimōn* or divinity).

The doctrine of CXIV has been discussed above in commenting on
XCVI–CXII. (See especially pp. 252f.) Here I consider the literal
interpretation of this marvellously brief and symmetrical three-word
utterance: *ēthos anthrōpōi daimōn*, 'character, for man <is his>
daimōn'. The meaning of the sentence depends on the sense given to
daimōn.

On the simplest view *daimōn* signifies one's destiny, one's prosperity or misfortune. Although in Homer and other authors the word is often used synonymously with *theos* 'god' (as in LVII, D. 79), the root meaning of *daimōn* is 'one who distributes or assigns a portion'. ____ This etymological value shows up in the two common compounds: *eudaimōn* 'with a favorable *daimōn*', 'happy', 'prosperous', 'fortunate'; and *kakodaimōn*, 'with a bad (unfavorable) *daimōn*', 'unlucky', 'miserable'. Hence the most obvious sense of CXIV is that it is a man's own character, not some external power, that assigns to him the quality of his life, his fortune for good or for ill. His lot is determined by the kind of person he is, by the kind of choices he habitually makes,[376] and by the psychophysical consequences they entail or to which they correspond. And since the fate of the psyche after death will be a direct prolongation of its life and death, one's destiny now and to come is a function of one's basic choice between a noble and a bestial career. The cause is not in the stars but in ourselves.

This primary meaning of CXIV is further enriched if we take *daimōn* literally as 'god' or 'divinity'. For the gods of Heraclitus, the immortals who live our deaths and are dead in our lives, can only be the elemental powers and constituents of the cosmos, from which our life comes and to which it returns. (Again the terminology of Heraclitus anticipates that of Empedocles, who designates his four elements as *daimones* in fr. 59.) The character of a man is thus identified with the corresponding element: moisture for the sensualists and topers, wasteful fire for the choleric, damp or smoky vapors for the souls of most men, a gleam of light for the wisest and best. These cosmic divinities are not merely emblematic of different kinds of lives, like Aphrodite and Artemis in Euripides' *Hippolytus*.[377] They constitute the physical explanation or psychophysical identity of the particular life in question, the elemental equivalent of a given moral and intellectual character. So read, CXIV offers a concentrated résumé of the doctrine of the dozen fragments just discussed.

A third reading emerges as a special case of the other two, if we recall Hesiod's use of *daimones* for the spirits of the golden race, become watchmen of justice after their death. I have suggested that in CX (D. 63) these guardian spirits are identified with the wisest and best souls, looking down from above as radiant light or astral fire. For the select souls too it is the character of the man that determines his fate as *daimōn*, as occupant or visitor in the highest region of mortality, the celestial terminus of the upward path.[378]

CXV

CXV (D. 14)   The mysteries current among men initiate them into impiety.

CXV is preceded in Clement by a list of mystery mongers: 'night-wandering sorcerers (*magoi*), Bacchoi, Lenai, mystic initiates (*mystai*): it is these he threatens with the afterlife, for these he prophesies the fire'. Most editors have recognized in this list of imposters the original context of CXV. But the authenticity of the list has recently been challenged on the grounds that the entire outburst could well have been added by Clement.[379] The five Greek words in question (from *nyktopoloi* 'nightwandering' to *mystai* 'mystic initiates') are syntactically blended with Clement's text in such a way that we cannot be sure whether or not they come from Heraclitus. It seems to me more probable that they do, for the following reasons.

CXV cannot stand alone; it calls out for *some* context. What context would be more appropriate than this reference to representative types of mystery religion? Of the five words in the list, *Lēnai* is a rare archaic form more likely to have been used by Heraclitus than by Clement, as Reinhardt agreed.[380] Secondly, an early mystic sense for *Bacchoi* ('elect', 'chosen by the god'), implied in a verse quoted by Plato (*Phaedo* 69C–D: 'many are the *narthēx*-bearers, few the Bacchoi'), is confirmed by a new gold tablet found in South Italy, dated about 400 B.C., which speaks of 'the long sacred way travelled <in the underworld> by famous *bacchoi* and *mystai*'.[381] This helps to establish the credentials of three words on our list. As for the other two ('nightwandering *magoi*'), nothing much hangs on their authenticity; but I am inclined to regard them also as genuine. Heraclitus will thus have seasoned his attack on Greek cult with a further sally against the holy men of the Persians.[382] However, the brunt of the attack is directed against the religion of his countrymen: Dionysian and Eleusinian mysteries here, phallic and orgiastic ritual in CXVI (D. 15), Apollonian purification rites and anthropomorphic cult generally in CXVII (D. 5). (And compare the contempt for funeral rites in LXXXVIII, D. 96.)

CXV tells us that initiation into the mysteries is impious, but does not tell us why. Perhaps Heraclitus has in mind some specific features of the ritual, some explicit sexual symbolism, so that (as in the mention of 'shamelessness' in CXVI) he is calling attention to the fact that in the name of piety men will perform, and applaud others who perform, acts which they normally regard with ridicule or disgust: *tantum religio potuit suadere malorum*.

But even if this conjecture is correct, it does not go to the heart of the matter. The central claim of the Eleusinian mysteries is to provide a life-giving experience, a beatific spectacle: 'Blessed is he among men who has seen these rites; but he who has not shared in them will never have a portion of similar blessings when he dies.'[383] In an echo of these verses Pindar announced that the one who has seen the mysteries 'knows the end of life and its god-given beginning'; Sophocles added that 'for these alone there is life in Hades; for others everything is evil'.[384] For Heraclitus the basic impiety of the mysteries will consist not in obscene symbolism but in the projection of a false picture of life and afterlife — in the invention of lies and swearing to them, in the promise of a magical connection between some ritual act and the future destiny of the psyche.

The same condemnation will fall on those esoteric cults represented by the 'Orphic' gold tablets, with their detailed topography of the next world and instructions for finding the right road. By distorting the true relationship between life and death, by seeking special exemption from the laws of cosmic justice which establish a necessary connection between the habitual conduct and character of a man and his destiny in this life and beyond, the spokesmen for such mysteries play the role of false witnesses in the gravest of all matters. Their impiety will be fittingly punished by Justice herself, in the natural course of events (LXXXVII, D. 28B).

Heraclitus' polemic is not directed against vulgar superstition, the cult of the uneducated masses, as some commentators suppose. The religion under attack is that of Pindar and Sophocles; it includes those western mysteries that attracted the tyrant Theron of Acragas and the heroic figures buried in the Timpone Grande and Timpone Piccolo at Thurii.[385] Heraclitus is not an aristocrat or conservative in religious matters. He is a radical, an uncompromising rationalist, whose negative critique of the tradition is more extreme than that of Plato a century later. Plato breaks only with current beliefs about the gods; in matters of cult he follows the principle that custom is king. Not so Heraclitus. Despite his great respect for *nomos* as the legal order and moral cement of the community, in matters of piety and psychic destiny he denounces what is customary among men (*ta nomizomena*) as a tissue of folly and falsehood.

CXVI

CXVI (D. 15)   If it were not Dionysus for whom they march in procession and chant the hymn to the phallus (*aidoia*), their action would be most shameless (*anaidestata*). But Hades (*Aidēs*) and Dionysus are the same, him for whom they rave and celebrate Lenaia.

What does Heraclitus mean by identifying Dionysus with Hades, and phallic cult with Bacchic frenzy? The statement is a riddle, and we must be satisfied with partial solutions.[386]

The most obviously correct interpretation takes Hades here as representative of death and the phallic Dionysus as representative of sexual vitality. So understood, the riddle reformulates the equivalence (i.e. interchangeability) of life and death expressed in XCII (D. 62) and XCIII (D. 88).[387] A second, deeper reading regards Dionysus not only as god of vitality and procreation but also as god of drink and madness. I have suggested that XCVIII (D. 20) depicts sexual activity as a waste of psyche, an expense of life-force liquefied as semen, just as drunkenness is a partial death and darkening of the soul by liquefaction (CVI, D. 117). The 'death' of psyche by the 'birth' of fluid in ejaculation coincides in the long run with the birth of the son that will supplant his father. Thus the desire of men 'to live . . . and to leave children behind' is really a desire for their own death and replacement.

The identification of the god of sexuality with the god of death, reinforced by the word play on 'shame', 'phallic song', 'shamelessness', and 'Hades', restates in symbolic form the contempt for the life-death of men who sate themselves like cattle (XCVII, D. 29). What is new in CXVI is the characterization of the phallic god in terms of ritual madness.[388] The Lenaia appear here as a festival of Bacchic frenzy, not a wine festival (as some have supposed).[389] Dionysus is the god of wine; but CXVI does not mention either wine or drunkenness. The point of CXVI lies in the reference to ritual madness as an explanation of the identity of Dionysus with Hades. The final comment on phallic worship would thus be the thought expressed in CXVII: 'anyone who *noticed* someone doing this would think he was mad'. A perceptive observer of ritual *mania*, recognizing it as insanity, would see the appropriateness of worshipping the god of sensuality and procreation with acts of madness. For he would recognize Dionysus as Hades, the invisible (*a-idēs*) figure of Death, and recognize madness itself, like drunkenness, as a kind of psychic death, a darkness of soul at maximal distance from the light of sound thinking (*sōphronein*). It is true witlessness and forgetfulness of self, 'not knowing what one is doing awake, just as men forget what they do in sleep', to waste one's psyche in sexual indulgence or darken it in madness (and we would add: or with drugs), not realizing that what passes for enhanced vitality is a sheer pursuit of death.

It would be a mistake, I think, to see Heraclitus as an apostle of chastity, some St Paul or Gandhi come before his time. What concerns him is not so much action or abstention but lucidity: to know what we are doing. As human beings we sate ourselves like animals; we want to see our children grow up and outlive us. (We also lose control of ourselves in anger, and occasionally moisten our souls with drink.) Heraclitus is not calling for some ascetic reform of human existence in which these features would disappear. Our condition is one of mortality, and Heraclitus offers no way out. What he does offer is insight into this condition, recognition of the deadly tendencies within life itself, and admiration for those few men whose gaze is enlightened by wisdom. For these will look beyond the cyclical fate that must be ours in any case and choose 'one thing in exchange for all' — the light of wisdom, symbolized and embodied in the gleam of cosmic fire.

The pessimism of Heraclitus is not that of Schopenhauer or certain Eastern mystics, who see the cycle of human existence as slavery and seek liberation by deliberate renunciation. His pessimism lies closer to the lesson of Solon in Herodotus: 'thus the god made plain that it was better for a man to be dead than to live' (I.31.3). This is not a recipe for suicide but for bearing death, your own death and the death of those dear to you, with courage and the peace of mind that comes from bitter wisdom.

The word play at the center of CXVI calls for some comment. The identification of Dionysus and Hades, fertility and insanity, is mediated by verbal connections between genitals (*aidoia*), shame (*aidōs*), shamelessness (*anaidestata*), and Hades (*Aidēs*). The sacred phallus is designated as 'pudenda', objects of shame or modesty (*aidoia*). For all the Greek delight in male nudity in art, in real life the genitals were normally covered; and the public display of an erect penis would probably be a source of mirth, if not embarrassment, as certain jokes in the *Lysistrata* make clear. Hence the paradox, expressed in the double sense of *aidōs* ('shame', but also 'reverence'), that the display of a giant phallus in grossly exaggerated form is treated not with shame but reverence and respect. The obscene song and solemn procession would be acts of utter shamelessness — *anaidestata* — if not done in the name of Dionysus. For a Greek of traditional piety that makes all the difference. But a sane man will see what is going on. What prevents this behavior from being outrageous in his eyes is

just the identity of Dionysus as the 'unseen' (*Aidēs*), the god of
death. Compare CXI, D. 98: 'souls smell in *Aidēs*', in the land where
they cannot see. Other levels of meaning are generated by the play
on the god's name, and there is no hope of cataloguing them all.[390]

CXVII

CXVII (D. 5)   They are purified in vain with blood, those polluted with blood,
as if someone who stepped in mud should try to wash himself with mud. Anyone
who noticed him doing this would think he was mad. And they pray to these
images as if they were chatting with houses, not recognizing what gods or even
heroes are like.

CXVII is remarkable for its length and its clarity. The absence of anything enigmatic in this text might almost cast doubt on its authenticity
if different portions were not cited by good and independent sources
(Clement, and Celsus in Origen). And a few stylistic features reveal
the hand of Heraclitus: the double construction of *haimati* 'with
blood', to be taken both with the preceding verb ('are purified') and
with the following participle ('polluted');[391] the play on *miainomenoi*
'polluted' and *mainomenoi* 'mad'; and the characteristic use of
gignōskō 'to recognize' for philosophic insight. If Heraclitus speaks
here with unusual clarity and undisguised sarcasm, perhaps for once
his spontaneous indignation breaks through the restraints of an indirect and allusive style. But there is probably a more deliberate
motivation for this straightforward language.

I assume that CXVII appeared as climax and conclusion to the
critique of religious practices in CXV (D. 14) and CXVI (D. 15); that
critique is here generalized and its philosophical foundation laid bare.
Whereas CXV–CXVI are directed against specific cults of Demeter
and Dionysus, the target in CXVII is not only the Apollonian rite of
purification[392] but the general practice of Greek religion as centred
on temples and cult statues.

In this polemic Heraclitus' predecessor is Xenophanes, who accused
Homer and Hesiod of ascribing to the gods 'whatever is a scandal and
a reproach among men' (frs. 11–12), and attacked both the principle
of theogony and the very notion that the gods have human form (fr.
14): if horses and oxen could produce images they would represent
their gods as hippomorphic and bovine (fr. 15). Xenophanes' irony
on this subject anticipates Heraclitus' attack on images (*agalmata*).
And the principle of Xenophanes' critique is the same: the customary

religion of the Greeks (and others) is systematic impiety, since it rests on a failure to 'recognize what gods are like'.[393]

The point of Heraclitus' critique is nonetheless new and personal. What Xenophanes attacks is a false conception of the gods. Heraclitus shows how such theological error leads to *action* that is shameful and ridiculous. The explicitness of the similes and the direct statement of the thesis in CXVII are perhaps required because his goal here is so difficult: to shock his reader or auditor into a realization of what is in some sense 'obvious', that behavior endorsed by the strongest sanctions of the society will reveal itself to a thoughtful observer as odious and absurd, since if it were *not* done in the name of the gods it would count as stupidity or insanity. The plain comparisons to washing with mud and talking with houses serve the literary function of Montesquieu's visiting Persian: to suggest the simplicity of vision of the child who sees that the emperor has no clothes.

The best parallel to this critique of idolatry is found not in Greek literature but in the Old Testament, and this accounts for some of the sympathy which a writer like Clement feels for Heraclitus. A man cuts down a tree, half of it he burns in the fire and warms himself, 'and the rest of it he makes into a god'; he falls down before it and 'prays to it and says "Deliver me, for thou art my god!" ' (Isaiah 44.17). The affinity is real, though wholly negative. Heraclitus and the Old Testament are at one in their rejection of anthropomorphic cult; their new conceptions of deity are entirely different. Heraclitus' god is neither personal nor transcendent; it is wholly immanent in the world and identical with the order of the cosmos over time. Heraclitus might have spoken like Spinoza of *Deus sive Natura*: 'god, that is to say the nature of things'. But like a true Greek he more often speaks of 'gods' in the plural. When he does refer to the divine as unique, we are confronted with a new paradox.

CXVIII

CXVIII (D. 32)   The wise is one alone, unwilling and willing to be spoken of by the name of Zeus (*Zēnos onoma* 'the name of life').

With deliberate antinomy Heraclitus here presents his positive conception of the divine, to be more fully spelled out in the next five fragments (CXIX–CXXIII). The aphorism is unusually dense and puzzling, full of conflicting forces mysteriously under control. The most striking features are: (1) the complex subject expression, with its echo of 'wise' and 'the one wise' from other fragments, but with the ambiguous addition of *mounon* 'only'; (2) the focus on 'the name of Zeus', with the old genitive form *Zēnos* (instead of the usual *Dios*, as in XLV, D. 120); and (3) the formal contradiction between denial and affirmation, which is even more explicit in the Greek ('is not willing and is willing').[394]

(1) The neuter adjective *sophon* 'wise' occurs in three other texts: XXVII (D. 108), XXXVI (D. 50) and LIV (D. 41). (See the discussion of these texts above, pp. 171f.) Now in XXXVI wisdom defines a certain mode of listening and speaking, just as in XXXII (D. 112) *sophiē* specifies a type of speaking, perceiving, and acting. In these cases, as in the reference to the best soul as 'wisest' (*sophōtatē*) in CIX (D. 118), Heraclitus implies that wisdom can and should belong to a human soul.[395] But this implication is tacitly challenged in XXVII (D. 108), where what is wise is 'set apart from all'. Other statements emphasize that the cognitive distance between men and gods is so great that what passes for wisdom among us is mere folly in comparison with their insight (LV–LVIII, D. 78, 82–3, 79, 70). These remarks help to explain the insistence in CXVIII that there is only *one* thing wise, the supreme divinity. In a coincidence that can scarcely be accidental a similar assertion in LIV (D. 41) begins with precisely the same three words: *hen to sophon* 'one the wise' (LIV, D. 41). But that text goes on to describe this singular wisdom in terms that might at least in principle apply to human beings: 'to know (or 'to master', *epistasthai*) the plan (*gnōmē*) by which it steers all things through all'. In commenting on LIV I have argued that this ambiguity is fundamental and irreducible: wisdom in the full sense is accessible only to the divine ruler of the universe, since it means mastering the plan by which the cosmos is governed. For human beings such wisdom can serve only as an ideal target, a goal to be pursued by *homo-logein*, by agreement with the *logos*: putting one's own thought, speech, and action in harmony with the universal course of things.

CXVIII describes this wisdom from the divine point of view, as the supreme cosmic principle, whose unity and uniqueness are underlined by the word 'alone' (*mounon*), ambiguously placed between the subject phrase 'the wise one' (or 'one, the wise') and the predicate: 'does and does not wish to be called "Zeus" '. Taking *mounon* with the subject, we can read the noun phrase as a complete sentence: 'the wise <is> one alone'. This formula rules out any irreducible plurality

within the divine power of wisdom and guidance. But Heraclitus is
no monotheist. Like Plato, Aristotle, and all other Greek thinkers
outside the Biblical tradition, he is uninhibited in his use of 'god'
(*theos*) in the plural. The monism of the philosophers takes the form
of 'henotheism', the conception of a single *supreme* god, as in Xenophanes fr. 23: 'one god, the greatest among gods and men'. By
employing the impersonal neuter form 'the wise one' (*hen* instead of
the masculine *heis*) Heraclitus suggests an even more radical break
with the anthropomorphic conception of deity, a precedent for the
impersonal (or transpersonal) One of Plotinus. And the violence of
this rupture with traditional theology is further indicated by the
initial negation: the wise one is *not* willing to be identified with Zeus.

A second reading will construe *mounon* ('alone', 'only') with what
follows; and this can be done in two ways: with the infinitival phrase
('the only thing to be called by the name of Zeus'), or with the noun
onoma 'name' ('to be called only by the name of Zeus', 'by the name
"Zeus" alone').[396] The former construal fits the affirmative clause:
cosmic wisdom is the only thing that can be designated as supreme
ruler. The latter construction matches the more emphatic denial: this
wisdom will not accept any *one* name as uniquely appropriate, for it
may equally well be called 'Fire', 'War', 'Justice', or 'Attunement'
(*harmoniē*). Indeed, it may be 'named according to the pleasure of
each one' (CXXIII, D. 67).

(2) The phrase 'to be spoken of (*legesthai*) by the name of Zeus
(*Zēnos*)' means 'to be called "Zeus" ', but it must mean more than
that. Heraclitus uses the verb *legesthai* where we might expect
kaleisthai 'to be called' or *onomazesthai* 'to be named'. And we find
'Zeus' in the genitive, where the nominative construction would be
more usual. The genitive construction permits him to employ the old
poetic form *Zēnos* instead of the standard prose form *Dios*. And it
calls our attention to the word *onoma* 'name'.

I think it would be a mistake to regard these unusual features of
diction as insignificant and unrelated to one another. They converge
in focussing interest on the correct *name* for divine wisdom. The
Greeks were always concerned to name the gods appropriately, to
call them by names pleasing to them so as to win their good will.
Now it seems obvious that the supreme principle would be willing to
be called 'Zeus', since this is the traditional name for the reigning
deity, father of gods and men. (Compare the formula for War in
LXXXIII, D. 53.) But this concession to traditional usage comes only
after, and despite, the more emphatic claim that the wise One is *un-*

willing to be so called. The denial that this name is pleasing may, I
have suggested, be read as a denial that any single name is uniquely
privileged. But it can more easily be understood as a rejection of the
traditional conception of deity, associated with the name 'Zeus' in
ordinary cult and in the poets' description.

The form *Zēnos* points to a deeper reading. For an author who
delights in word play, *Zēnos* recalls the verb *zēn* 'to live'. According
to the *Cratylus*, Zeus is so called because he is 'the cause of life (*zēn*)
. . . through whom life belongs in every case to all living things'
(396A7ff.; cf. 410D). Such etymological play with the name for
Zeus was rampant in the archaic period.[397] And this particular
etymology is clearly presupposed by Aeschylus in the *Suppliants*
(584f.). Now for Heraclitus as for Aeschylus 'etymology' must be
taken literally: an *etymos logos* is a 'true statement' hidden in the
form of a name. In LXXIX (D. 48) the name of the bow asserts the
deeper unity between life and death. In CXVIII the name *Zēnos*
affirms that the supreme deity is also a principle of life, like the
'everliving fire' in which it is manifest.[398]

As for the verb *legesthai* here instead of 'to call' or 'to name', its
use is probably motivated by the etymology: in this name (*onoma*) a
statement (*logos*) is hidden. And we might detect overtones of the
larger significance of *logos* for Heraclitus.

(3) Why does Heraclitus formulate CXVIII as an explicit contradiction? This antithetical form can be seen as exhibiting in its own
structure the dialectical moment in his general doctrine of opposition:
a strong sense of the positive force lurking behind a negation. (See
above, pp. 188f.) But the contradiction can also be understood
within the context of his attitude to language and assertion (*legesthai*),
which is one of profound ambivalence: a definite statement on
matters of such supreme importance can be taken both as true and as
false. This ambivalence reflects neither an intrinsic defect of language
nor a conception of reality as incoherent or irrational. It springs
rather from a grave sense of risk in communication, a risk amounting
almost to a certainty that he will be misunderstood. The need for
two-tongued statement is a consequence of the epistemic deafness of
his audience. If Heraclitus must, like the oracle, 'neither declare
(*legei*) nor conceal but give a sign', that is because his listeners cannot
follow a plain tale. If they had what it takes to comprehend his
message, the truth would already be apparent to them. But since
words alone cannot make them understand 'when their souls do not
speak the language', he must resort to enigma, image, paradox, and

even contradiction, to tease or shock the audience into giving thought to the obvious, and thus enable them to see what is staring them in the face. If they succeed, they will understand not this sentence alone but the unified world view that Heraclitus means to communicate. And central to such understanding will be a recognition that the principle of cosmic order is indeed a principle of life, but that it is not willing to be called by this name alone. For it is also a principle of death. Human wisdom culminates in this insight that life and death are two sides of the same coin. And cosmic wisdom is truly spoken of only when identified with both sides of the coin.

Thus the linguistic forms of antithesis and paradox combine with ambiguity and resonance for the expression of a total view, no part of which is fully intelligible in separation from the whole.

CXIX–CXXII

CXIX (D. 64)   The thunderbolt pilots all things.

CXX (D. 65)   Hippolytus (immediately following CXIX): [By 'thunderbolt' he means the eternal fire. And he says this fire is intelligent (*phronimon*) and cause of the organization of the universe. He calls it 'need and satiety' (D. 65). According to him 'need' (*chrēsmosynē*) is the construction of the world order, 'satiety' (*koros*) is the conflagration (*ekpyrōsis*). For he says . . .] (What follows is CXXI.)

CXXI (D. 66)   Fire coming on will discern (*krinei*, literally 'separate') and catch up with all things.

CXXII (D. 16)   How will one hide from (*lathoi*, 'escape the notice of') that which never sets?

I group these four texts together because they agree in conceiving the supreme principle of the universe as cosmic or celestial fire. In the case of CXX, however, it is only Hippolytus' commentary that connects 'need and satiety' with the concept of fire. I postpone for a moment the discussion of Hippolytus' interpretation.

The imagery of the helmsman in CXIX (*oiakizei* 'pilots', from *oiax*, the tiller of a ship) recalls the 'steering' of all things in LIV (D. 41). The latter is introduced by the phrase *hen to sophon*, 'the wise is one', which is repeated in CXVIII for the divine intelligence that rules the cosmos. That intelligence, ambivalently identified with Zeus, is represented by his characteristic weapon in CXIX, where the fiery thunderbolt stands as symbol for the counterpoint themes of unity ('the wise one') and totality ('piloting *all things*') that form the warp and woof of cosmic order.

The metaphor of the helmsman guiding the ship of state is as old as Greek lyric poetry. And the cognate metaphor for cosmic governance is probably as old as Greek philosophy. Anaximander seems to have said of the Boundless that it 'contains all things and steers (*kybernan*) them all'.[399] The metaphor of cosmic steering becomes a standard one in Ionian natural philosophy, but its use in CXIX and LIV may be a direct echo of Anaximander's words.[400] However, Heraclitus never takes over a motif without altering it. In CXIX the new philosophic theme of an intelligent regulation for the cosmos is invoked in terms of the mythic ruling power of the supreme god, as directly experienced in the most terrifying of natural events: the lightning bolt and the crash of thunder.

CXXI takes up the theme of fire (which connects the thunderbolt of CXIX with the cosmic fire of XXXVII, D. 30, the *prēstēr* of XXXVIII, D. 31A, and the 'fiery Zeus' of XLV, D. 120) and explicates its control over 'all things' (*panta*) by means of three verbs: (i) it comes upon (*epelthon*) all things, (ii) it will discern or decide or distinguish them (*krinei*), and (iii) it will seize or catch hold of them all (*katalēpsetai*). Cosmic guidance is thus reinterpreted in terms of cosmic justice, as indicated by the direct parallel to LXXXVII (D. 28B), where Dikē herself is subject of the third verb: she '*will catch up with* those who fabricate and bear witness to lies'. But in CXXI the scope of justice is universal: it will catch up with all things.

The notion of cosmic justice, introduced by Anaximander, is systematically developed by Heraclitus.[401] Justice as expressed by *dikē* normally implies punishment, as Heraclitus himself seems to have pointed out (LXIX, D. 23). And both punishment and compensation are suggested by the word *antamoibē* 'requital', which denotes the exchange of all things for fire in XL (D. 90). I recall these points here because the authenticity of CXXI was challenged by Reinhardt on the grounds that it imports into Heraclitus' text the Christian notions of hellfire and Last Judgment which Bishop Hippolytus wished to find there.[402] But justice, judgment, and punishment of some sort are represented in the fragments in any case. CXXI introduces the notion of hellfire only if we interpret judgment in the specifically Christian sense, and there is no reason to follow Hippolytus in this regard. Instead, consider the literal meaning of the three verbs.

(i) Fire comes upon or 'attacks' all things (in Herodotus *epelthein* is often but not always used for the advance upon an enemy); (ii) it will discern, distinguish, or judge all things (*krinei*), and (iii) it will catch up with and seize hold of them (*katalēpsetai*), which should mean that they will literally catch fire. The universal approach of fire is depicted as hostile and threatening, but not exclusively so. For *krinein* may mean to select someone for special honors, to judge a contest in his favor, as well as to judge him guilty or subject to punishment. The verb has the same ambivalence as 'requital' (*antamoibē*) in XL (D. 90). According to the merits of the case, the seizure of a thing by fire will entail either its punishment or its reward, its promotion upwards to enhanced life or downwards to elemental death.

As executor of universal justice, Fire here plays the role of Justice herself and her ministers the Furies in XLIV (D. 94).[403] Now Justice is also identified with Conflict and opposition (LXXXII, D. 80). If Heraclitus' thought and imagery are coherent, the Fire which figures as justice must stand not only for the principle of cosmic guidance (like the thunderbolt of CXIX) but also for the cosmic structure of opposition, as reflected in the measured kindling and extinction of XXXVII (D. 30). Ultimately these two notions will coincide: it is precisely *by means of polar opposition* that wisdom orders the universe and distinguishes the upward and downward paths of reward and punishment.

To make sense of this, however, we must distinguish two roles for fire in Heraclitus. In the first place fire is conceived as one elemental form among others, an alternative to earth or water or clouds and wind. It is not easy to find in the fragments an unambiguous reference to fire in this narrow, elemental sense.[404] But the ordinary sense of fire is obviously presupposed by every use of the term. On the other hand, when the everliving fire of XXXVII is identified with the world order or *kosmos* as such, it is presented as the system of *all* elemental forms that emerge as it is kindled and quenched. If we accept (as I propose) a pattern of cosmogony and universal conflagration for Heraclitus, then this trans-elemental role is embodied in the primordial Fire that precedes and alternates with the formation of the world. We need not return here to the controversial issues of cosmogony and ecpyrosis: in a general conflagration the fate of all things will be the same, so this can throw no special light on the judicious *discernment* by fire. Insofar as Heraclitus has such a total conflagration in view, CXXI tells us only that cosmic justice and symmetry require that at some point all things return to the source from which they first emerged.

On any reading of XXXVIII (D. 31A), in which water, earth, and the like are presented as 'reversals' of fire, as on any interpretation of the exchange of all things for fire in XL (D. 90), we must allow for some privileged role for fire that sets it apart from the other elements. There must be some sense, symbolical if not physical, in which fire represents the world order as a whole and the principle of cosmic justice. How are we to conceive this role of fire within the present constitution of the universe?

I will suggest in a moment a view (not very easy to understand) according to which fire passes *physically* through all other natural forms and phenomena. But first we recall that fire appears both as representative of death, in the funeral pyre, and also as the highest afterlife for pre-eminent souls who, as a beam of light (*augē*), are associated with, or absorbed into, the celestial fire of the sun and stars (above, pp. 250f., 256). Secondly, in natural phenomena such as the lightning bolt, the fiery *prēstēr*, and the 'all-seeing sun', fire is the embodiment and instrument of cosmic wisdom. It is just this traditional conception of the sun as 'eye of Zeus' or 'eye of Justice' that explains the allusion to divine insight as *a sun which never sets* in CXXII (D. 16), an unsleeping eye whose notice one cannot hope to escape.[405]

Underlying the imagery of CXXII, then, we find the analogy between sun and cosmic fire that is also implied by the solstitial 'turnings (*tropai*) of fire' in XXXVIII (D. 31). The traditional role of the Sun as observer must be taken over by its cosmic analogue, since the sun itself is under higher surveillance (XLIV, D. 94) and, extinguished each night, it is unavailable as a possible observer for half of a man's lifetime. The conception of cosmic fire as a kind of super-sun thus unites the mythical ideas of divine justice associated with Zeus and Helios and the new Ionian view of rational order as pervading the entire natural world. Without following Reinhardt in recognizing a direct quotation in the comment (in CXX) that 'this fire is intelligent (*phronimon*)', we can see this as an accurate statement.

Our interpretation of CXXII is confirmed by a passage already referred to in Plato's *Cratylus*, where he is expounding the doctrine of flux and offers two connected etymologies for 'Zeus' and 'just' (*dikaion*). Plato here mentions the view that there is something which pervades or passes through all things and is cause of everything that comes about (412D). This universal causal factor is the swiftest and finest of all things.

And because it administers (*epitropeuei*) all things by moving

through (*dia-ion*) them, it was rightly called by this name *dikaion*
'just' . . . And someone said it was right to call it Zeus [in the
accusative *Dia*] as the cause: for the cause is that because (*dia*) of
which things happen. (412D8–413A5)

Socrates claims he has been able to learn these doctrines only with
great difficulty, as secret lore; and he found that his informants could
not agree on any further answer to his persistent question: what is
just?

One of them says it is the sun that is just (*dikaion*); for it alone by
moving through (*dia-ion*) and burning (*kaon*) administers all
beings. But when I tell this to someone else . . . he laughs at me
and asks if I think there is nothing just once the sun has set. When
I persist in asking what he takes justice to be, he says it is fire. But
this is not easy to understand. Another says it is not fire itself but
the very heat which is present in fire. Another one claims to laugh
at all these views and says the just is what Anaxagoras meant:
intelligence (*nous*). For this is the supreme power and, being mixed
with nothing else, it sets all things in order by moving through
them all. (413B3–C7)

How far this account is based upon Plato's own reading of Heraclitus,
how far it reflects the exegesis of earlier Heracliteans, we can only
guess. The connections between the sun, elemental fire, supreme
intelligence, and the cosmic causal factor are all to be found in the
fragments.[406] What Plato adds is that the fiery wisdom of the universe sets things in order *by moving through them*. And perhaps this
is a natural interpretation of CXXI: 'fire coming on (*epelthon*) . . .
will catch up with all things'. This view of fire as literally penetrating
everything in the world would fully agree with other pre-Platonic
attempts to conceive the causal action of the supreme principle in
terms of physical presence and penetration.[407] Heraclitus must also
have thought of his divine principle as in some sense all-pervasive,
immanent in the natural order and in all of its constituents, as the
'pantheistic' tendency of CXXIII (D. 67) will make clear. The Greeks
before Plato and after Aristotle seem able to conceive of the spiritual
or intelligent ordering of the world only in terms of a rarified, all-
pervading physical presence, like the ether of pre-Einsteinian physics.
Even in the fourth century A.D., Augustine was able to free himself
from this corporeal view of God only by the study of Neoplatonic
metaphysics. The Stoics speak of the supreme deity in pre-Socratic
fashion, as breath (*pneuma*) or rational fire (*pyr noeron*), a power
which orders all things by 'passing through them all'.[408]

I have left for the end the phrase 'need (*chrēsmosynē*) and satiety (*koros*)' (CXX, D. 65), whose authenticity is guaranteed by independent citations in Philo and Plutarch. All three authors reflect a Stoic interpretation which identifies the two terms with successive stages in the cosmic cycle: 'Need is the construction of the world order (*diakosmēsis*), Satiety is the universal conflagration (*ekpyrōsis*).' I see no way of deciding whether or not this interpretation is based upon something in the lost context of CXX. The Stoics may simply have taken their clue from Theophrastus, who construed the related pairs War-Peace and Strife-Agreement as a reference to these cosmic periods 'of the opposites the one that leads to generation and coming-to-be is called "war" and "strife"; the one leading to the conflagration is called "agreement" and "peace" ' (D.L. IX.8: see Appendix IIA). In the exegesis of CXX 'Need' takes the place of 'Strife', 'Satiety' replaces 'Peace' and 'agreement'. The substitution was an easy one, given the parallel pairs of CXXIII.

Perhaps the only safe conclusion from such reports is that Heraclitus presented 'Need and Satiety' in some close connection with fire. (Cf. 'hunger' and 'satiety' in CXXIII.) The actual phenomenon of fire may be characterized intuitively in terms of 'need' (or 'hunger') for fuel, and 'repletion' or 'satiety' when it burns itself out. In Greek *koros* 'satiety' suggests *hybris* and carries connotations of disaster. (Hence the Stoic interpretation of *koros* as the destruction of the world order.) We recall the analogy between *hybris* and destructive fire in CIV (D. 43). If the kindling and extinction of fire is taken as a figure for the cosmic order, this pattern may be redescribed as Need and Satiety.

For a similar pairing of Hunger (*limos*) and Satiety, see LXVII (D. 111).

CXXIII

CXXIII (D. 67)   The god: day and night, winter and summer, war and peace, satiety and hunger. It alters, as when mingled with perfumes it gets named according to the pleasure (*hēdonē*) of each one.

CXXIII consists of two distinct sentences connected by the particle *de*. The first of these announces as its topic 'the god' (*ho theos*) and offers as comment four pairs of antithetical nouns.[409] The second sentence begins with a verb 'it alters' or 'it becomes different' (*alloioutai*) without any subject expressed, and continues with a complex comparative clause containing a subordinate clause of time: 'just as, when it is mingled with perfumes, it is named according to the pleasure of each one'. Again no subject noun is provided for either clause (unless we add one, as many editors have done). There is thus a sharp formal contrast between the two sentences: the first consists of nine nouns in the nominative, with no syntax, simply a list of names; the second sentence is all syntax, with three finite verb clauses but no subject noun. In the first the god is described by a formal pattern of antitheses; in the second by a verb of *process*, explicated in turn by analogy to another process. This elaborate formal asymmetry gives us a strong *prima facie* reason for resisting the editorial temptation to introduce a subject noun into the second sentence. I consider the two sentences in turn.

(1) This is the only definition of deity in the fragments. Other texts dealing with the gods may be divided into four groups. Group I develops the traditional contrast between divine insight and human ignorance, but tells us nothing further about the divine.[410] Group II posits a mysterious equivalence between gods and humans, immortals and mortals, suggesting some deeper unity in which these opposites are reconciled.[411] Group III speaks in mythical terms of specific gods: Dionysus and Hades (equated in CXVI, D. 15), Dike and her servants the Furies (XLIV, D. 94; cf. LXIX, D. 23 and LXXXVII, D. 28B), Apollo 'whose oracle is in Delphi'.[412] The references to Justice point to a fourth group, in which CXXIII will be included. These are the texts that invoke a supreme principle of cosmic unity which lies *beyond* the traditional Greek conception of the divine. In two cases the principle described in terms appropriate to deity is explicitly contrasted with gods (*theoi*) as normally understood: War, which has made some gods and others men (LXXXIII, D. 53); and the cosmic Fire, which 'no one either of gods or of men has made' (XXXVII, D. 30).

War and Fire thus appear as designations of the new super-Zeus, a principle of universal order and justice that must coincide with 'the wise one alone' of CXVIII (D. 32). It is this principle that we have just seen described as Thunderbolt, Fire, or a sun 'which never sets'.[413] It must be the same supreme principle that nourishes all human laws as 'the divine one' in XXX (D. 114): 'it prevails as it will and suffices for all and is more than enough'.

We thus find two quite distinct conceptions of deity in Heraclitus. The gods in general as opposed to men, including individual powers designated by traditional names (other than Zeus and Dike), are conceived as one member of a polar opposition (immortals-mortals, Hades-Dionysus), and hence as partial constituents which, if isolated, cannot be identified with the world order as a whole.[414] On the other hand there is 'the divine one' or 'the wise one', the principle of unity represented by War and Fire and identified with the *kosmos* that is 'common to all' (XXXVII, D. 30). Now the antitheses which follow make clear that 'the god' of CXXIII must also represent this universal principle of cosmic unity. But it is striking that the definition given in our sentence makes no use of the network of terms by which this concept is articulated in other fragments: cosmic Fire, unique wisdom, universal steering, the *logos* according to which all things come to pass. Instead, CXXIII displays the divine plan in typical instances of its constituent structure.

Four pairs of opposites divide into two groups. Day and night, winter and summer define the cosmic order of change and regularity within which human life is carried on. The last two pairs (war and peace, satiety and famine) represent extreme human experiences of disruption and restoration. But all four pairs are characterized by a common pattern: the alternation and interdependence of a positive and a negative term. Thus war and famine represent things dangerous and destructive, while peace and satiety represent what is positive and desirable. A similar positive-negative contrast underlies the antitheses of the first group: summer is the good season (*kalokairi* 'fair weather' in Modern Greek: the ancient name *theros* suggests 'crops'), whereas winter is named from 'storm' (*cheimōn*); daylight stands for life, but Night is the fearful power of darkness (hence her euphemistic name *euphronē* 'the kindly one', used throughout the fragments).[415] Now the regularity of the seasons and the changing ratio of day and night was recognized as the very pattern of cosmic plan, the work of an ordering intellect.[416] The formal symmetry of our sentence seems to make a similar point about the negative and positive extremes of human experience. By the 'measures' of cosmic order, peace and war, satiety and hunger are necessarily joined together within a total unity that is 'the god'. But whereas other fragments assert the unity of a specific pair of opposites, what our sentence adds is the thesis of unity for *all* the pairs.[417]

Except for war and peace, the antitheses of CXXIII all reappear in other fragments.[418] The pairing of war and peace is unique, since elsewhere War stands alone for the cosmic order (LXXXII, D. 80; LXXXIII, D. 53). We thus recognize a duality in the role of war, which figures here as one constituent of a particular antithesis and there as the principle of antithesis as such, just as we have distinguished a partial and a total conception of deity and a particular (elemental) and universal (cosmic) role for fire. There is no *one* term that can designate the principle of total order without ambiguity.

It would be pointless to debate whether these four pairs of opposites are to be attributed to the god as predicates or strictly identified with him as alternative descriptions. The logical dichotomy between the 'is' of predication and the 'is' of identity is a conceptual anachronism, which does violence to the simple directness of Heraclitus' language. God is in some sense defined by or identified with the opposites here, though of course he (or it) cannot be identified with any one, or with any pair, taken alone. Nor can the list be regarded as an *exhaustive* account of deity: the god will be strictly identical only with the total pattern of opposition, of which these four pairs are paradigmatic specimens.

This pattern is the order of the universe, its unifying structure as a balancing of opposites over time. The god identified in CXXIII is neither a physical substance nor an underlying element, nor any concrete body like elemental fire. This is obvious from the first sentence, but often forgotten in the exegesis of what follows.

(2) 'It alters, as when mingled with perfumes it gets named according to the pleasure of each.' What is it that alters or becomes 'other in kind' (*alloios*)? The god, surely. But not the god as some underlying subject or substrate that could *manifest* itself in the opposites taken one at a time, being actually and in itself an entity distinct from them all. This substratum-interpretation of CXXIII, which is encouraged by a superficial reading of the simile of incense as well as by the Aristotelian view of Heraclitean fire as material cause, is clearly ruled out by the preceding sentence. For there is no *one* subject which might become first day, then night, then winter or summer, war or peace. Days and nights are themselves part of, and modified by, summer and winter, just as they are qualified in turn by war and peace. The four pairs of opposites are in no sense *alternatives to one another*, as potential attributes of some one underlying subject, in the way that different fragrances may characterize a single fire. It is only between the two terms of any given pair that a change of this kind can be understood. So the verb 'it alters' must refer to a change from any one term to its opposite — or, more generally, to every change between opposites. This is the divine structure of cosmic process according to Heraclitus. It is a misreading of the simile to suppose that there is some process by which cosmic fire might change

from day to winter, from peace to famine, or from one pair of opposites to another pair. And it is the same misreading that leads so many editors to insert 'fire' or some other noun as subject of the clause 'when it is mingled with perfume'.[419] For the altar flame is of course distinct from the incense or spices that are thrown upon it. All the more reason why Heraclitus should have avoided here any explicit mention of fire. His simile holds not between the transformations of the god and the mingling of fire with incense but between the different manifestations of the god and the alternative *naming* (of the fire — or of the god?) when so mingled. As there is one fire called by many names, so there is one divine system of unity and opposition that has just been designated by four pairs of opposites.

As it stands, the subject of this clause (as of the entire second sentence) is *nameless*: it acquires a name only from the spices with which it is mixed, and in which the namer takes 'pleasure'. Since the remote subject of the preceding sentence is 'the god', and since we are given *no* subject here, the text suggests that it is the god himself who appears as fire mingled with incense: the cosmic god has his epiphany in the flame burning on the altar. Once the text is 'corrected' by the editors we find no such mysterious identity between the universal deity and the sacrificial fire, indeed no mystery at all but a transparent and misleading simile.

The final phrase, 'named according to the pleasure (*hēdonē*) of each', may be read in two ways. According to an old technical use of *hēdonē* for a flavor or perfume, it means simply that the unnamed fire receives the name of each spice that is added to it.[420] But this is not the ordinary sense of *hēdonē* (for example, in Herodotus); and even if Heraclitus alludes to this special usage here, it is difficult to believe that he meant to exclude the standard meaning of the word 'pleasure'. On that reading the phrase with *hekastou* will mean not 'according to the flavor of each spice' but 'according to the pleasure of each man (who so names it)'. It is not that the naming of the divine by means of opposites is arbitrary or subjective, depending upon personal whim, but rather that the positive and negative values of opposing names are relative to the human perspective and to the personal experience of the individual. Mankind perceives the contrast, the otherness (*alloios*) of daylight and nocturnal darkness, hunger and surfeit, but not the unity which binds each pair together, and which is the same principle of antithesis throughout: 'It is disease that makes health sweet and good, hunger satiety, weariness rest' (LXVII, D. 111).[421]

Hippolytus tells us that CXXIII was found 'in the same section' as CXX—CXXI (D. 65—6).[422] This is one of the very few cases where my arrangement of the fragments rests on documentary evidence. (But Hippolytus' remark does not include CXXII, D. 16, which I have grouped here because of its thematic link with what precedes.)

CXXIV

CXXIV (D. 10)   Graspings (*syllapsies*): wholes and not wholes, convergent divergent, consonant dissonant, from all things one and from one thing all.

The form of this fragment recalls the first sentence in CXXIII (D. 67): a topic is posed by the opening word, then explicated by a series of opposing terms. But whereas the surface structure of CXXIII was clear, with a subject ('the god') singled out by the definite article, in CXXIV the initial term is itself enigmatic and we scarcely know what is being asserted of what. Both in form and content these two fragments serve as complements to one another, providing a kind of summary of Heraclitus' thought. They might well have been placed together here, at or near the end of the book.

(1) As first word, and the only term not paired with an antithesis, the plural form *syllapsies* emerges as the topic upon which the following pairs will comment. But what does this word mean? Most commentators, groping for some clue, assign to *syllapsies* a sense that will fit the rest of the sentence: 'Zusammensetzungen' (Snell), 'things taken together' (Kirk), 'connections' (Marcovich), 'assemblages' (Bollack-Wismann). But none of these senses is attested for *syllapsis* (Attic *syllēpsis*) in archaic or classical usage. Such renderings tend to short-circuit the process of understanding, by taking as point of departure an interpretation that can only be reached by an analysis of the whole sentence.[423] Before Aristotle (for whom the word can mean biological 'conception' or 'pregnancy'), the only sense attested for *syllēpsis* is the bodily notion of 'seizing, laying hold of, arresting, apprehending' (LSJ s.v. *syllēpsis* II; this is still the standard meaning of the term in Modern Greek). Now the cognate verb *katalēpsetai* is twice used by Heraclitus in this sense of personal capture (LXXXVII, D. 28, and CXXI, D. 66; cf. *elabomen* and *katelabomen* in XXII, D. 56). If we are to take Heraclitus at his word, our interpretation must begin with the literal sense of grasping or seizure, as in the capture of someone trying to escape. Commentators have generally neglected this ordinary meaning of the word because it makes CXXIV harder

to understand. But who ever supposed that Heraclitus was an easy author?

This initial sense of *syllapsies* becomes less puzzling once we realize that CXXIV characterizes the structure of the universe and remember that this structure is an order of justice involving punishment and reward. We are then free to connect the image of seizing a fugitive with other statements about the impossibility of escape (CXXII, D. 16; XLIV, D. 94; cf. LXXXVII, D. 28 and CXXI, D. 66). By this initial echo of the themes of fire and Justice laying hands on guilty ones, the term *syllapsies* will recall the dimension of cosmic justice that is similarly invoked by the term *antamoibē* 'requital' for the mutual exchange between fire and all things in XL (D. 90).

Other, less usual senses of *syllapsis* (or *syllēpsis*) are nonetheless essential for deciphering CXXIV. (1) *Syllēpsis* is etymologically a 'taking-together', a physical conjunction or concatenation of sounds or the like, as in the cognate *syllabē*, 'syllable'. (2) *Syllēpsis* can designate the cognitive act of collecting together, comprehending, or summing up. This sense of the noun is unattested in classical usage, but well represented for the corresponding verb *syllambanein* 'to comprehend'; it might easily be understood here as a recondite *hyponoia*.

Since Snell's study of our fragment in 1941 (*Hermes* 76, 84–7), it has been recognized that *syllapsies* must be taken here in sense (1) or (2). We need not choose between the two, any more than we need to choose between the two sides of the action-object ambiguity: between the act of grasping and the things grasped. 'Graspings' may be understood here both in the physical and the cognitive sense, both as act and as object. *Syllapsies* will denote the pairwise structuring of reality and also the act of intelligence by which this structure is gathered together.

(2) 'Wholes and not wholes.' It is the neuter form of these two terms (*hola kai ouk hola*) which obliges us to go beyond the usual meaning of *syllēpsis* as 'seizure (of a person)'. If it is not a question of someone being captured, what kind of apprehending is going on here? Answer: things whole and things not whole.[424] In cognitive terms the contrast between 'wholes' and 'not wholes' points to the most abstract and general feature of intellectual synthesis: combining objects in thought and seeing them together as larger unities. Of all conceptual antitheses, only the opposition of unity and plurality is of comparable generality. (See the contrast of 'one' and 'many' in the final pair of CXXIV.) In form the opposition of *wholes* and *not*

wholes is even more general, since it exhibits the basic logical pattern of affirmation and denial: Yes and No. Both terms also express in their plural form the idea of the manifold as such. And in terms of semantic content, the notion of 'wholes' indicates a subordinate diversity of parts and thus a greater richness of structure, a more organic unity, than the contrast of *one* and *many* alone. We might say that the notion of 'whole' expresses the concept of unity as dynamic rather than static: each unit is built up out of an internal plurality and grouped in turn within some wider plurality. In the language of set theory, each set short of the universal set is both a whole (since it is a unit including one or more members) and not a whole, since it is not all-inclusive. The literal sense of *holos* is 'complete, lacking in none of its parts'. Strictly speaking, there can be only one whole, one unity from which nothing is lacking. (Hence *to holon* comes to mean 'the universe'.) But all unities short of the universe itself will be both wholes and not wholes.

Beginning with the cognitive notion of bringing things together as totalities in thought, we have been led to speak of the correlative unity of structures or objects synthesized. But these structures remain general and abstract. Terms like *whole* and *part, positive* and *negative, one* and *many*, indicate purely formal features that can apply (like the concepts which Ryle has called 'topic-neutral') to any subject matter whatsoever. Thus there is a crucial difference of type between such abstract opposites and the more concrete, 'substantive' oppositions illustrated in CXXIII: day and night, summer and winter, peace and war, satiety and famine. It is in virtue of this distinction that CXXIV and CXXIII supplement one another as a summary of the doctrine of opposites. Unlike the formal antitheses of CXXIV, the opposites of CXXIII are directly instantiated in human life and in nature, like the terms of XCIII (D. 88): *living* and *dead, waking* and *sleeping, young* and *old*.

Understood as forms of 'combinations' (*syllapsies*) in the world, then, terms like *wholes* and *not wholes* are logically of a higher type: we must think of them as applying to some particular substantive term, such as *day* or *night, life* or *death*. One can say of each day or each individual life that it is a distinct *whole*, with beginning, middle, and end. But we can also, and even more truly, say that it is *not a whole*, since it is only a part of some larger unity: of the diurnal cycle of day-and-night, or of the Heraclitean cycle of life-and-death by which immortals live the death of mortals. Thus the topic-neutral opposites of CXXIV give us a formal characterization of the view expressed in the claim that Day and Night are one (XIX, D. 57), and generalized in the statement that 'all things are one' (XXXVI, D. 50).

(3) 'Convergent, divergent.' Intuitively, the pair of participles *sympheromenon diapheromenon* suggests local motion: the movement of plurality together (*syn-*) in the direction of unity, balanced by the movement apart (*dia-*) to diversity. This spatial imagery may be taken as a figure for the dynamic tension between totality and partiality, unity and diversity that runs through all cases of opposition. But we should also take these participles literally, as depicting an actual process of alternating motion towards unity and diversity, as in the concluding antithesis: 'from all things one and from one thing all'.

Even more unmistakable is the metaphorical sense of *sympheromenon* and *diapheromenon* as 'agreeing with', 'being advantageous to' (the usual sense of *sympherei* in the active voice), and 'quarrelling with', 'being hostile to'. So understood, this antithesis echoes the references to Agreement and Conflict in so many other fragments, and specifically in LXXVIII (D. 51): 'how in variance it agrees with itself'. Recall the pairing of *peace* and *war* in CXXIII. Peace and conflict, amity and hostility are the forms in which the principles of unity and diversity are directly manifested within the social life of mankind.

(4) 'Consonant, dissonant.' *Synaidon* and *diaidon* mean literally 'singing together' and 'singing apart'.[425] There has been much learned attention devoted to the state of musical practice and terminology in Heraclitus' day, and it has been emphatically denied that *harmoniē* in LXXVIII (D. 51) and LXXX (D. 54) can refer to the harmony or 'concord' of several notes struck or sung together, like chords in unison.[426] But in any case the musical antithesis, following as it does here upon 'coming together-disagreeing', must be significantly related to the *harmoniē* or 'attunement' of the lyre in LXXVIII, since the latter is precisely said 'to agree in variance with itself'. I leave it to historians of Greek music to decide (if they can) what forms of consonance and dissonance Heraclitus may have had in mind. There are several obvious applications: the strings of the lyre may sound either in agreement with one another or out of tune; the singer himself may sing either in harmony or in discord with his instrument; and several unaccompanied human voices may sing together with or without the desired accord.

Music is a strikingly specific instance of unity and diversity; and we may ask what accounts for this special role of music for Heraclitus. There is no doubt of the privileged status enjoyed by music and the lyre in the aristocratic culture of archaic Greece. (Think of the scene in *Iliad* IX, where Agamemnon's ambassadors find Achilles in his hut singing to the lyre.) And the formal patterns of Greek music were regarded as familiar examples of a unity and 'agreement' that requires as its basis an objective diversity of sounds and tones. (This is the thought which Aristotle, following Plato, ascribes to Heraclitus in LXXV, D. 8.) But I suspect that Heraclitus was also influenced by the kind of Pythagorean speculation concerning the musical numbers and the cosmic role of harmonic ratios that is reflected in the fragments of Philolaus.[427] For if we see in Heraclitus' development of the theme of musical *harmonie* a reaction to Pythagorean ideas, there will be a direct connection between this emphasis on music and his conception of cosmic order in terms of 'measures' and proportion (*logos*).

(5) 'From all things one and from one thing all.' As final determination of the concept of 'graspings', Heraclitus here names the themes of unity and plurality which dominate the fragment and characterize his thought throughout. (It is easy to imagine these words as closure for the book, or at least as closing the positive statement of doctrine. They would thus form a ring pattern with 'all things are one' in XXXVI, D. 50.) However, Heraclitus does not refer to plurality as such (*polla* 'many') but to a plurality that is total and all-inclusive: *panta* 'all things'.[428] It is not the numerical contrast between the one and the many that is the focus of concern, but the world-constituting antithesis between unity and totality: the one and the all.

Since this final chiastic pairing of antithetical terms provides a kind of summary for all that has gone before, any elaborate commentary would be repetitious. I call attention only to the dynamic, emergent form of the contrast: 'X out of Y, and Y out of X'. In cognitive terms we might understand these two moments as alternating phases of synthesis and analysis, the seeing-together and seeing-apart which characterizes intelligence in general and the understanding of opposites in particular.[429] But beyond this dialectical structure of cognition, there is surely some reference to the monism expressed in XXXVI (D. 50): 'all things are one'. And the reciprocal movement from pluralized totality (*panta*) to unity (*hen*) and back again recalls the exchange of all things (*ta panta*) for fire and fire for all things in XL (D. 90). Whatever interpretation fits the universal exchange for fire must also apply somehow to the alternation between all things and one. I have given my reasons for finding a Heraclitean allusion to some vast cosmic cycle involving the emergence of the world order from fire and its reabsorption into the same principle, as in the pattern of Stoic ecpyrosis (above, pp. 134ff., 145ff.). At the very least, the 'turnings' (*tropai*) of fire in XXXVIII (D. 31) will imply a succession of cosmic seasons marked by the prevalence of fire at one extreme and its withdrawal to some minimum position in the opposite phase, like the sun at winter solstice. On either reading, the alternation of one and all things in CXXIV will correspond to the kindling and quenching of cosmic fire in XXXVII (D. 30). The history of early Greek philosophy suggests an obvious parallel in the cosmic cycle of Empedocles, described in terms that echo CXXIV (Empedocles fr. 17.1–20; cf. fr. 26). Other parallels do not require a cycle of cosmogony and world-destruction. Thus in the Milesian pattern of *apokrisis* or separating-out, all things are separated from the Apeiron, or from the boundless Air; and this process of dispersion must be continually balanced by a movement of contraction and condensation (So in Anaxagoras, frs. 2, 4, and 12–16.)

Hence the physical interpretation of 'one thing from all, all things from one' will include, but need not be limited to, a cycle of alternating cosmic periods. The abstract form of this antithesis excludes any univocal reference to such a cosmic pattern. That pattern will serve, like conflict and amity, musical accord and dissonance, as a paradigm of the unity-in-opposition manifested by every system of rational structure. The kindling and quenching of cosmic fire, mirrored in the alternation of day and night, summer and winter, is of significance for Heraclitus because it reveals the *same* pattern as the alternation of waking and sleeping, youth and age, life and death, satiety and hunger. It is this general pattern of unity whose formal structure is articulated by the 'graspings' of CXXIV.

By way of conclusion, I offer a paraphrase of CXXIV that states more fully the thought that Heraclitus has deliberately schematized in his elliptical style. (The words in italics are added to make the fuller statement explicit.)

'Graspings, *that is to say groups holding together, apprehensions bringing things together: these are* wholes and not wholes; *they characterize a system which is* convergent, divergent, *structured by cooperation and by conflict; this system is* consonant, dissonant, *held together by harmony and discord alike;* from all *its components* a unity *emerges*, and from *this* unity all things *emerge.*'

CXXV

CXXV (D. 124)   Theophrastus: [The fairest order in the world ('the most
beautiful *kosmos*'), says Heraclitus, is a heap of random sweepings.]

Since even the text of Theophrastus is badly preserved, there is no
hope of recovering the original passage which he cites. At least the
play on *kosmos* ('adornment' and 'world-order') must belong to
Heraclitus. And some reference to a random collection must also be
authentic, if the quotation is to have any point in Theophrastus' context. The implied production of the fairest celestial arrangement from
a random assortment of refuse would be a striking illustration of the
paradoxical connection of opposites.

 Beyond this any interpretation must be a conjecture. My best
guess at Heraclitus' point is that the structure of the universal system
described in CXXIII and CXXIV is so strict and so all-pervasive that
chance and providence must coincide: any random arrangement of
material, any arbitrary sample of human life or evidence from nature
must exhibit the same pattern and illustrate the same plan (*gnōmē*).
This thought would not be too remote from Aristotle's comment on
the anecdote about the visitors who came to meet Heraclitus, but
hesitated to enter when they found him warming himself at the
kitchen fire. Seeing them at the door, he called out, 'Enter with confidence, for here too there are gods.' Citing this story in justification
of his study of the structure of animals great and small, Aristotle
remarks: 'in all these things there is some element of nature and
beauty'.[430]

Appendix I:
Dubious quotations from Heraclitus

I translate here, for the sake of completeness, the eight fragments listed as genuine by Diels but not included in my own translation and commentary. Reasons for omission differ from case to case. D. 67a and D. 125a seem to me straightforward forgeries, like some of the examples which Diels listed as spurious (D. 126a–139); D. 46 may belong in the same category. On the other hand, there is no reason to doubt the authenticity of the single word listed as D. 122, but also no hint of a sentential context and hence no way to construe it as a meaningful fragment. In the case of the two citations from Iamblichus (D. 68 and 69), the situation is rather similar: we seem to have a term quoted without any reliable indication of the original context. (I have included a comparable quotation from Iamblichus among the fragments proper, D. 70, LVIII, since it fits plausibly into a context provided by other fragments.) Many editors have accepted D. 49a as a genuine quotation, but I can only see it as a thinly disguised paraphrase of the river fragments (L and LI), modelled on the contradictory form of CXVIII (D. 32), and influenced by the thought of XCII (D. 62): we are and are not alive.[431] The text of D. 4 is in a class by itself: preserved in Latin by Albertus Magnus in the thirteenth century A.D., with no hint of a Greek source, it seems nonetheless to preserve a Heraclitean kernel; and I have used it with some hesitation in the commentary on LXX–LXXII.

I should add that among the fragments included in my text and commentary there are at least two of doubtful authenticity: XLI (D. 76) and CI (D. 115). Also, several of my 'fragments' are doxographic reports rather than verbal citations: XXIII (D. 105), XXIV (D. 38), XLIII (D. A13 and A5), and CXIII (D. A15 and D. 12).

D. 4 (M. 38, p. 188)   Albertus Magnus: Heraclitus said that if happiness lay in bodily delights, we would say that cattle are happy when they find bitter vetch (*orobus*) to eat.

D. 46 (M. 114, pp. 573ff.)   Diogenes Laertius: He said that conceit (*oiēsis*) was a sacred disease [i.e. epilepsy] and seeing was being deceived.[432]

D. 49a (M. 40c², pp. 199f.; cf. p. 211)   Heraclitus Homericus: (Heraclitus the obscure says . . .) 'Into the same rivers we step and do not step, we are and we are not.'

D. 67a (M. 115, pp. 576ff.)   Hisdosus Scholasticus: Heraclitus gives an excellent comparison of the soul to a spider and the body to the spider's web. As the spider, he says, waiting in the middle of the web, notices as soon as a fly breaks any thread and then quickly runs to the spot, as if she suffered until her web is repaired, just so does the soul of a human being, when any part of the body is harmed, move swiftly to that place, as if disturbed by the wound of the body, to which it is tightly and proportionately linked.[433]

D. 68 (M. 88, p. 469)   Iamblichus: In the holy seeing and hearing of shameful things we are released from the harm that is caused by the corresponding deeds <as in the cathartic effect of comedy and tragedy on the emotions> . . . And therefore it was reasonable of Heraclitus to call these practices 'remedies' (*akea*), as having a healing effect upon the soul.[434]

D. 69 (M. 98g, p. 518)   Iamblichus: Hence I posit two kinds of sacrifices. The first are those of wholly purified men, such as may occur rarely in the case of a single man, as Heraclitus says, or a very small number; the other kind are immersed in matter, corporeal, and produced by change.[435]

D. 122 (M. 111, p. 565)   Suidas: Heraclitus used the form *anchibasiē* ('stepping near').

D. 125a (M. 106, p. 543)   Tzetzes: May your wealth never fail you, men of Ephesus, so that your wretchedness may be fully exposed.[436]

Two texts listed by Diels among the spurious fragments are of some doctrinal interest:

D. 136 (M. 96b, p. 509)   Scholia to Epictetus: 'Souls killed in war are purer than those <that die> in diseases.' This is a late commentary on C (D. 24).

D. 137 (M. 28d¹, p. 135)   Aetius: 'Things are altogether determined by fate (*heimarmena*).' See on XLIIIB (n. 180).

Appendix II:
Doxographic reports

(A) From the Life of Heraclitus in Diogenes Laertius (IX.7–11), following an epitome from Theophrastus' *Opinions of the Natural Philosophers*.

7. In general his opinions are these: all things are composed out of fire and dissolved into it. Everything takes place according to Fate, and things are harmoniously fitted together by the transformation of opposites.[437] Also, all things are full of souls (*psychai*) and divine spirits (*daimones*). He discussed all the phenomena which occur in the cosmos, and said the sun is the size it appears (cf. XLVII, D. 3). Another saying of his: 'You will not find out the limits of the soul by going, even if you travel over every way, so deep is its *logos*' (XXXV, D. 45). And he said that conceit is a sacred disease [i.e. epilepsy] and seeing is being deceived (D. 46: see Appendix I above). His book contains some brilliant, clear passages, which even the dullest can easily understand and hence get some spiritual enrichment (literally 'elevation of soul'). The brevity and density (*baros* 'weight') of his style are incomparable.

8. In detail his doctrines are these: Fire is the elementary principle (*stoicheion*) and all things are an exchange for fire (cf. XL, D. 90), produced by rarefaction and condensation. But he does not expound this clearly. Everything occurs through opposition (cf. LXXXI, D. A22), and the whole world flows like a river (cf. L, D. 12 and LI, D. 91); but the universe is finite, and there is one world (cf. XXXVII, D. 30). It is generated from fire and ignited again in a conflagration according to certain cycles, alternating for all time (cf. XLIIIA, D. A13); this takes place in accordance with Fate. Of the opposites, the one leading to generation is called War and Conflict (cf. LXXXII, D. 80, and LXXXIII, D. 53); the one leading to the conflagration (*ekpyrōsis*) is called Agreement and Peace (cf. LXXVIII, D. 51 and CXXIII, D. 67). Change is a way up and down (CIII, D. 60), and through this the world is produced.

9. As fire thickens it becomes moist and as it condenses it becomes water; and water thickens and turns into earth (cf. XXXVIII, D. 31A). And this is the way down. But in turn the earth dissolves, and from it water arises, and from water everything else (cf. XXXIX, D. 31B), since he derives almost everything from the exhalation (*anathymiasis*) out of the sea. And this is the way up.

Now exhalations arise from both earth and sea, some of them bright and pure, others dark. Fire is augmented by the bright exhalations, moisture by the other ones. He does not indicate what the surrounding heaven (*to periechon*) is like. But in it there are certain bowls (*skaphai*) turned over with the hollow part facing us, and bright exhalations gather together in these and produce flames, which are the heavenly bodies.

10. The brightest and hottest is the flame of the sun; for the stars are farther

away from the earth and for this reason they are less bright and give less heat (cf. XLVI, D. 99). And the moon, although it is closer to the earth, does not travel through a pure region. But the sun lies in a translucent, unmixed region and at an appropriate (*symmetron* 'proportionate') distance from us. Hence it is hotter and gives more light.

Eclipses of the sun and moon occur when the bowls are turned upright. The moon's monthly change of shape is produced as the bowl in her case[438] turns little by little. Day and night, months and seasons and years, rainfall and wind and the like take place according to the different exhalations.

11. The bright exhalation produces day when it catches fire in the circle of the sun; but when the opposite exhalation prevails it produces night. And as heat increases from the bright exhalation it makes summer; but when moisture from the dark exhalation becomes excessive it produces winter (and rainstorm, *cheimōn*).

He gives an explanation of other things along the same lines. But he tells us nothing about what the earth is like, or even about the bowls. Such were his doctrines.

Commentary on the Theophrastean doxography

It is hard to know what to make of this report. The careful way in which the gaps are noted — 'Heraclitus says nothing about the structure of the heavens, nothing about the earth' — shows that it is not an unscrupulous invention but a conscientious attempt to make sense of the Heraclitean text. And in the first portion of the detailed report (section 8 and the first paragraph of section 9) we can see what Theophrastus' procedure was in interpreting this book, since we happen to have most — perhaps all — of the texts he used. This passage shows how Theophrastus, with the avowed goal of reconstructing a physical theory out of Heraclitus' enigmatic words, has pressed into service utterances that might properly bear a different sense. For example War and Strife, Peace and 'Agreement', are all interpreted in terms of the 'upward and downward path', and the latter in turn identified with the process of elemental transformations by which the world is generated from fire. The *tropai* or 'reversals' of XXXVIII, D. 31A are similarly understood as water 'turning into' earth by condensation: *pēgnumenon trepesthai* (DK I, p. 141, l. 26).

Now if we look through the fragments where the original text is unmistakable, we do not find a single word about the celestial bowls and the two kinds of exhalations described in sections 9–11.[439] Nor do we find any clear reference to the heat of the sun, the position of the stars, the region of the moon, nor any word about eclipse, lunar phases, the cause of rainfall and other seasonal changes, not a single word about any specific meteorological phenomenon except the thunderbolt (CXIX, D. 64) and the mysterious *prēstēr* of XXXVIII

(D. 31A). One very partial fragment does refer to the seasons (XLII, D. 100), and the lost context may have contained some information on which Theophrastus is relying. But can we believe that *this* context, or other fragments which are wholly lost, were so entirely different from the quotations that survive as to justify the reconstruction of a physical theory of the kind that Theophrastus provides?

For my part, I cannot believe it. It seems likely that some lost text of Heraclitus spoke of one or more 'bowls' in connection with sun or stars, but quite unlikely that Heraclitus intended to formulate the childish doctrine which Theophrastus has ascribed to him. As Kirk noted, the theory of bowls will not explain what it is supposed to, namely the phases of the moon and the shapes of sun and moon when eclipsed. All the more reason not to ascribe it to Heraclitus as a serious doctrine, in the absence of direct evidence.[440] As for the two exhalations and the mixed region of the moon, they represent something that Heraclitus *might* have said: the kind of meteorological theory that is attested for the Milesians, Xenophanes, or other early authors.[441] There are significant parallels in the doxography for Xenophanes.[442] But the distance between what we find in the fragments and in the doxography is so great as to convince me that Theophrastus was fundamentally misled by his assumption that Heraclitus was a *physikos*, a natural philosopher; and hence he systematically misread these riddles and allusions as the disguised statement of a physical theory.

In consequence, I have made little or no use of the doxography to reconstruct doctrines not directly attested either in literal quotations or in paraphrases where the style of Heraclitus is still recognizable as a partial guarantee of authenticity. My only conscious exception to this rule is in the case of the number 10,800 for the Great Year, where the reliance is restricted to a single number and its application. (See above on XLIII.) But in the case of the celestial bowls, where we have no corresponding information from the fragments, we must simply suspend judgment. The problem is, as West has put it, 'to unravel Theophrastus' knitting', that is, to isolate the threads of evidence from which he has woven his fabric of doctrine. For the bowls I do not see that we have any reliable clues for such detective work, and I offer no hypothetical solution.

In the case of the dual exhalation the situation is different. 'He had Heraclitus' book before him, and his dual-exhalation interpretation however Aristotelian, must have been an interpretation of something in the book' (West, p. 133). I see no reason to suppose (with Kirk) that Theophrastus was correct in attributing a systematic theory of exhalations to Heraclitus but mistaken in distinguishing two *kinds* of exhalation. This is just the sort of detail for which Theophrastus would generally be quite reliable. If he is unreliable in the case of Heraclitus, it is not because of anachronism or carelessness in detail but because of an error in principle, a mistake as to the nature of the writer and the character of his work. Hence he construes as meteorological and astronomical theory what must have been intended as something rather different. But the opposition of bright and dark in the doctrine of vapors is just what seems most authentic in Theophrastus' report. It corresponds to the pre-scientific opposition between the murky lower region of mist (*aēr*) and the bright sky above (*aithēr*).[443] And it is echoed in the fragments themselves by the description of the dry soul, the wisest and best, as a 'gleam of light' (*augē*: see above on CIX, D. 118). Here we are able to make sense of Theophrastus' doxography as a narrow physical reading of a doctrine whose primary concern was with the fate of the psyche after death.[444]

In conclusion, I note that my scepticism with regard to the doxographical report is greater than most recent interpreters but not much greater than Zeller's.[445] It was first Burnet (pp. 147ff.) and then, curiously enough, Reinhardt (*Parmenides* pp. 181–3) who made use of the doctrine of bowls and exhalations to reconstruct a physical theory for Heraclitus. They have been followed in different ways by Gigon, Kirk, Guthrie, and Marcovich. Thus we have the paradoxical situation that at the time when doxographical reports concerning other pre-Socratics were regarded with increased suspicion, the doxography on Heraclitus came to enjoy more authority for Reinhardt and his successors than it had possessed for Zeller!

(B) The Doxography from Sextus Empiricus, *Against the Mathematicians* VII (= *Against the Logicians* I). 126–34 (DK 22.A16)

126. Like most of the natural philosophers . . . Heraclitus regarded sense-perception (*aisthēsis*) as unreliable and proposed reason (*logos*) as the criterion of truth. He refutes the claims of sense-perception in the following words: 'Eyes and ears are poor witnesses for men if they have barbarian souls' (XVI, D. 107); which is the same as to say that it is the mark of barbarian souls to rely upon irrational sense-perceptions.

127. The reason (*logos*) which he declares to be judge of truth is not any ordinary sort but the *logos* which is shared or common (*koinos*) and divine. We must briefly explain what this is. Our natural philosopher believed that the medium which surrounds us (*to periechon*) is rational (*logikon*) and intelligent.

[128. Passages from Homer, Archilochus, and Euripides are cited to show that this is an old and widely held view.]

129. According to Heraclitus it is by drawing in this divine reason (*logos*) in respiration that we become intelligent, and <it is by the same principle that> in sleep we become forgetful, but in waking we regain our senses. For in sleep the passages of perception are shut, and hence the understanding (*nous*) in us is separated from its natural unity with the surrounding medium; the only thing preserved is the connection through breathing, which is like a root <of this natural union>. So when separated, our understanding loses its former power of memory.

130. But when we awake it goes out again through the passages of perception as through so many windows, and by contact with the surrounding medium it regains its rational power. Just as coals that are brought near the fire undergo a change and are made incandescent, but die out when they are separated from it, just so does the portion of the surrounding medium which resides as a stranger in our bodies become nearly irrational (*alogos*) as a result of this separation, but by the natural union through the multitude of passages <when they are re-opened> it attains a condition which is like in kind to the Whole [i.e. to the divine Reason of the universe].

131. Now it is this common and divine Reason, by participating in which we become rational, that Heraclitus proposes as the criterion of truth. Hence whatever appears in common to all men is reliable, for it is grasped by the reason that is common and divine; but an appearance that presents itself to only one person is unreliable on the opposite grounds.

132. Thus at the very beginning of his work *On the Nature of Things* our author refers in a way to the surrounding medium when he says 'Although the *logos* is so, men fail to comprehend . . . ' [There follows a citation of fragment I, with three words omitted.]

133. In this passage he explicitly presents the view that it is by participation in the divine Reason that we perform all our actions and all our thoughts. And a little later he adds: therefore one should follow what is common . . . 'Although the *logos* is common, most men live as though their thinking were a private possession' (III, D. 2). But this *logos* is precisely an explanation of the way in which the universe is organized. Therefore to the extent that we share in the memory of this common reason, to this extent we know the truth; but whenever we go our private way we are deceived.

134. Thus in so many words he expressly declares the common reason (*logos*) to be the criterion of truth, and he claims that what appears to all in common is reliable, since it is judged by common reason; but what appears to each one privately is false.

Commentary on IIB

I have rendered the entire context in Sextus because it presents the fullest example of an ancient commentary on Heraclitus, from an essentially Stoic point of view, and also because the sections on sleep and the rationality of the circumambient medium or *periechon* have been taken by some scholars as a reflection of authentic Heraclitean doctrines not fully preserved in the extant fragments.[446]

Sextus' commentary is striking in two respects. Except for the assumption that Heraclitus is a physicist, this interpretation has nothing in common with the doxographical tradition represented in Diogenes (Appendix IIA), but presents itself as an independent reading of Heraclitus' text. And it interprets this text just as freely and (from the modern point of view) just as arbitrarily as it provides allegorical commentary on Homer and Archilochus in section 128. The procedure is to give the meaning in advance, and then cite the literal text as confirmation. (Compare Cleanthes' interpretation of D. 12 given above as CXIIIB, where the same technique is used. The procedure is familiar to us from traditional methods of citing Scripture.) Thus the personal 'discourse' or 'report' of Heraclitus is identified with the cosmic Reason (or, more cautiously, in section 133, with the *exegēsis* or 'explanation' of the cosmic governance);[447] and this cosmic Reason is identified in turn with the surrounding medium or circumambient air (Stoic *pneuma*); while the alienating darkness of sleep, alluded to in such suggestive terms by Heraclitus in I, LXXXIX (D. 21) and XC (D. 26), is explained as a strictly mechanical process of separation from the cosmic Reason due to the closing of our passages of perception in sleep. The result is a coherent physical exegesis of Heraclitus' doctrine of sleep, maintaining the essential distinction between the private (or cognitively deprived) and the common (and cognitively reliable) ranges of experience that are so sharply contrasted in III (D. 2), where the text quoted by Sextus is not entirely free from Stoic contamination,[448] but remains faithful in principle to Heraclitus' thought. Sextus' interpretation also preserves, in its own way, a genuine Heraclitean sense of identity between the *logos* of the human psyche and that of the universe as a whole.

The physical identification of the 'common *logos*' with the circumambient atmosphere or *pneuma* cannot be supported by any evidence from the fragments: it is part of the hermeneutical rules of correspondence by which the Stoics found their own truth in Heraclitus' text. And this doctrine is also un-Heraclitean in its unambiguous precision: it states a psychophysical theory which happens to be false, but which some ancients believed to be true. But it preserves no hint of that poetic resonance and density that make Heraclitus' own statements on sleep profoundly meaningful for a modern reader, who can no longer take seriously the ancient theory stated in the commentary.

The commentator's text has virtues of its own; and the image of the dying embers brought back to radiance by contact with the fire is one that we do not easily forget. In the quasi-mystic view of human intelligence as an alienated spark cut off from the divine Mind, there is a kind of gnostic poetry that illumines this prosaic piece of antiquated physics. Such a reading of Heraclitus is worthy of Cleanthes, or even Posidonius.

Historians of Hellenistic philosophy may determine how far our text bears any trace of the personal style or doctrine of a particular author. Regardless of its source, this ancient reading is of interest in its own right, but without any authority for the modern interpretation of Heraclitus.

Appendix III:
Heraclitus and the Orient, apropos of a recent book by M.L. West

Three out of the seven chapters in West's *Early Greek Philosophy and the Orient* (Oxford, 1971) are devoted to Heraclitus. The question is, as he says, a 'perpetual' one: proposed in antiquity by the forged correspondence between Heraclitus and Darius, reopened early in the nineteenth century by Schleiermacher and Creuzer, it is unlikely to be closed soon. Scholarly fashions may come and go, but here there is a genuine problem that will remain. In the case of Heraclitus more clearly than for any other author of early Greece, we can find striking textual parallels with the half-mythic, half-philosophic speculation of ancient India and Iran. I take this much to have been established by West and by the scholars who preceded him in this line of comparative research.

Individual scholars may disagree on whether any particular item belongs on the list of significant parallels. For example, I am not convinced that the points of correspondence between the story of Heraclitus' death and the Persian purification rite that West describes are 'too striking to be fortuitous' (West, p. 200); nor do I believe that a Hellenistic story can be used as evidence for Persian influence in the earlier period. On the other side of the ledger, West dismisses the usual parallel to an Iranian judgment by fire (p. 170), because he follows Reinhardt in rejecting CXXI (D. 66) as inauthentic (p. 114, n. 1). Since I accept the fragment in question, this point of similarity will belong on my list but not on West's. However, I wish to avoid these particular issues of controversy and simply take for granted some minimal list of significant or intriguing parallels, beginning with the central role of fire in the general world view and the verbal parallel between the Heraclitean wise One (*hen to sophon*) and the Iranian worship of the 'Wise God' (= Ahuramazda), and ending perhaps with the juxtaposition of LXXXVIII (D. 96: 'Corpses should be thrown out quicker than dung') and the Persian practice of exposing dead bodies in lieu of burial (West, p. 184). Assuming some such list of parallels, the question I want to discuss is: what do we make of them?

West's thesis is explicitly 'diffusionist'. For him, all such parallels are to be evaluated from the point of view entitled 'the gift of the Magi': where they are significant at all, they reflect the many ideas which Greeks of the late sixth century borrowed from Eastern wisdom. I think there is here a methodological mistake in the posing of the question. Of course the possibility of direct (or indirect) borrowing cannot be ruled out; but there is no reason to assume that significant parallels are to be regarded only, or even primarily, as evidence for historical diffusion of ideas from one culture to another. I happen to believe that West's thesis is correct in at least one case (namely the Eastern, ultimately Indian origin of the doctrine of transmigration), though the evidence is probably not clear enough to convince anyone inclined to scepticism. And in another case — the contempt for anthropomorphic cult and temple worship — the possibility of direct influence is established by Herodotus' report that this was a striking peculiarity of Persian religion (I.131.1; West, p. 192). Even here, however, we must raise the question: what do we mean by *influence*? It would be strange indeed to suppose that Xenophanes and Heraclitus despised the worship of cult images *because* they found out that the Persians despised it. It would be much less strange to suggest that their own critical reflection on the implications of idolatry was somehow stimulated or encouraged by the shock of contact with a religion from which such a cult was conspicuously absent. (We may then come to see Herodotus' remark about Persian belief in non-anthropomorphic gods as an expression of *Greek* thought, presupposing and prolonging the critical reaction of men like Xenophanes and Heraclitus. For of course Herodotus does not present us with a naive or culture-free report on Persian religion, a neutral description that could antedate the reaction of that earlier generation which encountered the Persians for the first time. On the contrary, Herodotus' own view of the Persians is conditioned by that earlier reaction.)

In other cases the diffusionist hypothesis must stand on very shaky ground, since even the *possibility* of historical contact is not easy to conceive. In West's collection of parallels, perhaps none is more striking than the echo of XC (D. 26) in the Brhadaranyaka Upanishad: 'When both sun and moon have set . . . what is the light of man then? The self becomes his light then . . . For, having fallen asleep, he transcends this world, — the forms of death' (West, p. 183). The parallel is genuine; but how can we understand it in terms of influence or borrowing? Are we to imagine Heraclitus somehow able to procure and read the Sanscrit text, written perhaps a century or more before his time? Or that some obliging multilingual Magus gave him a literal rendering into Greek? For what is striking here is not only the general conception but the specific imagery: the self or soul as a man's light in the night; the dream experience as a link between the world of the living and the other world of the dead. I find it neither possible nor necessary to believe that Heraclitus' words were inspired by some intermediate text in which these thoughts from the oldest Upanishad were transmitted to the Greeks. It is far more plausible to suppose that, just as in the case of the parallel cited from Proust in note 287, we have an example of thinkers very remote from one another in time and place who are sufficiently akin in turn of mind or speculative temperament to give expression to similar thoughts in similar language.

This example illustrates what is most valuable and most defective in the comparative method as practised by West and many of his predecessors. What is valuable is the reminder that a Greek thinker like Heraclitus may have more in common with an early Indian mystic like Yajnavalkya (and also, I have suggested, with a seventeenth-century metaphysician like Spinoza) than with the philosophers of his own time and place. The minimal and by no means negligible benefit of the comparative approach is to free us from a narrow historicism that is easily generated by the techniques of traditional philology. But the accompanying defect is the unspoken and uncriticized assumption that wherever such resemblances are documented, they are to be regarded as *prima facie* evidence of historical contact. For this assumption stultifies the comparative enterprise by enlisting its results in advance under the banner of a new and more implausible form of historicism.

If the comparative method in these areas tends to provoke such strong resistance (and even West seems to display an allergic reaction to the work of Georges Dumézil, probably the greatest comparativist of our time), that is not simply because the specialist feels uncomfortable when confronted by texts he cannot control. It is also because those who make use of the comparative method do not always have a clear view of what they are doing. To assume that we must seek for an historical 'explanation' whenever important resemblances are found between the Upanishads or the Avesta and certain ideas of Heraclitus or Parmenides — and also between the Egyptian notion of *ma'at* and the Indo-Iranian conception of *ṛta-aša* (West, pp. 177–9) — is not only to prejudice the inquiry unnecessarily. It also tends to produce historical fiction, as in West's concluding hypothesis of the stimulating flow of Magi refugees westward to Ionia after Cyrus' conquest of Media (pp. 240f.). To call this historical fiction is not to say that we know such creative stimulus from the Magi did *not* take place, but only that we have no good reason to believe that it did.

In general, the straight historical use of the comparative method tends to trivialize interesting comparisons by reducing them to points of evidence for a weak case.[449] Even if this particular historical thesis were correct, it would raise more questions than it answers. Why were Greek thinkers impressed by such Oriental wisdom, and how did they transform it? But we could begin to give useful answers to these questions only if we had a clear picture of just what kind of material was available to the Ionians — if we knew, for example, what kind of 'theogony' the Magi sang at a Persian sacrifice (according to Hdt. I.132.3), and what they told their Greek interlocutors about it. But this we do not and probably cannot know. Hence the comparisons are likely to prove more enlightening if we leave aside all thought of historical contacts, and consider what other ways there are of accounting for resemblances of the sort cited by West. I will conclude by mentioning four or five other applications of the comparative method, each one of which might shed some light on the thought and language of Heraclitus.

First of all, a striking parallel between speculative thought in two different cultures may reflect something like a human 'universal'. For the purpose of intellectual and textual comparisons of the sort we are considering, such cultural universals can be distinguished into two kinds. The first kind I will call a conceptual universal, like the innate ideas posited in some recent theories of linguistic universals. These will represent very general traits of language and rationality. Perhaps the clearest example is the contrast between Yes and No, affirmation and negation, with the associated fact that many concepts tend to come in pairs of opposites, like night and day, wet and dry, good and evil. Heraclitus' doctrine of opposites can thus be seen as one specific articulation of a general feature of rational discourse. We should expect to find parallels everywhere, from China to Africa and from Australia to pre-Columbian America.

A second type of universal seems to depend less upon language as such than upon fundamental features of the human condition and the order of nature. (Some of Heraclitus' opposites will fall under this heading, for example male and female, life and death, sleeping and waking. The distinction between natural and linguistic universals is not always easy to draw — e.g. for night and day, summer and winter. I propose this merely as a convenient device for listing data whose full discussion would raise major philosophical problems.) Thus the importance of fire in human life and the role of the sun as a representative of the order of nature (both daily and annually) are items that may impress themselves upon reflective minds in any cultural tradition. So again we should expect to find some parallel to Heraclitus' conception of fire and sun almost anywhere we look.

A third type of parallel which is less universal and more distinctly culture-bound will depend upon the possession of similar social or religious institutions, regardless of whether or not these have a common origin. Many cultures make use of fire for burnt-offerings to the gods (or to the Lord God), keep sacred fires always lit, or regularly light fires according to certain prescribed forms. In any culture where the role of fire is thus ritually developed, Heraclitus' reference to the everliving fire of the cosmos and his association of fire with justice will have a rich and specific resonance that is lacking in a society without a fire cult.

A special case of the cultural affinity just mentioned is the situation where institutional or conceptual similarities reflect the inheritance from a common past, so that the parallels are true cognates of one another. Thus the ritual and mythic role of fire in Iran, India, and Greece may present features derived from a common Indo-European origin. A more obvious example of cognate parallels is provided by the Indo-European verb 'to be' (*es-), with a present participle meaning 'real' or 'true'. This linguistic kinship between Greek and Sanscrit partially explains (since it makes possible) the parallel developments of the concepts of Being and Not-Being in Parmenides and the Upanishads (West, p. 224).

Last of all, I would include parallels that rest upon resemblances between individuals rather than between cultures: an affinity of spiritual or intellectual temperament of the sort I have suggested between Heraclitus and Yajnavalkya and between Heraclitus and Spinoza. (And one might glance here at stylistic parallels between the aphorisms of Heraclitus and those of Nietzsche or Wittgenstein.) 'Heraclitus strikes a prophetic note that has reminded more than one reader of Zoroaster' (West, p. 193), as other readers have compared Hesiod to an Old Testament prophet. If such comparisons are soundly based and carefully formulated, they may provide us with a typology of moral and intellectual temperaments, the counterpart for intellectual history to the character- or personality-types of psychological theory. Such individual typologies might (or might not) show interesting correlations with social typologies of the sort defined by Max Weber. What they would in any event have in common with Weber's 'ideal types' is the theoretical abstraction from any historical connection: thus when we compare feudalism in Japan with the feudalism of medieval Europe we do not even consider the question whether one is derived from the other.

In some cases it may turn out that a resemblance of type is accompanied by an historical link. If I am correct in recognizing a likeness of kind between the thought of Heraclitus and that of Spinoza, this typological affinity does not exclude the possibility of an actual historical link, via the Stoics. But in this case it is the resemblance of type that helps us to understand the historical connection, and not the other way round.

Notes

1 Both synchronism and acme are given by Suidas (DK 22.A1a); acme alone by D.L. IX.1 (ibid. A1). The acme or *floruit* dates reflect the artificially precise report of a prose excerpt from Apollodorus' *Chronika* (in verse). I see no reason to saddle Apollodorus himself with such arbitrary simplifications, as many scholars do. He probably referred more vaguely, but soundly, to the reign of Darius (just as he apparently dated Anaximenes by reference to Cyrus, and the long-lived Xenophanes by both kings, Cyrus and Darius). The Apollodorean date is echoed, rather than confirmed, by the forged correspondence between Heraclitus and Darius. It may originally have been based upon an intelligent reading of XVIII (D. 40).

2 Or 470, if one takes the latest possible date for Xenophanes' death. Hecataeus lived until 494, at least. It is tempting to explain the dyadic structure of XVIII ('Hesiod and Pythagoras, and likewise Xenophanes and Hecataeus') by the assumption that Pythagoras (like Hesiod) was dead when Heraclitus wrote, Xenophanes and Hecataeus still alive. Even so, we would not have a precise date, but a more narrowly limited period, perhaps 505–490 B.C. Cf. Marcovich, PW 249, who assigns the book to a date 'around 490 B.C.'. For other evidence pointing towards this date, see comment on LXIV.

3 D.L. IX.6.

4 Ibid. Ancient temples were regularly used for storing treasure, and were open to private individuals only under exceptional circumstances. There are parallels to the depositing of a book which make the story plausible in Heraclitus' case.

5 'The Artemesium must have been incomparably the most opulent Greek temple of its time', A.W. Lawrence, *Greek Architecture* (Pelican History of Art, 1957), p. 136.

6 John Boardman, *The Greeks Overseas* (Penguin, 2nd edition, London, 1973), p. 96.

7 One late 'quotation' has him saying: 'May your wealth never fail you, men of Ephesus, so that your wretchedness may be fully exposed' (D. 125a: see Appendix I). Although this is pretty clearly not a genuine quotation, the spirit is that of XCVII (D. 29), where 'the many' who 'sate themselves like cattle' must in fact be the rich. Heraclitus' repeated references to satiety (*koros*) recall the words of Solon: 'satiety begets crime (*hybris*), when great wealth falls to men whose understanding is not straight' (fr. 5.9).

8 Compare LXVI (D. 33) with LXIII (D. 49). Heraclitus must have in mind an exceptional statesman like Solon of Athens, Bias of Priene, or (in his view) Hermodorus of Ephesus. His insistence upon the rule of law would

exclude any approval of tyranny, which for the Greeks meant *illegal* monarchy. Compare the report in Clement (DK 22.A 3) that Heraclitus persuaded a certain tyrant Melankomas to give up his unconstitutional rule.

9   H. Diels, *Herakleitos*[2], p. vi.

10   D.L. IX.6. One group of these early Heracliteans seems to have developed a full-scale physical system, from which a few details are preserved in the Aristotelian *Problemata*. See below, n. 372.

11   See commentary on CV (D. 85), and compare Democritus fr. 64 with XVIII (D. 40), 158 with XLVIIIA (D. 6), etc.

12   *De Victu* I.5—24, printed as DK 22.C 1. The early (i.e. pre-Platonic) date of the *De Victu*, for which I argued in *Anaximander* (p. 189, n. 2), is confirmed by R. Joly, *Recherches sur le traité pseudo-hippocratique 'Du Régime'* (Paris, 1960), p. 209; but some scholars (e.g. West, p. 122) still assign the treatise to the mid-fourth century. This would testify to an even more continuous stylistic influence of Heraclitus, as in the much later Hellenistic 'Hippocratic' treatise *De Nutrimento* (DK 22.C 2).

13   D.L. II.22; compare IX.12. For Socrates' response see p. 95.

14   See DK 22.C 4 for the most Heraclitean section of Cleanthes' *Hymn*, and comment on CXIII (D. 12) for a possible citation from his commentary. Deichgräber (pp. 28—30) has made a good case for assigning to Cleanthes the epigram on Heraclitus quoted on p. 95. I would not be surprised if the passage on sleep from Sextus Empiricus (see Appendix IIB) represented the commentary of Cleanthes.

15   At least one of these authors is earlier than Cleanthes: Heraclides Ponticus, a contemporary of Aristotle and associate of Plato.

16   See DK 22.C 5. Lucian represents Heraclitus as the weeping philosopher in contrast to the laughing Democritus, in a tradition that goes back at least as far as Seneca and is represented in Montaigne's essay 'On Democritus and Heraclitus'. Lucian is also said to have composed a deliberately nonsensical version of Heraclitus' text which he submitted to an unwitting philosopher of renown, who obligingly responded with a profound commentary. (The story is told by Galen, cited from an Arabic translation by Deichgräber, p. 29, n. 25.)

17   So rightly Deichgräber, p. 20; similarly West, p. 112.

18   I. Bywater, *Heracliti Ephesii reliquiae*. In his 1967 edition M. Marcovich again arranged the fragments in topical sections; but the 1972 edition by Bollack and Wismann retains the order of Diels.

19   See the citation on p. 21, with n. 45.

20   I here repeat the view expressed in 'A new look at Heraclitus', p. 190. Since all the evidence is indirect, it may be an exaggeration to ascribe so much artistry to the original composition; but I believe it is an exaggeration in the right direction.

21   So likewise West, p. 113n, following Walzer.

22   Any modern arrangement must operate with a serious handicap, since we do not know how much of Heraclitus' book has been lost. For an attempt to calculate the original dimensions of the work, and some interesting parallels to the order proposed here, see H. Gomperz, 'Ueber die ursprüngliche Reihenfolge einiger Bruchstücke Heraklits', *Hermes* 58 (1923), 20ff. Gomperz estimates that nearly half of the book has been preserved in quotation or close paraphrase.

23   Reinhardt, *Parmenides*, p. 219.

24   D.L. IX.5. What the words imply is that, for the ancient commentator

whose view is cited, 'the work fell naturally into these three parts' (so Burnet, quoted and corrected by West, p. 112). Deichgräber (pp. 18–20), followed by Kirk and Marcovich, connects this tripartition with Stoic divisions of philosophy. But there is no Stoic classification in which politics (or ethics) could be sandwiched in between physics and theology. And *politikos logos* must be taken here in its broader Aristotelian sense, to include moral philosophy as a whole.

25 He attacks indiscriminately both the poets who were generally accepted as the teachers of Greece – Homer, Hesiod, Archilochus – and the new wise men of the scientific tradition: Pythagoras, Xenophanes and Hecataeus of Miletus. In his contemptuous reference to empty learning he names Hesiod in the same breath with the latter three (XVIII, D. 40).

26 Compare Hesiod, whose Muses proudly insist upon their power to tell 'many falsehoods like unto truth' (*Theogony* 27). And Pindar, one of the most conservative fifth-century spokesmen for the older moral view, can reject a well-known story about gods tasting human flesh, on the grounds of piety alone (*Olympian* I.52).

27 To this extent I fully agree with the conclusions of Hugh Lloyd-Jones, *The Justice of Zeus* (Oxford, 1971), ch. II, though I think he underestimates the intellectual distance between this moralizing view and the tragically amoral outlook expressed by Achilles at the end of the *Iliad*, that Zeus distributes good and evil to men as he pleases (*Il.* XXIV.525–33; cf. Lloyd-Jones, p. 27).

28 See my *Anaximander*, esp. pp. 238ff., for the connections between the Milesian view of the cosmos and the new conception of deity as a cosmic god.

29 The extreme point of Homeric egoism is reached in the momentary wish of Achilles that all the Achaeans and Trojans might perish, while he *and Patroclus* should alone return victorious from Troy (*Il.* XVI.97–100). The qualification 'and Patroclus' is absolutely crucial, as the sequel shows.

30 See A.W.H. Adkins, *Merit and Responsibility: a Study in Greek Values* (Oxford, 1960).

31 See Helen North, *Sophrosyne*, pp. 10f. and passim.

32 Compare the first naive attempt to define *sōphrosynē* in Plato's *Charmides*: to walk and talk in a quiet, decent manner, and in general to act with 'quietness' or restraint (159B).

33 For the question when *sōphrosynē* was first explicitly recognized as *aretē* or 'excellence', the crucial text is Heraclitus XXXII (D. 112). Although in later usage, for example in the Platonic dialogues, *sōphrosynē* is regularly counted as one of the canonical virtues for which *aretē* stands as the genus, the two terms were originally contrasted with one another. See the funeral inscriptions cited below, in n. 95.

34 The best-known discussion is that of E.R. Dodds, 'From shame-culture to guilt-culture' in *The Greeks and the Irrational*. Cf. Adkins, *Merit and Responsibility*, p. 76, for a somewhat different account.

35 I do not mean to deny that changes took place in the moral ideals of Greece during the archaic period; what I doubt is that the Homeric poems can serve as a reliable historical document for the psychology or sociology of any definite period or stage of culture.

36 *Laws* IV, 714A. (This prefigures the fuller definition of law by St Thomas: 'an ordering of reason for the common good'.) I do not doubt that Plato, who was a careful reader of Heraclitus, is here consciously echoing XXX (D. 114), as again in *Laws* XII, 957C. The word play is even more natural

for Heraclitus, since in his dialect *noos* and *nomos* differ by a single letter. For the philosophical implications of the play on *xyn nōi, tōi xynōi* and *tōi nomōi*, see comment on XXX. Heraclitus has, in effect, anticipated Aristotle's remark (*Politics* I.2) that man is the most social (literally, 'political') of animals because of his possession of *logos* as the capacity for rational communication.

37   See XLVII—XLVIII (D. 3 and 6). As Diels observed, 'die Naturwissenschaft verdankt ihm nichts' (*Herakleitos*², p. ix).

38   Indicative in this respect, though surely apocryphal, is Aristotle's tale about how Thales made a fortune by forecasting a heavy olive harvest (*Politics* I.11 = DK 11.A 10).

39   For the borrowing from Babylon see Hdt. II.109; the contribution of Anaximander is mentioned by D.L. II.1 (DK 12.A 1), Suidas (12.A 2) and Eusebius (12.A 4). For a general defense of this tradition see 'On early Greek astronomy', *JHS* 90 (1970), 99—116.

40   See DK II.B 1—2 and the use of the Big Dipper in navigation, ascribed to Thales by Callimachus (DK 11.A 3a). Again, what is of interest is not the historicity of the ascriptions but the general sense for the practical bent of early natural philosophy. Anaximander's map of the earth, which is better attested, points in the same direction.

41   Cf. Xenophanes A 33, 5—6; and *Anaximander*, p. 185.

42   Among the early cosmologists the atomists (and their later followers, the Epicureans) seem to have been alone in developing the conception of an organized physical cosmos without the correlative concept of a divine organizing principle.

43   See DK 13.A 7, 2—3.

44   Similarly 'it scatters and again gathers; it forms and dissolves, and approaches and departs' in LI (D. 91) suggests the condensation-rarefaction cycle of Anaximenes' air. Some such text in Heraclitus may have served as the basis for Theophrastus' claim that he, like Anaximenes, produced all things from the first principle 'by thickening and rarefaction'.

45   Theophrastus cited in D.L. IX.6.

46   Cited in D.L. IX.15.

47   Diels, *Herakleitos* (1st ed.), p. vii.

48   It may be no accident that Heraclitus has himself expressed the formal structure of these two principles: 'out of all things one, and out of one thing all' (CXXIV, D. 10).

49   A. Lebeck, *The Oresteia*, pp. 1f.

50   Compare, for example, William Empson's *Seven Types of Ambiguity*, first published in 1930, with the remarks on ambiguity in Roman Ingarden, *The Literary Work of Art* (pp. 142—4 and 253—4 in English tr. by G.G. Grabowicz, Evanston, 1973), original ed. 1931.

51   See in particular Anne Lebeck, *The Oresteia*, p. 3: 'It should be a basic principle in interpreting Aeschylus that when language and syntax are most difficult, the poet has compressed the greatest number of meanings into the smallest possible space. Pursuing the customary methods of classical scholarship one is sometimes tempted to treat ambiguity as if the author were at fault, as if the clarity of normal diction were beyond his grasp. Yet that ambiguity characteristic of Aeschylus is not easy to achieve; it comes about neither by accident nor inability but by design.' I suggest the same is true *a fortiori* of Heraclitus.

52   Readings may differ in other ways, for example by an ambiguous reference, as in the question whether the lion cub at *Agamemnon* 717ff. is

taken as allusion to Helen or to Clytemnestra. I am not sure that examples of this type of ambiguity are to be found in Heraclitus. Linguistic density in the fragments is often a function of allusion to earlier texts, as in the Homeric and Archilochean references of *polemos xynos* 'war is shared' in LXXXII (D. 80) (see commentary); but perhaps all such cases can be analysed in terms of different senses for a given word, in this case *xynos*.

53 Some of the Hippocratic treatises may be contemporary with Herodotus, or only slightly later. But the dating is controversial, the texts often unsatisfactory, and there is no systematic means of surveying the Hippocratic data at all comparable to Powell's *Lexicon*.

54 For the Homeric (and occasionally post-Homeric) use of the verb *einai* in the sense of 'be alive', see my *The Verb 'Be' in Ancient Greek*, pp. 241—3.

55 For examples in Herodotus, see *The Verb 'Be' in Ancient Greek*, pp. 352ff.; for the application to our fragment, ibid. p. 354, n. 26. This reading was anticipated by Burnet (p. 133, n. 1); recently accepted by West, pp. 115f. and E. Hussey, *The Presocratics*, p. 39.

56 I mention for courtesy's sake two other readings presented in the scholarly literature. Both involve punctuating before *aiei*, but the first keeps the construal of 'is' as copula by taking the demonstrative pronoun *hode* as predicate: 'the *logos* is this one, is as follows'. (So, after Kranz and others, Kirk, p. 33: 'the Logos which is as I describe it'; Bollack-Wismann, p. 59: 'du discours qui est celui-la'; also accepted as possible by Guthrie, I. 425n.) The second reading takes 'is' as independent verb but gives it a stronger existential rather than strictly veridical sense: 'this *logos* is real' or 'it really exists'. This may be what is intended by Snell's translation: 'diese Lehre hier, ihren Sinn, der Wirklichkeit hat'; but there is a natural tendency to slide from the sense of existence to that of truth. So also in Marcovich's rendering: 'this Truth, real as it is'. Cf. Fränkel (*Dichtung und Philosophie*[2], p. 423): 'Diesem Logos . . . der in Ewigkeit gilt.'

57 D.L. IX.16. The epigram is plausibly assigned to Cleanthes by Deichgräber, p. 30.

58 Compare the fifth-century proems of Herodotus and Thucydides. Long before Hecataeus, Hesiod introduced his *Theogony* with a similar contrast: 'This word (*tonde mython*) did the Muses speak to me first of all . . . "we know how to tell many lies resembling truth; and we know, when we want, to utter what is true".' (*Theogony* 24ff., cited as a precedent for Hecataeus by F. Jacoby, *Die Fragmente der griechischen Historiker* I (Berlin, 1923), p. 319.)

59 The treatise of Alcmaeon (a western Dorian writing in the tradition of Ionian science, probably in the early fifth century) begins: 'Alcmaeon of Croton, son of Peirithous, said as follows' (DK 24.B 1). Since Alcmaeon, like Hecataeus (and Hesiod in the *Theogony*), begins with a mention of his own name in the third person, Diels suggested that Ion's work too might have begun 'Ion of Chios says the following (*tade*)'. A number of scholars (including Diels) have supposed that Heraclitus' fragment I was also preceded by such a signature or 'seal': 'Heraclitus of Ephesus says the following (*tade*)'. But for such a personal signature there is really no evidence (unless one relies heavily on the initial particle *de*, attested only in Hippolytus). The demonstrative pronoun traditional in such proems occurs at the beginning of our preserved text, and again in the second sentence: *ho logos hode* 'this account'.

60 I follow Bywater and Bollack-Wismann in excluding the words that precede III, 'therefore one should follow the common', as an interpretative

paraphrase added by Sextus. (So likewise West, pp. 118f.) The interpretation is not incorrect; but the tone of moral exhortation and the explicit statement of what is about to be conveyed implicitly are quite uncharacteistic of Heraclitus' own style.

61   See Powell's *Lexicon* under *koinos*, esp. sense 2, where *koinōi logōi* appears as an equivalent to *koinēi gnōmēi* (*chrasthai*), 'to make common cause', 'adopt a common policy'.

62   This latent value of *xynos* in III as a signal for *noos* 'understanding' would be guaranteed if Marcovich (and others) were right in supposing that III follows upon XXX (D. 114). What would in that case be an echo of an earlier thought becomes in my arrangement an example of the proleptic hint of things to come.

63   Cf. Kirk and Raven, p. 188.

64   It is only with the Stoics that *logos* comes to be regularly used as an equivalent of *nous*, the faculty of 'reason' as a power of the human soul. Even in Aristotle this notion is ordinarily expressed by derivative terms such as *to logikon* (*meros tēs psychēs*) the rational (or calculating) part of the soul, or by the phrase *to logon echon*: the rational faculty is not *logos* itself but 'what has (is characterized by) *logos*'. Thus in Aristotle's terminology *logos* remains the principle of rationality (argument, calculation) immanent in thought and speech.

65   See H. Fränkel, '*Ephēmeros* als Kennwort für die menschliche Natur', in *Wege und Formen* (3rd ed.), pp. 23–39, with an accurate assessment of our fragment there, p. 31, n. 6. Compare his *Dichtung und Philosophie* (2nd ed.), p. 424.

66   The thought is proverbial, even formulaic, in its earliest occurrences: cf. *Il.* XVII.32. The familiar jingle *mathos-pathos* (or *mathein-pathein*) is not attested before Aeschylus and Herodotus, but something like it is presupposed by Heraclitus' phrase *mathontes ginōskousin*.

67   Archilochus fr. 67a, verse 7: 'recognize (*gignōske*) what a see-saw pattern change (*rhysmos*) holds men in its power'.

68   Thus I concur in the conclusion of Kirk and Bollack-Wismann, though not in all of their arguments.

69   For the early Ionic use of *philosophein* see Herodotus I.30.2: Solon goes travelling in order to learn more than most men know. It is true that the expression *philosophoi andres* might have been added by Clement: see Marcovich, p. 27; Wiese, p. 259, with note 3; Reinhardt in Wiese, pp. 317f. Reinhardt wanted to take *histores* as 'eyewitness'; he pointed to the juridical parallel between *histores* here and *martyres* 'witnesses' in XV (D. 101a).

     Wiese, followed by Marcovich, would construe *eu mala* with *chrē*, thus giving the sense: 'A man who loves wisdom [or, 'who wants to be wise'] *really must be* a judge [or 'eyewitness'] of many things.'

70   Such is the usual rendering of the text. In my own translation ('listen like children to their parents') I have followed a suggestion of West, p. 127.

71   See my article 'On early Greek astronomy'.

72   As Reinhardt saw long ago: 'Der Tag ist eine erleuchtete Nacht, die Nacht ein verfinsterter Tag' (*Parmenides*, p. 182 commenting on D. 99; cf. Kirk, p. 165).

73   For the rejection of XX as a distinct fragment see Kirk, pp. 157–61; for its defense see Marcovich, pp. 320f. and Bollack-Wismann, pp. 299–301.

74   Seneca, who renders the phrase as 'one day is equal to all' (*unus dies par omni est*), offers as the first of several interpretations one that coincides in effect with our explanation of XIX: 'if a day is the time of twenty-four

hours, all days are necessarily equal to one another, because the night
possesses what the day has lost' (*Epistles* 12.7, in Marcovich, p. 319).
75 For detailed discussion, see E.N. Roussos, 'Archilochos kai Erakleitos',
Philosophia, Yearbook of the Research Center for Greek Philosophy at
the Academy of Athens, 1975–76, pp. 103–32 (German summary, pp.
128–30).
76 See the juxtaposition of different versions (pp. 164f.) in G.S. Kirk, 'The
Michigan Alcidamas-Papyrus; Heraclitus fr. 56 D; The riddle of the lice',
Classical Quarterly 44 (1950), 149ff.
77 As Kirk points out, loc. cit. p. 159. Cf. LVII–LVIII, where human wisdom
is assimilated to that of a child; also the contrast between men and boys in
LXIV (D. 121) and CVI (D. 117).
78 Here I agree with Marcovich, p. 342, and Bollack-Wismann, p. 298.
79 Edward Hussey writes me that, although he accepts XXV as authentic, he
regards the phrase 'choosing what he liked from these compositions' as
indefensible in the Greek, because of the unusual construction of *eklego-
menos*, which would normally mean 'selecting these treatises (from some
larger set)'. I believe with Reinhardt (*Parmenides*, p. 235 n.) that this
anomaly is the sign of an archaic style rather than a forgery.
80 For a recent attempt at reconstruction, see West, ch. 1. For the stories
connecting Pythagoras with him, see Kirk and Raven, pp. 50–2.
81 Not in prose, but suggesting a technical tradition, was the 'Nautical
Astronomy' ascribed to Thales (or to Phocus of Samos), and a similar
hexameter work assigned to Cleostratus of Tenedos (DK 6 and 11.B 1–2).
Vitruvius (VII, Preface 12) mentions two important sixth-century descriptions of archaic temples recorded by the architects: an account of the
Samian Heraion by Theodorus of Samos, and one of the Artemesium in
Ephesus by Chersiphron and Metagenes. These astronomical and architectural manuals, together with the treatises of the Milesians, give some
idea of the sixth-century technical literature to which Heraclitus must be
referring.
82 See the quotation from Timaeus in DK (D. 81) and Marcovich 18b, p. 71.
83 The last clause can also be construed: 'to recognize that the wise is set
apart from all'; but this does not represent a significant conceptual difference.
84 Some interpreters have tried to give a less paradoxical reading to these two
words, at the price of ignoring their natural sense. There is nothing in
Herodotus to suggest that *edizēsamēn* could bear the much tamer meaning
'I asked myself questions'. Nor is there any evidence that the verb means
'to consult an oracle'. In the one case in Herodotus (VII.142) where the
verb takes 'oracle' (*manteion*) as its object, the sense is not 'to consult
(the oracle)' – that has already been done – but 'to investigate it', 'to
search out (its meaning)'. (So Guthrie, I, 418.)
85 Cf. Plato, *Charmides* 164E7; Helen North, *Sophrosyne*, pp. 10ff.; Wilamowitz, 'Erkenne dich selbst', in *Reden und Vorträge* II (Berlin, 1913), p.
173.
86 See Marcovich, p. 96, and further discussion on XXXII.
87 Or even 'for all (human) laws', with *nomois* understood (so Marcovich). As
far as the human-cosmic duality is concerned, this reading falls on the
human side and is thus roughly equivalent to 'for all men'.
88 For the triple word play on *noos-xynos-nomos* see the Platonic echoes
cited above, n. 36); and compare the echo in Cleanthes' *Hymn to Zeus*
24f. quoted by Marcovich, p. 89.
89 Compare Semonides of Amorgus, fr. 1.1–2 Diehl: 'Zeus controls the

accomplishment of all there is, and disposes it as he wishes' (*hokēi thelei*: cf. *hokoson ethelei* in XXX).

90   The doubts go back as far as Schleiermacher; they were recently generalized by Kirk (p. 56), who describes all three citations as 'weak paraphrases'. Similarly Marcovich (pp. 89f., 563; cf. pp. 96f.).

91   Pp. 129 and 257 of Hense's edition of Stobaeus, Vol. I = Wachsmuth-Hense Vol. III. For the general character of Stobaeus' work see Hense's article in PW IX, 2549ff.

92   This does not apply to CI (D. 115), which is not ascribed to Heraclitus by Stobaeus (but only by modern editors), and hence need not have been taken from the same source as those preceding (D. 108—14).

93   Saying something about the virtue in question does not mean using the abstract noun *sōphrosynē*. The fact that XXIX and XXXII, like Aeschylus, Sophocles and Herodotus, employ the verb *sōphronein* but not the noun tells in favor of their authenticity.

94   It is natural, though not inevitable, to take *megistē* with the following *sophiē* as well as with the preceding *aretē*. Note that the form *sophiē* occurs in the verbatim fragments only here, and in XXV (D. 129), where Heraclitus is speaking of human excellence. When the neuter form *sophon* occurs, there is generally some human-cosmic ambivalence.

95   See North, *Sophrosyne*, p. 13, n. 47: the formula is found in the epitaph for Protomachus ascribed to Simonides (fr. 128.4 Diehl) and in four sixth-century inscriptions (P. Friedländer, *Epigrammata*, nos. 6, 31, 71, 85 (= *IG* I^2, 988, 974, 986, 972)). These early parallels should suffice to answer the charge (Kirk, p. 390, following Heidel) that the first three words of the fragment 'can safely be rejected as a banal paraphrase in the language of late fifth-century ethical investigations'.

96   Here again it is natural, though not inevitable, to construe *alēthes* as direct object of both infinitives.

97   Note repetition of 'and' (*kai*); cf. the two-fold pattern of heroic excellence described in the Introduction, p. 12 above.

98   Reinhardt (*Parmenides*, p. 223, n. 1, followed by Kirk, p. 391), rendered it thus: 'das Wahre sagen und tun (durch Tat und Wort der Wahrheit dienen) in richtiger Erkenntnis'. Marcovich (p. 96) complained, with some reason, that '*alēthes poiein* does not seem to make good sense'.

99   See LSJ s.v. *alētheia* I.2.

100   For this value of *alētheia*, see *The Verb 'Be' in Ancient Greek*, pp. 364f.

101   *Apology* 21B3. See U. Hölscher, *Anfängliches Fragen*, pp. 136—41.

102   For the latter interpretation, see Snell, 'Die Sprache Heraklits', in *Gesammelte Schriften* (1966), pp. 144f.

103   Cf. Hölscher: 'Die Dunkelheit der Gleichnissprache . . . entspricht dem Rätselcharakter des zu Sagenden . . . Paradox ist seine Rede, weil seine Wahrheit paradox ist' (*Anfängliches Fragen*, p. 141).

104   This was correctly seen by Schleiermacher, p. 14. Compare E. Rohde, *Psyche* (Engl. tr. W.B. Hillis, London, 1925), p. 316, n. 64; 4th German ed. (Tübingen, 1907), II, 69, n. 1. The Sibyl was sometimes dated in the eighth, sometimes in the sixth century B.C. Only in the later tradition is her birth put back much earlier, centuries before the Trojan War. From this, together with the original dating, arose the view that the Sibyl must have lived a thousand years (and hence wanted to die)! (See Rohde (Engl. tr.) pp. 315f., n. 61 and Rzach, PW 2nd series, II, 2078f.) What Plutarch gives here is a spiritualized version of the Sibyl's long life.

105   Kirk and Raven, p. 212, n. 1; Marcovich, p. 405; and Bollack-Wismann, pp. 270—2.

106 See Rohde, *Psyche* (English tr.), p. 293.
107 For the former view, see A. Bouché-Leclercq, *Histoire de la divination dans l'antiquité* II (Paris, 1880), 136ff., followed by Rzach, PW 2nd series, II (1923), 2075, and by A.S. Pease in the *Oxford Classical Dictionary* s.v. 'Sibylla'. The latter view is that of Rohde, *Psyche* (Engl. tr.), p. 292 with n. 58 (on p. 314).
108 See Pausanias X.12.1 and Parke and Wormell, *The Delphic Oracle* I (Oxford, 1956), p. 13.
109 Thus Guthrie, p. 414; Kirk and Raven, p. 212 n; Hölscher, *Anfängliches Fragen* p. 143; and my remarks in 'A new look at Heraclitus', p. 193 column 2.
110 'Lob der Sibylle bei Heraklit sehr unwahrscheinlich', Reinhardt, 'Nachlass' 86, in Wiese, p. 317.
111 *Parmenides* p. 201. Similarly Snell, *Die Entdeckung des Geistes* (3rd ed.), p. 36. For the historical background, see Snell, ch. IV, esp. pp. 103ff., 116f.
112 The culprit here is Burnet, whose paper 'The Socratic doctrine of the soul', in the *Proceedings of the British Academy* VII (1915—16), 235—59, is a brilliant piece of special pleading for the thesis that before Socrates 'the *psychē* is never regarded as having anything to do with clear perception or knowledge, or even with articulate emotion' (p. 254), a thesis which can scarcely convince anyone who reads without bias the texts that Burnet himself cites. (He does *not* cite Heraclitus.) Dodds has served as unwitting accomplice by relying upon Burnet in his own discussion of the fifth-century conception of *psychē*. When Dodds writes (*The Greeks and the Irrational*, p. 139) that 'the *psyche* is spoken of as the seat of courage, of passion, of pity, of anxiety, of animal appetite, but before Plato seldom if ever as the seat of reason; its range is broadly that of the Homeric *thumos*', we can agree 'broadly' but must take exception to the phrase 'seldom if ever'. In Antiphon 4.1.7 a soul that can deliberate (*bouleusasa*) looks rational; and at *Antigone* 227 the Watchman's *psychē* is precisely giving him good advice, participating in deliberation. So there is no reason to set apart as special exceptions *Philoctetes* 55, which (as Burnet handsomely admitted, p. 256), 'seems to imply that it [viz. the *psychē*] is the seat of knowledge', and *Philoctetes* 1013 which implies 'that it is the seat of character' (Burnet). Compare Jebb's note to *Antigone* 176.
113 This view of the psyche is as old as Anaximenes and, in a sense, as old as Homer, for whom the psyche is the breath of life which a man 'expires'. It was one of the merits of Burnet's article (cited in preceding note) to point out that the 'prevailing notion in the time of Socrates was that the souls of the dead were absorbed by the upper air, just as their bodies were by the earth' (ibid. p. 248), citing Eur. *Supplices* 533 (the *pneuma* goes to the *aithēr* as the body to the earth) and the Potidea inscription of 432 B.C.: 'the *aithēr* received their *psychai*; the earth their bodies'.
114 Or, keeping the MS form with Bollack-Wismann: 'one will not find them out, even if one travels . . . '.
115 It has also been suggested that we think of some physiological process involving the soul's movements within the body: either its capacity to 'move to all parts of the body at need'; or the fact that its 'bonds' or 'limits' (*peirata*) are in the blood, on the assumption that the psyche is an exhalation from the internal fluids of the body. The first view is that of Kirk and Raven, relying upon the more-than-dubious fragment D. 67a (which compares the soul within the body to a spider within its web); the second is that of Marcovich (pp. 366f.).

But there is no good evidence for a connection between psyche and blood in Heraclitus: this is a Stoic view (see p. 260 and n. 371), though of course one with older antecedents (as in Empedocles B. 105). I think the physiological view is a mistake in both its variants.

116   In later authors *echei logon* can mean 'it has something to be said in its favor', 'it is reasonable', but this usage is not found in Herodotus. The earliest example seems to be Soph. *Electra* 466; compare 'to live *kata logon*' (reasonably, according to a rational principle) in Democritus fr. 53.

117   The anecdote (cited above, p. 95) contains an echo of Aeschylus, *Suppliants* 407: 'we need a deep thought (*phrontis*) to save us, like a diver who goes to the bottom with his eyes open'.

118   See the critical study of this alleged monism of the Milesians by Michael C. Stokes, *One and Many in Presocratic Philosophy*, chapter II, especially pp. 32—64, with whose results I am in general agreement. Stokes concludes that 'there is no reason to associate with them [viz. the Milesians] the view that all things were one, or that one thing was many things, or any similar doctrine' (p. 63). Stokes agrees, however, that 'the Milesians may have described their cosmogonies in terms of one and many', where the unity is understood genetically, as the original source from which the present plurality of things is derived (p. 64).

119   For this meaning of *kosmos* as a technical usage, see the two texts from Plato (*Gorgias* 508A) and Xenophon (*Memorabilia* I.1.11) discussed in *Anaximander*, pp. 219f.

120   For the pre-philosophical usage of *kosmos*, my account in *Anaximander*, pp. 220ff. must be supplemented by H. Diller 'Der vorphilosophische Gebrauch von *kosmos* und *kosmein*', *Festschrift Bruno Snell* (Munich, 1956), pp. 47ff. My earlier discussion does not sufficiently recognize the primacy of the military and moral or political sense of *kosmos* as 'disciplined array', 'troops (or equipment) in good order', 'behavior showing obedience to command'; I overestimated the purely visual notion of 'something physically neat and trim'. This is a subordinate idea which can be derived from the moral-military sense, since neat appearance is a natural concomitant of disciplined order. Compare J. Kerschensteiner, *Kosmos*, p. 7.

121   A strong suggestion of the technical use would come at the very beginning, if we followed Diels and other editors in reading *kosmon tonde* with Plutarch and Simplicius, instead of (or in addition to) *kosmon ton auton hapantōn* with Clement. On purely documentary grounds Clement's reading has the greater authority, since he is the only author to cite XXXVII in full (as well as XXXVIII—XXXIX). Simplicius, who cites only half of it without any mention of fire, and Plutarch, who cites even less, must be quoting from memory or following some inferior doxographical source. (Similarly, J. Kerschensteiner, *Kosmos*, pp. 101f.) In any case *kosmos hode* 'this world order' is a banal phrase, found in every author from Anaxagoras to Plato who employs *kosmos* in the technical sense; whereas the formula in Clement is unusual and ambiguous in the way characteristic of Heraclitus, for *ton auton hapantōn* can mean either 'the same (human) order for all men' or 'the same (world) order for all things'. Thus Clement's reading is both more authoritative and also more Heraclitean. If we interpolate this authentic text with the banal phrase from Simplicius and Plutarch (as nearly all editors have done, with the honorable exception of Bollack-Wismann), we tend to eliminate the primary reading of *kosmos* in its pre-philosophical sense.

122 The few exceptions to this proposition cannot be decisive for the point at issue. Most scholars accept the secondary evidence for a 'great year' in Heraclitus (below, XLIII = DK A 13), although it is not confirmed by an original quotation. But whether or not this great year is to be interpreted as involving major cosmic transformations will depend in turn upon one's understanding of the extant fragments.

123 This is the sense that has been given to these words by many eminent scholars. Thus Cherniss: 'This fragment asserts that it is *this cosmos* that is fire; I cannot believe that is reconcilable with an *ekpyrōsis* or with world-periods of any kind.' (*AJP* 56 (1935), 415: Cherniss and others rely upon the editorial interpolation of *tonde* 'this' into Clement's text, but that is probably not crucial for either side.) Similarly Kirk, p. 336; Guthrie, p. 455, and many others. Compare Burnet, p. 162, and Reinhardt, pp. 175f.

124 *Anaximander*, p. 225, n. 2. In the eighteen years since these lines were written, I have not found any reason to change them.

125 So likewise Vlastos, 'On Heraclitus', in Furley and Allen, pp. 423ff.

126 See *Anaximander*, p. 150, for confirmation of the accuracy of this account.

127 There has been some debate about whether or not we should punctuate after 'it ever was and is and will be', and before 'fire everliving'. Since Heraclitus wrote without punctuation marks, the issue is not one of text but of interpretation. Here as elsewhere I think we must have it both ways. As Reinhardt demonstrated, the three forms of the verb 'be' clearly have their full existential (or 'vital') value in the formula for eternity, re-echoed in *aeizōon*, 'everliving'. But these verbs *also* serve as copula, with 'everliving fire' as predicate. The notion that 'be' in Greek must be *either* existential *or* copulative, but not both at once, is one of those superstitions that should have been discarded by now. See *The Verb 'Be' in Ancient Greek*, pp. 80, 139—41, 164—7, etc.

128 J. Bronowski, *The Ascent of Man*, p. 123.

129 My rendering follows a suggestion of G.E.L. Owen that the nominative form *gē* 'earth' requires the same subject for the preceding verb *ēn* 'it was'.

130 *Vermächtnis*, p. 51; more cautiously Marcovich and others cited by him, p. 286.

131 The Theophrastean interpretation is given in Appendix IIA. The fullest Stoic exegesis, referring XXXVIII to cosmogony and XXXIX to the ecpyrosis, is preserved by Clement in the quotation of these fragments; see von Arnim, II, No. 590, and below, n. 135. For the influence of the Theophrastean doxography on the Stoa, see J. Kerschensteiner, 'Der Bericht des Theophrast über Heraklit', *Hermes* 83 (1955), who perhaps underestimates the extent to which the Stoics also studied Heraclitus' own words.

132 I say 'transformation' since it is not entirely clear whether the temporal process in XXXIX is a continuous interchange of land and sea within the present world order or some larger cosmic cycle. I suspect it is both. See p. 144.

133 Herodotus uses the term four times, twice in sense (1) and twice in sense (2A). Senses (1) and (2) are as old as Homer; sense (2A) is first attested in Hesiod. See my 'On early Greek astronomy' p. 113, with nn. 50—2.

134 So rightly Snell, 'Die Sprache Heraklits' in *Gesammelte Schriften*, p. 134. But in denying that this process of 'turnings' is depicted as a sequence spread out in time, Snell abandons his own principle of taking Heraclitus' imagery at full strength. For the temporal value of 'turnings' in archaic Greek literature see Hesiod, *Theogony* 58: 'as the seasons turned around' (*peri d' etrapon hōrai*); Semonides 1.8 (Diehl): 'the turnings-round of the

years' (*eteōn peritropai*, again referring to the cycle of the seasons).

135 See D. 31 = Marcovich, p. 278. The Stoic interpretation is as old as Chrysippus (von Arnim II, No. 579): 'the change of fire is as follows: it turns (*trepetai*) through air into water'. It may well go back to Zeno (ibid. No. 581 = D.L. VII.142); compare von Arnim I, 102 = Arius Didymus fr. 38 Diels, where we find the doctrine expressed with Heraclitus' own term *tropē*. Zeno seems to have derived his physics directly from a reading of Heraclitus; hence Cleanthes' long commentary on the latter.

136 See Anaxagoras fr. 16, with parallels in Anaximenes A 7.3 and probably also in Anaximander A 27. In Melissus B 8.3 'from water, earth and stone arise' seems to be cited as a fact of everyday experience, as in *Timaeus* 49Bff. It is not so much a fact of observation as a theoretical way of describing certain phenomena of drying, freezing and sedimentation. The theory which determines this description is just the Ionian cosmogony.

137 Thus the account of Chrysippus continues: 'and out of water, as earth comes into existence, air is evaporated [or 'exhaled', *anathymiatai*]. As air is thinned out, the sky is poured around (*aithēr pericheitai*) in a circle. The stars with the sun are kindled from the sea' (von Arnim II, No. 579; see the parallel doctrine assigned to Zeno and Chrysippus ibid. 581 = D.L. VII.142). The Stoics are developing Heraclitus' remarks in the light of the traditional Ionian cosmogony; so already Theophrastus in D.L. IX.9—11 (see Appendix IIA). Despite Reinhardt, they may have had one or two lost sentences of Heraclitus to help them out. The sun and stars 'kindled (*anaptontai*) from the sea' in Chrysippus might well be the echo of a lost Heraclitean text (just as *pericheitai* in Chrysippus echoes *diacheetai* in XXXIX).

138 *Theogony* 846. Even if the verse were post-Hesiodic, as some editors have thought, it would still be older than Heraclitus. As Wilamowitz observes (in his comment on *Lysistrata* 974) the production of *prēstēres* by Typhoeus in the *Theogony* prefigures the connection between *typhōn* (whirlwind) and *prēstēr* in Aristophanes (loc. cit.).

139 Some authors (including LSJ) suggest a derivation from *prēthō* 'to blow'; but that is not the sense Aristotle sees in *prēstēr*. Similarly, *prēstēres anemoi* in *Theogony* 846 must be 'burning' (not 'blowing') winds. In the *Lysistrata* passage (973ff.) what *prēstēr* adds to *typhōn* is precisely the notion of fire, as Wilamowitz remarks, following the scholiast.

140 This includes the metaphorical use in Euripides fr. 384 Nauck, where 'the twin *prēstēres* flowing down' are jets of blood from lacerated eyes.

141 For recent discussion taking *prēstēr* in this sense, including a photograph of a Mediterranean waterspout, see J.J. Hall, '*Prēstēros aulos*' in *JHS* 89 (1969), 57—9 with Plate VI; and further comments by P. Plass, ibid. 92 (1972), 179f. This phenomenon does occur in the Aegean area; but the connection between waterspout (or tornado) and lightning storm is not regular enough for this to be what Herodotus, Aristophanes, and Xenophon are speaking of. Aristotle describes the *prēstēr* not as 'a variant of the *typhōn*' (as Hall claims, p. 57) but as a development from the same raw material as thunder and lightning, hurricane (*eknephias*) and whirlwind (*typhōn*). Hall, following Burnet and LSJ, may have been misled by the closer connection between *prēstēr* and whirlwind in Hellenistic and Roman authors. Lucretius VI.423ff. certainly describes a waterspout in his account of *prēstēr*; but that is not true of any classic Greek author, as far as I can see. (For confusion in Lucretius' account, see Bailey's commentary, p. 1618.) Herodotus and Xenophon are both referring to disas-

ters on land; and they have in mind fire, not water. Aristophanes (*Lysistrata* 973ff.) and Aristotle (*Meteor.* 371a 14ff.) both describe a *typhōn* (not a *prēstēr*) as lifting things off the ground, like a tornado. Friends long familiar with Greek weather tell me this can be paralleled nowadays in localized wind storms, but that there is no Greek equivalent to the great 'twisters' of the central plains of North America.

142 For the close connection, amounting sometimes to identification, between *prēstēr* and thunderbolt (*keraunos*), see West's note to *Theogony* 846.

143 Burnet had a theory to account for this. 'This must mean that, at any given moment, half of the sea is taking the downward path, and *has just been* fiery storm-cloud, while half of it is going up, and *has just been* earth' (*Early Greek Philosophy*, p. 149, italics added). Heraclitus' words admit many interpretations, but I doubt that this is one. The text indicates that earth and *prēstēr* represent stages following upon sea (and this is clear also from the phrase 'before it became earth' in XXXIX). If Burnet has made them precede the sea, that is not by sheer perversity but in order to render possible his generalization of this law for 'each of the three aggregates, Fire, Water and Earth': each one is 'made up of two equal portions ... one of which is taking the upward and the other the downward path' (ibid. 163). Here the motivation for calculating from the preceding phase is clear. For of course half of fire can at any given moment be taking the upward path *only* if one counts from the stage before. And similarly for the half of earth that is supposed to be on the downward path. (Burnet does not call attention to the fact that, contrariwise, for the half of fire on the downward path, and the half of earth going upwards, one must count as we expect, prospectively.) The artifice here in the interpretation of Heraclitus' words 'half earth, half *prēstēr*' is worthy of Clement and the Stoics. And in fact the introduction of the upward and downward path into the commentary on XXXVIII–XXXIX is due to Theophrastus (in D.L. IX.9 = DK 22A 1.9; cited with approval by Burnet, p. 148).

144 Kirk, p. 330; cf. Kirk and Raven, p. 201. Kirk's view of XXXVIII (D. 31A) is accepted by Vlastos (in Furley and Allen, p. 419), though he differs on XXXIX (D. 31B).

145 See Xenophanes A 33.5–6 and my suggestion in *Anaximander*, p. 185, that the sinking of the earth into the sea was regarded by the Milesians as necessary 'reparation' to the moist for an excessive victory of the dry.

146 As far as I can see, this holds true on any reading of this controversial text. On my version (the text of Clement-Eusebius accepted by Diels and Marcovich), the sea is measured according to the same *logos* as 'before it became earth'. On the most reasonable alternative (proposed independently by Cherniss and Wiese; and cf. Bollack-Wismann, p. 134) the sea is measured 'in the same *logos* which was at first' (*hokoios prōton ēn*), whatever that may be. In any case the construction of *metreetai eis ton auton logon* is that of measurement 'up to' a definite mark or limit previously established, as in the refilling of an empty container. (See Powell, *Lexicon*, s.v. *es* A.IV and C.1–3, p. 146.)

147 It is an interesting question why the Stoics followed Heraclitus not only in foreseeing a world conflagration but also in beginning the cosmogony from fire. This can scarcely be for physical reasons; as a plausible process, world formation begins for the Stoics in almost Milesian fashion with primeval moisture, associated with *aēr*. The initial step, from Fire to moisture, is metaphysical dogma rather than physical theory, dictated by requirements of symmetry and the authority of Heraclitus. But I suspect it was fire that

brought the Stoics to Heraclitus rather than Heraclitus that brought them to fire. Zeno's choice of fire as first principle may have been decided by its dynamic role as power of transformation in the arts. Cf. the Stoic notion of *pyr technikon* 'fire the artificer'.

148   For cosmic cycles in Milesian thought, see *Anaximander*, pp. 184f.; compare pp. 47—53.

149   Cf. gold as object of search and desire in VIII (D. 22) and the metaphor of Pindar's *First Olympian*: 'gold is a gleaming fire'.

150   See Zeller-Nestle I.2 (1920), pp. 796ff.

151   As formulated, Zeller's interpretation presupposes the anachronistic reading of sixth-century monism which I have rejected above (p. 131), following Stokes. It remains to be seen whether Zeller's view could be reformulated without such anachronism.

152   Zeller-Nestle I.2, pp. 865ff. Zeller rightly sees that the only ancient testimony that appears to tell against this interpretation of Heraclitus, the oft-quoted passage in Plato's *Sophist* 242C—D, is not a definite statement on the point at issue (pp. 875f.). And he also sees that the statement in Aetius (DK 22.A10) that 'the cosmos is generated not in time but only in conception' *presupposes* the existence of a literal cosmogony, as in the similar interpretation of Plato's *Timaeus*.

153   Burnet, p. 145 with note 1. This view of fire as a figure of stable form maintained by constant change seems profoundly true to Heraclitus' intention; and (like many others) I have unconsciously echoed Burnet's remark on other occasions.

154   And cf. XLIX (D. 126), LXVII (D. 110—11), XC (D. 26), etc.

155   The same holds for XLI (D. 76) whether or not it is an authentic fragment, since its form is directly parallel to that of CII (D. 36).

156   It is passages like this one on the bow and the lyre which justify Plato's contrast between the austere Heraclitean Muses, who insist that things are always one and many, 'always coming together in divergence', with the softer Sicilian Muses who relax this tension of 'always' and substitute an alternating pattern of unity and plurality, Love and Strife (*Sophist* 242C—D). If Plato had denied the importance of periodicity for Heraclitus, he would simply be mistaken. But all he says is that, unlike Empedocles, Heraclitus does not *need* this periodic pattern in order to conceive the unity of opposites.

157   Burnet, p. 150: 'And yet the "measures" are not absolutely fixed.' He goes on to speak of the alternation of day and night, summer and winter. So in referring to the measures of the sun he sees periodic recurrence as a kind of exception that proves the rule: 'Of course there is a certain variation, as we saw; but it is strictly confined within limits, and is compensated in the long run by a variation in the other direction' (pp. 161f.). Note the ambiguity between 'in the long run' here, where the diachronic stipulation is indispensable for any pattern of symmetry, and the occurrence of the same phrase in the earlier quotation from p. 150 (above, on p. 149), where it seemed incidental.

This down-playing of periodic phenomena is all the more unconvincing, since for the meaning of 'measures' here Burnet correctly refers to Diogenes fr. 3, where they are exemplified *only* by periodic recurrence: the measures 'of winter and summer and night and day and rainfall and winds and fair weather'.

158   Burnet, p. 161, followed by Kirk (pp. 347f.): 'the simile quite clearly precludes complete alternation, for in the exchange of gold and goods neither

element is ever absorbed into the other (as *ta panta* would have to be in *pyr*), but the total of each remains the same'. Similarly Marcovich, p. 295.

159   See Reinhardt, *Parmenides*, pp. 168ff.; more fully in Wiese, pp. 238—46.

160   Ibid. 177. Note that this is not an objection but a confirmation for those of us who regard the philosopher of Ephesus as reacting to his older contemporaries in nearby Miletus. It is one of the eccentricities of Reinhardt's book that he wished to explain Heraclitus' thought as a response instead to Parmenides in faraway Italy. Parmenides' poem was almost certainly unknown to Heraclitus, although it may have been composed during his lifetime.

161   Cf. 'Heraklits Lehre vom Feuer', in *Vermächtnis*, pp. 55ff. Reinhardt concedes that the term *metra* can have a temporal aspect, as in Heraclitus XLIV (D. 94) and Diogenes fr. 3, but in effect denies the relevance of this for the interpretation of XXXVII—XL.

162   Vlastos, who clearly posed this question, does not offer a clear answer in physical terms. His implied answer is that the priority of fire is due to the fact that it is intelligent and governs the cosmos ('On Heraclitus', in Furley and Allen, p. 424). With this I agree, but it does not help us interpret the exchanges of XL (D. 90) or the 'reversals' of XXXVII (D. 30). Vlastos does suggest (ibid. p. 421) that XL 'identifies fire as the thing that remains constant in all transformations and implies that *its* measure is the same or common measure in all things . . . Thus . . . the invariance of *its* measures is what accounts for the observance of the *metron* in all things.' This is a gallant defence of a hopelessly lost cause. For if all things observe the measure, fire is not in any discernible way privileged in remaining 'constant in all transformations'. We are left with the fact that there is no physical basis for the priority of fire in Heraclitus' system if we follow Burnet and Reinhardt in depriving it of the dimension of cosmogony.

163   Among recent scholars only Gigon and Guthrie have accepted it as an independent fragment; others regard it as an inaccurate paraphrase of CII (D. 36). See Guthrie, I, p. 453 with n. 2; Gigon, *Untersuchungen*, p. 99, *Ursprung*, p. 224. I previously argued for authenticity in *Anaximander*, p. 152, n. 1.

164   Compare Maximus' version of D. 62 with the fuller quotation in Hippolytus to judge this author's accuracy in citation: see texts 47b[3] and 47a in Marcovich, pp. 236f.

165   Maximus is scarcely an expert on Heraclitus. He seems to know only three fragments: the way up and down (CIII, D. 60); the gods living our life and we living their death (XCII, D. 62), and the citation under discussion here, which is presented less as an independent quotation than as an *interpretation* of D. 62. See the full context in Marcovich, p. 167 (text 33d[4]).

166   See W.C. Helmbold and E.N. O'Neil, *Plutarch's Quotations* (New York, 1959), p. 34.

167   According to Wiese, pp. 322—5, there are some 74 quotations or allusions in Clement's much less voluminous works. Clement accounts for 23 quotations in Diels' edition, whereas Plutarch accounts for 17. We may note that Hippolytus also accounts for 18, one more than Plutarch. But these quotations are concentrated in a single section of Hippolytus' work, and they reflect special research (whether by Hippolytus or by some predecessor) rather than a general familiarity with the text.

168   Helmbold and O'Neil, *Plutarch's Quotations*, p. IX. 'His memory was prodigious, and his confidence in it no less so, as when he asserts that such-and-such does *not* occur in Plato (*Mor.* 1115C—D); and sure enough it does

not. But he committed the kind of error that one almost always makes in citing from memory.' In quotations from Heraclitus Plutarch sometimes corrects himself, by giving a more literal version elsewhere. (See the two versions of XLIV, D. 94, in Marcovich, p. 274.) When we can check his version against verbatim citations, we usually find he has omitted or altered at least a word or two. (Compare Plutarch's versions of CIX, D. 118, with the text given by Musonius, Stobaeus, and Philo, and Clement, 68a¹–a⁷ in Marcovich, pp. 371–2.) Only in very short quotations can we confirm his literal accuracy (e.g. XXVIII, D. 101; LXXXVIII, D. 96; CXIV, D. 119; see Marcovich, pp. 53ff., 407, and 500).

169   Thus in XL (D. 90) the slight change from *antamoibē* (which I restore, with Diels and others) to *antameibetai* in the MSS may well be due to Plutarch himself, rather than to his copyists. On the other hand, in XXXIII (D. 93) the inferior parallel in Stobaeus (see Marcovich, p. 49) shows just how good Plutarch's memory can be.

170   *De primo frigido* 948F; and cf. *de Iside* 363D; both in Marcovich, p. 356.

171   See Kirk, pp. 343f. with Marcovich, p. 360, and Bollack-Wismann, p. 235.

172   *Anaximander*, p. 152 n.; cf. pp. 145ff.

173   So, for example, Kirk, p. 343; 'fragments 31 and 36 show quite clearly that he [sc. Heraclitus] believed that the main constituents of the world were fire, sea, earth — not air'.

174   Reinhardt, 'Heraclitea', in *Vermächtnis*, pp. 75–83; clarified by Kirk, pp. 295–303.

175   Kirk, p. 294, and Marcovich, p. 344, emphasize the dactylic rhythm of XLIIA (*hōras hai panta pherousin*); Reinhardt regards version B ('what the seasons bring') as better attested (*Vermächtnis*, p. 76). In either case Heraclitus may have used an old phrase to express a new idea.

176   It is rejected by Marcovich, p. 345, and by Bollack-Wismann, p. 287.

177   The term *epitropeuein* is applied to fire 'which begets and administers all other things' at *Theaetetus* 153A8, where Plato has just mentioned Heraclitus (152E) and the doctrine of flux. A few lines later he observes that the preservation of cosmic order depends upon the continuous movement *of the sun* and of the heavens generally.

178   That is suggested, but not established by the fact that in the same context of the *Cratylus* Plato paraphrases CXXII (D. 16): see above, p. 275. This shows either that Plato himself is interpreting the text of Heraclitus (in which case our bold step might well be justified) or that his Heraclitean sources were doing so.

179   DK A 1.8; see Appendix IIA.

180   Aetius I.27.1 (Diels, *Doxographi*, p. 322), in DK A 8. Contrast the purely Stoic interpretations of Heraclitean Fate given by Aetius in I.28.1 (also cited in DK A 8). This more confused tradition is responsible for an alleged quotation: 'Thus Heraclitus writes: "things are entirely fated" ' (Aetius I.27.1 = fr. 137, recognized by Diels as inauthentic).

181   *On Regimen* I.5 (DK I, p. 183, lines 5 and 7); compare I.10 (ibid. p. 185, 1. 17). Some such statement is presupposed by the view of Anaxagoras: 'he says that nothing occurs by fate (*heimarmenē*), but this is an empty word' (DK 59.A 66, from Alexander).

182   Reinhardt, *Parmenides*, pp. 188–90 (cf. p. 184); accepted by Kirk, p. 301.

183   The only exception I have noted is Bollack-Wismann, who accept the number 30 for a generation (p. 183), but refuse to speculate about any larger cycle (p. 287).

184   As Guthrie points out (p. 458, n. 4), Aristotle speaks of a 'great winter' with an excess of rain in connection with larger astronomical periods

(*Meteor.* I.14, 352a31). The idea of the cosmic year is clearly formulated by Plato at *Timaeus* 22C–23A, with alternate destructions of human civilization by flood and fire, referred to as 'winter' and as '(summer) heat' (*kauma*) at 22E6. (Cf. *Critias* 109D, *Laws* 677A.) It seems clear that Plato is here developing a pre-Socratic theory, not inventing one of his own. Contrast the myth of the *Statesman* (269Aff.), where Plato is making up his own version of the cosmic cycle.

185   In order to avoid this interpretation of the Great Year Reinhardt suggested a cycle of transmigrations such as we find in Empedocles and in Plato's *Phaedrus*: as the 'day' of the great year is a human lifetime, 'so must the year of the soul, its migration through the cycle of births, also last 360 such days, and consequently 30 times 360 solar years' (*Parmenides*, p. 199; followed with some hesitation by Kirk, p. 302). But there is not the slightest evidence for Heraclitus' belief in transmigration; and his attacks upon Pythagoras provide some evidence against it — particularly in the light of his insistence that men have no inkling of what is waiting for them at death (LXXXIV, D. 27)! (See below on XCII, D. 62.) Reinhardt's suggestion that 10,800 years is the period of the soul's transmigrations can only be seen as an arbitrary attempt to avoid the interpretation offered by Theophrastus: that this is a 'fixed time for the change of the cosmos according to some fated necessity'.

I am afraid the same must be said of other attempts to accept the period of 10,800 years while rejecting Theophrastus' account of it. The most influential way out is that of Burnet (pp. 157f.) developed recently by Vlastos (in his review of Kirk, *AJP* 76 (1955), 311) and accepted by Guthrie (I, 458). Vlastos sees quite clearly that, by analogy, the great year ought to be 'the period of the world's complete renewal', a kind of 'world-generation'. But in order to avoid the natural implications of this, he thinks of it (with Lassalle and Burnet) as 'the time required for every part of the fire which takes the "downward" turn at any given moment to return to its source, or, to look at it the other way round, the interval after which every part of water and earth existing at any given time will have been re-placed'. This he admits is only a 'likely guess', for it is difficult to find even a toe-hold for it in the fragments. But it can scarcely be regarded as likely, or even coherent, unless we can make sense of the notion of a *part* or *particle* of fire that preserves its identity throughout elemental change, or a part of water that preserves its identity until it is replaced. Now this idea is not only absent from the fragments but incompatible with Heraclitus' own conception of identity, which is that of a *pattern* (like night-and-day) and not of a formless 'glob' or fistful of matter. What remains the same is the river, not the water rushing by.

186   Aristotle, *Meteorologica* II.6, 363a31–b6, with Lee's diagram in the Loeb edition, p. 187. Also W.A. Heidel, *The Frame of Ancient Greek Maps* (New York, 1937), pp. 17ff. For possible evidence of this system on Babylonian maps of the sixth century B.C., see *Anaximander*, p. 83 n. 3.

187   See 'On early Greek astronomy', pp. 106ff. with nn. 25 and 27.

188   George A. Megas, *Greek Calendar Customs* (Athens, 2nd ed. 1963), p. 133.

189   For the Greek use of the Bear — first Ursa Major, then Ursa Minor — as a fixed point for steering by night, see the passages in PW II, 1173, 40–8, and the reference to Thales in Callimachus (DK 11.A 3a, vv. 118–20).

190   I see that this solution (proposed earlier in 'A new look at Heraclitus', p. 197, col. B) was guessed long ago by G. Teichmüller, *Neue Studien zur Geschichte der Begriffe* I (Gotha, 1876), p. 16, cited by Marcovich, p. 338.

191   Hesiod puts the evening rising of Arcturus 60 days after the winter solstice,

and hence a month before the actual equinox; Geminus lists it for 24 February. Spring comes early in Greece. The dawn or heliacal rising of Arcturus corresponds to the middle of September, and thus more closely to the autumnal equinox (dates from Wilamowitz on *Erga* 567 and 610; cf. PW III, 718 for dates according to a variety of ancient sources).

192   See texts in Marcovich, pp. 312f.

193   The reference to a human foot in Aetius may not have formed part of the original text. The Theophrastean doxography (D.L. IX.7) says only 'the sun is the size it appears'. From repeated statements in Aristotle, where Heraclitus' name is not mentioned, we know that 'the sun is a foot long' was a stock example of an *appearance* that educated men do not accept as true. (Texts in Marcovich, pp. 307f., Deichgräber, pp. 25f.) Aetius' version may represent a doxographical tradition in which these two items have been unscrupulously combined. Compare the way in which Heraclitus' account of solar extinction and rekindling becomes more detailed in later sources (Marcovich, p. 313, texts b^2 and b^3).

194   See B. Snell, 'Die Sprache Heraklits', in *Gesammelte Schriften*, pp. 132ff.

195   The words of XLIX serve so well as an explication of Anaximander's fragment that W. Bröcker once suggested that Heraclitus was *quoting* here from Anaximander! That seems unlikely; but scarcely more so than Bollack-Wismann's rejection of XLIX (p. 345) as the pseudo-Heraclitean formulation of a banal idea.

196   For cases of systematic ambiguity see the construal of *ekeinōn* (twice) in XCII (D. 62), and *pantōn* in XXVII (D. 108), XXX (D. 114), XXXI (D. 11? etc. Compare the double construction of *aiei* in I.1 and the three forms of 'to be' in XXXVII (D. 30) above, n. 127.

197   So Reinhardt, *Parmenides*, pp. 177, 206f., and others since. Cf. Burnet, pp. 145f.

198   Aristotle, *Met.* Gamma 5, 1010a14. Edward Hussey suggests that Cratylus himself may have been the first to formulate Heraclitus' statement in this way ('you cannot step *twice* into the river') in order to correct him. If so, both Plato and Aristotle were deceived by Cratylus as to what Heraclitus actually said.

199   *Crat.* 439C–D; cf. *Theaetetus* 182C, etc.

200   This is, in effect, Bywater's reconstruction, following another version in Plutarch; see his fr. XLI. For a supposed third 'fragment' referring to the river, see D.49a in Appendix I.

201   For a survey of scholarly opinion see Marcovich, pp. 207f., who rejects all three pairs as un-Heraclitean. Similarly Bollack-Wismann, p. 268.

202   A careful study shows that Plotinus cites 11 fragments, 6 of them in full; see Evangelos Roussos, *O Herakleitos stis Enneades tou Plotinou* (Athens, 1968), p. 80 (p. 98, German summary). But these tend to be the more familiar sayings; only in the present case does he quote a text not otherwise known. Roussos agrees with Richard Harder that the quotations reflect Plotinus' own reading of Heraclitus. See also Wilhelm Halbfass, 'Plotins Interesse an Heraklit', *Festschrift für Karl Deichgräber*, Göttingen, 1968 (typescript of the Seminar für Klassische Philologie); W. Burkert, 'Plotinus, Plutarch und die platonisierende Interpretation von Heraklit und Empedocles', in *Kephalaion. Studies . . . C.J. de Vogel* (Assen, 1975), pp. 137–46.

203   See LXXVIII–LXXXIII, and above all CXV–CXXV. These correspond to the *theologikos logos* in the division cited in the Introduction (above, p. 9, n. 24). The remaining section, LV–LXXVII, together with earlier fragments

like XXX—XXXII, will represent the *politikos logos*, the discourse on man and society.

204 See Kirk, p. 389, and Gigon, *Untersuchungen*, p. 144. The texts of Bywater and Walzer are comparable. Diels thought he could keep ὁτέη as a feminine form of ἧτις, but he was mistaken. It is not just that this particular form is unattested: there is simply no such thing as a feminine stem for τις (= Latin *quis*). That was pointed out by Bechtel in 1924 in reference to this very fragment (*Die griechische Dialekte* III (Berlin, 1924), 171); and it is remarkable that classical scholars fifty years later continue to print this text with linguistically impossible forms. (That includes the dative ὁτέηι, proposed by Deichgräber.) Even Marcovich (pp. 447f.), who cites Bechtel (and Schwyzer, *Griechische Grammatik* I (Munich, 1938), 616, where the absence of feminine forms of τις is conspicuous), lists four 'likely' emendations of which two are linguistically unacceptable. We have, in fact, only the choice between ὅκη (ὅπη) 'how' and ὅτεῳ (= ᾗτινι) 'by which'. Unless someone produces an Ionic parallel for ὅτεῳ with a feminine antecedent, we had better stick to ὅκη, as in CVI (D. 117).

205 Kirk, p. 388, argues that a mechanical corruption from *kybernatai* is more probable; I am not sure. The present middle, which Kirk accepts, reads more smoothly, but seems stylistically weak. All the early parallels (except Diogenes fr. 5) have the verb in the active voice: Anaximander A 15 (= Aristotle, *Physics* 203b11), Parmenides fr. 12, and the passages from Pindar and the *De Victu* cited by Kirk (ibid.). So likewise Heraclitus' own use of *oiakizei* in CXIX (D. 64); compare Anaxagoras fr. 12 (*kratei*, *diakosmēse*). The stylistic difference between active and passive here seems more decisive than that between present and aorist.

206 Cf. *epistatēs*, 'supervisor', 'overseer'. For this sense of the verb see Archilochus fr. 1 (Diehl): 'I am a master (*epistamenos*) of the desirable gift of the Muses'; fr. 66 *hen d' epistamai* 'there is one thing I am good at'. The same imagery with a different verb (the causative of *epistamai*) occurs in Hesiod. *Works and Days* 659: 'at the place where the Muses first set me over (*epebēsan* 'made me master of') sweet song'.

207 See IV (D. 17), XIX (D. 57) and XXVII (D. 108); cf. XXIX (D. 116), LXI (D. 97), and LXXXV (D. 28A).

208 The inference becomes explicit in Diogenes fr. 3: 'It would not be possible for things to be so distributed without intelligence (*noēsis*), so that there are measures (*metra*) of all things, of winter and summer and night and day and rainfall and winds and fair weather.' For the notion of universal 'steering' in Anaximander, Xenophanes, Anaxagoras and Diogenes, see the passages cited p. 272, with n. 400.

209 So Bollack-Wismann, p. 240.

210 For the traditional thought, see Semonides of Amorgos fr. 1.3 West: 'There is no understanding (*noos*) in men, but day by day (*ephēmeroi*) we live like cattle knowing nothing.' Cf. J. Mansfeld, Chapter I of *Die Offenbarung des Parmenides*.

211 So Marcovich (pp. 488f., with others) and Bollack-Wismann (pp. 248f.). The authenticity of the *Hippias Major* is irrelevant to the question of its reliability as a source for Heraclitus. I am convinced that the dialogue is artistically and even intellectually too crude to be a work of Plato. But the author is a careful writer who reproduces Platonic doctrine with considerable accuracy and could have cited Heraclitus correctly if he wished.

212 See 'A thought pattern in Heraclitus', *AJP* 59 (1938), 309–37; German translation in *Wege und Formen* (3rd ed.), pp. 253ff. Fränkel needlessly

apologized for his use of mathematical terminology; he forgot that one of the basic senses of *logos* is precisely 'ratio', 'geometrical proportion'. But Heraclitus' pattern is the formal development of an older mode of expression, as in the quotation from Semonides in n. 210 above: as cattle stand to us (in understanding), so do we stand to the gods.

213　Cf. XL (D. 90): as gold is to merchandise, so is fire to all things. The same pattern emerges from the juxtaposition of VIII (D. 22) with IX (D. 35), and from LX (D. 87) with LXI (D. 97). See on LXI.

214　Cf. IV (D. 17), XIX (D. 57), XXVII (D. 108), etc.; also *gnōmē* in LIV (D. 41); *gnōsis* in XXII (D. 56).

215　See Hipponax (73 Diehl) and Demodocus (6 Diehl), cited by D.L. I.84.

216　Aristotle, *Nic. Ethics* V.1, 1130a1 and *Rhet.* II.13, 1389b23f. For further details see Crusius in PW III (1899), 383—9.

217　D.L. I.87 and 88. This is the first of the sayings attributed to Bias in the list of Demetrius of Phaleron (DK I, p. 65). Cf. Bruno Snell, *Leben und Meinungen der Sieben Weisen* (3rd ed. Munich, 1952), pp. 12 and 102.

218　D.L. I.88; cf. PW III, 388, 32—4.

219　See DK 22.A 3a and Marcovich, pp. 538f.; discussion by Münzer, 'Hermodorus (3)' in PW VIII (1913), 860. It has been conjectured that the Roman story reflects some historical fame of Hermodorus as lawgiver or judge in Ephesus. For the slim evidence, see R. Schottlaender, 'Heraklits angebliche Aristokratismus', *Klio* 43—5 (1965), 25f. Cf. Marcovich, PW 252.

220　So Vlastos, 'Equality and justice in early Greek cosmologies', in Furley-Allen, p. 72, n. 92. Cf. Bollack-Wismann, p. 333.

221　The usual classification of Heraclitus as a disgruntled aristocrat, like Theognis of Megara, does not do justice to the breadth and independence of vision manifested in the fragments. For a sounder view see Schottlaender (cited above, n. 219) and Vlastos, p. 70, n. 82 in the article cited in preceding note.

222　See Herodotus VI.43.3. The date would fit Marcovich's suggestion that Heraclitus' book was composed around 490 (PW 249).

　　The egalitarian sentiments attributed to the Ephesians in LXIV (D. 121) need not reflect an advanced democratic regime; a narrow oligarchy of jealous peers is also capable of eliminating an outstanding rival. But Heraclitus' emphasis on the responsibility of *all* Ephesians in Hermodorus' exile strongly suggests something like a popular vote.

223　For the connection between *koros* and the rich and mighty in Solon see, in addition to the passage quoted, frs. 3.9; 4.6; 5.9.

224　As we have seen (n. 8), Heraclitus' insistence upon the legal power of a single man ('if he is the best') cannot be understood as a plea for tyranny or even for constitutional monarchy; the former is excluded by his commitment to the rule of law, while the latter was not a relevant option for a Greek city of his time.

225　Bywater and others have assumed that these two sentences form a continuous text. Kirk (p. 130) and Marcovich (p. 390) prefer to separate them and thus cut the link between Heraclitus' moral outlook and his conception of opposites.

226　*Nic. Ethics* I.8, 1099a25; *Eud. Ethics* I.1, 1214a1.

227　No. 10 in the list of Demetrius of Phaleron, DK I, p. 64.

228　Cf. *Theaetetus* 176 A: 'It is not possible for evils to be destroyed; for it is necessary that there be always something opposed to the good. These evils have no seat among the gods; but they circulate of necessity in this region and in mortal nature.' The dualistic motive that follows ('therefore one must endeavor to flee from here to there as quickly as possible') is Plato's own. But his conception of the 'mortal region' is faithfully Heraclitean.

229 Kirk, Marcovich, and Bollack-Wismann accept LXVIII as a reliable paraphrase. I do not share their optimism.

230 It is possible to suppose, on one reading of LII—LIII (D. 84), that by contrast to human beings the deity itself, as the all-pervading structure of the world, experiences rest and weariness together, as a single process of constant change.

231 This is suggested by the context in which Clement quotes LXIX, and perhaps also by an imitation in one of the spurious 'Letters of Heraclitus'. So Marcovich, p. 229. But on Letter VII see now Leonardo Tarán in *Eraclito: Testimonianze e Imitazioni*, ed. Mondolfo and Tarán (Florence, 1972), pp. 336, 345f.

232 The root sense of *dikē* is that of *deiknymi* 'to point, indicate' and Latin *in-dex* 'pointer', *iu-dex* 'right-pointer, judge'; so also *dico* in the legal sense of 'pronounce judgment', 'plead a lawsuit', 'make decisions' (cf. *dictator*).

233 The addition of chickens here depends upon whether or not Columella is to be trusted as a source of LXXII. Many scholars have thought there is also a genuine kernel to the medieval Latin citation listed as D. 4 (Marcovich fr. 38; compare Kirk, pp. 84ff.), which mentions the peculiar taste of cattle for bitter vetch (*oroboi*).

234 See Zeller, Fränkel and others cited by Marcovich, p. 183. Kirk (pp. 78—80, 83f.) rightly rejects this view.

235 *De Victu* I.10 (p. 12, 1. 4 ed. Joly), cited by DK I, p. 185, 1. 12. *De Nutrimento* 19 (DK I.189, 15), cited by Kirk, p. 75.

236 Sextus Empiricus, *Outlines of Pyrrhonism* I.40; Loeb ed. Vol. I, p. 26.

237 This difference will not be so great if one follows Michael of Ephesus in interpreting *syrmata* in LXXI as *chortos* 'fodder', the natural food of donkeys. So in the late and distorted citation D. 4, bitter vetch is mentioned as fodder for cattle.

238 For a vague version, see Reinhardt, p. 204; a naive or confused view is ascribed to Heraclitus by Kirk, pp. 80, 83f. and Guthrie I, 445, among others.

239 So Zeller, pp. 832ff.: 'he concludes . . . that the thing *in itself* is both healthy and destructive at the same time'; it was a mark of his lack of logical training that he was satisfied with the thought that 'everything has opposed properties in itself'.

240 Translation and bracketing here reflect the text as given by Kirk and printed above, p. 62. My own translation there is slightly freer.

241 See Dodds' commentary on Plato, *Gorgias* 456B4, where LXXIII is cited with Platonic and Hippocratic parallels; for other examples see Gigon and Marcovich on D. 58. It is possible that the proverbial phrase is older than Heraclitus; but the next attested example is a generation later, in Aeschylus' *Agamemnon* (verse 849), and I am willing to believe (with Kirk, p. 91) that the proverb originated with Heraclitus.

242 Marcovich accepts an emendation of Wilamowitz: 'they produce the same effect as the diseases'. But this again commits Heraclitus to a negative comment that weakens the thought of crucial ambivalence.

243 The MSS give *grapheōn*, corrected by Bernays, Diels and other editors to *gnapheiōi* 'in the fuller's shop' (or 'for the carding tool'?), by Bywater to *gnapheōn* 'of the fullers or carders' (i.e. the path of their comb, according to Burnet), and by Marcovich to *gnaphōn* 'of the carding-rollers'. Kirk (pp.

97ff.) and Bollack-Wismann (p. 202) have tried to make sense of the transmitted text, by referring respectively to the path of the pen in writing ('the
path of letters' or 'of writers') or to some rotating instrument for painting
figures ('the path of the painters').

244   See Hdt. I.92.4, with parallels in Marcovich, p. 164.

245   See R.J. Forbes, *Studies in Ancient Technology* IV (Leiden, 1964), p. 21.
Compare H. Blümner, *Technologie und Terminologie der Gewerbe und
Künste bei Griechen und Römern* I (2nd ed. Leipzig, 1912), pp. 110ff.
(for combing) and 177ff. (for carding).

246   For some continuity between ancient and modern Greek technology in
this connection see A.W. Parsons, 'A Roman water mill in the Athenian
Agora', *Hesperia* V (1936), 70—90.

247   The words 'He says "it is one and the same" ', which Diels and others take
as continuing the text of LXXIV, are probably an addition by Hippolytus
designed to provide the transition to CIII (D. 60) by equating the two
paths. So rightly Bollack-Wismann, pp. 202f.

248   Kirk, p. 104; cf. Marcovich's table opposite p. 160, and Stokes, *One and
Many*, p. 91.

249   Aristotle cites the view of people 'who think Heraclitus claimed that the
same thing can both be and not be (so)', in *Metaphysics* Gamma 3,
1005b25; cf. 1012a24—34.

250   Compare Stokes, *One and Many*, pp. 91 and 97. But I see no reason to
credit Heraclitus with the fallacious inference that therefore *straight* and
crooked were the same (as Stokes and others do, following the interpretation of Hippolytus). Even if he said 'the straight and crooked path of the
roller is one and the same (path)' — if the fuller text accepted by Diels and
Marcovich belongs to Heraclitus — he was saying something obviously true.
It is only the gloss of Hippolytus that turns this into a confused assertion
of the identity of contraries.

251   See Marcovich, pp. 429f. As Diels pointed out, the Homeric image of the
thunderbolt and the notion of cosmic guidance by a blow (*plēgē*) are combined by Cleanthes in his *Hymn to Zeus* (DK 22.C 4), following up a
Heraclitean thought; cf. CXIX (D. 64).

252   *Il.* XVII.447 = *Od.* XVIII.131. The parallel was noted by Nestle (in Zeller,
p. 911 n. 2) and substantiated by Marcovich, loc. cit.

253   This third, most esoteric level of interpretation, generally rejected by recent
commentators, was accurately perceived by Chrysippus (von Arnim II, no.
937, cited by Marcovich as 31b[1]); and apparently also by Theophrastus,
who quotes LXXVII in connection with the circular motion of 'those
things which are naturally such as to move in this way', i.e. the heavenly
bodies. The same thought underlies some Heraclitean sections of the
Cratylus, where the notion of the cosmic *logos* is connected with the
celestial rotation. Cf. *Cratylus* 408C with 413B, 417C.

254   For this theme of the *logos* as a kind of objective discourse see above, p.
98.

255   Of course, *if* there was a mistake in Hippolytus' text, we could explain it
by the two preceding occurrences of *homologein*. But the fact that an
error might have occurred cannot count as evidence that it did. And the
only thing brought forward to show that there is in fact an error in
Hippolytus' text is some entirely arbitrary speculation about what Plato
could or should have made Eryximachus say.

256   For the three citations in Plutarch see Marcovich, pp. 122f. The exception

occurs in one of Plutarch's latest and most allegorical works, *On Isis and Osiris*, where he is scarcely interested in exact quotation. The same mistake occurs independently in one manuscript of one of the other two quotations in Plutarch, where other manuscripts faithfully preserve *palintropos* (see Kirk, p. 211). The fact that an author like Proclus (who does not quote but simply alludes to LXXVIII) makes the same mistake is of no interest whatsoever: he may be influenced by Plutarch's *De Iside*, or he may be independently misled by his memory of the Homeric formula, like Plutarch himself in one case and his copyist in another.

257   Frs. 27 Diels = 92 Bollack, 96 Diels = 462 Bollack. Like Heraclitus, Empedocles plays on a plurality of senses for *harmoniē*, among which the concrete meaning of 'link' or 'joint' is conspicuous.

258   This last, more general sense is possible in *Pythian* VIII.68, probable in fr. 125 (Bowra): *aoidan te kai harmonian aulois epephrasato*. It is frequent later, e.g. in Aristotle, *Poetics* 1447a22 and passim, where *harmonia* regularly means 'melody' or simply 'music'.

259   See my 'Pythagorean philosophy before Plato', in *The Pre-Socratics* ed. A.P.D. Mourelatos (Doubleday, 1974), pp. 176—8, 183—5.

260   In Plato *harmonia* in this sense becomes practically a synonym for *symphonia* 'sounding together', which again has both literal (musical) and figurative (moral and social) meanings. This assimilation of *harmonia* to *symphonia*, where the musical application is primary and applications to carpentry, for example, are lacking, accounts for the loss of the older physical and structural notions in post-Platonic uses of *harmoniē*.

261   For a later parallel to this wider sense, compare the *harmonia* of Zeus which mortal plans cannot transgress in Aeschylus, *Prometheus Bound* 551. An echo of Heraclitus here is not out of the question.

262   Cited by Burnet (pp. 163f.) with approval; rejected by Kirk (p. 216) on the grounds that 'the action of the hands . . . could not possibly be described as *harmoniē*'. That is true, but irrelevant. The point is to see the structure or fitting of the bow as an illustration of 'how in variance it agrees with itself'.

263   LXXV, D. 8. Even if Aristotle is only paraphrasing LXXVIII and CXXIV, his paraphrase is an apt commentary. Cf. *Symp.* 187A—B.

264   For the defence of this reading see above, pp. 195f. The exact sense of *palintonos* is itself not entirely clear. Hdt. (VII.69.1) uses it for the curving shape of an oriental bow; and LSJ suggests that the bows are bent 'the opposite way to that in which they are drawn'. Kirk (p. 214), who reads *palintonos harmoniē* in LXXVIII, understands it to refer to tension in the strings or in the instrument: 'a connection working in both directions'.

265   For the importance of polar contrasts in early Greek thinking, and thus for the traditional background of Heraclitus' doctrine of opposites, see above all H. Fränkel: 'qualities can only be conceived together with their opposites', *Dichtung und Philosophie*, p. 77, and passim; cf. the summary pp. 657f.

266   See 'the name of Dike' in LXIX (D. 23) and 'the name of Zeus' in CXVIII (D. 32). There is a general reference to the ways in which deity (or per haps fire) 'is named' (*onomazetai*) in CXXIII (D. 67).

267   See Parmenides fr. 1.38, 53; 9.1; 19.3. For the influence of this Eleatic theory of names, see my article on the *Cratylus* in *Exegesis and Argument, Studies . . . Presented to Gregory Vlastos* (Van Gorcum, 1973), pp. 154—7.

268   For the Aeschylean passages, see Kirk, p. 119.

269   In rendering *harmoniē* as 'structure' I am encouraged by the example of
        Edward Hussey, *The Presocratics*, pp. 43f., who translates LXXX as 'Latent
        structure is master of obvious structure' (p. 35).

270   This is at least a reasonable possibility. See the reference above in n. 259.
        Unfortunately, the later story that the cosmic music, inaudible to everyone
        else, was heard by Pythagoras alone, cannot be counted as historical
        evidence.

271   There are also mythic precedents for this notion, for example in Hesiod's
        claim that Tartarus is as far below the earth as the earth is below heaven:
        nine days' fall for a brazen anvil (*Theogony* 720ff.). But such measures,
        with their picturesque and anecdotal quality, belong to an essentially dif-
        ferent, pre-geometric and pre-scientific world view.

272   The literary procedure is thus the same as in IV (D. 17) above, p. 103.

273   See the passage from Solon's praise of Lawfulness (*Eunomiē*), 'who makes
        crooked *dikai* straight and . . . stops the wrath of grievous Strife (*Eris*)', in
        fr. 3.36 above, p. 180.

274   *Works and Days* 11–26. An Homeric allusion is of course compatible with
        the biographical fact (which seems to me certain) that Hesiod is here cor-
        recting the genealogy which he himself had given earlier at *Theogony* 225,
        where he followed Homer in recognizing only evil Eris.

275   Diels' emendation *chreōn* is not a happy one, despite its success with later
        editors. The reading *kat' erin kai chreōn* (without even so much as a *te*
        before *kai*) is very clumsy Greek for *kat' erin kai kata chreōn* 'according
        to conflict and according to what is right (and necessary)'; I cannot believe
        that Heraclitus penned this phrase. The rhythm of the clause, built around
        panta kat' erin, preceded by *kai ginomena* and followed by *kai* . . . , leads
        us to expect another participle in the middle voice at the end, which is just
        what the manuscripts provide. Despite the feeble support some editors
        find in a battered papyrus of Philodemus (see Kirk, pp. 238ff.; Marcovich,
        p. 132), there is really no justification for Diels' reading beyond the wish
        to find an exact echo of Anaximander's wording in LXXXII. Of the
        emendations suggested, Bywater's *krinomena* is by far the best, since it
        provides us with the needed middle participle and one with a real point:
        'all things are both generated and *judged* (or *selected*) according to con-
        flict'. Strife would thus appear (not only as begetter but also) as judge or
        magistrate, in the role we find Time playing in Solon and Anaximander.
        Attractive as this reading is, it is too tendentious to be admitted into the
        text, as Bywater himself recognized.

276   Several commentators compare Pindar's famous phrase *nomos ho pantōn
        basileus* 'custom, the king of all, both mortals and immortals' (fr. 153
        Bowra), which may have been influenced by Heraclitus' wording.

277   See, e.g., *Iliad* XIII.244: *deiknys sēma brotoisin* 'showing a sign to mortals'
        (cited by Kirk, p. 247n.). The verb can also be understood as a synonym
        for *epoiēse* in the next clause, as Marcovich and others assume. But that
        would not explain why Heraclitus uses *both* verbs.

278   Gigon, *Untersuchungen*, p. 119, followed by Marcovich (p. 147) and others.
        Diskin Clay suggests to me an alternative version: battle shows the differ-
        ence between men and gods by revealing the mortality of the former; gods
        may be wounded, but not killed (as in the case of Aphrodite and Ares in
        Iliad V).

279   See the different and equally arbitrary inferences drawn on this score by
        Plutarch, Clement and modern scholars in Marcovich, p. 401.

280 For the background of this distinction between divine knowledge and human guesswork in early Greek poetry, see J. Mansfeld, *Die Offenbarung des Parmenides*, pp. 4—11.

281 Note that *ginōskei* 'recognize', which normally has a strong positive value for Heraclitus, is here used ironically for the failure of genuine cognition.

282 So Wiese (pp. 214f.), who reads *apistiēi* in the dative and translates: 'aufgrund seiner Unglaublichkeit'. As he points out (p. 217), Plutarch's understanding of LXXXVI (D. 86) is a better clue to the original meaning than the gnostic interpretation given by Clement.
    I hesitate to change the manuscript reading of *apistiē* to the dative (as most editors do), since that obliges us to provide an unspecified subject for 'it escapes being recognized'. In this form, and taking *apistiē* as 'incredulity', LXXXVI becomes an uninteresting repetition of VII (D. 18).

283 Clement cites these words immediately after LXXXV, introducing them with the phrase *kai mentoi kai* 'and furthermore' (DK 'aber freilich'), which were formerly ascribed to Heraclitus; thus LXXXV and LXXXVII were regarded as the continuous text of a single fragment (D. 28). Recent discussions agree that the phrase just quoted is Clement's device for joining the two citations, whether or not they belonged together in Heraclitus' text. (See Marcovich, p. 75, and above all Wiese, p. 193.) Bollack—Wismann, who follow Reinhardt in omitting *kai mentoi kai*, still print the two sentences together as a single fragment. With Marcovich, I prefer to leave this question open.

284 So Gigon, *Untersuchungen*, p. 128; Marcovich, pp. 76f.

285 Marcovich, pp. 407ff. lists quotations of this fragment by ten or twelve different authors, from Strabo to Julian. It is reflected in the Hellenistic stories of the death of Heraclitus covered with cow-dung in D.L. IX.3—4.

286 There is a radical incompatibility between Heraclitus' attitude to the corpse and the frame of mind revealed in the elaborate burial arrangements for the bodies interred in those South Italian graves where the 'Orphic' gold tablets were found. See the reference below, n. 385.

287 'Suddenly I was asleep, I had fallen into that deep slumber in which are opened to us a return to childhood, the recapture of past years . . . the transmigration of the soul, the evoking of the dead . . . all those mysteries which we imagine ourselves not to know and into which we are in reality initiated almost every night, as we are into the other great mystery of annihilation and resurrection' Marcel Proust, *Within a Budding Grove*, tr. Moncrieff, Vol. II, pp. 165f. (= *A la recherche du temps perdu*, Éd. Pléiade, I, 819f.).

288 The lexicon cites no parallel use of the middle voice of *haptō* to mean 'kindle', except for a highly artificial Hellenistic verse from Callimachus (*Hymn to Artemis* 116). Normally the middle is passive in this use, which would give the sense: 'a man in the night *is kindled* as a light for himself'. As secondary reading or hint, this construction answers exactly to the passive form *aposbestheis* 'when he is quenched'.
    An older parallel for the middle of *haptō* with accusative object is *Od.* XI.278, where the wife-mother of Oedipus hangs herself by 'fastening [to herself] a noose' (*hapsamenē brochon*). This suggests a third construal of the phrase in XC: 'fastening to himself a light'; which would explain the dative pronoun (*heautōi*) and anticipate the sense of *haptetai* in the sequel.

289 This point was rightly seen but overstated by the commentator whose gloss *apothanōn* 'having died' was later introduced here into the text. The correct text was restored by Wilamowitz, accepted by DK and Marcovich.

290   Pindar fr. 116 Bowra. Cf. Rohde, *Psyche* (English tr.), p. 415. There may be some secondary allusion in XC to the outward resemblance between sleep and death.

291   See Kirk and Raven, p. 208, and other passages cited by Marcovich, p. 245. This physical theory of sleep is developed in the Stoic commentary in Sextus (DK 22.A 16, 129), translated in Appendix IIB.

292   Compare the paraphrase of XCII by Numenius (in D. 77): 'We live their death and they [sc. the *psychai*] live our death.'

293   Compare Xenophanes A 12 (Aristotle, *Rhetoric* II.23, 1399b5): 'Xenophanes said that those who claim the gods were born are just as impious as those who say they die. For in both cases it follows that at some time the gods are not.' What is new in Xenophanes' assertion is the attack on divine genealogies such as Hesiod's *Theogony*; what is taken for granted is that it is sacrilege to speak of a god's death.

294   Hdt. II.61; cf. II.86.2, 132.2 and 170.1.

295   Fr. 112.4. For the 'startling' and 'unique' character of this claim see Zuntz, pp. 190f.

296   See Zuntz, p. 301 (Tablet A1, verse 8) and p. 329 (Tablet A4, verse 4); published again by G.P. Carratelli, *La Parola del Passato* 29 (1974), 116. The tablets themselves belong to the fourth century, but their text is probably older than Empedocles.

297   For the textual corruption at the beginning of XCIII, see note on the text above, p. 70.

298   As Plato and Plutarch put it, echoing something Heraclitus must have said. See above on LI (D. 91).

299   In addition to Tablets B1 and B2 in Zuntz, pp. 359ff., see also the new text in Carratelli (1974), p. 111, cited in n. 296.

300   This old view of the continuity of life is expressed in a recent text from an American Indian culture: 'The life cycle of the Creation is endless. We watch the seasons come and go, life into life forever. The child becomes parent who then becomes our respected elder. Life is so sacred, it is good to be a part of all this.' (From an Indian poster published by *Akwesasne Notes*, Mohawk Nation, Rooseveltown, N.Y.)

301   No definite form is preserved through elemental transformation unless one posits some microstructures common to water and earth, as in ancient atomism and in modern chemistry, but not in the physics of Heraclitus.

302   For the imagery, and I suspect for the deeper thought as well, compare Plato, *Laws* X.903–4, where the divine player or *petteutēs* (903D6), called the 'king' (904A6), places human souls in the position for a rebirth that is appropriate to their character. (The verb for 'transpositions' of souls is *metatithenai* at 903D6, *metapesonta* at 904D1, *metebalen* at 904D7, etc.) That mysterious Platonic passage is literally haunted with Heraclitean reminiscences. In addition to those just mentioned, see the echo of CXIV (D. 119) at 903D7, XCVI (D. 25) at 903E1, and probably CXXIV (D. 10) in 'many from one and one from many' at 903E6f. The 'ensouled (*empsychon*) water' which comes from fire at 903E6 is almost certainly an echo of passages like XXXVIII (D. 31A), XL (D. 90), and CII (D. 36).

   It is difficult to explain Plato's choice of the term *petteutēs* except on the assumption that he understood the *pessoi*-game of XCIV in the way suggested, as a rule-like series of transpositions between the living and the dead according to some pattern of cosmic order. Despite differences in physical and psychological doctrine, Plato here, like Heraclitus, is attempting to construct a 'scientific eschatology' in which 'the next world is simply

the physical universe'; see T.J. Saunders, 'Penology and eschatology in
Plato's *Timaeus* and *Laws*', *Classical Quarterly* 67 (1973), 232—44,
especially pp. 237f. and 241ff.

303 On this point, but not in the detail of their interpretation, I follow Bollack-
Wismann, p. 183.

304 See H. Fränkel, 'Heraclitus on the notion of a generation', *AJP* 59 (1938),
89—91, followed by Kirk, 298f. The erroneous view recurs in Marcovich
(pp. 556ff.) and Bollack-Wismann (p. 183).

305 See the citation in DK A 19 and Marcovich, p. 552. A defense of this view
can scarcely be supported by the quicksand of a passage in Aetius, cited by
Diels as A 18 and by Marcovich as 108c. Aetius is our most unreliable
doxographer; and here he explicitly refers to Heraclitus in connection with
a *Stoic* view of the periods in human life.

306 See *Laws* VI.772D—E for the wider interval; IV. 721A and VI.785B for
the narrower one.

307 J.K. Campbell, *Honour, Family and Patronage* (Oxford, 1964), pp. 83ff.

308 'When the father dies, it is as if he were still alive, for he has left a copy of
himself behind him' (Ecclesiasticus 30.4).

309 LSJ lists two epigraphical occurrences of *moros* for a measure of land. In
Herodotean prose, where the word occurs eight times, it always signifies a
violent death. A ninth occurrence in Herodotus, in the hexameter verse of
an oracle at IX.43.2, has the Homeric sense of 'destiny' or 'allotted portion
(of life)'.

310 For the threat of lying in the *borboros* or mire see *Phaedo* 69C6 with
Burnet's note. For the standard mystic promise of bliss see quotations on
p. 263; cf. L.R. Farnell, *Greek Hero Cults and Ideas of Immortality*
(Oxford, 1921), pp. 373—80.

311 In addition to the standardized praise of the dead in Athenian funeral
orations, compare the fate of Tellus the Athenian, 'most fortunate of men'
according to Solon, 'whose end of life was most brilliant', since he fell in
battle after having routed the enemy, and who (like the victors at Mara-
thon) received not only a public funeral but the signal honor of being
buried on the spot of his triumphant death (Hdt. I.30.5). Solon's second
story in the same context, concerning the glorious (though not military)
death of Cleobis and Biton, by which the god showed that 'it is better for
a man to be dead than to live', can also be read as a partial commentary
on XCVI.

312 The words 'or rather, to rest', inserted after 'they want to have their
moroi' in the citation of XCVIII, must belong to Clement, not to Heraclitus. But Clement seems to have taken the term from another Heraclitean
text (LII, D. 84A); as Walter Burkert says, 'Clemens hat offensichtlich
Heraklit mit Heraklit interpoliert'. See the article cited above, n. 202.

313 The alternative destinies of imperishable fame (*kleos aphthiton*) or long
lifetime (*aiōn*) are first announced at *Il.* IX.410—16. The passage at
XVIII.98—126, which expresses Achilles' decisive choice, also contains the
curse on 'strife' (*eris*, in verse 107), alluded to by Heraclitus in LXXXI
(D. A22).
    The words and imagery of these Homeric passages seem to be echoed in
many of the fragments. Compare the sweetness of wrath at *Il.* XVIII.109f.
with CV (D. 85). At XVIII.95 Thetis addresses her son as *ōkymoros* 'early-
doomed'; cf. *moros* in XCVI and XCVIII. The heroic destiny or *moira*
(suggested in XCVI) is mentioned at XVIII.120, where Achilles is comparing his lot to that of Heracles. 'Everflowing fame' (*kleos aenaon*) in XCVII

is a Heraclitean variant on 'imperishable fame' (*kleos aphthiton*) at *Il.*
IX.413 — one of those traditional 'formulae' which in fact occurs nowhere
else in the extant epic!

314   Simonides fr. 4 Bergk = D.L. Page, *Poetae Melici Graeci* (Oxford, 1962),
531. The phrase 'everflowing fame' seems to occur nowhere else in Greek
literature. If we could believe that Heraclitus completed his book after
480 B.C. (which is the earliest possible date for Simonides' poem), he
might be alluding here to Simonides' praise of those who had fallen at
Thermopylae. But the date is late for Heraclitus. Since so much archaic
Greek poetry has been lost, it seems likely that Heraclitus and Simonides
are echoing some earlier use of the phrase. Or perhaps each one independently chose the epithet *aenaos* 'everflowing' for immortal fame, because
of its phonetic associations with the idea 'ever renewed' or 'forever young'
(*aei neos*). Compare *aeinaos timā* 'everflowing (i.e. ever new) honor' in
Pindar, *Olympian* 14.12, generally dated to 476 B.C. It is also possible
that both Pindar and Simonides were influenced by the language of
Heraclitus.

315   For the construction of *morous genesthai* as final-consecutive after
kataleipō, cf. *Od.* III.271: Aegisthus left the bard on the island 'to become
a prey for birds' (*kallipen . . . kyrma genesthai*).

316   See text A1 from the gold tablets, discussed in Zuntz, pp. 320ff.

317   The authenticity of *peras* in XCIX seems confirmed by the fact that in
parallel texts about the beginning and the end of the circle, the word for
end point is not *peras* but *teleutē*. See passages from Hermippus (fr. 4)
and three Hippocratic treatises cited by Kirk, pp. 113f.

318   For the discussion by G.S. Kirk, 'Heraclitus and death in battle', see commentary on CIX (D. 118).

319   CI is quoted only once, in Stobaeus, who assigns it to 'Socrates'. Since it
follows immediately upon XXX (D. 114), cited under the title 'Heraclitus',
most editors have attributed this quotation to him. It was omitted by
Bywater and recently questioned by Marcovich (p. 569).

320   See *De Anima* I.2, 404b29 and I.4, 408b33ff. The commentators identify
the view as that of Xenocrates. See Xenocrates, frs. 60—5, ed. R. Heinze.
Could the title 'Socrates' in Stobaeus be a mistake for 'Xenocrates'? Cf.
West, p. 128, n. 3.

321   See citations in Walzer under fr. 115; also Marcovich, p. 569. Gigon, *Untersuchungen*, p. 105, conjectures that 'the measure of the soul augments
itself . . . through continuous nourishment from the blood'.

322   This holds also for the dubious XLI (D. 76) in its most respectable form,
that of Plutarch: 'death of fire is birth for air and death of air is birth for
water'. If XLI is not genuine, Plutarch (unlike Maximus) has at least perceived and preserved the Heraclitean association of death with the downward path.

323   See Anaximenes A 7.3, Anaxagoras A 42.2 and B 15—16, and above, p.
137.

324   For a few protests against the misinterpretation of psyche as fire see Reinhardt, *Parmenides*, p. 194, followed by Nestle in Zeller-Nestle, p. 816n.
Similarly Gigon, *Untersuchungen*, p. 110 ('the soul must be conceived as
air'), and Bollack-Wismann, who translate *psychai* by 'souffles' (pp. 88,
145f.).

325   See Aetius in DK 22.A 15; Philo, *de aet. mundi* 111 in Marcovich, p. 353.
We can ignore Macrobius (in DK ibid.), whose report that the soul is 'a
spark of stellar essence' might be a distorted version of CIX (D. 118). Even
less reliable is the excerpt from Aetius that assigns a fiery soul to 'Par-

menides and Hippasus and Heraclitus' (Theodoretus in DK 18.A 9 =
Marcovich 66f[4], p. 358).

326 See Anaximenes A 23 and B 2; cf. the passages from Diogenes and Aristophanes cited p. 247 with n. 350.

327 Gigon (*Untersuchungen*, p. 103) also connects CIII with CII.

328 For the elemental reading see Theophrastus in D.L. IX.8–9 (see
Appendix IIA), with other texts in Kirk, pp. 107f. An upward and downward path for the psyche is hinted at in Plato (see especially *Gorgias* 493A)
and becomes dominant in Neoplatonic commentary. Cf. Plotinus' preface
to the citation of LII–LIII (D. 84A–B; full text in Marcovich, p. 301).

329 Negative potentialities are alluded to in CXXI (D. 66), where fire appears
as universal judge and executioner. But the connotations there are not
wholly negative, as we see from the parallel to Justice in LXXXVII (D.
28B).

330 Cf. the epigram cited at Hdt. V.77.4 (= Simonides fr. 100 Diehl), with
parallels in Marcovich, p. 532.

331 *Parmenides*, p. 196, n. 2; supported by parallels in Marcovich, p. 383 (note
4 to text a[1]). Marcovich suggests (p. 386) that the phrase 'to fight against
thymos' was also proverbial, but the parallels he cites (p. 383, note 1)
may all be influenced by Heraclitus. The fragment was a famous one:
answered by Democritus (fr. 236), cited three times by Aristotle, and as
often by Plutarch. It is scarcely surprising if we find echoes of it in
Euripides and Plato. Cf. Diels, *Herakleitos*[2], p. xii: 'Euripides is full of
⟨the impact of Heraclitus⟩, and Plato . . . owes him more than he later
realized.'

332 Burnet, p. 140 n. 2, followed by others cited in Marcovich, pp. 386f.

333 *Republic* 375B and *Laws* 863B, cited by Marcovich in this connection (p.
383, note 1 to a[1]).

334 Out of 19 occurrences of *thymos*, Powell's *Lexicon* classifies 6 as meaning
'anger', 5 as 'courage', and 2 as 'spirit' with a martial connotation. Of the
6 remaining examples, 3 employ *thymos* in a fixed formula for 'heed' or
'attention' which reflects the intellectual range of the word in Homer. In
only 3 out of 19 examples does Powell note a generalized, neutral sense of
'desire'; and in none of these is there any special reference to sensual desires
that might be regarded as a weakening or softening of the spirit. (The three
occurrences in question are I.1.4 'they bought those wares of which they
had most *thymos*'; II.129.2 'he satisfied the *thymos* of the man who complained of his decision by giving him something else'; VIII.116.2 'he had a
thymos to behold the war'. And the cognate verb *thymoumai*, which
occurs 10 times in Herodotus, always means 'to be angry'. The verb 'to
desire' in Herodotus is *epithymein*, as in Democritus fr. 70. The Platonic
contrast between *thymos* and *epithymia* is thus already implicit in the
Ionic use of the two corresponding verbs.
  For further support for this interpretation see W.J. Verdenius, 'A
psychological statement of Heraclitus', *Mnemosyne* Series 3, Vol 11
(1943), 115–21.

335 Cf. Bollack-Wismann, p. 254, who point to the etymological link between
thymos and *anathymiasis*. Similarly Verdenius in the article cited in the
preceding note.

336 Bollack-Wismann, p. 323, who continue: 'L'homme est conduit, parce
qu'il n'est pas en état de se conduire. Il est plutôt entraîné qu'il n'est
guidé, par un enfant, qui, à ses côtés, fait figure d'adulte, à cause duquel
il régresse, par contraste, dans l'âge où l'on ne sait pas même marcher.'

337 Thus Kirk (p. 340), followed by Marcovich (p. 360), dismisses D. 77 as

'simply a reworking of fr. 36 [CII] and possibly of fr. 117 [CVI]'. See, *contra*, Guthrie's defense of CVIII (I, 433, with note 4), following Gigon (*Untersuchungen*, p. 109).

338   This is the second half of D. 77, given by Marcovich as 47d^4.

339   Since in CVIII we are dealing with a paraphrase at second hand, it seems pointless to 'correct' the text of Porphyry (as Diels and others have done) in order to avoid a contradiction with CII (D. 36). It looks rather as if Numenius wanted to replace the literal sense of CII ('it is death for souls to become water') with an allegorical view, according to which Heraclitus meant not physical death but the sensual delight of the soul in descending into bodily form.

340   See texts 68a^1, a^2, a^3, a^4, a^8, and a^9 in Marcovich, pp. 371–4. We may add a second Plutarch citation if Sieveking's likely correction *augē* for *hautē* is accepted in a^5. This is also the form of the quotation in Marsilio Ficino (ibid. a^{12}).

341   So in Clement (Marcovich a^7), and also once in Plutarch (a^6) if Marcovich's correction there is accepted.

342   So in Aristides (Marcovich a^{10}) and Porphyry (a^{11}). This is rendered as *lux sicca* in Ficino and in the Latin translation of Galen in Marcovich, note 5 to a^8.

343   This version in Porphyry (b^1) must be regarded as an abbreviation of the fuller text (including *augē*) implied by his citation in a^{11}. The short version is attested in Synesius (b^2), Eustathius (b^3), and other Byzantine authors (b^4, b^5).

344   The reading *auē* (for *augē*) is attested, apparently for the first time, in two corrections added by a later hand (A^2) in an inferior fourteenth-century manuscript (A) of Stobaeus, which according to Hense (prolegomena, pp. XXXVI–XXXVII, to *Stobaei libri duo posteriores*, Vol. I) is full of conjectures and mistaken 'corrections'; in each case the better manuscripts have *augē*. But *auē* appears again in the sixteenth-century edition of Stobaeus by Trincavelli (for which see Hense, op. cit. p. XXXIII); it was endorsed by Stephanus and has had a brilliant fortune ever since. In this connection one may cite Sandys' judgment on Stephanus: 'In his recensions of the Classics his alterations of the manuscript readings were capricious and uncritical, and he is accordingly denounced with some severity by Scaliger as a corrupter of ancient texts' (*A History of Classical Scholarship* II (Cambridge, 1908), 176). It is not clear why his authority has been so great among editors of Heraclitus.

345   Diels was right, therefore, finally to resist this Renaissance 'correction' and to preserve the ancient text in his second edition of Heraclitus (1909) and in the *Fragmente der Vorsokratiker*, after having yielded to it in his first edition (1901). Diels' virtuous example was unfortunately not followed by Kranz, Walzer, or Marcovich, nor apparently by any modern editor except Bollack-Wismann.

346   See texts a^6 and a^7 in Marcovich. (It may be noted that Stobaeus cites CVI and CIX, D. 117–18, side by side.) This construal ('dry soul') underlies the variant (3) represented in Porphyry and later authors. The construction of 'dry' with 'soul' is attested in a^6 whether or not one accepts Marcovich's restoration of *augē* (as I do); it is similarly presupposed in a^5 (where there is accordingly no need of adding *sophōtatē* as Marcovich suggests).

347   See text a^{11} in Marcovich (p. 374): 'When the soul succeeds in practicing the withdrawal from Nature (i.e. from the bodily realm of generation and

corruption), it becomes a dry beam of light (*augē xēra*), free from cloud and shadow; for it is moisture that gives rise to cloud in the air, but dryness produces from vapor a dry beam of light' (*Sent. ad intellig. ducentes* c. 29.3 = p. 15 Mommert).

348 Cf. Bollack-Wismann, p. 325. The most interesting consequence of the syntactic ambiguity is that it permits us to read the sentence both backwards and forwards, taking first *psychē* and then *augē* as subject (or topic): (1) 'the soul which is wisest and best is dry, (and is) a beam of light', and (2) 'a beam of light when dry (in a sky free of all humidity) is soul in its wisest and best condition'. The sentence is, in effect, a statement of identity.

349 See passages from Homer and Hesiod cited in *Anaximander*, pp. 140ff. For Anaxagoras the contrast between 'moist and dry, and hot and cold, and bright and dark' in fr. 4 seems to correspond to the opposition of *aithēr* and *aēr* in frs. 1 and 2.

350 Theophrastus, *De Sensibus* 44, in DK 64.A 19. This is the view mocked by Aristophanes in the basket scene from the *Clouds*, where the unusual word *ikmas* recurs (verse 233).

351 G.S. Kirk, 'Heraclitus and death in battle: Fr. 24D', *AJP* 70 (1949), 389f.

352 Ibid. p. 392.

353 This is not strictly compatible with Kirk's own statement that the psyche is 'made of fire, or a form of fire', loc. cit. p. 387: the soul must be made of water as well, if it can be described as a mixture of the two.

354 See D.L. IX.9–10, in Appendix IIA. Cf. Aetius in DK A 11–12. This is essentially the explanation of 'dry beam of light' given by Porphyry (cited above in n. 347). The less reliable doxography also explains *prēstēr* or lightning storm by 'the conflagration and quenching of clouds' (Aetius in DK A 14); which corresponds roughly to what we find in D.L.

355 Compare Aristotle's view of the effect produced on a man's prosperity or 'happiness' (*eudaimonia*) by events that befall his family after his death, according to popular belief: 'it would be strange if there was no connection between the children and the parents [who are dead], *at least for some time*' (*Nicomachean Ethics* I.10, 1100a29f.).

356 *Pensées* no. 265.

357 Spinoza, *Ethics*, Scholium to V.23.

358 Even the verb *epanistasthai* 'to rise up' (which seems to be guaranteed as the basis of Hippolytus' mention of resurrection, *anastasis*) is puzzling in this form, since in Hdt. it always means 'to rise in revolt against' (22 occurrences). The shorter form *anistasthai* would give the right sense; perhaps the prefix *ep-* is part of the textual corruption.

359 Some scholars deny any relation between CXI and CXII. Thus Kirk (p. 235n., followed by Marcovich, pp. 419f.) prefers to connect the smoke of CXII (D. 7) with the incense of CXXIII (D. 67).

360 Besides the context of CXII (*De Sensu* 5.443a22), see evidence from Anaxagoras and Hippocratic treatises in Kirk, *AJP* (1949), 388; also *Timaeus* 66D–E.

361 To be consistent, Kirk and Marcovich should regard CXII merely as a deformed echo of CXXIII; it is unlikely that Heraclitus would have repeated himself in this way, if CXII contains no independent thought.

362 On this assumption, Aristotle's reference to 'nostrils' in CXII is part of his own rewording, as is the phrase *panta ta onta* 'all beings'. Heraclitus would have spoken only of smell (*osmē*), as in CXI. Aristotle's mention of smoke

(*kapnos*), on the other hand, may well be authentic; this could be the Heraclitean word rendered by *anathymiasis* in Plutarch, Aristotle, and others. Cf. CXIIIB (D. 12).

363   *Cratylus* 403A6 reports this as the common view. Cf. Bollack-Wismann, pp. 282f.

364   *The Face on the Moon* 942F (tr. H. Cherniss in Loeb *Moralia* XII), with Cherniss' note on p. 195.

365   The thought appealed to Yeats: 'it is a ghost's right, / His element is so fine / Being sharpened by his death, / To drink from the wine-breath / While our gross palates drink from the whole wine'.

366   CXIIIB may be a citation from Cleanthes' four volumes of commentary on Heraclitus, but more probably from his two volumes on Zeno's natural philosophy (D.L. VIII.174). The last sentence in CXIIIB ('But souls too are exhaled from moisture') has sometimes been taken as part of Heraclitus' text (e.g. by Diels). Both style and diction are distinctly doxographic, however; and Bywater, Kirk, and Marcovich are surely right to include this in Cleanthes' exegesis.

367   This is explicit in Cleanthes and implied by Aristotle, whose text (CXIIIA = *De An.* 405a25ff.) continues: 'And <according to Heraclitus> what is in motion is known by what is in motion <namely, by the psyche as an everflowing exhalation>. For he like most theorists thought that reality (*ta onta*) was in motion <and hence that the soul as cognitive principle must be so likewise>.'

368   See texts on p. 247, with n. 350.

369   See Bonitz, *Index Aristotelicus* 44b36ff. An archaic use of 'exhale' in English recalls this old physiological sense: 'of animal fluids: to ooze through a membrane or blood-vessel' (*The Shorter Oxford English Dictionary*).

370   Von Arnim I, no. 128. The two texts are quoted together by Eusebius, in Diels, *Doxographi graeci*, pp. 470f.

371   So Walzer, p. 54 n. 2 (following Gigon), who cites von Arnim I, no. 140; cf. von Arnim II, 778, 781–83. The physiological notion of *anathymiasis* is ascribed to Heraclitus himself by Gigon (*Untersuchungen*, pp. 104f.) and Bollack-Wismann, p. 88.

372   It would be unwise to rely upon Aetius (DK A 15; cf. A 18), who simply assigns the Stoic view to Heraclitus. The Stoic doctrine may have been prepared (or reflected?) in the views of 'some among those who follow Heraclitus' (*tines tōn Hērakleizontōn*) that *anathymiasis* occurs within the body just as it does within the universe, so that odors in urine might be produced by the exhalation from food (Pseudo-Aristotle, *Problemata* XIII.6, 908a30, cited by Gigon, *Untersuchungen*, p. 106). These are presumably the same theorists referred to in the same terms at *Problemata* XXIII.30, 934b34, where their doctrine is 'that stones and earth are formed from fresh water as it dries and hardens, while the sun is produced by evaporation (*anathymiasthai*) from the sea' (cited in Mondolfo-Tarán, *Eraclito. Testimonianze e Imitazioni* (Florence, 1972), p. 120). These 'Heracliteans' have obviously gone far beyond their master in working out a detailed physical theory, even if we credit him with all the doctrine in the Theophrastean doxography.

373   This expression is puzzling, unless we compare the Theophrastean doxography: 'from water the rest arise, since he (Heraclitus) traces almost everything back to the *anathymiasis* from the sea' (D.L. IX.9; see Appendix IIA). Aristotle seems to take for granted some such doxography.

Was part of Theophrastus' work in existence before the *De Anima* was written?

374   Some editors read *nearai* 'young' (for *noerai* 'intelligent'): the fragment will then show that souls are always being generated anew (*nearai*), as the waters are continually flowing on. But this emendation does not fit the larger context, since we then lose the connection with perception in what precedes and follows.

375   For a recent discussion that emphasizes the impact of Heraclitus on Cleanthes see A.A. Long, 'Heraclitus and Stoicism', in *Philosophia* (Yearbook of the Research Center for Greek Philosophy at the Academy of Athens), 1975—76, pp. 133—53.

376   *Ēthos* 'character' is closely related to *ethos* 'custom, habit'. In the plural *ēthos* too can refer to customs or customary haunts. But in CXIV (as in Empedocles frs. 17.28 and 110.5, in other poets, and in Aristotle) *ēthos* means very much what we understand by 'character': the customary pattern of choice and behavior distinctive of an individual or a given type. Thus in LV (D. 78) human *ēthos* is contrasted with a divine nature.

377   Cf. Snell, *Scenes from Greek Drama* (University of California Press, 1964), p. 69: 'The goddesses become symbols of different ways of life, of different *bioi*.' Snell notices earlier steps towards a 'symbolic' interpretation of the gods in Empedocles and Sophocles. Here as elsewhere Heraclitus anticipates the new spiritual world of the late fifth century.

378   For a similar view of CXIV, see W.J. Verdenius, 'Some aspects of Heraclitus' anthropology', in *Images of Man . . . Studia G. Verbeke dicta* (Leuven, 1976), p. 34.

379   So Marcovich (p. 465), following Reinhardt and Wiese. What they have shown is that the five words in the list *might* be an addition by Clement, not that they *are*.

380   Compare M.P. Nilsson, *Griechische Feste* (Leipzig, 1906), p. 275. Reinhardt suggested that the *Lēnai* are conceived here as a female *thiasos* or sacred band, the ritual counterpart to the mythical Maenads ('Nachlass' No. 48, in Wiese, p. 315).

381   See p. 111 in the publication by Carratelli cited above, n. 296.

382   If Clement has added anything of his own to the list, it is likely to be these two initial words. But for a good case in favor of ascribing all five words to Heraclitus, and for the importance of a reference here to *night*, see Bollack-Wismann, pp. 92—4.

383   Homeric *Hymn to Demeter* 480—2. Heraclitus may be alluding to this old formula, that the one who has no share (*ammoros*) in the rite will not receive his portion (*aisa*) of good things hereafter, in his own promise that great dooms (*moroi*) will receive greater shares or destinies (*moirai*) in XCVI (D. 25).

384   Pindar fr. 121 Bowra; Sophocles fr. 753 Nauck, with other passages cited on *Hymn to Demeter* 480—2 by Allen-Sikes and in the recent commentary of N.J. Richardson (Oxford, 1974).

385   See Zuntz, *Persephone*, pp. 288—92 for a description of the graves. In at least one case, 'the dead man . . . must have been worshipped as a hero' (Zuntz, p. 289, following Cavallari).

386   I see no evidence for Marcovich's view (p. 253) that the identification of Hades and Dionysus is presupposed as 'a commonly accepted and known truth'. Herodotus reports it as a peculiarity of the Egyptian religion that they regard Dionysus (i.e. Osiris) as king of the dead (II.123.1). The sar-

casm of CXVI implies that men do *not* recognize the appropriateness of their phallic ritual, which lies precisely in this identification.

387 So Gigon, *Untersuchungen*, pp. 91f.

388 For the role of the phallic procession in the cult of Dionysus see Hdt. II.48–9; cf. the rural Attic Dionysia in Aristophanes, *Acharnians* 237ff., where a virgin carrying the sacred basket is followed by two slaves holding up a phallus (a large wooden pole topped by a leather penis, according to the scholiast); Dikaiopolis brings up the rear singing the phallic song (*to phallikon*) to Dionysus, and repeatedly reminding the slaves that the phallus must be held erect. For the official Athenian state ceremony, a colony was expected to contribute a phallus for its mother city. See van Leeuwen on *Acharnians* 243, and Meiggs and Lewis, *A Selection of Greek Historical Inscriptions* (Oxford, 1969), No. 49, p. 129, l. 13. Further details on phallophoria in Farnell, *Cults of the Greek City States* V, 197 and 243 (where Plate XXXIVb shows a Hellenistic relief with a phallus in a basket); also Deubner, *Attische Feste*, pp. 135f. and 141.

389 See Nilsson, cited above, n. 380; similarly Farnell, V. 208. The older view of the Lenaia as a wine festival is maintained by Verdenius in *Mnemosyne* (1959), 297.

390 Cf. Verdenius (*Mnemosyne* (1959), 297): 'the god of wine and life, whose rites are so "utterly unlike Hades" (*anaidestata*)'. Similarly Bollack-Wismann, p. 97.

I see no merit to the suggestion of Lesky, adopted by Marcovich (p. 253), that in reading the initial 'if'-clause we emphasize the negation rather than the name of the god, understanding 'If they did *not* perform these rites (they would be acting irreverently)', instead of 'If it were not *Dionysus* for whom they perform them.' The strong position of 'Dionysus' at beginning and end tells against this reading, which also makes the paradoxical identification with Hades irrelevant. The thought that the *omission* of a ritual would show a lack of reverence is more banal than what we expect from Heraclitus; and the verb *eirgastai* 'perform' would be a curious one to express the omission of an action.

391 Cf. the dual construction of *aei* 'forever' in I, and *ēn aei* ('existed forever' and 'was forever fire') in XXXVII (D. 30); also the multiple syntax of *mounon* 'only' in CXVIII.

392 For the role of pig's blood in the Apolline purification ritual, see Farnell, *Cults* IV, 303f.

393 For the influence of Xenophanes on Heraclitus, see Gigon, *Untersuchungen*, esp. p. 132. The remark on heroes in CXVII seems to have no precedent in Xenophanes and probably reflects Heraclitus' own view of superior souls as 'guardians' (CX, D. 63).

394 CXVIII is unique in presenting a direct contradiction, whereas other Heraclitean paradoxes assert the identity of contraries (like Day and Night in XIX, D. 57) or ascribe them to a common subject (as in CXXIII, D. 67). The contradictory form of CXVIII is imitated in the paraphrase that counts as fragment 49a in Diels-Kranz. See Appendix I.

395 The same may be said for 'men in love with wisdom' (*philosophous andras*) in IX (D. 35), if the wording is authentic. In XXII (D. 56) and XXV (D. 129) wisdom is attributed, ironically, to Homer and Pythagoras.

396 One other construal is grammatically possible but unnatural and uninteresting: 'the one wise is the only thing to be both unwilling and willing . . . '.

397 Cf. Pherecydes of Syros, fr. 1, where four different non-standard forms of the name are given.

398   The etymological value of *Zēnos* in CXVIII was recognized by Bernays and
      many others. It has been denied by Gigon (*Untersuchungen*, p. 139), Kirk
      (p. 392) and Marcovich (pp. 445f.) for reasons that do not seem cogent.
      One would like to know the source of Aristotle's report (*De Anima*
      405b27 = DK 38.A 10) that the theory that the soul is hot is supported by
      an etymology of *zēn* 'to live'. Philoponus (in DK, loc. cit.) says the view
      belongs to Heraclitus and derives *zēn* from *zein* 'to boil'. The etymology
      fits Aristotle's account, but the attribution to Heraclitus must be wrong.
      There could be a connection with other 'Heraclitean' citations in the
      Problemata; see above, n. 372.
399   *Physics* 203b11 = DK 12.A 15. Anaximander's name is given in the next
      sentence; and probably no one else would have said of *to apeiron* that 'it
      steers all things'.
400   Cf. Diogenes fr. 5: 'all men are steered (*kybernasthai*) by the intelligent
      Air, and it dominates them all . . . and it arranges all things'; and the same
      thought (without the image of the helmsman) in Anaxagoras' description
      of cosmic Intelligence (*nous*): 'the finest of all things and the purest, it
      possesses all cognition (*gnōmē*) concerning everything . . . It dominates all
      things that have life (*psychē*) and . . . knows them all (*panta egnō*) . . .
      Intelligence has set all things in order' (*panta diekosmēse nous*; fr. 12).
401   See on XL (D. 90), XLIV (D. 94), LXXXII (D. 80).
402   *Vermächtnis*, p. 66: if the sentence is authentic, 'then the Church Fathers
      were right, there is no helping it, Heraclitus was one of theirs'. Reinhardt's
      case against CXXI (D. 66) was accepted by Kirk (pp. 359ff.); rejected by
      Gigon (pp. 130f.), Marcovich (p. 435) and Bollack-Wismann (p. 218),
      rightly in my opinion.
403   Compare the imagery of Time as judicial magistrate in Anaximander's frag-
      ment and in Solon fr. 24.3 Diehl.
404   Unless 'the death of fire' is accepted as authentic in XLI (D. 76). Cf. also
      the 'blazing fire' (*pyrkaiē*) of CIV (D. 43).
405   Thus Helios is the divine spy in the Olympian adultery story, *Od.* VIII.
      270ff. and 302. See other Homeric references to the all-seeing Sun and to
      Zeus himself in this role in Kirk, p. 363, and Marcovich, p. 433. Hesiod's
      phrase about the all-seeing and all-knowing 'eye of Zeus' whose notice
      nothing escapes (*Erga* 267f.) is often echoed in later poetry, with or with-
      out reference to the sun. See Nauck, *Tragicorum Fragmenta Adespota* no.
      485 and passim; cf. no. 421 for 'the eye of Dike'; and no. 278 for lightning
      (*astrapē*) in this role.
406   For the possibility that the conception of the sun as viceroy or steward of
      the highest god (suggested by the repetition of the verb *epitropeuein* in
      Plato's text at 412D8 and 413B5) goes back to Heraclitus himself, see
      above, p. 156 on XLIIA (D. 100).
407   Thus for Anaxagoras *nous* is 'present where everything is' (fr. 14); the
      divine air of Diogenes 'penetrates (*aphichthai*) to every thing and arranges
      all and is present in every one' (fr. 5); Empedocles speaks of a god who is
      'holy intelligence (*phrēn*) alone, rushing through the whole world-order
      with rapid thoughts' (fr. 134).
408   *Dynamis dia pantōn diēkousa* (Cornutus), cited by Kirk (p. 362) in a
      possible reminiscence of CXXI; there are many Stoic parallels.
409   I have added 'and' for each pair, in order to make the English readable.
      The Greek consists of nine nouns, the first of which is distinguished by
      the definite article.
410   LV–LVII (D. 78, 83, 79) and LXVIII (D. 102). Cf. CXVII (D. 5): men do

not know what gods and heroes are like. In C (D. 24) there is a more unusual parallel between gods and men: both agree in honoring those who die in battle.

411 XCII (D. 62), with a comparable hint in LXXXIII (D. 53): War has shown some as gods, others as men.

412 XXXIII (D. 93). Cf. the Sibyl in XXXIV (D. 92), where the reference to the god may have been added by Plutarch.

413 CXIX–CXXII (D. 64–6 and 16). Cf. *aithrios Zeus* 'bright (fiery) Zeus' in XLV (D. 120).

414 For such particularized divinities cf. the *daimōn* of CXIV (D. 119), identified with a man's character.

415 Chiastic grouping brings 'peace and satiety' together in the middle, with the negative terms 'war' and 'hunger' at the extremes. The reversal of the chiasm in the first group (where 'day' and 'summer' are the extremes), may be only a stylistic variation; it may also reflect the relativity of positive and negative evaluations in the context of total order.

416 See Diogenes fr. 3 cited above, n. 208.

417 See Fränkel, *Wege und Formen*, p. 238.

418 For day and night see on XIX (D. 57); for the seasons, XLII (D. 100) and commentary on XLIV–XLV (D. 94 and 120), with a cosmic analogue to the seasons in XLIIIA (D. A13) and the 'reversals' of XXXVIII (D. 31A); for satiety and hunger, LXVII (D. 111) and the related pair in CXX (D. 65).

419 For a survey of the proposed emendations see Kirk, pp. 191–7, and Marcovich's critical note on pp. 413f.

420 For this sense of *hēdonē* see Anaxagoras fr. 4, Diogenes fr. 5, and other passages in Kirk, p. 197, LSJ s.v. *hēdonē* II.

421 Xenophanes fr. 38 is the earliest expression of a similar relativism: 'if god had not produced golden honey, they would have said figs were much sweeter'. But Xenophanes refers to one extreme only, and Heraclitus' comment may be understood as a correction: neither figs nor honey would be sweet at all if there were nothing bitter or sour.

422 See the text in Kirk, pp. 184 and 350, n. 1. Hippolytus clearly 'implies that the original arrangement was preserved in [his] source', as Kirk admits (p. 185). I see no reason why Hippolytus should mislead us on this, or why he should himself be misled, as Kirk seems to suggest.

423 These translations of *syllapsies* may be influenced by the alternative reading *synapsies* 'contact', 'juncture', even though this form is rejected in most recent editions of the text.

424 Bollack-Wismann, pp. 82f., limit the text of CXXIV to this question and answer, but without sufficient reason.

425 The verb *diaidein* occurs elsewhere only in the sense 'to contend against in singing', 'to compete in a singing context'. That sense is relevant here, as a continuation of *diapheromenon* 'quarrelling'. But most commentators rightly assume that Heraclitus is exploiting the etymological contrast with *synaidein* 'to accompany in song', 'sing in agreement with'. Cf. 'from notes at variance (*diapheromenōn*) comes the finest harmony' in LXXV (D. 8), which may be simply a paraphrase of CXXIV.

426 See especially Kirk, pp. 15, 169, 204, 208; and my discussion of *harmoniē* above, pp. 196ff.

427 See above, pp. 203f. Philolaus (fr. 6) uses as a technical term for one of the fundamental musical ratios the word *syllabē*, a cognate of *syllapsies*. In a musical context *syllapsies* would mean 'notes taken together'.

428 The neuter plural form *panta* occurs as a constant theme throughout the fragments: D. 1, 29, 41 (twice), 50, 64, 80, 90 (twice); it is also found in D. 7, 8, and 102, where the wording may not be authentic. In six or seven cases the form is ambiguous between the neuter ('all things') and the masculine ('all persons'): D. 30, 53 (twice), 108, 113 and two occurrences in D. 114. There are five unambiguous occurrences of the personal form in D. 56, 114, 116, 121 and 129. By contrast, the neuter plural *polla* 'many things' occurs only once (D. 35) or twice (if one adds *pleista* 'most things' from D. 57); although the masculine form *hoi polloi* 'most men' occurs with almost the same frequency as *pantes* 'all men': D. 2, 17, 29, 104.

429 So roughly Kirk, pp. 178f.

430 *De Part. An.* 645a17 = DK 22.A 9.

431 D. 49a is listed as authentic by Bywater, Diels, Walzer, Snell and Bollack-Wismann; rightly rejected by Kirk (pp. 373f.) and Marcovich (p. 211), following Gigon. The reliability of this author (an allegorical commentator on Homer named Heraclitus) as a source for the original text can be judged by comparing his version of XCII (D. 62) with the literal quotation in Hippolytus. See texts (a) and (b[1]) in Marcovich, p. 236.

432 For the Stoic definition of conceit or conjecture (*oiēsis*, Lat. *opinatio*) as a disease, see von Arnim III, pp. 103.6 and 104.35, cited by Deichgräber, p. 27. The second clause of D. 46 may be inspired by XVI (D. 107).

433 There is nothing Heraclitean in this view of the psyche. Both doctrine and imagery come from Chrysippus, as Marcovich has shown (*Phronesis* II (1966), 26f.).

434 If the context in Iamblichus is to be trusted, this one-word quotation must belong with CXV–CXVII in the critique of conventional cult practices, where Marcovich has placed it.

435 It seems likely, as some have suggested, that this 'fragment' is little more than a reminiscence of LXIII (D. 49).

436 Marcovich and Bollack-Wismann have recently defended the authenticity of this 'quotation', which seems to me patently forged (so likewise Bywater, Wilamowitz, Walzer, Kirk).

437 Reading *enantiotropēs* with DK. Hicks and Long read *enantiodromias* 'by the clash of opposing currents' (Hicks).

438 This is the sense; but it is difficult to construe the text as it stands.

439 Unless 'and souls are exhaled from moisture' in the ancient commentary on L (D. 12) is itself taken as a quotation from Heraclitus. But see above on CXIIIB.

440 See Kirk, p. 276. If Heraclitus referred to a bowl of the sun, he may have been alluding to the poetic conceit of Helios transported across the Ocean each night in a golden bed, first attested in Mimnermus (fr. 10 Diehl = 12 West). The parallel in Stesichorus (fr. 6 Diehl = 185 Page) speaks of a golden goblet or bowl (*depas*). Several recent commentators have assumed some connection between Heraclitus' 'doctrine' of *scaphai* or bowls and this mythic theme. See Marcovich, p. 333, who rejects the connection.

441 But Heraclitus can scarcely have explained day by the bright exhalation, night by the dark one, as Kirk points out (p. 272). This would be hard to reconcile with the unity of day and night proclaimed in XIX (D. 57). And XLVI (D. 99) seems precisely to deny that night is a positive reality.

442 'He [sc. Xenophanes] said . . . that sun and stars arise from clouds' (DK 21.A 32): 'The sun arises each day from little fires gathering together . . . the earth is being mixed with sea and in the course of time is being dissolved by the moist . . . all human beings will be destroyed when the earth

collapses into the sea and becomes mud; and then the process of generation will begin again' (ibid. A 33.3). Cf. 21.A 40, where gathering of little fires is derived from the moist exhalation (*anathymiasis*).

443   See *Anaximander*, pp. 140ff.

444   It is gratifying to find that West (pp. 187ff.) has arrived at a similar conclusion by travelling along a very different road. My interpretation of the dual exhalation in terms of two psychic destinies was reached independently.

There is a more than accidental parallel in the Stoic doctrine of two forms of *pneuma*: one of the psyche, which is hotter and drier, and one of vital 'nature' (*physis*), the nutritive or vegetative soul, which is damper and cooler (von Arnim II, 787). In a connected context, Galen naturally cites Heraclitus on the dry soul (CIX, D. 118; see 68a[8] in Marcovich, p. 373 = von Arnim II, 788).

445   See Zeller-Nestle, pp. 860f. The meteorological report is given in a note (861 n. 1) without comment.

446   See above all Kirk, p. 341; Kirk and Raven, pp. 208f. Other references in Marcovich, p. 583, who describes the passage as a 'sheer forgery'. I suspect it was typical of many ancient books that cited and expounded the text of Heraclitus.

447   At this point, Sextus (or perhaps his source) shows some awareness of the discrepancy between the literal sense of *logos* as 'discourse' in the text he cites and the cosmic sense of Divine Reason in the circumambient atmosphere imposed upon the text by his interpretation. So also in the phrase *tropon tina* ('he refers *in a way* to the surrounding medium') with which fragment I is introduced.

448   In the phrase 'therefore one should follow what is common', and in the substitution of *koinos* for *xynos*.

449   It should be noted that there is also such a thing as a *strong* case for historical borrowing. Herodotus tells us that the Greeks got astronomical equipment and knowledge from the Babylonians (II.109.3), and we believe him; not because he is reliable on matters of cultural origins (he is generally unreliable), but because in this instance there is the modern history of Babylonian astronomy to back him up, with a much earlier and more systematic tradition, and detailed resemblances (e.g. in the zodiac), which make it extremely implausible to posit an independent discovery by the Greeks. In science and technology, unlike mythic and philosophic speculation, the hypothesis of historical diffusion is probably a good one whenever it is chronologically possible at all. For this is the kind of thing societies do borrow from one another very often, as we can see from the diffusion of modern technology around the world.

Concordances

Diels-Kranz	This edition
1	I
2	III
3	XLVII
4	Appendix I
5	CXVII
6	XLVIIIA
7	CXII
8	LXXV
9	LXXI
10	CXXIV
11	LXXVI
12	L, CXIIIB
13	LXXIIA
14	CXV
15	CXVI
16	CXXII
17	IV
18	VII
19	XVII
20	XCVIII
21	LXXXIX
22	VIII
23	LXIX
24	C
25	XCVI
26	XC
27	LXXXIV
28A	LXXXV
28B	LXXXVII
29	XCVII
30	XXXVII

Diels-Kranz	This edition
31A–B	XXXVIII–XXXIX
32	CXVIII
33	LXVI
34	II
35	IX
36	CII
37	LXXIIB
38	XXIV
39	LXII
40	XVIII
41	LIV
42	XXI
43	CIV
44	LXV
45	XXXV
46	Appendix I
47	XI
48	LXXIX
49	LXIII
49a	Appendix I
50	XXXVI
51	LXXVIII
52	XCIV
53	LXXXIII
54	LXXX
55	XIV
56	XXII
57	XIX
58	LXXIII
59	LXXIV
60	CIII
61	LXX
62	XCII
63	CX
64	CXIX
65	CXX
66	CXXI
67	CXXIII
67a	Appendix I
68	Appendix I

Diels-Kranz	This edition
69	Appendix I
70	LVIII
71	V
72	V
73	V
74	XIII
75	XCI
76	XLI
77	CVIII
78	LV
79	LVII
80	LXXXII
81	XXVI
82	LVI
83	LVI
84A	LII
84B	LIII
85	CV
86	LXXXVI
87	LX
88	XCIII
89	VI
90	XL
91	LI
92	XXXIV
93	XXXIII
94	XLIV
95	CVII
96	LXXXVIII
97	LXI
98	CXI
99	XLVI
100	XLIIA
101	XXVIII
101a	XV
102	LXVIII
103	XCIX
104	LIX
105	XXIII
106	XX

Diels-Kranz	This edition
107	XVI
108	XXVII
109	CVII
110	LXVII
111	LXVII
112	XXXII
113	XXXI
114	XXX
115	CI
116	XXIX
117	CVI
118	CIX
119	CXIV
120	XLV
121	LXIV
122	Appendix I
123	X
124	CXXV
125	LXXVII
125a	Appendix I
126	XLIX
129	XXV
A5	XLIII
A13	XLIII
A15	CXIIIA
A19	XCV
A22	LXXXI
A23	XII

This edition	Diels	Marcovich
I	1	1
II	34	2
III	2	23b
IV	17	3
V	71–73	69b[1], 4, 3c, 1h[1]
VI	89	24
VII	18	11
VIII	22	10
IX	35	7
X	123	8
XI	47	113
XII	A 23	6a[1]
XIII	74	89
XIV	55	5
XV	101a	6
XVI	107	13
XVII	19	1g
XVIII	40	16
XIX	57	43
XX	106	59
XXI	42	30
XXII	56	21
XXIII	105	63a
XXIV	38	63b
XXV	129	17
XXVI	81	18
XXVII	108	83
XXVIII	101	15
XXIX	116	15f = 23e
XXX	114	23a
XXXI	113	23d
XXXII	112	23f
XXXIII	93	14
XXXIV	92	75
XXXV	45	67
XXXVI	50	26
XXXVII	30	51
XXXVIII	31A	53A
XXXIX	31B	53B
XL	90	54

This edition	*Diels*	*Marcovich*
XLI	76	66e[1]
XLII (A)	100	64
XLIII	A 13, A 5	65
XLIV	94	52
XLV	120	62
XLVI	99	60
XLVII	3	57
XLVIIIA–B	6	58a, c
XLIX	126	42
L	12	40a
LI	91	40c[3]
LII	84A	56A
LIII	84B	56B
LIV	41	85
LV	78	90
LVI	82–83	92b
LVII	79	92a
LVIII	70	92d
LIX	104	101
LX	87	109
LXI	97	22
LXII	39	100
LXIII	49	98
LXIV	121	105
LXV	44	103
LXVI	33	104
LXVII	110–111	71, 44
LXVIII	102	91
LXIX	23	45
LXX	61	35
LXXI	9	37
LXXIIA–B	13, 37	36a[1], c[1]
LXXIII	58	46
LXXIV	59	32
LXXV	8	27d[1] (= 28c[1])
LXXVI	11	80
LXXVII	125	31
LXXVIII	51	27
LXXIX	48	39
LXXX	54	9

This edition	Diels	Marcovich
LXXXIA–B	A 22	28c^2, c^5
LXXXII	80	28
LXXXIII	53	29
LXXXIV	27	74
LXXXV	28A	20
LXXXVI	86	12
LXXXVII	28B	19
LXXXVIII	96	76
LXXXIX	21	49
XC	26	48
XCI	75	1h^2
XCII	62	47
XCIII	88	41
XCIV	52	93
XCVA–B	A 19	108b^1, b^2
XCVI	25	97
XCVII	29	95
XCVIII	20	99
XCIX	103	34
C	24	96
CI	115	112
CII	36	66
CIII	60	33
CIV	43	102
CV	85	70
CVI	117	69
CVII	95	110a^3
CVIII	77	66d^1
CIX	118	68
CX	63	73
CXI	98	72
CXII	7	78
CXIIIA	A 15	
CXIIIB	12	40
CXIV	119	94
CXV	14	87
CXVI	15	50
CXVII	5	86
CXVIII	32	84
CXIX	64	79

This edition	*Diels*	*Marcovich*
CXX	65	79, 55
CXXI	66	82
CXXII	16	81
CXXIII	67	77
CXXIV	10	25
CXXV	124	107

Indexes

1. General Index

I have listed the first occurrences and principal discussions of each name and topic, but there is no attempt at a complete listing for items mentioned frequently throughout the whole book (such as fire and logos) *or for authors very frequently cited in the notes (such as Diels, Marcovich, Reinhardt).*

Adkins, A.W.H., 13; nn. 30, 34
aēr, 141, 154f., 239
Aeschylus, 7, 90ff., 201, 270; nn. 51, 241, 261, 268
afterlife, *see* death
aiōn, 71n, 227f., 231
aithēr, 162, 250, 293
aithrios, 162, 250; n. 413
ambiguity, deliberate, 91–5, 97f., 115f., 123ff., 167, 176, 181, 268–71; *see also hyponoia*
anathymiasis (exhalation), 147, 240, 243, 250, 256–60
Anaxagoras, 10, 139, 163, 165, 239, 275
Anaximander, 9, 16–19, 96, 108, 138, 144, 147, 161, 163, 166, 206f., 222, 226, 272
Anaximenes, 19f, 22f, 108, 136ff., 145, 239f., 248
antamoibē (or *antameibetai*), 20, 46–7nn., 146
Apollo: and Delphic oracle, 43n, 116, 122–6; bow and lyre as attributes of, 198, 200f.
Archilochus, 37n, 111
Arcturus, 160, 162–4; n. 191
aretē, 12ff., 43n, 120ff.
Aristotle, as interpreter of H., 93, 131, 199 (with n. 263), 259f.
arrangement of fragments, 6–9, 89–91, 132, 170, 213, 233, 281; nn. 24, 203, 422
Artemesium of Ephesus, 2; nn. 4–5, 81
augē, 76n, 77n, 245ff., 256f.

Babylonian influence on Greek astronomy, 16f., 109, 158; n. 449
battle, death in, 232, 236, 248ff.; *see also* war

Bear (Ursa Major), 51, 161f.; n. 189
Bernays, J., n. 243
Bias of Priene, 9, 57n, 175–8; n. 8
Bollack, (J.)-Wismann, (H.), 26, 28n, 46n, 56n, 111, 170, 178, 207, 234; nn. 18, 56, 60,73
bow: as image of unity, 192f., 198–202, 210; n. 262; name of, 201
bowls, celestial, 165, 291f.; n. 440
Bronowski, J., 137f. (with n. 128)
Burkert, W., nn. 202, 312
Burnet, J., 87, 135, 148–51, 170; nn. 24, 55, 112f.
Bywater, I., 6, 26, 28n, 44n, 46n, 183, 193; nn. 18, 60, 200

Calogero, G., 240
Campbell, J.K., 230, n. 307
Campbell, Lewis, 198
carding wool, 190–2
Carratelli, G.P., nn. 296, 299, 381
Censorinus, 156–8
Cherniss, H., 155, 258; nn. 123, 146, 364
childhood as a theme, 111 (with n. 77), 173f., 178f., 227–31, 235, 244
Chrysippus, nn. 135, 137, 253, 433
Clay, Diskin, n. 278
Cleanthes, 4f., 79n, 166, 259f., 296; nn. 14, 135, 251, 366–7, 375
Clement of Alexandria, as source, 5, 44n., 46n., 139ff., 148, 151, 246; n. 121, 283, 312
cognition, *see* wisdom
common, what is shared, 3, 14f., 101f., 117–19, 130, 180, 236, 252–4; *see also xynos*
communication, difficulty of, 99, 101, 124, 130, 270f.
comprehending, *see* wisdom

oracular style, 7, 91, 97, 123ff.
Oriental parallels and influence, 297ff.
Orphic doctrine and tablets, *see* gold tab-
lets; mystic doctrine of soul;
Pythagorean view of soul
Owen, G.E.L., x; n. 129

palintonos, corruption in LXXVIII (D. 51),
195f., 199; n. 264
palintropos, 65n, 198–200; correct reading
in LXXVIII (D. 51), 195f.; n. 256
panpsychism, 119, 128, 221f., 238
Parmenides, 136, 154, 192, 211; n. 160; on
names, 201 with n. 267
Pascal, B., 254
peirata, 128, 236; *see also termata*
periodicity, 150, 155–9, 166; *see* cyclical
change
Persians and Persian influence, 262, 297ff.
pessoi (game), 71n, 227; n. 302
Pherecydes of Syros, 113; nn. 80, 397
Philolaus, 196, 204, 285
philosophos, 31n, 105
phrēn, 57n, 175
phronein, phronesis, 29n, 41n, 43n, 101f.,
107, 119
physis, 33n, 99, 105
Plass, P., n. 141
Plato, as interpreter of H., 4, 148, 222f.;
nn. 177–8, 228
Plotinus, as a source, 5, 169; n. 202
Plutarch, as source, 5, 104, 110, 124–6,
153–6, 195, 246, 258f.; nn. 121,
166–9, 256
political theory, 2f., 15, 178–81, 184f.
polymathiē, 37n, 108, 110, 113, 171
Powell, J.E., 92; n. 61
prēstēr, 47n, 138–43, 239, 256, 272; nn.
138–42
priamel, 181f.
prolepsis, 90f., 112, 129
proportions and ratios, 155, 159, 174f.,
179, 203f., 285; *see also* measures
prose, early use in Greek, 96f., 113f. with
n. 81
Proust, M., n. 287
psychē, 35n, 45n, 75n, 107, 126ff., 165,
237–43, 251, 259ff.; nn. 112–13; *see
also* soul
punishment, *see* Justice
Pythagoras, 1, 10, 27, 37n, 39–41, 107f.,
113f., 172, 196 (with nn. 259, 270),
203f., 211f.
Pythagorean view of the soul, 220ff., 238;
notion of harmony, 158, 196, 203f., 285

readings of a text, *see* interpretation
Reinhardt, K., 8, 87, 126f., 135, 139, 146,
151f., 155f., 158f., 172; nn. 23, 72, 79

relativity, *see* justice; negativity; opposites
rest and weariness, 169f., 181f.
Richardson, N.J., n. 384
ring composition, 215, 235, 238, 285; cf.
cyclical change and structure
river image, 166–9, 223, 260; *see also* flux
Rohde, E., nn. 104, 106f., 290
rotation, cosmic, 194f.; n. 253
Roussos, E.N., x; nn. 75, 202

Sages (seven), wisdom of, 9, 13, 22, 116,
172, 177
Sarakatsani, marriage among, 230
satiety and excess, 180–2, 271; need and
satiety, 276; *see also koros*
Saunders, T.J., n. 302
Schleiermacher, F., 297; nn. 90, 104
Schottlaender, R., nn. 219, 221
seasons, 140, 145, 155–61; *see also* great
year
self-knowledge, 41, 116–18, 121f., 251f.
semen, as liquefied psyche, 248, 260
Seneca, 110 with n. 74
sexuality and phallic cult, 233f., 264f.
Sibyl, 45n, 124–6
Simonides, 234f.; n. 314
sleep as a theme, 99, 213–16, 255; in Stoic
doxography, 294f.
smell and the soul, 256–9
Snell, B., 87, 127, 282; nn. 102, 111, 134
Socrates, 4, 95, 127 (with nn. 112–13),
130, 172
Solon, 3, 9, 180; nn. 7–8
solstice, 159f., 159–62; *see also tropai*
sophiē, 120ff., 172; n. 94
sophos, 31n, 41n, 45n, 51n, 83n, 105, 115,
131, 171f., 268f.
sōphronein, 14, 41n, 43n, 116–23, 251–3
sōphrosynē, 13 with nn. 32f., 120
soul, H.'s view of, 126–30, 213ff., 243–63;
takes the place of air, not fire, 238–40,
248ff., 259; *see also psychē*
Spinoza, 119, 252, 254, 267, 299, 301f.
spurious and dubious fragments, 288f.; cf.
153–5, 237
steering as a theme, 170f., 271f.; n. 400
Stephanus (Henri Estienne), 246; n. 344
Stobaeus as a source, 5, 120
Stoic interpretation of H., 4f., 102, 104,
134ff., 145ff., 154–7, 260, 276, 294ff.;
nn. 115, 131, 135, 137, 147; cf. nn. 372,
408, 444; *see also* Cleanthes, Chrysippus
Stokes, M.C., nn. 118, 248, 250
style, *see* ambiguity; arrangement of fragments; interpretation; oracular style
sun, as principle of cosmic order, 155f.,
159–63, 250, 274; n. 177; size and
rekindling of, 163–5

2. Index of Passages discussed